NORTHWESTNET'S
GUIDE TO OUR WORLD ONLINE

March 1993
Fourth Edition

Jonathan Kochmer
and
NorthWestNet

NorthWestNet and Northwest Academic Computing Consortium, Inc.
Bellevue, Washington

The Internet Passport: NorthWestNet's Guide to Our World Online. 4th ed.
[Formerly, *NorthWestNet User Services Internet Resource Guide (NUSIRG)*.]

by Jonathan Kochmer and NorthWestNet

Editor and Production Supervisor:	Jan Eveleth
Executive Editor:	Dr. Eric S. Hood
Technical Editor:	Dan L. Jordt
Assistant Editor:	Anthony C. Naughtin
Contributing Author, "Using Supercomputers":	Lawrence E. Gales
Production Assistance:	Carol Brand
Cover Design:	Icon Imagery (Ross West)

Printed in the United States of America on recycled paper.

ISBN 0-9635281-0-6

A list of trademarks, registered trademarks, and copyrights mentioned in this book appear as "Trademarks and Copyrights" at the end of this book.

While every precaution has been taken in the preparation of this book, the authors and publishers take no responsibility for errors or omissions or for damage resulting from the use of the information herein.

NorthWestNet
Attn: The Internet Passport
15400 SE 30th Place, Suite 202
Bellevue, Washington 98007 USA

e-mail:	**passport@nwnet.net**
voice:	(206) 562-3000
fax:	(206) 562-4822

Table of Contents

Section I: Introduction

Section II: Basic Internet Tools

Section III: Community Forums

Section IV: Texts and Data

Section V: Resource Discovery and Retrieval Tools

Section VI: Targeted Interests

22. A Schoolhouse for the World: Using the Global Internet in K-12 Education 347

Appendices

About NorthWestNet

NorthWestNet is a regional computing and digital communications network founded in 1987 by the Directors of the Northwest Academic Computing Consortium, Inc. (NWACC). The NWACC mission is to promote research, education, and economic development by providing access to network communications, computing and electronic information systems and services throughout the Northwest. In 1988 NWACC was incorporated in the state of Oregon as a not-for-profit corporation. NorthWestNet is wholly owned, operated, and managed by NWACC. NorthWestNet is an independent, regional sub-unit of the Interim National Research and Education Network (NREN) currently managed and operated by the National Science Foundation (NSF).

A national movement is growing to build a permanent National Research and Education Network (NREN) to enhance the nation's and each state's educational, research, and economic competitiveness and productivity. NREN is designed to provide the primary information linkage among the nation's knowledge-based organizations including higher education institutions, scientific laboratories, and industrial research units. The general architecture of NREN has three levels: a Federally sponsored interstate foundation (backbone) network; midlevel networks providing broad, regional connectivity and expected to be partially self-supporting; and self-sponsored individual campus, government agency, industrial, and Federal laboratory networks distributing information to their end users.

NorthWestNet is a regional (midlevel) network which is cooperatively addressing the high-performance computing and networking needs of the Northwest within the scope of the NREN program. NorthWestNet serves higher education institutions, government agencies, not-for-profit organizations, industry, and business in six states (Alaska, Idaho, Montana, North Dakota, Oregon, and Washington). Since NorthWestNet was established in 1987, our network connectivity has expanded from 11 originator members to over 80 sites. Similar growth is expected over the next five years as NorthWestNet expands and enhances its marketing efforts and network services offerings.

NorthWestNet is financially supported by a grant from the National Science Foundation (NSF), institutional membership dues, and network service fees. In April 1991 the NSF confirmed renewal of NorthWestNet's core grant, first approved in 1988. Under the terms of the grant renewal, NSF has committed funds totaling nearly two million dollars distributed over the next three-year contract period. NWACC revenues and annual operating budgets for the next three fiscal years are expected to exceed 1.5 million dollars annually.

In 1989 NWACC initiated a strategic planning process to chart the future course for NWACC and NorthWestNet. The resultant plan recognizes the special needs of the northwestern U.S.—a geographically large yet sparsely populated area. Current markets for NorthWestNet services are rapidly expanding and broadening, extending past the conventional education and research communities to industry, government agencies and health care organizations. Technical and operational implementation of the NorthWestNet Strategic Plan are now in progress. NorthWestNet is already upgrading network equipment, operations, and user services offerings. The NorthWestNet Network Operations Center (NOC) facilities management agreement with the University of Washington was formalized in June 1991. NorthWestNet currently offers a variety of information and user support services.

- For the past four years, NorthWestNet has published for its membership an Internet users training manual. "The Internet Passport: NorthWestNet's Guide to Our World Online," formerly "NorthWestNet User Services Internet Resource Guide (NUSIRG)," is another step in our user services support. "The Internet Passport" will soon be available in both hardcopy and electronic formats.

- Technical seminars and training courses are presented each autumn at our NorthWestNet Annual Meeting. Seminars and workshops on a variety of topics are presented by regionally and nationally recognized network engineers, communications technicians, and user services specialists. A special training track for new NorthWestNet member institutions is also offered.

- Workshops for researchers and scholars providing training in the use of high-performance computing systems and networked information resources are offered periodically and are also held in conjunction with our Annual Meeting.

- To facilitate communication among participants in our numerous committees and working groups, NorthWestNet operates and maintains electronic mail exploders for the NWACC Board of Directors and Executive Committee, the NorthWestNet Technical Committee and Configuration Subcommittee, the User Services Committee and the Editorial Review Board.

- NorthWestNet maintains and offers via anonymous FTP a modest collection of regional and national networking policies, working papers, and operational documents on our network information server.

We are also vigorously pursuing the development of new programs focusing on high performance computing and parallel processing, electronic library resources and networked information services, K-12 educational networking, and health care information and delivery systems.

Over the next five years, NorthWestNet is committed to servicing the needs of its expanding membership by:

- Providing its members from education, government, not-for-profits, and industry with the ability to access and to share advanced computing and information systems (especially data bases and electronic library resources) using high-speed telecommunications facilities;

- Seeking, promoting, and supporting methods and tools that allow users to access and share information in an interactive, convenient, integrated, and easy-to-learn manner;

- Expanding NREN access to primary and secondary education, health care organizations, and economic development groups;

- Encouraging and enhancing education, research, and development by providing value-added network services in support of northwestern interests;

- Promoting affordable and, if possible, subsidized national and international electronic access for all regional education and research organizations;

- Encouraging and facilitating collaboration among educational institutions, government, not-for-profit agencies, industry, and business: opportunities include sharing of computing and information resources as well as collective procurement and technology transfer;

- Being a leader, both regionally and nationally, in the efforts to establish a regional electronic sharing of computing and information resources; and

- Being recognized by its membership and funding agencies as a provider of excellent quality services and support.

In June 1991, the NWACC Executive Director established a home office for the NorthWestNet staff in the principal market city of Seattle. The Executive Director provides leadership and manages the network under the general direction of the Executive Committee and the Board of Directors. The Executive Director's staff coordinates network operations, technical planning and management activities, network information service delivery, network user training and educational services, and marketing and general network administration.

The futures of NWACC and NorthWestNet are truly bright. In the Northwest's rapidly growing, technology-based and driven economy, the demand for computing, electronic communications, and information services is ever increasing. With our expanded and enhanced network and computing service offerings, NorthWestNet membership and revenues are both projected to continue increasing rapidly through the 1990s.

Prepared by:

Dr. Eric S. Hood
Executive Director
NWACC and NorthWestNet
October 1992

For further information contact:

NorthWestNet
15400 SE 30th Place, Suite 202
Bellevue, WA 98007

voice: (206) 562-3000
fax: (206) 562-4822

Preface

When people ask for education they normally mean something more than mere training, something more than mere knowledge of facts, something more than a mere diversion. Maybe they cannot themselves formulate precisely what they are looking for; but I think what they are really looking for is ideas that would make the world, and their own lives, intelligible to them. When a thing is intelligible, you have a sense of participation...

E. F. Schumaker
Small Is Beautiful

Once you get started, you'll start to understand...

Overheard in a crowd

Until very recently, using computer networks was like using a car at the beginning of the 20th century. Charlie Chaplin and Buster Keaton made comedies featuring wrestling matches with temperamental cars. It was funny because everybody knew you couldn't drive to the next town without getting greasy up to your elbows at least once. The technology was still being perfected, and sometimes it was hard to get where you were going.

It was also hard to figure out how to find the places you were looking for.

There's an old joke in New England about a city slicker asking for directions from a farmer sitting on his front porch. The farmer says, "You can't get there from here." As a person who grew up in a rural area, I've always thought this was short for saying, "well, I can give you directions, but unless you grew up in these parts, you probably won't understand anyway..."

But things have changed with automobiles, and they're beginning to change with computer networks.

Most of us use complex technologies like automobiles, televisions, or telephones every day without knowing exactly how they work. We take it for granted that when we turn on a radio we'll hear news or music, and that when we start a car we'll get to where we want to go.

Computer networks have jumped the first hurdle on the path which all technologies must run. They are now usually very reliable. Most of the time, you can press a few buttons and know that your message will be received by someone thousands of kilometers away, maybe even in a few seconds. Today, global computer networks like the Internet are being used daily by millions of people who don't know much more about computers than the average person knows about the inner workings of a television set.

The purpose of *The Internet Passport* is to help network users get over the second great hurdle of new technologies: now that computer networks are reliable, what can they be used for? And once you know what can be done, you'll learn "how to get there from here." You can think of *The Internet Passport* as a set of basic driving lessons, and a glove compartment full of "road maps" to the many interconnected routes and valuable services that together comprise a worldwide network of networks known as "The Internet."

How to Use Your *Internet Passport*

> *...a book is more than a verbal structure, or a series of verbal structures; a book is the dialogue with the reader, and the peculiar accent he gives to its voice, and the changing and durable images it leaves in his memory. That dialogue is infinite.*
>
> Jorge Luis Borges
> "For Bertrand Russell"

The Internet Passport is for anyone who uses or wants to use the Internet: from elementary school teachers at small and isolated rural schools, to the most sophisticated supercomputer users at major urban research institutions. Throughout, every attempt has been made to keep the text simple without being simplistic, and thorough without being thoroughly overwhelming.

No single book can provide complete documentation about the Internet, so your *Passport* is meant to be a generic framework upon which to build a collection of materials suiting your level of expertise and particular sets of interests. This book will have succeeded in one of its primary goals if each *Passport* user creates their own unique library of Internet documentation, just like everybody's glove compartment contains a different collection of road maps. Most of the online documents referred to throughout the book can be obtained, for free, from any computer connected to the Internet.

Every Internet user is different, but most network activities depend on the mastery of three basic skills: using electronic mail to communicate with other Internet users, logging in to remote computers with a service called Telnet, and obtaining online documents, software, and other materials via FTP. It is also a good idea to have an overview of the Internet as a whole. So you are encouraged to read through the chapters on the Internet, electronic mail, Telnet, and FTP first. Once you've mastered the basic "Internet-working" skills and concepts you should be able to use the remaining chapters in any order that suits your needs.

Most chapters have the following structure (where "x" is the topic of the chapter):

> What is x ?
> What is x used for?
> What do I need to know before I start using x?
> How do I access x?
> A sample session using x, with step-by-step explanations
> For more information on x

Because the Internet is able to support a tremendous diversity of hardware and software, it is sometimes impossible to present examples guaranteed to work for everyone. For instance, there are dozens of software packages for electronic mail. In such cases, a generic example using a "lowest common denominator" implementation is presented to illustrate the essential features of a particular Internet topic. When necessary, you should obtain appropriate documentation from your instructor or user services staff on how a particular application is used at your site.

The Internet is also a rapidly changing realm. Although every online resource and example in *The Internet Passport* was tested and checked repeatedly during the writing and editing, you may find that a few of the resources listed here have changed, moved, or maybe even no longer exist by the time you use this book.

Stylistic Conventions

Throughout this book, a number of typographic conventions are used to communicate what happens (or should happen!) during your Internet sessions.

Sample Internet sessions, or information which appears on a computer screen, will appear in shaded boxes, intended to approximate the three dimensionality of your monitor:

Inside such boxes, you will see characters that have been sent to your screen by a computer, either your computer, or a remote Internet computer to which you've connected. Such messages will be in a typeface known as `courier bold`:

```
Welcome to the Internet!
```

This font has also been used in tables for names of Internet computers or online files we may encourage you to obtain.

FTP host:	`nis.nsf.net`
directory:	`internet/documents/rfc`
filename:	`rfc1000.txt`

Of course, computers aren't of much value unless you can send commands or ask questions. Because what we as computer users want is often of the *utmost* urgency, a font called "`courier bold italic`" is used to indicate commands which you will type:

```
telnet answer.library.net
```

Sometimes, what the computer sends to your screen and what you enter as a reply may appear on the same line. In such cases, the computer's message will be in `courier bold` and what you type in response will be in `courier bold italic`:

```
Display what topic(s)?: all
```

In the screen snapshot above, you've been shown exactly what to type. Other times, you can supply information of your choosing, and sometimes, what kinds of information you should type, and possibly even the format in which it should be entered. Such user-supplied information is presented in `courier bold italic`, surrounded by angle brackets:

```
Display what topic(s)?: <a topic of your choice>
```

This doesn't mean that you should literally type "<a topic of your choice>", but rather, that you should type the name of a topic.

When some explanation about a command or its consequences might help you understand what is happening on your screen, you will see parenthetical comments on the screen (in regular courier):

```
telnet answer.library.net

(followed by login messages from answer.library.net)
```

Finally, there will be cases where several of these conventions may appear in a single, extended screen snapshot, as in the following:

```
Display what topic(s)?: all        (display all topics)
  1. Aeronautics and Aerospace
  2. Afro-American Studies
  3. Agriculture
  4. Algebra
  5. American Studies
  6. Ancient History
     ...
 20. Arabic Studies
 21. Archery
 22. Arctic Studies
 23. Art History

Select 1-23, n for next page, or q to quit:

20
            Welcome to the Arabic Studies Database
            -------------------------------------

Begin search, Display datasets, Help:

<enter a letter, b, d or h>
```

As you may see, the "20" that our hypothetical computer user typed is in italics, but it's a little hard to spot. So when you see a screen like this, you may have to squint every now and then to distinguish between what you will type, and what will be sent by the computer. Also note the ellipses ("...") in the middle of the screen. These will often be used when what the computer will display may be much longer than is convenient to include in the screen snapshot. In this case, you can assume that online resources for other topics have been displayed on your screen.

Your Comments and Suggestions

This document will be most effective if it is a continuing dialogue, between you, the Internet, and NorthWestNet User Services. If you have any comments or suggestions about *The Internet Passport*, feel free to drop us a line.

> NorthWestNet
> Attn: The Internet Passport
> 15400 SE 30th Place, Suite 202
> Bellevue, Washington 98007 USA
>
> e-mail: `passport@nwnet.net`
>
> voice: (206) 562-3000
> fax: (206) 562-4822

Acknowledgements

It is perhaps appropriate that this book, which is meant to teach you how to use the extraordinary wealth of information on the Internet, was written using the Internet itself as the main source of information. Only a very small number of traditional printed books were consulted during the preparation of this document. Therefore, primary thanks go to the Internet itself, for being such a treasure trove of documentation!

Most of the research and writing was done from my home, which became an "electronic cottage" in the global village by virtue of a personal computer connected to the Internet by a modem. *The Internet Passport* is proof of the ease with which the wealth of Internet resources can be accessed with minimal hardware and software requirements.

Snippets of information were collected from tens of thousands of postings in many Internet community forums, including Usenet, LISTSERV discussion groups, and Internet mailing lists. I thank everyone who so willingly shares their knowledge with the Internet community. Reading and answering typical questions from new Internet users posted in these forums was also invaluable for helping to determine what should be included in an entry-level Internet guide. Another useful source of information was existing, online Internet documentation written by Internet User Services staff around the world, and a large number of helpful documents about the Internet written by individuals on their own initiative, and freely distributed through the Internet. A rich collection of K-12 Internet resources prepared by Jim Flanagan of the Glenview School District in Illinois is just one of many such documents which made this manual possible.

The Internet Passport has benefited from reviews of the previous edition of this book; comments and suggestions made by John S. Quarterman were of particular value.

A number of my friends and housemates with no prior Internet experience—Martin Gaspe, Peter Marks, Spain McMillan and Sarah Scott—read and commented on the earliest drafts, and gave insight into how best to present this material to new Internet users. Almost as importantly, these and other friends eased the decompression process during re-entries from cyberspace to reality. And without the friendship of Cynthia Walcker, I may never have survived the weaving of this epic.

Like Vergil in his telling of *The Aeneid*, Jan Eveleth, NorthWestNet's new Director of User Services, joined this project *in media res* and steered this book to completion.

I am very thankful for the expertise of Larry Gales of the University of Washington, who wrote the chapter on Supercomputer Access, and to user services staff at the supercomputer sites for providing up-to-date descriptions of their state-of-the-art sites.

Preliminary drafts of chapters of *The Internet Passport* received thorough and expert review by User Services staff from a number of NorthWestNet member institutions: we would like to thank Marilyn Bushway (Oregon Health Sciences University), Thomas Bremer (North Dakota State University), Betsy Draper (North Dakota State University), Jessica Dubey (Reed College), Marvin Dunn (Reed College), Marty Hoag (North Dakota State University), Dick Jacobson (North Dakota State University), David McMullen (North Dakota State University), Tim Preuss (North Dakota State University), and Marty Zimmerman (University of Idaho). Kudos to Sheryl Erez of the University of Washington for thoroughly reviewing some of the materials not just once, but twice!

Every page of the penultimate (and antepenultimate!) draft of this book was vastly improved by the reviews and revisions by NorthWestNet staff: Carol Brand (Educational Services Specialist), Jan Eveleth, Eric Hood (Executive Director) and Dan Jordt (Director of Technical Services). And in our pursuit of perfection, a final proof was made by Eric Hood and Tony Naughtin (Manager of Member Relations). Any errors in the final copy were of course caused by cosmic rays corrupting the diskettes we carried to the printer. :-)

Yale University and my dissertation committee have graciously allowed an extended leave of absence from my research in evolutionary biology to work with NorthWestNet on Internet documentation. Rick Harrison (now at Cornell University) and Rob DeSalle (now at the American Museum of Natural History) have been particularly understanding, and I genuinely look forward to working with them again now that I am newly invigorated by my travels through the Internet.

Finally, I owe special and personal gratitude to my parents, Anne and Kenneth Kochmer, MD, and my brother, Casey, for a childhood suffused by a love of language and learning, and a familial belief that being a renaissance person is still possible and even desirable in the information age. Thanks to a number of Internet databases I learned about while writing this book, my father was able to develop a treatment for a frequently fatal disease he had contracted. I am delighted to report that he is still alive, and is now enthusiastically pursuing his own second career as a photographer. So in closing, as in opening, I must thank the Internet for being an invaluable resource.

Jonathan Patrick Kochmer

The Cottage
Seattle, Washington
December, 1992

NorthWestNet wishes to acknowledge and express appreciation for the financial support provided for this project by the Directorate for Computer and Information Science and Engineering through the Division of Networking and Communications Research and Infrastructure of the National Science Foundation under Grant No. NCR-9100415.

@ Section I @

Introduction

@ 1 @

Introducing the Internet

Like any child, I slid into myself perfectly fitted, as a diver meets her reflection in a pool. Her fingertips enter the fingertips on the water, her wrists slide up her arms. The diver wraps herself in her reflection wholly, sealing it at the toes, and wears it as she climbs rising from the pool, and ever after.

Annie Dillard, *An American Childhood*

An unbroken thread beyond description...
Stand before it and there is no beginning.
Follow it, and there is no end...

Lao Tzu, *Tao Te Ching*

The Internet is a worldwide network of networks which interconnects computers ranging from the simplest personal computers to the most sophisticated mainframes and supercomputers. This network of networks is used for an extraordinary range of purposes - long distance collaborations, retrieving free software and documents, accessing library catalogs, logging in to supercomputers - the list of current Internet activities and services is large and the range of possible future applications is· as unlimited as our imagination.

The Internet is huge, and in fact, no one is exactly sure just how huge. Because it is in direct communication with satellites far above us, it could even be said that the Internet is already bigger than the earth. And because the Internet is incredibly complex, there probably isn't a single person who understands everything about it. Remember this if you get confused and you'll probably feel better!

This chapter will give you a basic orientation to the world of the Internet, and the rest of this book will help you go where you want to go and meet who you want to meet.

1.1. What Is a Network?

The Internet is comprised of networks, but what's a network?

Every one of us, every moment, is surrounded by, embedded in, and in fact made up of networks.

As you read this page, light passes through your eyes into your nervous system, a complex network of cells that somehow allows you to make sense of the patches of light and dark on the page, and turns these words into meaning. In turn, the page you are reading was brought to you by a complex network of networks made up of people, vehicles, buildings, and more people. And when you travel to another country, you travel on networks of roads, buses, airline routes, and sea lanes.

Almost everything you see around you is part of or made possible by networks of networks. In both the human and natural worlds, networks provide communication, sharing of resources, and collaboration of many distinct parts as one big system, greater than the sum of its parts.

1.2. What Is a Computer Network?

You have probably seen or used simple computer networks made up of a few identical computers in an office or a store. Such simple networks may allow files to be transferred between computers, sharing of centralized hard disks, printers, and other services, and can be very useful in situations where all users are performing the same tasks.

But just as a small organism comprised of only a few types of nerve cells may be limited to a few simple behaviors, a network made up of computers using only one kind of operating system can only be used by people using that kind of computer, and can only offer a limited variety of applications.

1.3. What Is an "internet?"

An internet (note the lower case "i") is a computer network which allows computers with distinctive software and hardware to communicate, or "internetwork." Many kinds of computers can be connected to an internet, and each computer can serve a specialized role, allowing an internet to offer a wide variety of services to its users. For example, you could use one internet computer designed to perform complex calculations and then send the output to another internet computer designed to display colorful graphs.

1.4. What Is "The Internet?"

The Internet is a specific kind of internet. In *The Internet Passport*, the Internet will be defined as the network of networks which follow a set of rules known as the "Internet Protocol (IP) suite."

But what does this mean to you? It means that any computer which is connected to the Internet can communicate with any other Internet computer thanks to the rules of IP, and that a message sent from one Internet computer to another will get to the intended destination.

Two related terms you might encounter are "The Net," which among Internet users is shorthand for the Internet but may sometimes refer to whatever network that person happens to use, and "The Matrix," which is often used to refer to the Internet, as well as all other networks to which Internet computers may communicate. And finally, you should note that other sources may define the Internet more or less restrictively.

1.4.1. What Is the Internet Used for?

The Internet contains the electronic equivalents of conference rooms and cafes, libraries and bookstores, post offices and telephones, radio and television stations, newspapers and magazines, and a growing variety of services that have no counterparts in "the real world."

Accessing Computer Resources

No matter how humble your own computer might be, if it is connected to the Internet you can access the resources of thousands of computers throughout the world. With an Internet connection you can:

- access online library catalogs,
- copy computer files or software from archives,
- access databases for teaching or research,
- obtain free electronic books,
- use educational and information services,
- use directory services to find Internet users, and
- access supercomputer sites.

Although the Internet is made up of many diverse computers, together they can work like one worldwide computer system.

Communicating with Other People

People communicating with people is the essence of the Internet. Using the Internet you can:

- exchange electronic mail,
- find people throughout the world that share your interests, and
- engage in discussions and collaborations with other Internet users.

These services have created a truly global village where people communicate with each other not just because they happen to live in the same place, but because they share the same interests. This simple fact has profound consequences for everyone no matter where they live.

1.4.2. Who Uses the Internet?

The Internet is a global community of communities: as of 1992, it is estimated that there are several million Internet users in nearly 50 countries. These millions of people from all walks of life count on the Internet as an integral part of their day-to-day activities. When you use the Internet, you will be able to communicate with:

- researchers and students at universities,
- senior citizens,
- government officials,
- K-12 students and teachers,
- business people,
- librarians,
- health care service providers,
- agricultural extension agents,
- and other people who share your interests, whatever they may be.

1.5. How Does the Internet Work?

This section is meant to give you just a brief overview of the nuts and bolts of the Internet. If you don't really care about nuts and bolts, feel free to skip ahead to section 1.6. As a network user, you really don't need to know much about these details, just like you don't need to understand particle physics to use a toaster. If you want more detailed and technical descriptions about how the Internet actually works, you should consult the references listed in the bibliography of Internet protocols and standards at the end of this chapter.

1.5.1. The Internet Protocol Suite (IP)

An early precursor of today's Internet was the ARPANET, supported by the Advanced Research Projects Agency (ARPA), now known as the Defense Advanced Research Projects Agency (DARPA). Research on the ARPANET led to the development of today's Internet Protocol suite, or IP. But what is a protocol suite?

In international affairs, diplomatic protocols are established to allow people from distinct cultures to negotiate and come to agreement; similarly, each computer that is part of the Internet must use software conforming to a collection (or suite) of rules, namely IP, in order to communicate with other Internet computers.

The need to develop shared protocols is of special importance because of the diversity of computer software and hardware. All of these computers need to have a shared language to communicate! If software conforming to IP is installed in a computer, it can participate in the Internet.

1.5.2. About Packet Switching

To understand how information is moved through the Internet, it's often useful to draw analogies with postal mail. Although the following examples all deal with mail and electronic mail, the principles described apply to other forms of communication on the Internet.

Suppose you have written a letter to a friend in Brazil. Your letter is taken to a local postal office and sorted on the basis of the address information on its envelope. To get to Brazil, your letter may now be put into a truck carrying completely unrelated packages going to many other destinations. The particular routes chosen by the postal service to deliver your letter might vary depending upon the volumes of letters passing through different intermediate stations, or the availability of vehicles.

All of this is similar to what happens when a message enters the Internet, except everything happens much more quickly. When you send a message or command from your computer to another Internet computer, the circuits carrying your message might contain messages sent from other users of your Internet computer to many other locations. Depending upon conditions within the network between here and there, a message you send to a friend on the other side of the continent might go by a northern route one day, or a southern route another day. To you, it doesn't really matter, as long as the message gets to its intended destination in a timely fashion.

Returning to the postal mail analogy, suppose a furniture company wanted to mail a very large object to Brazil, such as a desk. They would have to dissemble it into units which were lighter in weight and smaller in size than the limits set by the postal service. Each package would require addressing information, as well as information about how the contents of this particular package were associated with the contents of the other packages, so that a fully functional desk could be reassembled at the destination. Each of the packages might get to Brazil by different routes, some by land, some by air, some through Texas, and some through California. It doesn't really matter as long as they all end up in Brazil at approximately the same time. And if one or more parts are missing, the client in Brazil would write a letter saying, "please send another front panel for the left bottom drawer."

Again, this is similar to what happens when you send a large file or message through the Internet. The file is broken into smaller parts, called "packets," each of which has addressing information and the information needed to reassemble the complete file at its destination. Each packet may take a separate route, and the packets are reassembled at the destination.

A network or service which works in this way is referred to as a "packet switched network." A message is broken up into component packages which can travel by different routes, and then be reassembled at the destination.

In contrast, the telephone networks of the world are mostly "circuit switched" networks. When you are having a telephone conversation with someone else, the circuit between you is dedicated solely to your conversation. If a word of the conversation is lost because of static interference, it is lost forever.

But in the Internet, the circuit carrying your message might be carrying messages and signals bound for multiple locations, yet gives the appearance, at the end points, of a dedicated line. And if something is lost in transmission, it can be sent again. All of this is possible because of the activities of the Transmission Control Protocol (TCP).

1.5.3. Transmission Control Protocol (TCP)

TCP, the Transmission Control Protocol, is what is referred to as an "upper layer protocol" used in conjunction with IP (written as TCP/IP). "Upper layer" means that TCP relies upon IP; other protocols could be (and sometimes are) placed atop IP for other purposes.

TCP guarantees that the packets sent through the Internet are properly packaged and transmitted in a reliable fashion. In Internet communications, individual files or messages are packaged into smaller units called "datagrams," each containing a portion of the actual data being transmitted, the relationship of the datagram to other datagrams derived from the same file or process, and all information required to send the data to a destination independently of other, associated datagrams. After being transmitted through the Internet by IP, the datagrams are then reassembled by TCP at the destination into an exact copy of the original data stream.

1.5.4. Internet Hardware (Router Rooters: "Go Internet Go!")

Physically, the Internet is composed of computers using software conforming to the rules of IP, and the transmission media, bridges, and routers that allow data to be moved between these computers.

The transmission media may be physical wires, such as telephone lines or twisted pair cables, or through the air, as in the case of microwaves or infrared light signals. But once computers are linked together by transmission media, how does information get to the right locations? This is the role of routers, which are responsible for moving the packets through a packet switched network such as the Internet.

A router receives packets of data and then forwards them toward their destination. By reading the packet's address information and using its internal "routing tables" to determine which path is optimal, a router will pass the packet on to the next router, which will repeat the performance until the packet has arrived at its final destination.

This relay race approach may strike you as slow and cumbersome, but in fact transmission of packets through the Internet can be remarkably speedy and efficient. For example, I have just run a command called "traceroute" from my computer here at NorthWestNet, in Seattle, Washington, to determine what path a message would take to reach a computer at the Artificial Intelligence Labs at MIT, in Cambridge, Massachussetts. The path reported goes south to San Francisco, then due east to Chicago, Cleveland, New York, and Hartford, involving 13 routers along the way. Using another network diagnostic tool called "ping," I found that the total round-trip time for the transmission of packets to Cambridge and back (involving 26 routers!) averaged less than 1/10th of a second.

1.5.5. *Bon Appétit* at the Information Diner: Internet Applications

The tremendous diversity of services described throughout the rest of this book are referred to as Internet applications. Unlike computer applications with which you may already be familiar, such as the word processor on your personal computer, Internet applications and the computers on which they are located are usually designed to be used by many people simultaneously. For this and other reasons, most Internet applications follow what is known as the "client-server" model.

Clients and Servers

In the old days (e.g., a couple of years ago), terminals and personal computers connected to mainframes and networks usually acted as "dumb terminals" which simply accessed and displayed the services provided by the mainframe. Most of the actual processing of information was done on the remote machine.

Today, many Internet applications are built from two interrelated components that have complimentary and active functions: "clients" and "servers." The concept is very simple if you think in terms of human clients and servers. A client makes a request and a server fulfills that request.

For example, when you sit down at a restaurant, you are a client. At your table, you will find a menu displaying what sorts of foods are available. You think about your choices, and then you tell the person waiting on you what you want to eat. Your request is passed on to the kitchen, and the cook prepares the meal. (Note that in this example, there are actually two servers: the waiter and the cook.)

Similarly, the client-server model involves client software installed on your local computer that performs basic functions such as displaying menus or negotiating connections to a remote computer, and a server that performs tasks such as searching databases and sending the results back to you. And just like the restaurant example above, one server may pass your request on to yet other servers before your request is fulfilled.

The client-server model has several advantages. Client software is often designed to let you work with the features of your computer that you know and love, such as pull-down menus, a mouse, or familiar commands. Since the client and server software are separate, developers can change the client and server software independently. And because the client software may handle a significant portion of the data processing of your request, the load on those computers (which many people access) may be reduced: the client-server model is intended to spread the computational load of the network more evenly among all the computers on the network.

1.6. People and Places, Names and Domains

To send a letter to someone or get to their home, you follow a set of rules used to read and write addresses. Similarly, to communicate and travel within the Internet global village, you need to know how to read and write Internet names and addresses.

1.6.1. Understanding Internet Addresses

Continuing the postal mail analogies, let's start with a typical postal address for a house in the U.S.:

> 11 Maple Street
> Seattle,
> Washington, 98103
> USA

You may not have thought of this before, but such postal addresses follow a precise set of rules. Each line provides increasingly general information about a location, from street to country. (Since streets are in cities, cities are in states, and states are in countries, this is called a hierarchical addressing scheme.) Let's call this the official address—the address a postal service actually uses to deliver a letter to the building.

Internet Protocol (IP) Addresses

To be a part of the Internet, a computer must be assigned an "Internet Protocol (IP) address." A computer used by people that has been assigned an IP address is known as "an Internet host." Like the postal addresses or telephone numbers whose rules you take for granted, IP addresses follow a specific set of rules: an IP address is made up of four numbers, separated by dots. For example, an Internet host at the University of Washington might be assigned the following IP address:

> `128.95.10.207`

This is the kind of address by which hosts and routers on the Internet "find" each other. When you need to read IP addresses, use the word "dot" for the periods: "one-twenty-eight dot ninety-five..." If such addresses look and sound forbidding and unfriendly, don't worry; the "Domain Name System" offers an easier alternative.

Domain Name System Addresses

Luckily for humans, who remember series of words more easily than series of numbers, the official IP addresses used in the Internet can be represented by words, instead of numbers. This is one of the tasks of "Domain Name System" software which allows numeric IP addresses to be represented in more nearly human-readable "domain names." The Internet host with the IP address 128.95.10.207 might have the following domain name:

> `my-mac.biology.washington.edu`

Domain names for Internet hosts are much like postal addresses. They are hierarchical, but the parts are separated by dots, instead of being on separate lines. Here's what our hypothetical domain name might mean:

`my-mac`	a particular Internet host (probably a Macintosh!)
`biology`	within the biology department
`washington`	within the University of Washington domain
`edu`	within the education-oriented domain of the U.S. Internet

So when you use the Internet, a domain name that you type ("norman.nwnet.net") is translated by Domain Name System software into the host's corresponding Internet address (192.35.180.15). (Notice that there is not a part-to-part correspondence between the domain name and Internet address: "192" does not mean "norman" and so forth.)

It's important to note that although the numeric IP address is the official Internet address, people often refer to domain names as Internet addresses as well. Though not strictly correct from a technical perspective, this usage is widespread and is sometimes used in *The Internet Passport* as well.

The Domain Name System is a method used for the management of parts of the Internet called "domains." The Internet host "my-mac" is in the domain called "biology." So someone, probably in this biology department, is responsible for keeping track of host names within this domain. Similarly, the domain "biology" is one of many domains within the domain "washington," and again, someone is responsible for those domains. Once a name has been used within a domain, it can still be used in other domains: there is nothing to prevent a domain administrator in the english department from assigning the name "my-mac.english.washington.edu".

Electronic Mail Addresses

Perhaps there will be a time when you could use a person's real name when you send messages to them over the Internet, but at the present, people on the Internet are known by their "userid," short for USER IDentification. (At your site, the userid may be known as "login name," "account id," or something similar.) Associated with most userids is an electronic mailbox, which is where messages to a person are received at an Internet host. Just like there may be many mailboxes in an apartment building there may be hundreds or even thousands of mailboxes on an Internet host, each assigned a unique name.

Userids can be constructed in many ways; this will be discussed in more detail in Chapter 2. But let's suppose that we have a friend "Sue D. Nimh" who has a mailbox named "sue" at the Internet host my-mac.biology.washington.edu. Her electronic mail address would be written as

> `sue@my-mac.biology.washington.edu`

where "@" simply means "at."

Notice that when someone says, "my Internet address is joe@ibmpc.school.edu," this is informal shorthand for saying the more technically correct, "I have a mailbox named 'joe' which is on a computer with the domain name 'ibmpc.school.edu'." So again, be aware that the term "Internet address" has yet another common meaning!

There are occasions when what is to the left of the "@" sign may serve roles other than a simple mailbox name. It could be an "alias" which means that messages sent to this address would be distributed to many mailboxes, or it could be forwarding information needed to send messages to networks beyond the Internet. Because the person administering each Internet host can locally set up mailboxes, aliases, and gateways at that host, whatever is to the left of the "@" sign is referred to as "the local part." So although "something@a.domain.name" usually means "a mailbox named 'something' at a host named 'a.domain.name'," it could have other meanings as well.

1.6.2. The Major Domains of the Internet

Just like the real world is divided into countries containing smaller units, the addresses found in the Internet world are divided into "top level domains" which contain "subdomains."

Consider the following three addresses:

```
cascade.nwnet.net          (host.subdomain.domain)
stis.nsf.gov               (host.subdomain.domain)
cnri.reston.va.us          (host.subdomain.subdomain.domain)
```

The first part of each of these DNS addresses is the name of an individual computer, or host. The rest of the address represents subdomains within domains, just like postal addresses represent streets within cities, and cities within states.

Sometimes domains and subdomains correspond to "real world" political boundaries; for example "cnri.reston.va.us" is an address for the Corporation for National Research Initiatives in Reston, Virginia, USA.

But more often than not, domains and subdomains reflect the naming structure of the Internet more than the structure of the world. Unlike political boundaries, boundaries of domains can overlap partially or entirely. To make this clear, let's look first at domain names which correspond to political boundaries, and then domain names which are based on categories of organizations.

International First Level Domains

Here's a list of the top level domain names of countries and territories which had Internet connectivity in September 1992 (as reported by Larry Landweber in the *Internet Society News*):

AQ	Antarctica	IN	India
AR	Argentina	IS	Iceland
AT	Austria	IT	Italy
AU	Australia	JP	Japan
BE	Belgium	KR	Korea
BR	Brazil	MX	Mexico
CA	Canada	NL	Netherlands
CH	Switzerland	NO	Norway
CL	Chile	NZ	New Zealand
CS	Czechoslovakia	PL	Poland
DE	Germany	PR	Puerto Rico
DK	Denmark	PT	Portugal
ES	Spain	SE	Sweden
FI	Finland	SG	Singapore
FR	France	TN	Tunisia
GR	Greece	TW	Taiwan
HK	Hong Kong	UK	United Kingdom
HU	Hungary	US	United States
IE	Ireland	VE	Venezuela
IL	Israel	ZA	South Africa

Within each national top level domain, there might be several distinct networks that are physically and administratively separate. Within Japan, both the JUNET and WIDE networks are part of the "jp" domain.

Similarly, a network may span several domains. NORDUnet, the Nordic Academic and Research Network, serves Iceland ("is"), Norway ("no"), Sweden ("se"), Finland ("fi"), and Denmark ("dk").

First Level Domains in the U.S.

Although there is a top level domain for each country, there are also top level domains based on kinds of organizations, instead of geographical location:.

COM	Commercial organizations
EDU	Educational and research institutions
GOV	Government agencies
MIL	Military agencies
NET	Major network support centers
ORG	Other organizations

Any Internet network within the U.S. might have hosts in two or more of these domains. For example, NorthWestNet has hosts in the com, edu, gov, net, and org domains.

1.7. The Structure of the Internet

The Internet is not just one network. In fact it is currently more than 7,000 networks, each of which may contain thousands or tens of thousands of computers!

In general, the boundaries between these many Internet networks are invisible to the average Internet user, just like the existence of regional phone companies is usually not apparent to you when you make a long distance phone call.

1.7.1. Kinds of Internet Networks

To give you a general understanding of how the Internet is structured, let's go through the major classes of Internet networks.

Government Sponsored National Networks

Many countries have government sponsored national Internet networks. For example, within the U.S., there are several distinct nationwide networks operated by various U.S. government agencies. The most widely used network of this sort in the U.S. is the National Science Foundation Network (NSFNET.) Other examples include the NASA Science Internet (NSI) and the Department of Energy's Energy Science Network (ESNET.)

Government Sponsored Regional Networks

Within national government sponsored networks, there may be government sponsored regional networks to serve specific geographic areas. In the U.S., there are nearly two dozen NSF-funded regional networks, each of which is connected to NSFNET at a "backbone site." For example, NorthWestNet is a regional network serving the six northwestern states, including Alaska, and is linked to NSFNET at the University of Washington in Seattle.

Supercomputer Access Networks

Several Internet networks are dedicated to providing local access to supercomputer sites. Examples within the U.S. include the Los Alamos National Laboratory network (LANL), the National Center for Supercomputer Applications Network (NCSANet), the Pittsburgh Supercomputer Network (PSCNET), and the San Diego Supercomputer Center Network (SDSCnet).

Statewide Networks

Within the U.S. many states currently have active statewide networks. Some, but not all state networks use the TCP/IP protocols. Similarly, there are provincial or district networks in other countries which may serve particular administrative regions within that country.

Metropolitan Area Networks (MANs)

Metropolitan Area Networks (MANs) are a more recent entry to the network world. As the name suggests, these networks are designed to provide network services to geographically-restricted metropolitan regions, for example, NCFN in Beijing, China. MANs are frequently used for local communications among government and other public service communities, including libraries, hospitals, and educational institutions.

Commercial Networks

There has been a rapid proliferation of commercial Internet networks in the past several years. Some of these commercial networks are "spin-offs" from pre-existing regional or international networks.

1.8. Who Runs the Internet?

No one person or organization runs the Internet. Instead it is a collective effort of many organizations each responsible for some subset of the net with the shared goal of providing global communications and network services. Quarterman (1990) and Marine et al. (1992) provide more thorough descriptions of the specific activities of Internet administrative and standards bodies.

1.8.1. Administrative Bodies and Organizations

Much of the research, development, and planning upon which the Internet is based is handled and coordinated by a variety of organizations.

The Internet Activities Board (IAB) and specific task forces within the IAB such as the Internet Engineering Task Force (IETF) and the Internet Research Task Force (IRTF) play technical, engineering, and administrative roles throughout the worldwide Internet. By the time you read this, the IAB and its task forces may have been incorporated into an organization called The Internet Society (ISOC).

1.8.2. Standards Bodies

The IAB, and its various, related task forces, are seen by many as the body guiding the development of Internet standards. A number of other organizations also help to create or participate in the evolution of related computing or networking standards. These standards bodies may be international, national, or regional groups of people from government, business, and educational institutions.

Among the standards bodies that you will most frequently hear about are the American National Standards Institute (ANSI), the Comite Consultatif International de Telegraphique et Telephonique (CCITT), the International Organization for Standardization (ISO), and the National Institute for Standards and Technology (NIST).

1.8.3. Internet NICs and NOCs

The day to day running and caring for specific Internet networks and their users are handled by Network Operations Centers (NOCs) and Network Information Centers (NICs.)

A network's NOC deals with the operational aspects of running the network, including installation and maintenance of the network's hardware and software; monitoring and troubleshooting of the network's activity; and establishing connections to new network sites. A NOC staff may also field questions from technical representatives from member institutions and from institutions which are contemplating connecting to the network.

A network's NIC provides centralized support for users and User Services staff throughout their network. Typical NIC activities can include preparing, distributing, and maintaining documentation for network users; publication of newsletters; maintenance of a central computer archive of information files or other resources; directory services for users of the network; and educational training classes for the users and network staff of member institutions.

NICs and NOCs may be actual parts of the network's administration, or they may be services provided by third party organizations.

1.9. Other Networks

There are a number of widely used computer networks which do not use the TCP/IP protocols, and thus are not technically part of the Internet. Services offered by these networks are usually limited to electronic mail and file exchange. In particular, it is not usually possible to do "remote logins," one of the special features of the Internet, to computers on such networks.

Nonetheless, you can communicate with users and computers on many non-Internet networks via e-mail messages sent to electronic mail "gateways." (See Chapter 5.) These e-mail gateways are responsible for translating messages between networks using different protocols.

Here are a few additional networks which you might hear about, and what they have to offer Internet users.

1.9.1. Corporation for Research and Educational Networking (CREN)

CREN is an umbrella organization which was responsible for two national networks, BITNET and CSNET. As of October 1991, CSNET was no longer operational. BITNET, however, is still a provider of educational networking.

BITNET—"Because It's Time Network"

This is a multi-disciplinary network designed to facilitate electronic communications among universities. Like the Internet, BITNET has associated networks such as EARN, the European Academic and Research Network, GULFNet in Saudi Arabia and Kuwait, and NetNorth in Canada.

BITNET is of interest to Internet users mainly because of a variety of valuable services such as mail servers and discussion lists. (See LISTSERV described in Chapter 10.) Although many computers in the world are on both BITNET and the Internet, there are computers which are only on BITNET, and you may want to communicate with users on these BITNET-only computers.

Users and services of BITNET are readily accessible to Internet users through gateways at several sites which are connected to both the Internet and to BITNET. For more information about electronic mail gateways, refer to Chapter 5.

1.9.2. FidoNet

FidoNet is an international network with more than 10,000 electronic "Bulletin Board Systems" (BBS's) in more than 50 countries. It is a grassroots, decentralized, not-for-profit network operated entirely through volunteer effort and it is based on simple technology. FidoNet is mainly used by networking hobbyists and in lesser developed nations. In several cases, e.g., in South Africa, FidoNet networks have been invaluable for demonstrating the value of networking and thereby have helped to create full-fledged Internet networks.

K12Net

K12Net is a spin-off of FidoNet designed specifically for K-12 students and teachers. Although K12Net offers more limited services than the Internet, many K-12 schools have found K12Net to be an effective way to start networking. Like FidoNet, K12Net may, in some cases, be a valuable stepping stone to the use of full service Internet networks.

1.9.3. UUCP

The UUCP network is a set of computers that exchange e-mail messages with the UUCP protocols. While using the Internet, you will encounter messages to discussion groups which have come from the UUCP network. The major UUCP networks are UUNET in the United States, EUnet in Europe, and ERNET in India. Many UUCP hosts are also part of the Internet and offer valuable archives of software and documents for Internet users. Addresses in UUCP are gradually being changed into a format that conforms with the Internet addresses.

1.10. Conclusion

Now that you have a general understanding of the Internet world, you are ready to begin your journeys.

Welcome to the Internet. You are now a member of the global village!

1.11. For More Information

1.11.1. Bibliography

Non-Technical Bibliography on the Internet and Related Topics

Aboba, B. *The BMUG Guide to Bulletin Boards and Beyond.* Berkeley, CA: BMUG, Inc., 1992.

Brand, S. *The Media Lab: Inventing the Future at MIT.* New York: Viking, 1987.

Brownrigg, E.B. "The Internet as an external economy: the emergence of the Invisible Hand." *Library Administration and Management*; 5(2):95-97. 1991.

Corbin, R.A. "The development of the National Research and Education Network." *Information Technology and Libraries.* 10(3):212-220. 1991.

Frey, D. and R. Adams. *!%@:: A Directory of Electronic Mail Addressing and Networks.* Sebastapol, CA: O'Reilly and Associates, 1990.

Hafner, K. and J. Markoff. *Cyberpunk: Outlaws and Hackers on the Computer Frontier.* New York: Simon and Schuster, 1991.

Holbrook, J.P. and C.S. Pruess. *CICNet Resource Guide.* Ann Arbor, MI: CICNet, Inc., 1992.

Kahin, B. "Information policy and the Internet." *Government Publications Review.* 18(5):451-72. 1991.

Kahin, B. (ed.) *Building Information Infrastructure: Issues in the Development of the National Research and Education Network.* McGraw Hill. 1992.

Kalin S.W and R. Tennant. "Beyond OPACs: the wealth of information resources on the Internet." *Database* 14(4):28-33. 1991.

Kehoe, B. *Zen and the Art of the Internet: A Beginner's Guide to the Internet.* Englewood Cliffs, NJ: Prentice Hall, 1992.

Krol, E. *The Whole Internet User's Guide and Catalog.* Sebastapol, CA: O'Reilly and Associates, 1992.

LaQuey, T. *The User's Directory of Computer Networks.* Bedford, MA: Digital Press, 1990.

LaQuey, T., and J. Ryer. *The Internet Companion: A Beginner's Guide to Global Networking.* Addison-Wesley, Inc.: Reading, MA, 1992.

Levy, S. *Hackers: Heroes of the Computer Revolution.* Garden City, NY: Anchor Press, 1984.

Malamud, C. *Exploring the Internet: A Technical Travelogue.* Englewood Cliffs, NJ: Prentice Hall, 1992.

Marine, A., S. Kirkpatrick, V. Neou, and C. Ward. *Internet: Getting Started.* Menlo Park. CA: SRI International, Network Information Systems Center, 1992.

McClure, C.R., J. Ryan, D. Lauterbach, and W.E. Moen. *Public Libraries and the Internet/NREN: New Challenges, New Opportunities.* Syracuse, NY: School of Information Studies, Syracuse University, 1992.

National Education and Technology Alliance. *NetPower: The Educator's Resource Guide to Online Computer Services.* Lancaster, PA: NETA, 1992.

Perry, A. *New User's Guide to Useful and Unique Resources on the Internet,* version 2.0. Syracuse, NY: NYSERNet, 1991.

Quarterman, J.S. *The Matrix: Computer Networks and Conferencing Systems Worldwide.* Bedford, MA: Digital Press, 1990.

Stockman, B. "Current status of networking in Europe." *ConneXions: The Interoperability Report* 5(7):10-14. 1991.

Stoll, C. *The Cuckoo's Egg: Tracking a Spy Through the Maze of Computer Espionage.* New York: Doubleday, 1989.

Vallee, J. *The Network Revolution: Confessions of a Computer Scientist.* Berkeley, CA: And/Or Press, 1982.

Bibliography of Internet Protocols and Standards

Comer, D.E. *Internetworking With TCP/IP.* Volume 1: *Principles, Protocols, and Architecture.* Englewood Cliffs, NJ: Prentice Hall, Inc.,1991.

Garcia-Luna-Aceves, J.J., M.K. Stahl, and C.A. Ward. *Internet Protocol Handbook: The Domain Name System (DNS) Handbook.* Menlo Park, CA: SRI International, Network Information Systems Center, 1989.

Lynch, D.C. and M.T. Rose (editors). *Internet System Handbook.* Addison-Wesley Inc.: Reading, MA. 1992.

Quarterman, J.S., and S. Wilhelm. *UNIX, POSIX, and Open Systems: The Open Standards Puzzle.* Addison-Wesley, Inc.: Reading, MA. 1992.

Stallings, W. *Handbook of Computer-Communications Standards* Volume 1: *The Open System (OSI) Model and OSI-Related Standards*; Volume 2: *Local Area Network Standards*; Volume 3: *The TCP/IP Protocol Suite.* New York: Macmillan, 1990.

Online Documentation of Internet Protocols and Standards

There are thousands of online documents that explain just about everything about the Internet. Appendix A explains how and where to obtain the "Requests For Comments" (RFCs) which define and explain many of the protocols upon which the Internet is based.

@ Section II @

Basic Internet Tools

@ 2 @

Electronic Mail

He opened the geography to study the lesson...they were all different places, that had those different names. They were all in different countries...and the countries were in continents, and the continents were in the world, and the world was in the universe. He turned to the flyleaf of the geography, and read what he had written there:

> *Stephen Daedelus*
> *Class of Elements*
> *Clongowes Wood College*
> *Sallins*
> *County Kildare*
> *Ireland*
> *Europe*
> *The Universe*

> James Joyce
> *Portrait of the Artist as a Young Man*

In the 6th century B.C., a postal system for government correspondence was established by King Cyrus of the Persian Empire. It took another 2,500 years until basic postal services became generally available to the average person. Today, we take postal mail for granted, and feel indignant when a birthday card gets to a relative a week late. But when you think about the tremendous volume of letters that are currently handled and shuffled throughout the world each day, it's amazing that anything gets anywhere at such a low cost.

But technology marches on: in the last 20 years a service called "e-mail" (electronic mail) has evolved. E-mail provides many of the same services as postal mail, but transmits messages in minutes or even seconds, instead of days or weeks. In fact, many e-mail users refer to regular mail as "snail mail." What would have seemed unimaginably fast to King Cyrus, seems quaint and slow to e-mail users!

2.1. What is Electronic Mail?

Like postal mail, e-mail is used to exchange messages or other information with people or services. Instead of being delivered by a postal service to your postal mailbox, e-mail is delivered by Internet software through a computer network to your computer mailbox.

E-mail is so quick, versatile, and easy to use that Internet users often avoid using postal mail, fax services, or even telephone calls except when they have to do so. Once you've gotten the hang of using e-mail, you'll find that you use it almost every day that you use the Internet.

E-mail can be used for the same purposes as postal mail:

- exchange correspondence with friends
- transfer documents
- obtain (electronic) books
- subscribe to (electronic) news services or journals
- get computer software
- obtain just about anything that can be stored on a computer

Internet users can even exchange sounds, graphics, and animations via e-mail, which is much like mailing cassettes or videos. About the only things you can't send through e-mail are physical objects, like carnations or chocolate chip cookies.

2.1.1. Electronic Mail Compared to Postal Mail

Because you probably already know how to write and send letters, it's easy to learn about e-mail by comparing it step by step to regular postal mail.

Suppose you wanted to write a letter to your aunt Susan Rose Allen to ask if you could stay at her farm the second week of July. You would simply:

1. write your letter;
2. put her name and address on an envelope; and,
3. give your letter to the post office. (See Example 1.)

Using e-mail is just as simple and involves exactly the same three steps:

1. write your e-mail message on a computer;
2. include the person's e-mail address; and,
3. send your e-mail message! (See Example 2.)

Instead of using pen and paper to write your letters, you need to use an e-mail software package (technically known as a "mail user agent") to compose and read your messages. Instead of being handled by postal workers, e-mail messages are moved electronically by computer throughout the Internet.

Example 1: A Postal Mail Letter on Paper

```
                                        James T. Allen
                                        NE 47th Ave.
                                        Seattle, Washington
                                        June 1, 1992


Susan Rose Allen
Idaho Creek High School
Apple Tree Lane
Idaho Creek, Idaho USA

Dear Aunt Susan,

Do you think I could visit you the second week of July?
I promise to help pick cherries from your orchard!  Well,
I'd better put down my pen and stop writing, the mail truck
is coming by in a few minutes. Please write back soon!

                                        Sincerely yours,

                                        James
```

Example 2: An E-mail Message Viewed in an E-mail Software Package (Pine)

```
PINE 3.03    VIEW MAIL    Folder:inbox  Message 1 of 3    100%

Date:     Mon, 6 June 92 14:22 PST
From:     jtallen@jrhs.lakeside.washington.edu
To:       sra@hs.idacrk.idaho.edu
Subject:  My first e-mail message!
----- Message Text -----
Dear Aunt Susan,

Thanks for letting me know I could visit starting July 15th.
When I'm there do you think your friend the geology teacher,
Bill Diaz, could take me prospecting again in the mountains?

Please send me a computer message back soon. This is my
*first* time using e-mail, and I want to be sure this gets
to you! I can't believe that it's so easy to use this
computer to send a message to you all the way in Idaho!

James

? Help M Main Menu P Prev Msg - Prev Page F Forward D Delete
O OTHER I Index N Next Msg SPACE Next Page R Reply S Save
```

2.2. Interpreting E-mail Addresses

Postal mail addresses probably seem commonsensical to you: there's a person's name followed by an address. In this section, you'll learn that e-mail addresses follow the same rules. Basically, an e-mail address like "sra@hs.idacrk.idaho.edu" means "a mailbox at an Internet host."

Anything to the left of the "@" sign is more technically known as the "local part" which can contain other kinds of information besides the name of a mailbox. For example as described in Chapter 5, the local part could contain information about gateways needed to send e-mail messages beyond the Internet. But in this chapter, we will be dealing only with mailbox names.

2.2.1. The Userid

Before you mail a regular letter, the first thing you should know is to whom it will be sent. Usually, you'll put that person's regular name on the envelope.

If you want to send e-mail to someone, you need to know both their "userid" and their host computer's Internet address. Userid is an abbreviation for USER IDentification, and is pronounced "user eye dee." At your Internet site, userids might be known as "login names," "user names," or "account names."

Userids may be assigned by the people who run your Internet host, or you may be able to pick your own. Susan Rose Allen's userid is "sra", which is made from the intitials of her real name; this is one of many ways in which userids are constructed. Here are some typical kinds of userids Susan might have at other Internet hosts and how they were constructed.

`allsusr`	(ALLen, SUSan, Rose)
`srallen`	(Susan, Rose, ALLEN)
`IdahoRose`	(a userid Susan picked for herself)
`nrg1234t`	(an arbitrary userid assigned to Susan)

So just because you know someone's regular name doesn't mean you can guess their userid. Chapter 21 explains how to get e-mail addresses from various Internet directory services, which is like using a phone book to get a phone number.

Let's look again at the beginning of the second and third lines of the simple e-mail message in Example 2. (We'll get to the "@hs.idacrk.idaho.edu" part in just a little bit.)

```
From: jtallen
To:   sra
```

The first line means that the message is from "jtallen" (James Trevor Allen) and the second line means that the message is going to the "mailbox" of the person with userid "sra" (Susan Rose Allen).

2.2.2. The Mailbox

An electronic mailbox is where incoming e-mail messages are stored, just like your real mailbox is a place for the postal service to put your mail.

Note that both postal and electronic mailboxes might be for one person or many people.

When an electronic mailbox is assigned to a person, it will usually have the same name as that person's userid.

When a mailbox is assigned to a group of people, it will often have a longer, descriptive name which indicates what these people have in common, like "idaho-fossil-hunters". Such mailboxes are often used for Internet mailing lists. (See Chapter 11.)

And when a mailbox is assigned to a computer program, it will usually have a name that describes what service the program provides, like "archive-server" or "whois."

Okay, now you understand that "sra" in Susan's e-mail address is her userid and the name of her Internet mailbox. But what in the world does "@hs.idacrk.idaho.edu" mean? It tells where the "sra" mailbox is located in the Internet world!

2.2.3. "@" an Internet Address

If you want to send a postal letter to somebody, knowing their name is not enough. You also need to know their address.

The same is true for e-mail: you need to know the Internet address for the mailbox if you really want your message to get delivered.

Luckily, Internet addresses (or more properly, domain names) are put together in almost the same way as postal mail addresses. Let's look at Susan Allen's postal mail address again.

> Idaho Creek High School
> Apple Tree Lane
> Idaho Creek, Idaho
> USA

There are four lines in this address, starting with the most local information (a school) and ending with the most general (a country). This standard way of writing an address helps the postal service find the right person in the right town, in the right state, in the right country. After all, there might be 10 Susan Allens in Idaho, 100 Susan Allens in the U.S., and 1,000 Susan Allens in the world.

The same is true of Susan's mailbox name, "sra." There might be many mailboxes with this name, but a full Internet address uniquely identifies Susan's.

Put Susan's complete postal and Internet addresses into the same format and compare them.

> Internet: **sra@hs.idacrk.idaho.edu**
> Postal: SusanAllen at HighSchool.IdahoCreek.Idaho.USA

Makes sense now, doesn't it!

2.2.4. Decoding Internet Addresses

Internet addresses usually follow a few simple rules similar to the rules of postal addresses.

- An Internet address has several parts separated by periods instead of being on separate lines.

- Many parts will be abbreviations, like "cs" for computer science.

- You read a computer's Internet address left to right; the first part is usually the name of a computer (a host), and the last part is an abbreviation for a geographic or administrative domain, like "au" for AUstralian hosts on the Internet, or "edu" for the EDUcational domain in the Internet.

- The particular words in each part of an Internet address may have no particular geographic significance, just like there may be no good reason why a street is called "Oak Street." Internet addresses may include arbitrary names like cartoon characters, famous persons, or brands of soda.

- Internet addresses may have various parts just like full postal addresses might have fewer or more lines than Susan's. But in general, you'll rarely encounter full addresses with more than five or less than two parts.

For more detailed information about Internet addresses throughout the world, see "Internet Addresses" in Chapter 1.

2.3. Electronic Mail Software (Mail User Agents)

When you write a letter, you might use a pen, a pencil, or a typewriter, and a piece of paper. The editor you use with your e-mail software is all of these things. However, when you write and receive e-mail messages, you use an e-mail software program, technically known as a "mail user agent." The mail user agent lets you see incoming e-mail messages and provides an editor for composing outgoing messages.

There are many kinds of e-mail software programs ranging from simple "line-at-a-time" packages, to full featured word processing interfaces. Your computer support staff should be able to help you get started with one of the e-mail software packages used on your Internet host computer.

If you're the self-starting kind of person (or if you just can't wait to use e-mail), you could try the online help system on your Internet host. Here are some general hints on finding mail software on some common types of Internet hosts.

Unix	The basic Unix mail software is called "mail". Common full screen mail software includes "elm" and "pine." Type "man mail", "man elm", or "man pine" for the "manual pages" of these mail packages.
CMS or VMS	Try typing "help mail". You should get some basic information on the locally installed mail software.

If you're working from a personal computer such as a Mac or an IBM PC, there might be one of many different mail software packages installed. Contact your local computer support staff for help in identifying the Mac or PC mail resources that might be available to you.

2.4. For Beginners, a Few Words of Advice

If you've read this far, you now know enough to start using e-mail!

No matter what kind of e-mail software you will be using, you should try sending your first few e-mail messages to yourself so you can get the hang of sending and receiving e-mail. You might also consider asking a friend who uses the Internet to be an electronic pen pal while you practice your e-mail skills. A little bit of practice locally will make using e-mail globally much easier!

2.5. E-mail Messages from Stem to Stern

Now that you understand that e-mail addresses contain a mailbox name and the Internet address of a computer, let's take a quick look at e-mail "envelopes" and e-mail "letters."

Your country's postal service has rules and regulations about how postal mail should be addressed and packaged. For example, the U.S. States Postal Service employs a cartoon character named Speedy Zip who urges you to "remember to use ZIP codes!"

Similarly, in order to guarantee that e-mail messages can get anywhere in the Internet, a set of rules have been established for the format of e-mail messages. These rules are spelled out in "Request For Comments" (RFCs) documents, especially RFC822. (See Appendix A for more information about RFCs.)

RFC822 states that all Internet e-mail messages must be divided into two parts: a "message header" which, like a postal envelope, displays address and delivery information, and the e-mail "message body," which is like a postal letter's contents.

2.5.1. The E-mail Message Header

The RFC822 document also defines the rules which all message headers must follow. Let's take another look at the message header of Example 2.

```
Date:     Mon, 6 June 92 14:22 PST
From:     jtallen@jrhs.lakeside.washington.edu
To:       sra@hs.idacreek.idaho.edu
Subject: My first e-mail message!
```

This message header shows some of the delivery information specified by RFC822: "Date," "From," and "To." Date is when the e-mail message was sent and it works like a postmark on a postal envelope; From is the Internet e-mail address from which the message was sent; and To contains one or more Internet e-mail addresses to which the message is being sent.

2.5.2. More about "To" and "From"

Most Internet e-mail software packages know the RFC822 rules and take care of the "Date" and "From" information for you. All you really have to worry about is supplying the right address(es) in the right format(s) in the "To" field.

Although the basic "To" field should contain a full Internet address, there are times when you can get away with less and times when you might want to add more.

Sending Mail within a Host

If you are sending e-mail to people with mailboxes on the same Internet host as your mailbox, you usually need only the mailbox name in the address. Suppose Susan sends an e-mail message to Bill Diaz at Idaho Creek High School. She might use only his mailbox name (wt_diaz) instead of his entire Internet e-mail address (wt_diaz@hs.idacrk.idaho.edu).

Sending Mail within a Domain

Similarly, you can sometimes type in just part of an Internet address if the destination host is in the same domain as your host. For example, at the University of Washington here in Seattle, there are a large number of hosts in the domain "u.washington.edu", including "milton.u.washington.edu" and "byron.u.washington.edu". A person using the host "milton" can send mail to someone using "byron" by using "mailbox@byron", instead of "mailbox@byron.u.washington.edu".

Customized Address Fields

You will often see e-mail addresses which look like these:

```
Susan Allen <sra@hs.idacreek.idaho.edu>, or
"S. R. Allen, Geode Crusher!" <sra@hs.idacreek.idaho.edu>
```

If you want to add a person's name or other information to a mail header, you can put the text on the "To" line, before their e-mail address, but be sure that the real e-mail address is surrounded by angle brackets (< and >)! If the text you are adding has anything but letters in it—for example, periods, commas, or numbers—then the text must be surrounded by quotes, as in the second example above.

2.5.3. Optional Message Header Fields that You Can Add

The following message header fields can be added in most mail software packages.

Subject:	The subject line should capture the essence of the message in a few words, for example "Subject: Does Santa Claus Exist??" If you don't write a subject, your outgoing message will say "Subject: (none)." Informative "Subject" lines make handling and storing e-mail much easier when other people check their mailboxes. Furthermore, when you've used the subject field, replies to your message will have the same subject line preceded by "Re:", for example, "Subject: Re: Does Santa Claus Exist??"
CC:	(Carbon Copy) Sending someone a "CC" of a message is like saying to them, "I wanted you to know I sent this material."
BCC:	(Blind Carbon Copy) A form of "CC" that is invisible to the people named in the "To" and "CC" fields, i.e., they won't see who, or if anyone, receives the BCC.
Reply-to:	If you want replies to be sent to a different e-mail address, put that e-mail address in this field.
Keywords:	Extra information about the contents of an e-mail message, that can be used later for classifying, sorting, and searching messages in very large message databases.

2.5.4. Message Header Fields Added by Mail Delivery Agents

Other message header fields may be added by mail delivery agents as the message is passed around the Internet.

Resent-< >:	The "<>" could be "From", "To", "Date", or "CC." These fields are added when a received message is forwarded to another person. Original message headers are left untouched, so the recipient of a forwarded message knows who the original sender was and when it was originally sent.

Received:	When an e-mail message has passed through a number of mail delivery agents on it's way to a destination, their Internet addresses and date of handling are put into "Received" fields, much like international postal mail might get postmarked repeatedly on it's way from Peoria to Bora Bora.
Message-ID:	A unique number is assigned by a mail delivery agent to a message which it has handled, for example:

`<36476234.AA583@ica.beijing.canet.cn>.`

Message-ID and Received fields are often used by postmasters to figure out why rejected e-mail messages have been "bounced." (See "Bounced Mail.")

2.5.5. The E-mail Message Body

The message body contains the actual message being sent. This could be regular text, like the message James sent to his Aunt Susan, or it might be computer code for software, graphics, or sounds. A blank line separates the message header from the body.

How Long Can My E-mail Messages Be?

Just like postal services cannot transport arbitrarily large or heavy packages, some Internet hosts won't accept e-mail messages above a certain size. A common limit currently is 100 Kilobytes, which is about 25 pages of printed text. When you need to transfer *really* big files, you'll use another basic Internet service called "FTP." (See Chapter 4.)

The Signature

E-mail users often include a brief file called a signature, or "sig," at the end of their e-mail messages. The sig usually contains a few lines of contact information and, depending on preference, nuggets of personal philosophy, pithy quotes, or simple pictures. For information on how to include a sig in your e-mail messages, ask savvy e-mail users or a computer consultant at your Internet host. Please refer to Chapter 4 before you launch your sig into the world.

2.6. Shipping E-mail

Beyond here there be daemons and dragons

Numerous Medieval Maps of the Unknown

The actual nuts and bolts (or more correctly, sockets and packets) of e-mail delivery are tremendously complicated, but this little summary should give a feeling of what's going on behind the scenes. The main players are the diligent SMTP, the ever vigilant mail daemons, your most wise Postmaster—and yes, even Elvis Presley plays a role.

2.6.1. Mail Delivery Agents

SMTP and BSMTP

Most of the handling of e-mail is done automatically by "mail delivery agents," special software programs and protocols such as SMTP (Simple Mail Transfer Protocol) which must be installed at every Internet host. When you are reading e-mail messages, you will occasionally see header information containing the terms SMTP or BSMTP. These are messages from the mail delivery agents, working diligently day and night to deliver your e-mail messages ("Neither snow, nor rain, nor heat, nor gloomy night stays their couriers from the swift completion of their appointed rounds.")

Bounced Mail: "Return to Sender; Uh-ddress Uhn-known!"

If you have supplied an incorrect address in an e-mail message, or if there is a problem with the mail delivery agents on the way to the destination mailbox, your message may be returned to your mailbox. This is called "bounced mail."

Mail Daemons Are Your Friends

When you catch bounced mail in your mailbox, you may see added information from a "mail daemon." A "daemon" is software programmed to respond to specific events in a computer, so a mail daemon is a software program that lies dormant until it detects a mail message coming through. Bounced mail may originate from other sources as well.

The information provided by mail daemons may help you figure out what's gone wrong when e-mail messages get returned to you. For example "user unknown" likely means that you've given an incorrect mailbox name in your mail header; "site unknown" likely means that you've given an incorrect Internet address, and so forth.

Most e-mail users don't need to know much more than this, but if your curiosity is piqued, references to the technical documents describing these protocols are provided at the end of this chapter.

2.6.2. Postmasters

Most Internet hosts or domains also have a person assigned to take care of any serious problems that may occur with e-mail at those sites. This person is usually assigned the mailbox name "postmaster@a.local.internet.address". (On the BITNET network, which is discussed in Chapters 1 and 10, the postmaster's userid is usually "POSTMAST@HOST".)

When you have e-mail problems, save the messages and show them to your local user services staff. If they are unable to figure out your problem, they may pass the information on to the postmaster.

2.7. Sample E-mail Session with Unix "mail"

Let's step through a sample e-mail session using Unix "mail", which is one of the most "bare-bones" mail software packages around. Although these particular instructions won't work for all e-mail software packages, the general steps will probably be the same no matter what e-mail software you use.

2.7.1. Sending an E-mail Message

In this example, you'll send a mail message to yourself.

Start the Mail Software

Type "mail" and your own full e-mail address on the same line. Even though your message would probably be delivered if you just entered your userid, this gives you some practice typing full e-mail addresses.

```
% mail <you>@<your.internet.host>
```

Enter a Subject

Most e-mail software gives you a chance to enter a subject for your message. Enter something short and informative to get in the habit of using subject lines.

```
Subject: My first e-mail!!!
```

Type a Message

Now you can type a message. How you do this will vary, depending upon what software you are using. Sophisticated mail editors will let you move around with arrow keys and "wrap" text to a new line while you're typing. As you can read in this sample message, others may be less sophisticated.

```
Okay, I'm in the editor. To end each line I pres thee return
key. Dang! I can't fix my spelling errors on the previous
line! Oh well, that's okay, I'm mailing this to myself
anyway. (I'll have to ask the compter consultant if we have
a full screen mail package I can use?). To send my message,
I have to type a period on a line by itself and then press
the return key. Let's see if this works:
.
```

Send Your Message!

Type a period on a line by itself and press enter. This sends your message and you should now be back at your Unix prompt. No matter what mail software you use, when you send your message it is transferred to your host's mail delivery agent.

2.7.2. Receiving E-mail Messages

Check Your Mailbox

Wait a little while (maybe get away from your computer to stretch your legs or eat a chocolate chip cookie) and then check your mailbox.

To look at the contents of your mailbox from Unix mail, type "mail" at the Unix prompt. This lets you use Unix mail as a mail reader. Typically, you will see messages from your mailbox in a list that shows the e-mail addresses of the senders, the subject lines, and other, optional information. Even if you haven't used mail before, there may be messages in your mailbox. And if you followed the last example and all went well, you'll find at least the one you've just sent.

```
% mail

Mail version 5.3 2/18/88. Type ? for help.

"/usr/spool/mail/user-id": 4 messages 4 new

N 1 friend@another.host      Mon Jun  1 09:15 17/356 "Long time no see!"
N 2 friend@another.host      Wed Jul 15 16:26 13/59  "Reply pleeeese!"
N 3 friend@another.host      Wed Aug 26 18:01 12/120 "Helllllooooooo!!"
N 4 you@your.internet.host Thu Aug 27 14:42 17/564 "My First email!!!"
```

Read Messages in Your Mailbox

Type a message number at the "&" prompt and that message will be displayed on your screen.

```
& 4
Message 4:

Date: Thu, 27 Aug 92 04:42:56 -0700
From: you@your.internet.host
Sender: you@your.internet.host
To: you@your.internet.host
Subject: My first e-mail!!!

Okay, I'm in the editor. To end each line I pres thee return

(etc.)
```

Even though you only entered a destination e-mail address and a subject, the mail software filled in the "Date," "Sender," and "From" fields for you.

If you want to reply to your message, you can type "R", and you will be put back into the simple line-at-a-time mail editor. You would then repeat the steps you went through when writing your original message.

Getting Help while Using Mail

Most e-mail software packages have some sort of help available. In Unix mail, type "?" at the "&" prompt and you'll see a list of commands. More sophisticated mail software packages may have an on-screen help menu.

Quit Your Mail Software

To quit Unix mail, just type "x" or "q" at the "&" prompt.

```
& x

Held 1 messages in /usr/spool/mail/you

%
```

If you're using another kind of mail user agent, check the help for that package. If you're stuck, try "quit", "exit", or "end".

2.8. For More Information

2.8.1. Mail Software Programs (Mail User Agents)

For more information about using specific electronic mail software, consult your local users service staff or your computer support staff. If you are using a mainframe computer, you may also be able to get help by typing "man mail" (on Unix computers), or "help mail" (on most other mainframes).

2.8.2. Bibliography

Quarterman's book offers one of the best semi-technical discussions of electronic mail on the Internet (especially Chapters 1-7, but the rest of the book is chock full of useful general information as well). Comer's book focuses on the technical details of e-mail format and delivery. Sproul and Kiesler provide an informative and well reasoned analysis of the effects of e-mail in organizational and personal behavior.

Comer, D.E. *Internetworking With TCP/IP*. Volume 1: *Principles, Protocols, and Architecture*. Englewood Cliffs, NJ: Prentice Hall, Inc., 1991.

Lane, G. *Communications for Progress: A Guide to International E-mail*. London: Environment and Development Resource Center, 1990.

Quarterman, J.S. *The Matrix: Computer Networks and Conferencing Systems Worldwide*. Bedford, MA: Digital Press, 1990.

Sproul, L. and S. Kiesler. *Connections: New Ways of Working in the Networked Organization*. Cambridge, MA: MIT Press, 1992.

2.8.3. Technical Information about Internet Mail Protocols

Many of the technical details about how e-mail is packaged and handled on the Internet are specified in the following Requests for Comments (RFCs):

RFC821:	Simple Mail Transfer Protocol
RFC822:	Standard for the format of ARPA Internet text messages
RFC886:	Proposed standard for message heading munging
RFC934:	Proposed standard for message encapsulation
RFC974:	Mail routing and the domain system
RFC1047:	Duplicate messages and SMTP
RFC1049:	Content-type header field for Internet messages
RFC1056:	PCMAIL: A distributed mail system for personal computers
RFC1082:	Post Office Protocol: Version 2: Extended service offerings
RFC1113:	Privacy enhancement for Internet electronic mail: Part I - message encypherment and authentication procedures
RFC1114:	Privacy enhancement for Internet electronic mail: Part II - certificate-based key management
RFC1115:	Privacy enhancement for Internet electronic mail: Part III - algorithms, modes, and identifiers
RFC1122:	Requirements for Internet Hosts -- Communication Layers
RFC1123:	Requirements for Internet Hosts -- Application and Support
RFC1153:	Digest Message Format
RFC1154:	Encoding header field for Internet messages
RFC1176:	Interactive Mail Access Protocol: Version 2
RFC1225:	Post Office Protocol: Version 3

These and all other RFCs can be obtained from mail servers (Chapter 3) and many FTP archives (Chapters 3 and 7). One currently authoritative FTP archive for RFCs is:

FTP host:	`nnsc.nsf.net`	
directory:	`rfc`	
filenames:	`rfc-index.txt`	an index of RFCs
	`rfc1000.txt`	each RFC is named
	`rfc1001.txt`	rfcXXXX, where "XXXX"
	`rfc1002.txt`	is the RFC number, e.g.,
		rfc822
	etc...	

2.8.4. Usenet Newsgroups about Internet Mail and Mail User Agents

The following newsgroups deal with various technical aspects of Internet mail and mail user agents. (For more on Usenet, see Chapter 9.)

Note: These newsgroups are not good places to ask beginning questions about using e-mail ! For such questions, try the following in this order: local documentation, friends at your Internet site, your local user services staff. If all else fails, post a note to the newsgroup "news.newusers.questions".

If you do wish to post a question to a newsgroup, first read Chapter 9. Pay special attention to issues of Usenet etiquette, and be sure to indicate what mail package you are running, what version, your operating system, and a detailed description of what is going wrong. (Questions like "My e-mail package is not working. Why not?" are not appropriate in these forums.)

Newsgroup Name	General Areas of Discussion
`bit.listserv.cw-email`	Discussion about using e-mail for intra-campus communications
`bit.listserv.mailbook`	Discussion about the Rice mail user agent for VM/CMS
`comp.mail.elm`	General discussion about the elm mailer for Unix
`comp.mail.headers`	Technical discussion of Internet mail headers
`comp.mail.maps`	Posting of "maps" for UUCP mail routing
`comp.mail.mh`	Discussion of the Rand Mail Handler
`comp.mail.misc`	Miscellaneous discussion about Internet mail
`comp.mail.multi-media`	Discussion about multi-media in Internet mail
`comp.mail.mush`	Discussion about the "mail user shell" package for Unix
`comp.mail.sendmail`	Discussion about Unix sendmail utility (not a mail package)
`comp.mail.uucp`	General discussion about UUCP mail
`de.admin.mail`	Discussion of administration of e-mail in Germany (in German)
`fj.mail`	Discussion about e-mail issues peculiar to Kanji character sets but you must be able to display Kanji characters to read the "fj" newsgroups

@ 3 @

Electronic Mail Servers:
Retrieving Files via E-mail

The real monuments to Montgomery Ward and Sears, Roebuck were the catalogs they sent by the hundreds of thousands to eager rural customers... Henceforth, it needn't really matter whether one lived in city or country, for the good life could be purchased by mail wherever one made one's home. The advent of the post office's rural free delivery in 1896 was an immediate consequence of the public demand that Ward and Sears had helped create, and it pointed the way to the roads, telephones, electrical networks, and chain stores that would transform the rural landscape of America in the twentieth century.

William Cronin
Chicago and the Great West

3.1. What Is a Mail Server?

In addition to exchanging messages with people, you can use e-mail to retrieve files from software programs on the Internet. Such services are sometimes called "mail servers," or more formally, "mail archive servers." You will also encounter the generic term "file servers."

Mail servers are similar to mail-order catalogs. Instead of ordering the latest Shill-Co slicer-dicer or a subscription to *Pork Belly Digest*, you can get shareware graphics packages, libraries of sophisticated mathematical algorithms from AT&T Laboratories, and even daily updates on agricultural markets.

3.2. How Do Mail Servers Work?

A mail server is a software program that has been assigned a mailbox at an Internet address just like an Internet user. Because it is just a software package and not a person, it handles your requests with robot-like and humorless precision.

To use a mail server, you send an e-mail message to the mail server's e-mail address and put precisely worded requests in the body of your mail message. Some mail servers accept commands placed in the Subject: line, but don't do this unless you are certain it's O.K. Like the people who work for mail-order catalogs, mail server software packages aren't interested in reading long, personal letters. They are efficient order-processors which expect certain precise commands in your e-mail message, like "get super-dooper.graf" or "send eigen-vector.corrector.c".

To get started using a particular mail server, you should send an e-mail message with the word "help" in the body of your message. Essentially, this is asking for an order form. Within a short time—often minutes, but sometimes as long as a day—you will receive a message in your electronic mailbox with a description of commands used by that mail server. Sometimes, detailed descriptions of what files are available (or at least instructions on how to order a catalog of files) will also be included.

Mail servers perform most of the same functions as the anonymous FTP hosts described in Chapter 7. In fact, most mail servers simply facilitate access to FTP archives by e-mail. This is great for people who only have e-mail access to the Internet. You will probably use FTP more frequently than mail servers, but there *are* times when using a mail server is preferable, or when it maybe your only option.

3.3. Table of Mail Servers

Here's a potpourri of mail servers in the U.S., Europe, and Australia to help get you started. There's something for nearly everyone here. This information is derived from a comprehensive and frequently updated list of mail servers maintained by Jonathan Kamens of MIT's Project Athena. In a nicely self-referential twist, his list is obtainable from a mail server as described in "For More Information" at the end of this chapter.

E-mail Address	Partial Description of Mail Server's Contents
`almanac@oes.orst.edu`	Information on agriculture , IBM PCs, electronic books, and more
`archive-server@ames.arc.nasa.gov`	NASA and space related files
`archive-server@ncsa.uiuc.edu`	Telnet and TCP/IP software for personal computers and other NCSA software
`info-server@hp4nl.nluug.nl`	Software for personal computers, Usenet archives, etc.
`mailserv@garbo.uwasa.fi`	Software for personal computers, network documents, Usenet archives, etc.
`mail-server@pit-manager.mit.edu`	Many files useful for new Internet users, such as "FAQ" (Frequently Asked Questions) files, for many Usenet newsgroups
`netlib@research.att.com`	U.S. AT&T Netlib: Large archive of sophisticated mathematical source code and algorithms
`netlib@draci.cs.uow.edu.au`	Australian AT&T Netlib server
`netlib@nac.no`	European (non-UK) AT&T Netlib server
`netlib@ukc.ac.uk`	UK netlib AT&T server
`netlib@uunet.uu.net`	Not to be confused with AT&T Netlib—a large general purpose collection including software for most kinds of personal computers, archives of Usenet newsgroups, and much more
`ps-file-server@adobe.com`	PostScript software
`service@nic.ddn.mil`	Internet information, such as RFCs and FYIs
`statlib@lib.stat.cmu.edu`	Statistical software

3.4. Sample Mail Server Session Using Almanac

In this example, we'll use e-mail to retrieve files from an unusually versatile and speedy mail server called Almanac, that is operated by the Oregon Extension Service. Part of this exercise is to teach you how to use mail servers, but it is also an exercise in using e-mail.

3.4.1. Getting Started with Almanac

As with most mail servers, the first thing you should do is to send e-mail with a message for help.

```
mail:     almanac@oes.orst.edu
subject:  (none needed)
message:  help
```

3.4.2. Handling the Reply from Almanac

The mail you get back from Almanac should be the *Almanac Users Guide*, which explains Almanac's many features. Here's what the first page looks like in the mail software, PINE.

```
PINE 3.03     VIEW MAIL     Folder:inbox  Message 1 of 414 1%

Date: Tue, 25 Aug 92 03:55:56 -0700
From: Almanac Information Server <almanac@oes.orst.edu>
Reply to: owner-almanac@oes.orst.edu
To: Jonathan Kochmer {NWNet} <info@nwnet.net>
Subject: RE: (null)
--------
## Regarding your request:
   help
                     Almanac Users Guide
                    Oregon State University
                     Extension Service
0. Table of Contents

You may move directly to any section of this guide by using
your text viewer's search option to locate the upper-case
search string for that section. The list below shows the
search strings for each section.
                        Section              Search String
              1      Introduction
              2      Mail Addresses              -ADDR-
              3      Receiving Help              -HELP-

? Help M Main Menu P Prev Msg - Prev Page F Forward D Delete
O OTHER I Index N Next Msg SPACE Next Page R Reply S Save
```

You can read your copy in your mail reader, save it to a file, or print it depending on your system's capabilities.

3.4.3. Requesting Specific Files from Almanac

Here's one last Almanac exercise for the road.

```
mail:      almanac@oes.orst.edu
subject:   (none needed)
message:   send quote
           send market-news wafv281
```

"Send quote" will send you a pithy little quotation, a network version of a Chinese fortune cookie; "send market-news wafv281" will send you information on last week's international arrivals of fruits and vegetables into the U.S. Here's how Almanac responded to my "send quote" and market news requests:

```
## Regarding your request: send quote

        "Those who can't write, write manuals."
                                  - anonymous

## Regarding your request: send wafv281

AVAILABLE DOMESTIC SHIPMENTS AND IMPORTS OF ORNAMENTAL CROPS

(AMTS ARE UNITS OF 1,000 STEM COUNT UNLESS DESIGNATED)

                  AUG  2    AUG 11   TOT THIS   TOT LAST    TOTAL
                  AUG  8    AUG 17   SSN THRU   SSN THRU     LAST
                  1992      1991     AUG 15 92  AUG 17 91

CARNATIONS
    CALIF CENT    2129      2800     75973      91165      133860
    CALIF SOUTH     69        52      2294       3442        4660
    BOLIVIA          4         4       458        307         473
    CANADA           -         -         3          -           1
    CHILE            -         -       167        897        1265
    CHINA            -         -         -          4           4
    COLOMBIA     12900     16049    730472     662910      988352
    COSTA RICA       -         -       397        402         736
    DOMIN REPUB.     -         -       230        209         211
    ECUADOR         86       258      9671      10495       14548
    FRANCE           -         -         -          6           6
    GUATEMALA      212       110      4427       3693        5601

(etc. for many pages)
```

I *wish* this were a cute and contrived example, but this is really what Almanac sent when I submitted my requests. Oh well, what does Almanac know anyway?!? It's just a computer program! But how *polite* and *sweet* of it to send me carnations... :-)

3.5. For More Information

3.5.1. General Information

Jonathan Kamens of MIT maintains two very useful files relating to mail servers.

"How To Find Sources"	Includes comprehensive listing of electronic mail servers; this file is packed with good advice on finding network sources.
"Mail Archive Server Software List"	An invaluable resource containing a list of mail server software with useful summary information for folks who want to set up a mail server.

You can get these files by mail server or by FTP.

By Mail Server

To get these files by mail server, send an e-mail message to:

`mail-server@pit-manager.mit.edu`

Include one of the following messages EXACTLY as shown below. If you miss a single "/" or "_" you won't get the file. (As I said, mail servers are humorless robots.)

send usenet/comp.sources.wanted/How_to_find_sources_(READ_THIS_BEFORE_POSTING)

or

send usenet/comp.mail.misc/Mail_Archive_Server_(MAS)_software_list

By FTP or Usenet Newsgroup

Both files are also available via anonymous File Transfer Protocol (FTP) and periodically posted to the newsgroups "comp.sources.wanted" and "comp.mail.misc". (For more on FTP and Usenet, see Chapters 7 and 9.) As above, when you retrieve these files from the FTP host, be sure to enter the filenames exactly as shown below:

FTP host:	`pit-manager.mit.edu`
directory:	`pub/usenet/comp.sources.wanted`
filenames:	`How_to_find_sources_(READ_THIS_BEFORE_POSTING)`
	`Mail_Archive_Server_(MAS)_software_list`

@ 4 @

Electronic Mail Etiquette: "How to Talk Internet"

Undirected by culture patterns—organized systems of significant symbols—man's behavior would be virtually ungovernable, a mere chaos of pointless acts and exploding emotions, his experience virtually shapeless.

Clifford Geertz
The Interpretation of Cultures

More often than not, what brings a stranger to his knees here is waving. Waving—it looks like a simple act, but it's almost as complicated as spoken Minnesotan.

Howard Mohr
How To Talk Minnesotan

Many travellers take little phrase books to help them communicate in foreign lands. Such books may offer invaluable phrases like "How do I get to the 'Islands of the Dreadful Hummingbirds?'" or "I collect paperclips. Do you have a hobby?" Apart from a selection of phrases, the best of these books also alert you to the unspoken nuances of etiquette and behavior that are woven into the fabric of a culture. Abiding by some simple rules can make your visit more pleasant and can help you avert a cultural faux pas.

This is equally true when travelling the world online.

There are a number of generally agreed upon do's and don'ts you should understand before you enter the world online and after reading many mail messages from many other people—in other words, after becoming enculturated to the ways of the net—you will probably understand why these principles make good sense.

First, consider two examples of e-mail messages.

Example 1 illustrates the intelligent and tasteful use of e-mail rules of etiquette and style. It is easy to read, written in an informative manner, and generally is an exemplar of e-mail etiquette.

Example 2 may seem extreme, but as everyone who has used the Internet can attest, messages such as this *do* occur! The text of Example 1 was carefully contorted into Example 2 by violating nearly every rule of etiquette espoused in this chapter.

Example 1: E-mail Following Suggested Etiquette Guidelines

```
Date:   Wed 8 June 92 10:45 MST
From:   Bill Diaz <wt_diaz@hs.idacrk.idaho.edu>
To:     Jim Allen <jtallen@jrhs.lkside.wash.edu>
CC:     Susan Allen <sallen@hs.idacrk.idaho.edu>
Subject: Prospecting in Ponderosa Canyon? You Bet!

Jim,

I'm *delighted* to hear you're visiting this summer! You wrote:

> When I'm there, do you think that geology teacher Bill Diaz
> could take me prospecting again in the mountains?

You bet, I'd be glad to have you come along!  I've planned a trip
from July 24-27, if that fits with your plans. Here's a few things
to get ahold of before you visit:

        a geological hammer, and plastic sunglasses
        a good field guide for rocks and minerals
        a *light* sleeping bag (remember how HOT
           you were in that down bag last summer? :-)
        a sturdy pair of hiking boots

If you need advice, feel free to contact me!  Take care,

Bill
```

Example 2: E-mail Violating Suggested Etiquette Guidelines

```
Date:   Wed 8 June 92 10:45 MST
From:   wt_diaz@hs.idacrk.idaho.edu
To:     jallen@jrhs.lkside.wash.edu
i'm delEted to hear that you're visiting us in idaho creek again this
 i'd be happy to have you come prosepcting. i've already planned
 a m july 24-27. here's some things you should probely bring along:
^Z logical hammer, a g   od field guide f      rocks and minerals, a
      light sleep if    king boots, and      sunglasses with plastic
      boots would be    Free to MAil ba      ser-id. Here's my sig!/-
 ^   ^           /  \      /\       /\  \  |  /  /'tis a gift to be sim
      ^ _      /----\  /  \     /  \  \ | / /'tis a gift to be free
   /  \     /      \/----\   /----\  \ /  /+------------------
    /    \   /"home is\     \ /      \ o /   |__   o   |    |
   /     \ / where the\     \        \ /    | \  |    |    |
  /        \heart is"   \                   |_/ _|_  _|_  _|_
tel: (208) 999-1234 (home) 999-4321 (woodshed) 999-3456 (car fax)
user-ids: wt_diaz@hs.idacrk.idaho.edu (INTERNET) wt_diaz@idacrkh
```

4.1 The Format of E-mail Messages

Many e-mail etiquette principles arise from the current state of terminal technology in networks. Although some lucky people have extraordinarily powerful graphics workstations that can display characters and graphics of varying fonts, sizes, and colors, most folks on the Internet still eke by with simple, text-only displays limited to 80 columns and 24 rows of text.

4.1.1. Screen Size

Be brief. What you need to communicate can usually fit in a screen of text.

Try to keep your e-mail messages narrower than 65 characters and/or spaces wide; short lines are easier to read on a computer screen, and other people's terminals may not be able to display longer lines. This also leaves room for text to be moved to the right when it is quoted by others. (This point is described in greater detail below.)

Blank spaces between paragraphs or other logical units of text make it easier to read the message. Along the same lines, keep your paragraphs short; in general, fewer than 15 lines should be about right. Large blocks of text can make it difficult to keep one's place within a screen or when moving between screens. (Unfortunately blocks of text that are proportioned correctly for a computer screen often seem disjointed when printed.)

4.1.2. Stylistic Conventions of Text-Only Messages

Using standard capitalization and mixed-case text is preferable in both written and electronic communication. messages in all lower case can cause problems. it creates a halting, uncertain reading pattern. on the other hand, USING ALL UPPER CASE IN A MAIL MESSAGE IS LIKE SHOUTING WHEN YOU SPEAK!

Emphasis can be subtle and effective. For example, use asterisks, underlines, or other special characters around words or phrases, like *this*, or like _this_, or >>even<< like that!

4.1.3. Control Characters and "The Sorcerer's Apprentice" Phenomenon

Avoid using control sequences (like "ctrl d") or special keys (like "tab"). Even if they seem to work fine while you are editing your mail document, such special characters may do really bizarre things to your file when someone else reads it with their e-mail software. (Using control characters is in fact how the weird slanted columns were generated in Example 2.)

4.2 The Content of E-mail Messages

Strive to be concise, clear, and polite in your own writing and flexible in your interpretation of the mail you receive from other people. This conforms to an old networking axiom: "Be precise in what you send, and forgiving of what you receive."

The following set of points deals with stylistic considerations that are based on the often neglected fact that the readers of e-mail messages are actually real people!

4.2.1. Of Relevance to All Outbound Messages

Use short, informative subject lines. In most cases, software for receiving e-mail displays only the first 15 or 20 characters. Since your subject line is the first impression your message makes on your recipient, be sure to distill the essence of your message into a few choice words that hit the proverbial nail on the head.

Most mail software packages have a CC (Carbon Copy) option allowing your mail to be sent to those who are at least marginally interested in what you have sent to the person indicated in the "To" field. This might be a boss you are trying to impress with your unending torrent of high-quality, work-related memos, or it might be yourself, if you need a reminder in your mailbox to "MEET THE DEADLINE!"

Begin your message with the name of the person to whom you are writing. Even though the person's e-mail address is in the mail header, starting your text with their real name makes your message more personal. Similarly, many mail software packages allow you to add a person's real name to the "To" field (see Chapter 2). Most people prefer to be known by their real names rather than by a userid. If you've never met the person to whom you're sending e-mail, a more formal title (Ms. Allen) or more generic salutation (Hello!) may be appropriate.

For some unknown reason, e-mail messages rarely begin with "Dear <insert name here>." Although this salutation is standard practice in regular letters, it is conspicuously absent in e-mail exchanges. (This is one of the *many* peculiarities of computer mediated communication that is worthy of analysis. If anybody takes this on, please let me know!)

In face-to-face conversation, subtle body language and intonation let us know how our speech affects the other person. These cues are completely absent when using e-mail.

Since e-mail doesn't contain direct physical cues, a number of conventions peculiar to e-mail have taken hold. In particular, the classic "smiley" is used to indicate that the previous statement was meant in a light-hearted or humorous way. Smileys, when looked at sideways, look vaguely like stick drawings of human faces. There are hundreds of smileys that can be made with the basic characters of a keyboard, each of which conveys a different emotion. Here's a small audience of smileys and their less fortunate relatives, dubbed "weepies," "frownies," or "anti-smiles":

:-)	the basic smiley	:-(	the basic frowney
;-)	the winking smiley	:-o	"OH NO!"
;^}	a more sinister winking smiley	>:-/	Sick of smileys

You get the idea. Hundreds of such ASCII glyphs are possible and there are in fact smiley hunters prowling through the net with collecting jars in hand. Although smileys serve a purpose, as with all things, moderation is best.

As a courtesy end the text of your message with your name. You may also want to include your first name, nickname, e-mail address, organization—whatever seems appropriate to the context.

Never forget that your e-mail is read by another human being—someone who's feelings and beliefs may be very different from yours! This is always important, but especially now as the Internet becomes a global community. The underlying humanity of the net can be easy to forget when you are sitting at a computer terminal writing a mail message to someone you have never met in person and about whom you may know virtually nothing—except that they are human.

4.2.2. The Infamous Signature: *John Hancock* Lives to See the Internet

With some mail software, you can automatically append a file called a "signature" (or "sig") to every outgoing mail message you send. As people grew weary of always typing their names, e-mail addresses, and other information at the end of every message, it seemed reasonable to automate the process. Thus, the signature file was born.

If you use a sig, remember the following:

- Keep your sig short, fewer than five lines is enough. Simple is best.

- Don't include ASCII graphics made of letters and characters (like a 24 row map of the Indian Ocean) or lists of all possible telephone numbers, postal, and e-mail addresses at which you can be contacted. At the very least, they take up space in other people's computers.

4.2.3. Of Relevance to Replies and Forwarded Messages

With most mail software, the reply and forward features allow you to automatically include someone else's mail message in your outgoing message. Pare the original text down to the minimal needed to establish context.

There are some stylistic conventions used when replying to e-mail messages. Symbols such as ">" or "|" are commonly added by the mail software in the first column of the message to which you are replying. This is sometimes referred to as "quoting." Where the message you received contained quoted material as well, these symbols may become layered.

```
>>> When did Henry IV of England live?
>> Henry IV lived in a flat near Shrewsbury in 1934.
> Are you sure? Last I checked with British Telecom, he was
> living in Nottingham.

Close, but not quite. Henry IV lived from 1366-1413 in
Bolingbroke and London!
```

True e-mail artists have a way of efficiently interspersing their comments with the original message, as in the following hypothetical e-mail reply (derived from W. Shakespeare, "Henry IV, Part 1", Scene III, Act 2):

```
On Wed, 16 Nov. 1402, The Earl of Worcester wrote:

> But, for mine own part, my lord, I could be well contented
> to be there, in respect of the love I bear your house.

You could be contented, why are you not then?

> The purpose you undertake is dangerous.

Why, that's certain: 'tis dangerous to take a cold, to
sleep, to drink: but I tell you, out of this nettle,
danger, we pluck this flower, safety.

> the friends you have named uncertain; the time itself
> unsorted; and your whole plan too light for the
> counterpoise of so great an opposition.

Say you so, say you so? I say unto you again, you are a
shallow, cowardly hind, and you lie. What a lack brain is
this! By the Lord, our plan is a good plan as ever was
laid; our friends true and contstant: a good plan, good
friends, and full of expectation; an excellent plan, very
good friends. ;-)

Your cool-headed friend
Hotspur
```

Do *not* include the entire original message unless you absolutely have to. This wastes resources used for transmitting and storing mail and, more importantly, the time of the person who has to locate the single word at the end of the message wherein you so eloquently doth declaim "NOT!"

Before sending off your e-mail message:

- Review what you have written and correct grammar and spelling errors.

- Make sure you've said everything you needed to say.

- Make sure you haven't said things you didn't need to say.

And finally, finally, finally, make shure you've yewsed korrect speling and grammer, splling errers end bad grammers make it harder for uther peeple to reed what you wrought. :^) Here's my sig!:

THE BASIC RULES OF E-MAIL ETIQUETTE

Be brief.

Keep line lengths to less than 65 columns.

Use blank spaces between paragraphs to help the reader's eye.

Use mixed upper and lower case.

Use capitals AND special characters for *emphasis*!

Keep your paragraphs short. Fewer than 15 lines is best.

Avoid using control characters or special keys.

Begin text with the real name of the person to whom you're writing.

If useful, include parts of the mail message to which you are replying.

End the text of your message with your real name.

If you use a "sig," keep it short and simple.

Review what you've written BEFORE you send it.

If possible, include the person's real name in the "To" line of the header.

Use the CC option if available and appropriate.

Summary of the points of e-mail etiquette in a format suitable for framing and placing next to your terminal

4.3 For More Information

4.3.1. Online Information

The following articles appear in the newsgroup "news.announce.newusers" as "periodic postings." Although written with Usenet in mind, many of the principles they espouse are relevant to all electronic mail communication. For more on Usenet, see Chapter 9.

Offutt, A.J., and G. Spafford. "Hints on Writing Style for Usenet." 1992.

Templeton, B., and G. Spafford. "Emily Postnews Answers Your Questions on Netiquette." (A tongue-in-cheek, very funny, but very informative essay on what not to do in electronic mail, especially in Usenet postings.) 1992.

Von Rospach, C. and G. Spafford. "A Primer on How to Work With the Usenet Community." 1992.

4.3.2. Bibliography

Goode, J. and M. Johnson, "Putting Out the Flames: The Etiquette and Law of E-mail." *Online* 15(6) (1991):61-65.

Quarterman, J.S. "Etiquette and Ethics." *ConneXions*—The Interoperability Report. (Advanced Computing Environments, Mountain View, CA.) 3(4) (1989):12-16.

Shapiro, N.Z., and R.H. Anderson. "Towards an Ethics and Etiquette for Electronic Mail." Santa Monica, CA: Rand Corporation, 1985.

@ 5 @

Electronic Mail Gateways: Sending Messages to the Great Beyond

Toto, I have a feeling we're not in Kansas anymore!

Judy Garland, in *The Wizard of Oz*

Although the Internet connects many countries and millions of people, there is a wide-variety of non-Internet networks as well.

You may want to exchange e-mail messages with people using these networks or may want to access services those networks provide. This chapter explains how you can communicate with people or services on many non-Internet networks by using electronic mail gateways.

5.1. What Are Electronic Mail Gateways?

Mail gateways are computers that allow e-mail messages to be transmitted between networks that use differing methods of addressing and packaging information.

Many computer networks are not part of the Internet and do not use the Internet Protocols (IP). Recall that if you want to send an e-mail message anywhere in the Internet you would use the standard Internet address format.

        `mailbox@an.Internet.host.address`

Addresses on other networks may use very different formats. Consider the format of an MCI e-mail address.

        `Firstname Lastname (123-4567)`

Internet mailers cannot read an address like this, because it contains information and symbols that are not part of an Internet address; likewise your postal service would be baffled by a letter with an Internet address. Furthermore, the actual way in which mail messages are packaged in other networks may be considerably different.

Mail gateways are able to resolve differences in both addressing and packaging when transmitting information between networks.

5.2. How to Use Electronic Mail Gateways

You need to know four things to send mail to users and computers on other networks:

1) the addressing convention of the network to which you are sending mail;

2) how to present the foreign network's address in your mail header so the Internet mailers won't reject it;

3) the Internet address of a gateway computer connected to the other network; and,

4) the e-mail address of the person or computer on the other network.

All of the information you need to answer questions 1-3 for many of the more commonly used non-Internet networks is provided in Table 1. It's up to you to supply the destination e-mail address.

The basic strategy used by mail gateways to transmit messages from the Internet to other networks is very simple:

• the Internet address of the appropriate e-mail gateway is put in the Internet address field;

• and sometimes, address information from the alien network is put in the userid field of an Internet e-mail address.

For example, suppose you want to send an e-mail message to a friend in France who uses the EARN network (a portion of the BITNET network). The typical e-mail address within the BITNET network looks like this:

    `user@host`

To send an e-mail message to our friend from a computer on the Internet, we need to include their whole e-mail address and the Internet address of an Internet-BITNET gateway.

Here's a general example of the e-mail address you would enter.

    `user%host.bitnet@An.Interbit.Gateway.Address`

where "An.Interbit.Gateway.Address" is one of the several computers providing Internet gateway services to both the Internet and to BITNET. (See Table 1 for a listing of these gateways.)

"C'est tres facile, non?" "You betcha!"

5.2.1. Table of Mail Gateways from the Internet to Other Networks

This table summarizes the information you need to send e-mail messages to some of the many non-Internet networks. It is derived from a more complete guide maintained by John Chew. (Refer to the end of this chapter for information on obtaining the "Inter-Network Mail Guide.")

For each network:

1) the first row contains the electronic mail address syntax used in each non-Internet network;

2) the second row shows how you modify that network's native electronic mail address syntax to send mail from the Internet to that network.

America Online	1) `userid`
	2) `userid@aol.com`
Applelink	1) `userid`
	2) `userid@applelink.apple.com`
BITNET	1) `userid@site`
	2) `userid@site.bitnet`
	At many Internet sites, you can address mail to BITNET users with the syntax above. If this doesn't work, try the following syntax:
	`userid%host.bitnet@An.Interbit.Gateway.Address`
	where "`An.Interbit.Gateway.Address`" is one of the following:

	`CORNELLC.CIT.CORNELL.EDU`
	`CUNYVM.CUNY.EDU`
	`MITVMA.MIT.EDU`
	`VM1.NODAK.EDU`

CompuServe	1) `7xxxx,yyy`
	2) `7xxxx.yyy@CompuServe.Com`
EASYnet/ DECNET	1) `host::user`
	2) `user@host.enet.dec.com`
ESnet	1) `userid@host`
	2) `userid@lbl.dnet.nasa.gov`
FidoNet	1) `Firstname Lastname at 1:2/3.4`
	2) `Firstname.Lastname@p4.f3.n2.z1.fidonet.org`
JANET	1) `userid@A.Janet.Domain.Address` (e.g., "`uk.ac.ox.vax`")
	2) `userid@Address.Domain.Janet.A` (e.g., "`vax.ox.ac.uk`")
MCI	1) `FirstName LastName (123-4567)`, where `123-4567` is an MCI phone id #
	2) `1234567@mcimail.com`
PeaceNet	1) `userid`
	2) `userid@cdp.igc.org`
Sprintmail	1) `Firstname Lastname at AnOrganization`
	2) `/G=Firstname/S=Lastname/O=AnOrganization/ADMD=TELEMAIL/C=US/@Sprint.Com`
THEnet	1) `userid@host`
	2) `userid%host.decnet@utadnx.cc.utexas.edu`

5.2.2. Using the Mail Gateways Table

As the previous example demonstrates, you need to know the Internet addresses of gateways which are appropriate for sending e-mail to users on non-Internet networks. Suppose you wanted to send an e-mail message to a friend who has an account on the FidoNet network. They've told you that their FidoNet address is the following:

```
Kelley Meithisson at 3:56/67.4
```

First make sure that you, and they, have got everything in this address right. Simple transcriptional errors are one of the more frequent causes of Inter-gateway mail problems.

Look in the first column to find Fidonet. Read across to the line labeled "1)." This shows a typical FidoNet userid and address which corresponds to your friend Kelley's address information above. Now look at the next line labeled "2)." This shows how Kelley's FidoNet address should be translated by an Internet user so that an e-mail message will be successfully sent to a FidoNet user. According to line 2, Kelley's FidoNet address should be translated to:

```
Kelley.Meithisson@p4.f67.n56.z3.fidonet.org
```

This address is now acceptable to mailers that conform to the Internet standards. When it arrives at the Internet-Fidonet gateway, it will be translated to a FidoNet address format and delivered within the FidoNet network to Kelley.

5.3. For More Information

5.3.1. Online Table of Gateways

"The Inter-Network Mail Guide," by John Chew, is a comprehensive and usually up-to-date table of gateways between the Internet and many other networks available by anonymous FTP. (For more on FTP, see Chapter 7.)

FTP host:	`ra.msstate.edu`
directory:	`pub/docs`
filename:	`internetwork-mail-guide`

Chew's document is also posted periodically to the following newsgroups, which are good forums for asking and answering questions about gateway problems.

`news.newusers.questions`	a good newsgroup for simple gateway problems
`comp.mail.misc`	a good newsgroup for obstinate gateway problems

It is also available from the following LISTSERV list:

```
mail:     listserv%unmvm.bitnet@cunyvm.cuny.edu
subject:  (none needed)
message:  get network guide
```

(For more on Usenet and LISTSERV, see Chapters 9 and 10.)

5.3.2. RFCs about Gateways

The following RFCs give some insight into the nuts and bolts of some gateway protocols:

RFC987:	Mapping between X.400 and RFC822
RFC1026:	Addendum to RFC987: (mapping between X.400 and RFC-822)
RFC1137:	Mapping between full RFC 822 and RFC 822 with restricted encoding
RFC1148:	Mapping between X.400 (1988) / ISO 10021 and RFC 822
RFC1168:	Intermail and commercial mail relay services

5.3.3. Bibliography

The following three reference books are invaluable resources for understanding the intricacies of electronic mail gateways specifically and intercommunication between networks generally:

Frey, D., and R. Adams. *!%@:: A Directory of Electronic Mail Addressing and Networks*. Newton, MA: O'Reilly and Associates, 1991.

LaQuey, T.L. *The User's Directory of Computer Networks*. Bedford, MA: Digital Press, 1990.

Quarterman, J.S. *The Matrix: Computer Networks and Conferencing Systems Worldwide*. Bedford, MA: Digital Press, 1990.

@ 6 @

Telnet: Using Computers throughout the Internet

If you're studying the eruption of a volcano, a computer model is better *than being there.*

Joseph Deken
The Electronic Cottage

========

Telnet allows you to use Internet computers throughout the world. Note that Telnet is not a network; it is one of the TCP/IP protocol applications that makes the Internet possible and useful.

Some of the many services that Telnet allows you to access include:

- library catalogs;
- databases;
- supercomputers;
- directories of e-mail addresses;
- and a huge variety of information services.

When you run a Telnet session with a computer thousands of kilometers away, the activities of that computer seem to be unfolding in real time right on your computer's screen. It's really quite amazing!

Telnet that supports 3270 terminal emulation (usually called "tn3270") is required for remote sessions to and from IBM mainframes. For the time being, assume that what applies to Telnet applies equally to tn3270. But as you'll find out later in this chapter, effective use of tn3270 often requires special attention and preparation.

6.1. Telnet Basics

Most Internet computers already have Telnet software installed. When you use Telnet, your local software (i.e., the Telnet "client") communicates with the remote software (i.e., the Telnet "server") on the computer whose services you want to access. All of this happens behind the scenes. What you see on your screen is the computer service you have requested.

6.1.1. Levels of Telnet Access

In practice, there are two levels of Telnet access.

- "Guest Telnet" allows you to login to an Internet host to use special, publicly available service(s) on the remote computer.

- With "full privilege Telnet" you can login to any other Internet computer on which you have an account.

6.1.2. Telnet Etiquette

All Telnet etiquette derives from one simple fact: somebody, somewhere, has been generous enough to let people on the Internet use their computer. In exchange for this generosity, these systems should be used with the utmost consideration and respect.

Some services request that you not use them during specific hours of the day, usually during standard business hours. If this is the case, honor this request and remember to take into consideration any difference in time zones between you and the site to which you would like to telnet.

6.2. Using Telnet

6.2.1. Getting Started

From most hosts on the Internet, starting a Telnet session is fairly straightforward.

Typically you just type "telnet" followed by the Internet address of a computer to which you want to connect.

```
telnet an.internet.host.address
```

If you are working from a computer with a graphical user interface such as the Apple Macintosh, a DOS machine running Windows, or a specific workstation, you might start Telnet by clicking an icon.

If you can't figure out how to start Telnet, try your local online help system or get help from your user services staff. Here are some of the more common requests you might use to get online help.

Unix   **man telnet**
VMS, VM/CMS, some Unix machines   **help telnet** or **help tcpip**

Command Mode

When you type telnet without a host address, you may find yourself in Telnet command mode. The prompt "telnet >" usually appears. This may also happen if you've misspelled the host's name or the host is unreachable. In the following example, I attempted to telnet to a (so far as we know) non-existent host and was presented with the telnet prompt:

```
telnet alpha.centuri.gov
alpha.centuri.gov: host unknown
telnet>
```

From this prompt, you can issue a variety of Telnet commands, of which the most commonly needed are "open" and "quit".

Open is used to open a telnet connection to a remote host.

```
telnet> open <an.internet.host.address>
```

Not surprisingly, quit is used to end any current remote sessions and exit Telnet, returning you to your operating system's prompt.

For more on what commands are available in command mode, see the sections "Ending a Telnet Session" and "Help!" later in this chapter.

6.2.2. A Sampler of Destinations

Here's a list of a few of the many Telnet sites on the Internet that offer valuable and interesting services. Enjoy!

Service Type and Name	Internet Address	Login Name
Internet Front Ends		
UNC BBS	`bbs.oit.unc.edu`	`bbs`
Services	`wugate.wustl.edu`	`services`
Library Catalogs		
CARL	`pac.carl.org`	none needed
MELVYL	`melvyl.ucop.edu`	none needed
Directory Services		
DDN NIC	`nic.ddn.mil`	none needed
Paradise	`hypatia.umdc.umu.se`	`de`
Databases		
PENpages (Agriculture)	`psupen.psu.edu`	`pnotpa`
FEDIX (Grants, Scholarships)	`fedix.fie.com`	`fedix`
Spacelink (NASA and Space Sciences)	`spacelink.msfc.nasa.gov`	`newuser`

6.2.3. Login Name and Password

One usually uses Telnet to engage in an interactive session with a Telnet host or service. In such cases, you have to supply a login name and maybe a password much as you would with your own computer account.

Sometimes a login screen displays information needed to use the service. For example, users of the University of North Carolina "Extended Bulletin Board Service" (whose Internet address is "bbs.oit.unc.edu") see the following message when they login:

```
telnet bbs.oit.unc.edu

Trying...
Connected to lambada.oit.unc.edu.
Escape character is '^]'.

ULTRIX V4.2A (Rev. 47) (lambada)

        *** ATTENTION EBBS USERS ***
        Type 'bbs' at the login prompt.

login: bbs
```

In this case you would simply type "bbs" at the "login:" prompt. But you will often need to know these login instructions before you access the service. Most reference lists of Telnet sites will give you this information.

6.2.4. Telnet Troubleshooting

If you type "telnet <an.internet.host.address>" and you don't get connected, read the error message that has appeared on your screen.

- "unknown host"—Most likely you have misspelled the computer's domain name, or the domain name might have changed, or the host may simply no longer exist.

- "foreign host not responding" and related messages—There's probably too much traffic somewhere on the Internet between you and the host, or the host is temporarily disabled in some way. Try again later.

- "maximum number of users exceeded" or something to that effect—This is likely to happen during the business hours of the site you are trying to reach, or on a system that has internally limited the number of simultaneous users accessing a specific service. Try again later.

6.2.5. About Terminal Emulation

When you want to use Telnet to access another Internet host, that host will often ask you for your "terminal type. You might be shown a list of options. Here is a terminal type list from pac.carl.org, an Internet host providing library catalog services:

```
telnet pac.carl.org

Trying...
Connected to pac.carl.org.
Escape character is '^]'.
Welcome to the CARL system

Please identify your terminal. Choices are:
1.ADM (all)
2.APPLE,IBM
3.TANDEM
4.TELE-914
5.VT100
6.WYSE 50
7.ZENTEC
8.HARDCOPY
9.IBM 316x

Use HARDCOPY if your terminal type isn't listed

SELECT LINE #:
```

Terminal type does not mean, "Is your computer a Macintosh SE or a Cray Y-MP?" but rather "What kind of terminal is your computer software emulating?"

Early on in the history of computers, each major computer company designed special terminals for particular purposes. For example, the Digital Electronics Corporation (DEC) developed the VT series of terminals (VT52, VT100, etc.) for accessing DEC computers; Tektronix terminals were developed for displaying graphics; and IBM developed the 3270 terminal for accessing IBM mainframes.

Today, you can use communications software that allows your computer to emulate one or more of these terminal types. The most commonly used terminal type on the Internet is VT100.

For more information about terminal emulation, ask a local user services person for help. The right answers to your questions depend heavily on the software and hardware installed at your site.

6.2.6. About tn3270

As alluded to above, 3270 refers to a special kind of terminal designed to interface with IBM mainframes, and tn3270 refers to software that emulates (or acts like) a 3270 terminal. Why is this important? Because you value your sanity.

The 3270 terminal implements the full-screen interface necessary for most IBM mainframe applications and relies heavily upon special features such as input areas and protected fields (areas where you can and cannot type, respectively), program function keys (the infamous "PF" keys), and other command keys ("PA," "clear") not employed by the standard VT100 emulation.

What this means to Internet users is that if you want to telnet to a 3270 based system, you must use a version of Telnet which emulates the 3270 terminal.

For users of IBM mainframes, this is usually no problem: you will typically use a program called "telnet" (which is actually 3270 based), and your remote IBM mainframe session will probably be just like your host mainframe session. So, "PF 12! PA1! and 'More...'" to your heart's content.

However, things are a bit trickier going between IBM mainframes and non-3270 based sites.

If you are going from a non-IBM mainframe to an IBM mainframe, you will need to use a version of Telnet called tn3270. Much of the time, tn3270 functions just the way your telnet software does. Simply type "tn3270" followed by the IBM host name. For example, "tn3270 orbis.ycc.yale.edu" would connect you to Yale's online library catalog, ORBIS.

However, even if you connect successfully, you may become confused or have trouble during your session; when prompted for "PF2", you may in fact have to type "esc 2" or some other initially nonintuitive incantation or permutation. And if your screen freezes (often accompanied by the word "HOLDING" in the lower right corner), and nothing will let you proceed, you either need to use a "clear" key if it has been assigned, or break your session ungracefully by using your Telnet escape command to quit the session.

To melt icy screens and resolve other quirks of the tn3270 world in future sessions, you may have to invoke special keymap files. For example, Unix users may be able to avail themselves of a file called "map3270" which allows tn3270 functions to be "mapped" to the keyboards of VT100 or other terminal types .

And if you telnet from an IBM mainframe to a service requiring VT100 emulation, the remote host may present you with an unintelligible, nonfunctional display, if it is not able to understand 3270 emulation.

Don't feel badly if this discussion has you confused—we are not alone. As with all issues that are site-related, your best bet is to talk with your local computer support staff.

6.2.7. What Is a Telnet Session Like?

What happens during your Telnet session from this point on depends upon the software and services of the computer you are accessing. It could be anything from an easy to use menu driven system giving information about the Internet to arcane, highly specialized programs designed to help you with very specific tasks like determining the locations of all telecommunications satellites within a 736.15 kilometer radius of Papete, Bora Bora.

Most all Telnet accessible services have some sort of online help system. If you don't see anything on screen about how to get help, try typing "help", "info", or "?". Commands like, "How does this thing work?" usually don't.

6.2.8. Ending a Telnet Session

Most Telnet services have a correct way of ending the session, usually a command like "logout," "logoff," "exit," "quit," or "bye." If the command to end is not obvious, try checking online help.

However, some services simply don't offer a way to exit. Or, for a variety of reasons, your session may suddenly display gibberish and not respond to commands.

If you must bail out of a Telnet session for some reason, try the "escape character" command. The most common version of this command is "control right bracket," symbolized as "^]". To issue this command, hold the key marked "ctrl" while pressing the "]" key. The Telnet escape character puts you in Telnet command mode and invokes the Telnet prompt ("telnet>") at which you can enter the command "quit". (Standard disclaimer: the procedure described here may not work with all Telnet software. Talk to your local computer support staff for more information.)

6.2.9. Help!

With most Telnet software, you can get help. Try starting Telnet without supplying an Internet host address, and then type "help" at the "telnet>" prompt. Most people never use the advanced Telnet commands, but you might as well know that they are available.

```
telnet

telnet> help

Commands may be abbreviated. Commands are:

close       close current connection
display     display operating parameters
mode        try to enter line-by-line or character-at-a-time
            mode
open        connect to a site
quit        exit telnet
send        transmit special characters ('send ?' for more)
set         set operating parameters ('set ?' for more)
status      print status information
toggle      toggle operating parameters ('toggle ?' for more)
z           suspend telnet
?           print help information
```

For more detailed information about these commands, you can type the command name followed by a
"?".

```
telnet> toggle ?

autoflush      toggle flushing of output when sending
               interrupt characters
autosynch      toggle automatic sending of interrupt
               characters in urgent mode
binary         toggle sending and receiving of binary data
crlf           toggle sending carriage returns as telnet
               <CR><LF>
crmod          toggle mapping of received carriage returns
localchars     toggle local recognition of certain control
               characters
debug          (debugging) toggle debugging
netdata        (debugging) toggle printing of hexadecimal
               network data
options        (debugging) toggle viewing of options
               processing
?              display help information
```

If this process doesn't work for you, ask your local computer support staff to assist you in finding help
for your Telnet software.

6.2.10. Telnet Ports

Just like there may be many doors leading into a building, there are many different "ports" leading
into most Internet hosts. Each of these ports is assigned a name, number, and purpose. The default
Telnet port is usually assigned to TCP port number 23. When you type "telnet
an.internet.host.address" the Telnet protocol assumes you mean "telnet an.internet.host.address 23".
This gives you a login screen where you must minimally provide a userid and password to continue.

However, some Telnet services may be assigned to other ports in which case, you will be required to
add a port number or name after an Internet address when you use Telnet. Here's an example of a very
simple service available on port 13 of many Internet hosts called "daytime." (Try using the Internet
address of your own Internet host.)

```
telnet <an.internet.host.address> 13

Trying...
Connected to an.internet.host.address.
Escape character is '^]'.

Thu Sep 10 14:58:44 PDT 1992

Connection closed by foreign host.
```

(Note that the exact syntax used to issue a port number may vary between Telnet software packages.)

A wide variety of Internet services, many of which are described throughout *The Internet Passport*, require specifying a port number. Some examples include the University of Michigan Weather Underground and the Knowbot Information Server.

6.3. What Happens behind the Scenes?

When you telnet to an Internet host, the Telnet program at your host and the Telnet program at the other host send messages back and forth to each other, in effect negotiating how they will communicate.

Some of the negotiations concern simple matters like how many columns of text your screen can display; others are more complicated issues dealing with exactly how information will be coded.

If the negotiations were conversations on which you could eavesdrop, you'd hear something like the following:

```
telnet <an.internet.host.address>

Trying...

Local Telnet:      "Hello 'an.internet.host.address'! Are you
                    there?"
Remote Telnet:     "You bet! Pleased to meet you. Let's talk."
Local Telnet:      "Will you put a carriage return and a line
                    feed at the end of every line that is sent
                    to Jonathan's screen?"
Remote Telnet:     "Yes, I will do that."
Local Telnet:      "Will you display output in 124 columns?"
Remote Telnet:     "No, I won't do that! Sorry."

...                ... more questions and answers

Both Telnets:      "Okay, we've come to an agreement and have
                    created a 'virtual terminal' for Jonathan's
                    Telnet session. Let's tell him that we're
                    ready!"

Connected to <an.internet.host.address>
Escape character is '^]'.

login:
```

Now that a method of communicating has been established, your screen displays the commands that you type and the responses from the computer to which you have connected. Throughout your Telnet session, the local and remote Telnet programs continue to send information back and forth across the Internet.

6.4. For More Information

6.4.1. Lists of Telnet Accessible Resources

Many of the chapters of *The Internet Passport* give information about Telnet accessible resources. In particular, try the chapters covering OPACs, Databases, Gopher, CWISs, WAIS, World Wide Web, and Directory Services.

"Special Internet Connections"

A frequently updated list of Internet resources that includes many Telnet accessible sites is maintained by Scott Yanoff. You can obtain this list in at least the three following ways:

1) From the newsgroup "alt.internet.services": The list is posted once or twice a month to this newsgroup. (For more on using Usenet, see Chapter 9.)

2) Via FTP:

FTP host:	`csd4.csd.uwm.edu`
directory:	`pub`
filename:	`inet.services.txt`

For more on FTP see Chapter 7.

3) By subscribing to the "special Internet connections" mailing list: Send the following e-mail message:

```
mail:    yanoff@csd4.csd.uwm.edu
subject: inet
message: (none needed)
```

If your host has the "finger" program, you can get up-to-date information about Yanoff's list by issuing the command "finger yanoff@csd4.csd.uwm.edu".

6.4.2. Technical Descriptions

Authoritative sources for technical information about Telnet (and most anything else about the Internet) can be found in Request for Comments (RFCs) documents.

Here's a partial list of relevant RFCs on Telnet:

RFC 854:   Telnet Protocol specification
RFC 855:   Telnet Option specifications
RFC 856:   Telnet binary transmission
RFC 857:   Telnet echo option
RFC 858:   Telnet Suppress Go Ahead option
RFC 859:   Telnet status option
RFC 860:   Telnet timing mark option
RFC 861:   Telnet extended options: List option
RFC 1184:   Telnet linemode option

Although RFCs are available from many other sources on the Internet, here are instructions on how to obtain RFCs from two definitive RFC repositories.

1) Via electronic mail messages to nic.ddn.mil's automated mail server:

```
mail:     service@nic.ddn.mil
subject:  rfcxxxx    (where xxxx is the RFC number)
message:  (none needed)
```

2) Via FTP:

FTP host: **nis.nsf.net**
directory: **documents/rfc**
filename: **rfcxxxx.txt**   (where xxxx is the RFC
                                                number)

6.4.3. TCP/IP Packages that Include Telnet

The document "Network Protocol Implementations and Vendors Guide" contains more than 300 pages of description of TCP/IP hardware and software. It is available at no charge via FTP and electronic mail.

FTP host: **nic.ddn.mil**
directory: **netinfo**
filename: **vendors-guide.doc**

```
mail:     service@nic.ddn.mil
subject:  netinfo vendors-guide.doc
message:  (none needed)
```

@ 7 @

Moving Files with File Transfer Protocol (FTP)

A man should keep his little brain attic stocked with all the furniture he is likely to use, and the rest he can put away in the lumber room of his library, where he can get it if he wants it.

Sir Arthur Conan Doyle
Five Orange Pips

FTP is a method used to transfer files between computers connected to the Internet. You can move your own files with FTP, but even better, you can copy files from numerous FTP archives throughout the world. By using FTP, the worldwide Internet becomes like a huge disk drive attached to your computer; the big difference is that you have millions of files to choose from!

7.1. What Is FTP Used for?

7.1.1. Getting Files from Anonymous FTP Archives

The most common use of FTP is to get files from Internet computers containing "anonymous FTP archives."

What kinds of files are in anonymous FTP archives? You name it!

- Software for most computers and for most purposes
- Informative documents (e-texts, e-journals, e-newsletters, archived discussions from LISTSERVS and more)
- Graphics
- Data
- MIDI sequences
- And much more!

There are more files in anonymous FTP hosts than any one person could ever use.

As of September 1992, it is estimated that there are nearly 2,000,000 files in more than 1,200 anonymous FTP hosts. It is also estimated that all together these files occupy more than 100 billion bytes of computer space. That's a lot of floppies!

Like most services on the Internet, FTP archives and the files they contain continue to grow in number daily. In Chapter 16, you will learn about a program called "archie" that allows you to keep track of this growing, ever changing wealth of files.

7.1.2. Full Privilege FTP

If you have full access privileges on two or more Internet hosts (e.g., your desktop computer and a mainframe) you can use FTP to copy files between these computers no matter where they are located.

7.2. Anonymous FTP Archives

Because most people on the Internet use FTP primarily for accessing anonymous FTP archives, most of this chapter will focus on the use of anonymous FTP. Almost everything described here applies equally well to the use of full privilege FTP, except you would need a userid and password.

7.2.1 The Organization of Anonymous FTP Hosts

Most FTP hosts are organized as directories and subdirectories of files. This hierarchical file system can be illustrated as an upside-down tree.

Here's a diagram of part of a typical FTP host, ftphost.nwnet.net.

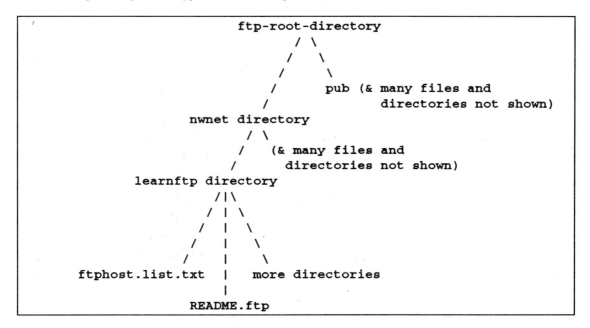

```
                    ftp-root-directory
                         / \
                        /   \
                       /     \
                      /       pub (& many files and
                     /              directories not shown)
             nwnet directory
                   / \
                  /   (& many files and
                 /       directories not shown)
         learnftp directory
                /|\
               / | \
              /  |  \
             /   |   \
            /    |    \
  ftphost.list.txt  |   more directories
                    |
              README.ftp
```

The "root" of this tree is the FTP root directory, which is where you start when you enter an FTP host. Directories are like the branching limbs of an apple tree and files are like the apples you pick.

Each directory usually describes what it contains. In this example, "nic" stands for "network information center," "nwnet" is for "NorthWestNet," and so forth.

To get to a file, you go down the tree (remember, it's upside-down and the root is at the top) along a "directory path." For example the directory path leading to "README.ftp" in the illustration above is "nic/nwnet/learnftp." Other paths lead to thousands of other files in the FTP host. Because the root is not a named directory, all path names are presented on the assumption that you proceed from the root.

Keep this image of an upside down tree in mind whenever you use FTP hosts, and navigating through FTP directories should be much easier. If you move onto one branch and want to look at another, you need to back up the tree until you reach a trunk common to both branches.

Some people prefer to think of directories and files in terms of folders and papers: folders can hold individual documents (files), or even other folders, and so on. For example, you might have a folder in your desk called "Letters." Inside this folder, you might have folders labeled "Amie," "Doug," and "Sarah," holding letters to and from these friends.

7.2.2. Case Sensitivity

Case sensitivity means that upper and lower case characters are treated differently by a program or operating system. And as you might infer, to a case insensitive system "a rose, is a 'Rose,' is a 'ROSE,' is a 'rose.'"

As a general rule, FTP hosts on Unix or Macintosh computers are case sensitive, while FTP hosts on DOS, VM/CMS, or VMS are not case sensitive. In a case sensitive FTP host, what you see is what you should type, UPPER.&.lower.case, exactly as displayed.

If you don't know an FTP host's operating system, how can you tell if it's case sensitive? Well, as Yogi Berra may have said, "you can observe a lot just by looking." If the directory listing of an FTP host shows mixed case in the file names, the host is case sensitive and you must type filenames exactly as shown. If all you see is lower case, the host is still probably case sensitive but there just aren't any mixed case filenames in sight. And finally, if everything you see on the screen is in upper case letters, the site is probably case insensitive.

7.3. Before Using Anonymous FTP, "README.FIRST"!

Anonymous FTP hosts can contain a huge amount of material. Luckily, the folks who maintain FTP hosts often provide three kinds of files that can help you understand an FTP host's structure and contents: "README," "INDEX," and "ls-lR" files.

7.3.1. README Files

Well organized FTP hosts often have filenames containing the word "readme" in many of their directories. Readme files usually contain understandable and informative descriptions about what's in a directory, and possibly even subdirectories within that directory. Typical names are "Readme," "READ.ME," "READ_ME," "README.1st," "00README," "$README," and so forth. These names are chosen so that they will appear conspicuously when you display the contents of a directory.

7.3.2. INDEX Files

INDEX files usually list the names of the files contained in an FTP host directory, sometimes with a very brief description of the contents of each file.

7.3.3. "ls-lR" Files

An ls-lR file is a complete drawing of an FTP host "tree" complete with branches (directories) and apples (files). "ls-lR" is the Unix command for a recursive directory listing. When executed, this command lists all the files and sub-directories in a directory, followed by all the files and sub-directories within each sub-directory. (Do not attempt to run this command on a FTP server! Because there are typically so many directories and files available, it may take an inordinate amount of time to process the command.)

Some of the really gargantuan FTP hosts like wuarchive.wustl.edu may have so many files that the ls-lR file from their root directory may be megabytes in size! In addition to being great reference material for the serious FTP user, these seemingly endless lists of filenames in ls-lR files make great reading for insomniacs.

7.3.4. Anonymous FTP Etiquette

There are a few very important rules of etiquette when using FTP just as there are when using e-mail. FTP etiquette is based on the fact that you are using another institution's computer that has been generously made available to the Internet community.

Life always involves tradeoffs. In the case of FTP, you need to consider tradeoffs of space and time—how far the FTP site is from your host and what the local time is at the FTP site.

When to FTP

Although you should feel free to FTP *from* your Internet host, any time day or night, you should avoid using anonymous FTP hosts between 8am to 5pm *their* local time, since the computer is probably being used by folks at that institution for work activities. Heavy anonymous FTP activity can interfere with the functioning of a host computer for its primary tasks, which do not usually include the running of anonymous FTP. For your convenience, many FTP hosts will display the local time at the host site when you first login. Of course, if you are aware of any explicit time restrictions on access to an anonymous FTP host different that the 8am to 5pm exclusion rule, honor them.

It may sometimes be difficult for you to avoid using FTP during working hours, especially if you are using FTP for work-related activities and the site you want to FTP to is in your time zone. But since the Internet makes it easy to access computers anywhere in the world, you may be able to find an FTP site in a different time zone that has what you need. Query the archie service to see what FTP host options you might have. (To learn more about archie, see Chapter 16.)

Where to FTP

You might think that this means you should use the most distant FTP host possible when you're working during the day. But this is not true for a number of reasons. U.S. and Canadian users in general should not need to access FTP hosts outside of North America since most of the world's FTP files still originate from North America.

FTP users from outside North America can often use FTP hosts in their countries that duplicate the contents of U.S. FTP hosts.

Is an Anonymous User Really Anonymous?

When you access an anonymous FTP host, you will login as "anonymous" when you are asked for an access name. Does this mean that you are truly an "anonymous" user? No, not really.

After you've entered "anonymous," you will be asked for "your ident" or "your real ident" as a password. Many sites may ask you to respond by typing in your userid, <you>@<your.internet.address>. Providing your e-mail address voluntarily is a demonstration of your willingness to be forthright and honest about who you are while using the resources of the FTP host. In fact, some FTP hosts automatically get your host's Internet domain address when you first login and will compare it with the address you entered.

Transfer logs containing the e-mail addresses of people who have transferred files from an FTP site are sometimes used to notify folks who have transferred a file that is later found to have problems. And on rare occasions, an FTP host administrator may have to track down a person (not you, of course!) who is abusing FTP privileges in some way.

7.4. Getting Started with Anonymous FTP

On most mainframes, workstations, and many personal computers, you should be able to start an FTP session simply by typing "ftp".

If you are using a computer with a graphical user interface, such as the Apple Macintosh, DOS machines running Windows, and some workstations, you might be able to start FTP by clicking an icon.

If you don't know if FTP is available or don't know how to access it, ask your user services staff.

You can also try your local online help system. Here are some of the more common forms of help syntax you might use.

Unix	`man ftp`
VMS, CMS, some Unix machines	`help ftp` or `help tcpip`
Macintosh (from a pull down menu)	`find telnet` or `find tcp`

7.4.1. The Essential FTP Commands

The following FTP commands are sufficient for most FTP sessions:

Command	Meaning or Action
ftp	start an FTP session
open <FTP.host.address>	access the FTP host at its address
cd (and **cdup**)	change directories down (and up)
dir (or **ls**)	display the contents of a directory
ascii	prepare FTP for a text-only transfer
binary	prepare FTP for a binary file transfer (usually used for getting program files)
get <filename>	copy a file from FTP host to your computer
quit	end your FTP session

7.4.2. Simple Sample Anonymous FTP Session

In this sample session, you will log into an anonymous FTP host and then copy files to your own Internet computer. The exercise assumes you are using a Unix system. If you aren't, you may need to vary some of the commands to suit your system.

The same sample session is presented in two formats. On the first page, the commands, and what they do, are explained step by step. On the second page, you see what the session looks like on-screen.

While you are connected to the FTP host, explore! There are many computer files on this FTP host, probably many more than you could fit into your own computer. You will encounter files with name endings such as ".Z," ".tar," ".exe," ".bin," but you may not want to retrieve them until you've read Chapter 8, which explains how to handle such files. After you quit you should have on your computer copies of the files README.ftp, ftphost.list.txt, or any other files you copied during your FTP session.

What you want to do:	What you type:
1) Start the FTP program:	`ftp`
2) Select an FTP host:	`open ftphost.nwnet.net`

3) Identify yourself:
 	
    type an FTP login name
 	
    type a password
	
	`anonymous`
	
	`your e-mail address`

4) Move to the "learnftp" directory	`cd nic/nwnet/learnftp`
5) List the contents of the "learnftp" directory	`dir` (or `ls`)

6) Copy the files "README.ftp" and "ftphost.list.txt" to your computer (They will be copied to the directory from which you started FTP.)	`get README.ftp`
	
	`get ftphost.list.txt`

7) Explore an FTP host:
 	
    a) Go back to "root" ("/") directory
 	
    b) Display contents of root directory
 	
    c) Enter a directory
 	
    d) Display contents of that directory
 	
    e) Get another file
	
	`cd /`
	
	`dir` (or `ls`)
	
	`cd <directory-name>`
	
	`dir` (or `ls`)
	
	`get <filename>`

8) Repeat any of these steps in any order as desired!	
9) Quit an FTP session (use at anytime)	`quit`

What You May See On-Screen During Your FTP Session

```
ftp

ftp> open ftphost.nwnet.net

Connected to shivafs.cac.washington.edu.
220 shivafs FTP server (Version 4.191 Feb 14 17:09:49 PST 1991)ready.

Name (ftphost.nwnet.net:<you>): anonymous

331 Guest login ok, send ident as password.

Password: <you>@<your.internet.address>

230 Guest login ok, access restrictions apply.

ftp> cd nic/nwnet/learnftp
250 CWD command successful.

ftp> dir
200 PORT command successful.
150 Opening data connection for /bin/ls (ascii mode) (0 bytes).
total 228

-rw-rw-r--  2 20080     55     1863 Nov 19  1991 README.ftp
drwxrwxr-x  2 20080     55      512 Aug 25 17:46 compressed-files
-rw-rw-r--  2 20080     55   168372 Oct 21  1991 ftphost.list.txt
-rw-rw-r--  2 20080     55    49462 Oct 21  1991 ftphost.list.txt.Z

226 Transfer complete.
295 bytes received in 0.14 seconds (2 Kbytes/s)

ftp> get README.ftp

200 PORT command successful.
150 Opening data connection for README.ftp (ascii mode) (1863 bytes).
226 Transfer complete.
local: README.ftp remote: README.ftp
1886 bytes received in 0.086 seconds (21 Kbytes/s)

(You can explore the FTP host by using commands like "cd ..",
 "cd <directory-name>, "dir", "ls", and other commands, as described
 in the rest of this chapter.)

ftp> quit
221 Goodbye.
```

A Sample List of FTP Hosts

The ftphost.list.txt file you may have gotten from the host ftphost.nwnet.net contains a comprehensive list of anonymous FTP hosts throughout the world.

Because this huge list can be slightly intimidating for beginners, a very brief list of some of the more useful, well organized, voluminous, or interesting anonymous FTP hosts in North America, Europe, Asia, and Australia is provided below. Try a site near you.

And please, don't forget: in the immortal words of Jon Granrose, "anonymous FTP is a privilege, not a right."

Internet Address (and Country)

archive.cis.ohio-state.edu	(USA)	nis.nsf.net	(USA)
ftp.apple.com	(USA)	pit-manager.mit.edu	(USA)
ftp.uni-kl.de	(Germany)	plaza.aarnet.edu.au	(Australia)
ftp.uu.net	(USA)	src.doc.ic.ac.uk	(United Kingdom)
ftphost.nwnet.net	(USA)	toklab.ics.osaka-u.ac.jp	(Japan)
gatekeeper.dec.com	(USA)	ux1.cso.uiuc.edu	(USA)
inria.inria.fr	(France)	wuarchive.wustl.edu	(USA)

7.5. Full Privilege FTP

If you have computer accounts on two or more computers on the Internet, you can use full privilege FTP to move the files between these Internet hosts.

Using full privilege FTP is essentially just like using anonymous FTP with one big exception: since you are working with your own accounts, you have the privileges needed to actually add, delete, and reorganize files on that remote host. You can put files into your account with the "put" command, make directories ("mkdir <directory-name>"), and even delete files on the remote computer ("delete <filename>").

To use full privilege FTP, from your system prompt simply type "ftp" followed by the Internet address of a computer on which you have an account.

```
ftp <your.host.internet.address>
```

Next, enter the userid and password for your account on the remote Internet host.

```
Name (your.host.internet.address): <your userid>
Password required for YOUR-USERID.
PASSWORD: <your password>
230 User YOUR-USERID logged in.
```

7.6. More Details about FTP Commands

The information presented up to this point is the bare minimum you need to use FTP, and with what you've learned so far, you could probably fill enough diskettes to overload the springs of a medium-sized automobile. But if you're interested in quality rather than quantity, please read on. You are encouraged to work through these examples while actually exploring any FTP host of your choice. Here we go!

```
ftp any.old.FTP.host

Connected to any.old.FTP.host.
220 an FTP server (Version 4.191 Thu Feb 14 17:09 PST 1991)
ready.

Name (any.old.ftp.host:yourname): anonymous
331 Guest login ok, send ident as password.

Password: <you>@<your.internet.address>
230 Guest login ok, access restrictions apply.

ftp>
```

Now you should be at the root directory of "any.old.FTP.host." What does it have to offer? Most FTP hosts support two commands to display listings of a directory's contents: "ls" and "dir."

7.6.1. "ls": A Quick Peek at What's in a Directory

"ls" is good for a quick peek at the contents of a directory. It is an abbreviation for the command "list." (But you could think of it as short for "look see"!) Only the names of the files and directories are listed.

```
ftp> ls
README.NOW
doc
etc
ls-lR
nic
pub
zebra.jokes
```

Notice that ls doesn't show whether an entry is a file or a directory: If you tried to "get pub", you'd probably get a message saying something like "550: pub: not a plain file."

7.6.2. "dir": More Detailed Information about the Contents of a Directory

You should use dir when you want a better view of what's in a directory. In addition to the file and directory names, dir also lets you know which entries are files or directories, the size of the files, and the date the files were most recently changed.

The file size is an especially important piece of information. You need to be certain you have enough space on your computer to receive the files you want to transfer. Some files, particularly graphics, can take several megabytes of disk space.

The format in which all this information is presented depends upon the operating system used by the FTP host computer. Although many FTP hosts are Unix based, you will encounter some that are based on VMS and VM/CMS, so a brief comparison of what these dir listings would look like in these three operating systems is given to save you future headaches. Each example has an explanatory key at the top to help you figure out how each operating system presents the information.

"dir" Display from a Typical Unix FTP Host

```
                               File Size
File System Information        in Bytes    Date Info.     File or Dir
===========================    =========   ==========     ============

ftp> dir
-rw-r--r--  1 20800  system        7463    Sep 21  2:01   README.NOW
drwxr-xr-x  1 bin    system        2048    Oct 23  4:02   doc
drwxr-xr-x  1 bin    staff          512    Feb 29  1991   etc
-rw-r--r--  1 20800  system     1458364    Oct 14  1:30   ls-1R
drwxr-xr-x  1 bin    system        1024    Jun 23  1989   nic
drwxr-xr-x  1 bin    system         512    Apr 22  1990   pub
drwxr-xr-x  1 bin    system         512    Apr 01 00:01   zebra.jokes
```

In the very first column, a "-" means that the entry in that line is a file, a "d" means that the entry is a directory. So "doc" is a directory, and "README.NOW" is a file. (The rest of the file system information is beyond the scope of this document.)

Notice that directories have an entry in the file size column. This does not mean that the directory only contains that amount of information! In fact, a directory showing a file size of 512 might have many megabytes of files within it.

"dir" Display from a VMS FTP Host

```
File or Dir       File Size
Name;Version      in Kbytes   Date Info.        File System Info.
==============    =========   ===============   =====================

ftp> dir
README.NOW;10         7       15-SEP-1992 2:01  [274,164]  (RWED,RWE,,)
DOC.DIR;1             0       23-OCT-1992 4:02  [274,164]  (RWED,RWED,,)
```

In a VMS FTP host, a directory is indicated by a name ending with "dir," e.g., "DOC.DIR." Note that the file sizes are given in Kilobytes instead of bytes ("7" here corresponds to "7,463" in the Unix dir display!)

"dir" Display from a VM/CMS FTP Host

```
                           File Size Info.
                        ===================
filename, type, mode    # cols  # lines  Kb   Date Modified      Disk
===================     ======  =======  ==   ===============    ======

ftp> dir
$README   NOW    V        1       156     7    9/15/92 02:01:50  DSK191
A         FILE   V        1         8     1   11/09/91 14:00:50  DSK191
ANOTHER   FILE   V        1         8     1    1/09/91 14:00:50  DSK191
```

VM/CMS doesn't use a hierarchical file structure, so there are no directories to see. Instead, there will be a long list of files in one "flat" directory. Like VMS, VM/CMS displays file size in Kilobytes.

Directing the Output from "dir" or "ls" to a Local File

If the FTP host you are using does not have INDEX or ls-lR files, you may find it useful to send directory listings to your local computer for local browsing or printing.

In the simplest case, you just type "ls" or "dir" followed by a name for an output file on your local host. For example, at the "ftp>" prompt, you could type:

```
ftp> dir <filename>
```

The dir display will be sent to your local host, and stored using the filename you provided.

7.6.3. "cd": Changing Directories

In order to move around an anonymous FTP host, you need to go up and down the directory tree. This is done with various forms of the "cd" command. If you are still in an FTP host, try some of the following versions of cd to get a feeling for how they work.

All FTP Hosts

Three forms of cd should work on most any FTP host.

`cd <directory name>`	Moves you "down" into the directory you have named.
`cdup`	Moves you up in the directory tree to the directory immediately above.
`cd <directory path>`	Lets you move down multiple directories with one cd command. The exact syntax used for <directory path> depends upon the syntax of the operating system. In an earlier example on a Unix host, we used the directory path nic/nwnet/learnftp.

Unix FTP Hosts

In addition to the universally available cd commands described above, Unix FTP hosts support the following cd commands:

`cd ..`   Moves you "up" to the parent directory

`cd ../..`   Moves you "up" two levels in the FTP host

`cd /`   Moves you back to the FTP host's root directory (Really handy if you're feeling a bit disoriented in a big FTP host!)

`cd ../../<directory name>`   Moves you "up" two levels in the FTP host, and then down into a directory

VMS FTP Hosts

In addition to the universally available cd commands described above, certain implementations of FTP on VMS systems support the following cd commands:

`cd [-]`   Move back to a parent directory (like the Unix "cd ..")

`cd [-.-]`   Move up two levels in the directory (like Unix "cd ../..")

VM/CMS Hosts

Because VM/CMS does not have a hierarchical file structure, you can't really move up and down directories! However, you can sometimes move between minidisks (which are loosely analogous to directories) with the following command:

`cd [username.minidisk]`   vaguely like "cd"; e.g., "cd anonymou.191".

7.6.4. "get": Copying a Single File from an FTP Host

Basic Syntax

The basic syntax of the "get" command is "get <filename>". This will copy the file named <filename> to your computer maintaining the same name. For example:

```
ftp> get README.FIRST
```

The file "README.FIRST" has now been copied to your computer, and has been put into your computer as a file with the same name in the directory from which you started FTP.

Creating Informative and Functional Filenames

You can also change the name of a file by typing the desired new name after the file's original name.

```
ftp> get README.FIRST topic.readme
```

In this example, FTP would transfer the file "README.FIRST" to your Internet host with the new name "topic.readme".

This ability to rename while copying is very handy for a number of reasons.

Although files stored in FTP archives usually have informative and easy to use names, you will inevitably encounter some extremes. Some FTP archive maintainers prefer cryptic filenames. For example, a hypothetical software packaged called MAUS-GRAF could be called "mg" in one FTP archive. Other FTP archive maintainers may go to an expository extreme and store the same file as "Before_You_Copy_This_MAUS-GRAF.exe_file_FEED_YOUR_KATZ".

Strive to create concise and meaningful names for files you've ftp'ed. If the operating system of your Internet host uses a hierarchical file system with directories, thoughtful organization and naming of directories can help tremendously by providing positional information. I personally might store the above file with the filename "MausGraf.exe" in the directory path "Katz/fed".

Of course, you must be aware of the file naming conventions used by your computer's operating system. For example, IBM PCs running DOS require that filenames fit the following format: "A:filename.ext" where "A:" indicates a disk drive and path, "filename" is a name no longer than eight characters in length, and "ext" is a filename extension no more than three characters long. Consider the following example:

```
ftp> get <a.file.with.a.long.name> <a:tinyname.doc>
```

This would result in a file on your A: disk drive with a suitable DOS name. Other operating systems, such as Unix and Macintosh OS are less restrictive about filename lengths, but may still prohibit the use of certain characters in filenames.

Previewing a File's Contents with the "get" Command

When you access a Unix FTP site, you may be able to preview a file before actually copying it to your own computer. For example, when connected to a UNIX based FTP site from a UNIX host, you can use the following nifty trick:

```
ftp> get <filename> |more
```

The contents of the file will then appear on your screen, one page at a time. To display the next page, press the space bar on your keyboard. (You have piped your get command to the "more" program on your local Unix host, so the information is being sent to "more" instead of being written to your disk.) If you want to stop previewing the file before you get to the end, type "q" to quit.

7.6.5. "mget" and "mput": Moving Multiple Files

There may be times when you want to move several files to or from an FTP host. Depending upon the version of FTP installed on your Internet host, you may be able to use the "mget" command. Similarly, "mput" can be used to put multiple files in a full privilege FTP session. (Although all examples in this section use mget, the instructions apply equally to mput.)

To use mget and mput to their fullest potentials, you should learn a little about wildcards, and the FTP commands "verbose" and "prompt."

Wildcards

Most FTP software supports "wildcards," special symbols that mean "any character or string of characters might be in this place." There are two main wildcards in the FTP world: "?" is a place holder for a single character in that location, and "*" can stand for one or more characters.

Using "?" is straightforward: "wor?" could stand for anything from "wora" to "worZ", "wor1" to wor9", and depending upon other special characters available to the FTP host, "wor!", "wor." and so forth.

Using "*" is a little more complicated and takes a bit more attention and foresight on your part. For example, "*ism" might mean anything from "prism" to "intro.to.anitdisestablishmentarianism", and "cat*" might stand for anything from "cats" to "catalog.of.all.stars.dimmer.than.magnitude2". A further complication is that the "*" does not necessarily reach beyond the file delimiter symbol (".") in DOS based FTP hosts. So "cat*" would not represent "cats.doc" from a DOS host; you would have to use "cat*.*" to represent the file.

So how about some practical applications of wildcards? Suppose that you are a xylophone buff, and after reading the README.FIRST file for a "xylophone.history" directory you've decided you want to get every single file in the directory. If you are in the "xylophone.history" directory, at the FTP prompt just issue mget with a wildcard.

```
ftp> mget *
```

All the files from that directory will be copied to your Internet host.

You can also use the wildcard to help specify a subset of files, for example, only those which contain the word "marimba" in the filename.

```
ftp> mget *marimba*
```

Before you try the mget command, be sure that you have enough room on your Internet host to accommodate the incoming files. Also, if your host has restrictions on filenames, you may have trouble using mget if the filenames in the FTP archive are not in the correct format.

"verbose" and "prompt" Commands

When you issue the mget command, your FTP session will usually provide a prompt before getting each file, at which you must type "y" or "n".

```
ftp> mget cat*

mget catalog.of.all.stars.dimmer.than.magnitude2? n
mget cats.and.aardvarks? y

200 PORT command successful.
150 Opening data connection for cats.and.aardvarks
226 Transfer complete.
local: cats.and.aardvarks: remote: cats.and.aardvarks
4987 bytes received in 0.031 seconds (1.6e+02
Kbytes/s)

mget cats.and.abalones? y
```

If there are many files, from "cats.and.aardvarks" to "cats.and.zoot.simms", this could be a long session spent typing "y" after each prompt. Furthermore, the FTP session is being "verbose": it is displaying the results of your request, the speed of the transfer, and other information which you may not be interested in seeing.

When you are confident that your mget or mput request is well specified and won't involve many unwanted files, you can toggle the "prompt" mode off.

```
ftp> prompt
Interactive mode off.
```

For the rest of your session, you will not be prompted about each file when you use mget or mput. If you want prompts to reappear, just enter "prompt" again.

Similarly, you can toggle FTP verbosity: typing "verbose" at the FTP prompt will suppress the informative messages that, during a long FTP session may be more annoying than helpful.

7.6.6. "ascii", "binary," and "image"

"ascii", "binary", and "image" are commands that specify how the requested files should be transferred. File formats you may encounter during an FTP session are explained in more detail in Chapter 8.

- "ascii" is used for text-only files, such as standard text documents.
- "binary" (or "image") is used for non-text files, such as software, graphics, and executable files.

When you want to get a file in one of these formats, you should specify the proper transfer mode at the FTP prompt.

```
ftp> ascii
200 Type set to A.
ftp> get <an.ascii.file>

ftp> binary
200 Type set to I.
ftp> get <a.binary.file>
```

7.6.7. Help!

If you want more information on FTP, you will generally find that the best online help is available from your computer's regular help system, e.g., "help ftp", or on Unix hosts, "man ftp".

Local Online Help

For a listing of all the commands available to you, type help at the command prompt while using FTP.

```
ftp> help
Commands may be abbreviated. Commands are:

!            cr           ls           prompt       runique
$            delete       macdef       proxy        send
account      debug        mdelete      sendport     status
append       dir          mdir         put          struct
ascii        disconnect   mget         pwd          sunique
bell         form         mkdir        quit         tenex
binary       get          mls          quote        trace
bye          glob         mode         recv         type
case         hash         mput         remotehelp   user
cd           help         nmap         rename       verbose
cdup         image        ntrans       reset        ?
close        lcd          open         rmdir
ftp>
```

(The exact commands available to you will depend on the FTP software your system is running.)

Now type help for any command, and you'll see a concise definition of what the command does.

```
ftp> help cd
cd                        change remote working directory
```

But in general this help is terse and primarily useful as a reminder about what you've learned elsewhere.

Remote Online Help

If the FTP host you are accessing is using a different version of FTP, there might be more or fewer FTP commands at your disposal. These are displayed by using the "remotehelp" command, available from some Internet host systems. Say you were using FTP from a Unix Internet host to a remote FTP site running VM/CMS. Here's what you'd see:

```
ftp> remotehelp

214-The server-FTP commands are:
214-ABOR, ACCT,*ALLO, APPE,  CWD, DELE, HELP, LIST, MODE
214-NLST, NOOP, PASS, PASV, PORT,  PWD, QUIT, REIN, RETR
214-RNFR, SITE, SYST, STAT, STOR, STOU, STRU, TYPE, USER
214-The commands preceded by  '*'  are unimplemented
214-Data representation type may be ASCII EBCDIC or IMAGE.

214-For information about a particular command, type
214 HELP SERVER command.
```

Even if you know the remote commands, actually using them can be tricky. For example, to get help on one of the commands above, you would not literally type "help server <command>" as is suggested, but rather "remotehelp <command>".

7.7. For More Information

7.7.1. List of Anonymous FTP Sites

Jon Granrose has maintained a very useful "List of Anonymous FTP Sites" for several years.

FTP host:	**pilot.njin.net**
directory:	**pub/ftp-list**
filenames:	**README**
	help
	index
	...and many others

If you worked through the FTP example to ftphost.nwnet.net, you have already retrieved one version of this file (ftphost.list.txt).

7.7.2. Usenet Newsgroups

The following Usenet newsgroups deal with anonymous FTP archives and FTP from administrative and technical perspectives:

comp.archives	Announcements about new and updated FTP files
comp.archives.admin	Discussion about FTP archives, access, administration, etc.
comp.protocols.tcp-ip	Discussion about TCP/IP protocols, including FTP
comp.protocols.tcp-ip.misc	Discussion about TCP/IP protocols, including FTP, under various operating systems
comp.protocols.tcp-ip.ibmpc	Discussion about TCP/IP protocols, including FTP, on IBM PC computers

Read Chapter 9 for details on Usenet.

7.7.3. Mailing Lists

A number of the larger FTP hosts have mailing lists for people interested in the maintenance and activity of that particular FTP host. In general, information about such mailing lists will be displayed when you access the FTP host.

See Chapter 11 on how to locate and use mailing lists.

7.7.4. Technical References

The following documents are essential reading for anyone who wants a detailed understanding of the nuts and bolts of how FTP works:

Comer, D.E. *Internetworking With TCP/IP*. Volume 1: *Principles, Protocols, and Architecture*. Chapter 23. Prentice Hall, Inc., Englewood Cliffs, NJ. 1991.

The following RFCs contain specifications for the File Transfer Protocol:

RFC783:	TFTP Protocol
RFC913:	Simple File Transfer Protocol
RFC959:	The File Transfer Protocol
RFC1068:	Background File Transfer

You can obtain RFCs by FTP from many anonymous FTP hosts throughout the Internet, or by e-mail from a mail server.

Via FTP (this is only one of many anonymous FTP sources of RFCs):

FTP host:	`nis.nsf.net`	
directory:	`document/rfc`	
filename:	`rfcxxxx.txt`	(where xxxx is the RFC number. e.g., "rfc0913.txt" or "rfc1068.txt")

Via electronic mail messages to nic.ddn.mil's automated mail server:

```
mail:    service@nic.ddn.mil
subject: rfc xxx
message: (none needed)
```

@ 8 @

The ABC's of File Formats:
From ASCII to ZOO

Bless thee, Bottom! Bless thee! Thou art translated!

William Shakespeare
A Midsummer Night's Dream, III.i.

===

Electronic information can be stored in a variety of formats many of which require special handling or processing before the file can be used. It is often important to know about these formats when you are getting files from anonymous FTP archives.

Most FTP users at one time or another will obtain files from anonymous FTP archives that just don't seem to work as expected. Chances are that the files were compressed, archived, or in one of the special formats described in this chapter.

This chapter is by no means meant to be comprehensive, but it does provide a quick overview of some of the main formats in which files are stored on the Internet, along with an introductory table that gives information on how to handle them. These pointers explicitly refer to FTP, but they should also apply when using telecommunications and file transfer packages on personal computers.

8.1. ASCII Files

Many documents on the Internet are in a text-only format called "ASCII." ("ASCII" stands for American Standard Code for Information Interchange.) ASCII format files can be read on most computers without any special handling.

8.1.1. Recognizing ASCII Files

Typically, but not always, ASCII files in FTP archives will have a filename that ends with ".doc" or ".txt" such as "manual.txt". Sometimes, there may be no special ending as in the case of a "README" file.

8.1.2. Transferring ASCII Files

When retrieving ASCII files with FTP, set the transfer type, or "mode," to ASCII before you begin. Simply type "ascii" at the FTP prompt.

```
ftp> ascii
200 Type set to A.
ftp> get manual.txt
```

8.2. Binary Files

When people speak of "binary files" or "binaries," they typically mean executable or non-text files such as computer programs or graphical bitmaps.

8.2.1. Recognizing Binary Files

Binary files can have a wide variety of endings for their filenames. These endings depend, in large part, upon the operating system in which the binary is meant to work. For example, ".exe" (short for "executable") is a common filename ending for binary files meant to run in DOS.

In general you need to know ahead of time whether a file is binary or not. README files in FTP archives will often give you this information.

8.2.2. Transferring Binary Files

Not surprisingly, you must use the binary transfer type (or binary "mode") when transferring binary files with FTP. Otherwise your computer may try to translate the file into text format and the file will no longer function as a binary program. On the other hand, when you're not sure what format a file is in, try transferring it using binary mode. While ASCII mode will not allow you to successfully transfer binary files, binary mode can usually transfer both successfully.

You put FTP into binary mode by typing the word "binary" at the FTP prompt.

```
ftp> binary
200 Type set to I.
ftp> get <filename>
```

8.3. Archived File Groups

When several files are logically related in some way, they are sometimes put together and stored as one archived file. Combining several files into one archived file makes it easier for you to copy the information to your computer. (An archived file should not be confused with a file archive. The former is a file that contains many files in it and the latter is a collection of files put on an FTP server. So an FTP archive may contain many archived files!) You only need to use the FTP "get" command once to transfer the whole archive file to your computer. Once retrieved, you can execute a program on your local computer that will "unpack" the archive into its component files.

8.3.1 Recognizing Archived Files

There are many archive programs, each of which adds a special suffix to the file's name. Refer to Lemson's table for more information. (A portion of this table, "Table of Archive and Compression Programs," and instructions for retrieving the complete Lemson table are provided at the end of this chapter.)

Note that archived files are often compressed as well, so be sure to read the section on compressed files before wrestling with archived files.

8.3.2. "tar" (Tape ARchive) Files

The most commonly encountered archive format on the Internet is called "tar," an abbreviation for "tape archive." These tar archives are created and unpacked using the tar program on Unix computers.

Files which have been archived with tar usually contain the word "tar" at or towards the end of their filename.

On most Unix systems, you can type "tar -xf filename" to extract a tarred file. Type "man tar" for more detailed information on the tar program. Refer to the "Table of Archive and Compression Programs" at the end of this chapter for information on handling tarred files in other operating systems.

8.3.3. Self-Extracting Archives

Self-extracting archives are most commonly encountered with Mac software and typically have a filename ending in ".sea". Use binary mode when transferring these files with FTP. Once the file is transferred to your Mac, double-click on the icon of the self-extracting archive and it will unpack into all its component files and folders.

8.3.4. "SHAR" (SHell ARchive) Files

The concept of a "shell archive" evolves from the Unix community where the intent was to bundle multiple files within a Unix shell command file that is self-extracting. Usually, the author of the shell archive has provided comments and instructions at the beginning of the file. These instructions typically ask the recipient to delete the comment lines up to a marked point in the file, and then begin the extraction of the archive by invoking "sh" (on Unix).

Alternatively, your machine may have a program that automates this process even further. Refer to the "Table of Archive and Compression Programs" found later in this chapter for more information.

8.4. Compressed Files

As the name suggests, compressed files are files which have been made smaller so that they take up less space on a computer disk or other storage media. Because they are smaller than the original file, compressed files are also transferred more quickly over the Internet.

When you encounter a file whose name ends with ".Z" (for example, "really.big.doc.Z"), you're probably looking at a file which has been compressed with the Unix "compress" utility. You will also come across files whose names end with ".tar.Z". These files have been compressed and archived. To work with such a file, you would first uncompress it and then untar the archive.

There are many other compression programs for Unix and other operating systems, and each will add a particular suffix to the file's name. Refer to Lemson's table for more information. (Instructions for retrieving this table are provided at the end of this chapter.)

Compressed files, like archived files, should be transferred in binary mode during an FTP session.

8.5. GIF Files

"GIF" stands for "Graphical Interchange Format," which is a special format used for encoding graphical images. These filenames typically end with ".gif", for example, "mars-scape.gif" might be a GIF file displaying the surface of Mars. There are several FTP archives on the Internet specializing in GIF files. But be forewarned—many of these files are huge and can be time consuming to transfer and process. GIF files should be transferred in binary mode. They require special software to view them and can only be printed on some kinds of printers.

8.6. Postscript Files

PostScript, developed by Adobe Systems, Inc., is a programming language with powerful graphics and coding capabilities. Many Internet documents are distributed in both ASCII and PostScript format.

On the Internet, files which are in PostScript format conventionally have filenames that end with ".ps", for example, "rfc1125.ps".

To use Postscript files, you must have access to a printer with PostScript printing capabilities (typically a laser printer) or a PostScript previewing program. You should also be aware that some PostScript files may use special character sets (or fonts) that may not be available on your printer. If you're lucky, those fonts will translate to an available font. On rare occasions, a PostScript file may cause your printer to gag ungracefully. If this happens, ask your local user services staff for help. They may be able to change some of the code in the PostScript file so it will work with your printer.

Although some PostScript files can be transferred in ASCII mode, maximize your chances for a successful transfer and use binary mode.

8.7. Table of Archive and Compression Programs

The following table is derived from a comprehensive listing of compression and archiving programs maintained by David Lemson. You may already have some of these programs installed on your Internet host or personal computer. If not, you can obtain Lemson's master list, which gives instructions on which anonymous FTP hosts have these programs, or you can use archie, as described in Chapter 16, to search for these files.

Archive or Compression Program Name	Added File Extension	Name of program *you* use to process this file on your computer's operating system	
		DOS	Mac
ARC	.ARC	arc602	ArcMac
BinHex	.Hqx	xbin23	BinHex
compress	.Z	u16	MacCompress
PackIt	.pit	UnPackIt	PackIt
PKZIP	.ZIP	pkz110eu	UnZip
SHellARchive	.shar	toadshr1	UnShar
StuffIt	.Sit	unsit30	StuffItLite
tar	.tar	tar	UnTar
uuencode	.uu	toaduu20	uutool
ZOO	.ZOO	zoo210	MacBooz

Archive or Compression Program Name	Added File Extension	Name of program *you* use to process this file on your computer's operating system	
		Unix	VM/CMS
ARC	.ARC	arc521	arcutil
BinHex	.Hqx	mcvert	binhex
compress	.Z	uncompress	compress
PackIt	.pit	unpit	-
PKZIP	.ZIP	unzip41	-
SHellARchive	.shar	unshar	-
StuffIt	.Sit	unsit	-
tar	.tar	tar	-
uuencode	.uu	uudecode	arcutil
ZOO	.ZOO	zoo210	zoo

8.8. For More Information

A comprehensive table of nearly 100 programs for handling compressed and archived files is maintained by David Lemson. His document also gives detailed information on where all listed programs can be obtained.

FTP host: **ux1.cso.uiuc.edu**
directory: **doc/pcnet**
filename: **compression**

This file is available on other FTP hosts as well.

8.8.1. Usenet Newsgroups

Two newsgroups deal specifically with the theory and practice of file compression. (Chapter 9 explains how to use Usenet.)

comp.compression   General discussion about
                                            compression

comp.compression.research   High tech discussions about
                                            compression

There are several newsgroups devoted to the distribution of binary files for a variety of operating systems. Note that some of the newsgroups are for discussion, and some are solely for posting of binary files, so be sure to monitor the newgroups first before posting inappropriately! Here's a sampling of some newsgroups which may be of interest to you:

comp.binaries.acorn
comp.binaries.amiga
comp.binaries.apple2
comp.binaries.atari.st
comp.binaries.ibm.pc
comp.binaries.ibm.pc.archives
comp.binaries.ibm.pc.d
comp.binaries.ibm.pc.wanted
comp.binaries.mac
comp.binaries.os2
fj.binaries.mac   (to use the fj
fj.binaries.misc   newsgroups, you need
fj.binaries.msdos   to be able to handle
fj.binaries.msdos.d   files with Kanji
fj.binaries.x68000   characters)
alt.binaries.multimedia
alt.binaries.sounds.misc

@ Section III @

Community Forums

@ 9 @

Usenet: Discussions in the Cafes of the Global Village

"The time has come," the Walrus said,
"To talk of many things:
Of shoes—and ships—and sealing wax—
Of cabbages—and kings—
And why the sea is boiling hot—
And whether pigs have wings"

Lewis Carrol
Through the Looking Glass

Whether it's over Darjeeling in Djibouti or maté in Montevideo, the cafe has traditionally been a place for people to share ideas, argue politics, engage in pleasant conversation, and generally enjoy camaraderie and communication. At one table, Gyorgi from the Crimea may be passionately debating farm policy with Pauletta from Italy while at another table, Nancy and Xiabo may be drinking in the banter and chatter as quietly as they sip their tea.

In some ways, a service called Usenet has become like a cafe for the electronic global village—and not just one cafe, but thousands, each with its own Gyorgis and Paulettas debating fine points of some arcane topic, plain folks chatting about whatever interests them, and Nancys and Xiabos, unheard and unseen, who are listening, learning, and loving every minute of it.

9.1. What Is Usenet?

The term "Usenet," also sometimes called "netnews," refers to several things simultaneously:

- Usenet is a collection of thousands of topically organized "newsgroups," covering everything from supercomputer design to bungee cord jumping, and ranging in distribution from the whole world to single institutions.

- Usenet is a loosely defined worldwide network of computers, not all on the Internet, that receive Usenet newsgroups.

- But most importantly, Usenet is a collection of worldwide and local communities of *people* who communicate with other people.

As you will eventually discover, Usenet is also much more. But let's cover the basics, one by one: Usenet newsgroups, newsfeeds, and newsreader software.

9.2. Usenet Basics: Newsgroups, Newsfeeds, and Newsreaders

9.2.1. Newsgroups

The term "Usenet newsgroups" might suggest that Usenet is mainly concerned with news, but Usenet newsgroups are also forums for information, debates, questions and answers, and just plain chatting. They are very similar to the bulletin board rooms, special interest groups, or conference rooms provided by Bulletin Board Systems or various commercial network services.

Names

Each newsgroup has a distinct name that describes the topics discussed in the group. Here are the names of a few newsgroups to give you a sense of the diversity of topics and how newsgroups' names are put together.

```
alt.dreams                     misc.jobs.offered
alt.sport.bungee               news.newusers.questions
bionet.genome.arabidopsis      rec.bicycles.rides
bit.listserv.history           rec.food.recipes
biz.comp.services              sci.environment
comp.binaries.ibm.pc.wanted    sci.math.research
comp.robotics                  soc.college
k12.chat.elementary            soc.culture.nepal
k12.lang.francais              talk.politics.guns
misc.activism.progressive      talk.rights.human
```

Newsgroup names look similar to, but should not to be confused with, Internet addresses.

Newsgroup names contain a string of words or abbreviations separated by periods. Unlike Internet addresses however, the words and abbreviations of newsgroup names are usually painstakingly designed by members of the Usenet community to be informative in some way. The newsgroup named "sci.math.research" is exactly what the name says it should be: a group for discussion about mathematical research.

Newsgroup names are hierarchical. For example, "k12.chat.elementary" is a group in the main hierarchy created for pre-college (k12) users oriented towards casual discussion (chat) among elementary school students.

The Main Categories

Newsgroups are organized into a few top-level categories, within which may be hundreds of specific newsgroups.

There are seven "traditional" categories distributed through most of the Usenet world:

`comp`	computer hardware, software, and languages
`misc`	topics not easily pigeonholed into other categories
`news`	newsgroups about Usenet newsgroups and administration
`rec`	recreational activities and hobbies
`sci`	discussion about science ranging from popular to research levels
`soc`	discussions about cultures and current events around the world
`talk`	debates on controversial topics (e.g., abortion, mid-Eastern politics)

In addition, there are a rapidly growing number of top-level "alternative" hierarchies which may or may not be distributed globally:

`alt`	tentative, frivolous, or highly controversial topics
`bionet`	learned discussions among research biologists
`bit.listserv`	a wide variety of LISTSERV lists "gatewayed" to Usenet
`biz`	business and commercial topics
`de`	German Usenet newsgroups
`fj`	Japanese Usenet newsgroups
`gnu`	discussion about Free Software Foundation software
`ieee`	newsgroups relating to the IEEE
`k12`	newsgroups for pre-college students and educators
`vmsnet`	newsgroups for discussion of the VMS operating system

Many topics could fit comfortably in two or more main level categories. Consider the following music related newsgroups:

```
alt.exotic-music
comp.music
k12.ed.music
rec.music.makers
```

Although all these newsgroups deal with music, they are each aimed at distinct audiences.

Regional and Local Newsgroups

Most of the main level categories mentioned above are distributed globally, but Usenet also contains regional or local hierarchies, which range from institutional to continental in distribution.

Institutions	`uw`	University of Washington
	`yale`	Yale University
Cities	`pdx`	Portland
	`tor`	Toronto
States or provinces	`ab`	Alberta
	`or`	Oregon
Regions	`pnw`	Pacific Northwest
	`ne`	New England
Countries	`fnet`	France
	`nz`	New Zealand
Continents	`eunet`	Europe
	`na`	North America

Regional newsgroups provide forums for articles that probably wouldn't interest users elsewhere in the world, such as where the Yale MacIntosh Users Group will meet next week, or a listing of bicycle parts stores in New Zealand.

Usenet Articles

Within newsgroups are the actual articles that have been "posted" by Usenet users. Usenet articles are much like e-mail messages with header information used for sending the article through Usenet, address information about the person who wrote the article, and the message body containing information submitted by a Usenet subscriber.

Unmoderated and Moderated Newsgroups

Most newsgroups are "unmoderated," i.e. open for anyone to post messages as they see fit. But some newsgroups are "moderated," meaning that a person (the moderator) screens postings before they are released to the newsgroup. Here are some examples of moderated newsgroups:

Newsgroup Name	Moderator	Moderator's Address
`news.announce.newgroups`	David Lawrence	`tale@uunet.uu.net`
`news.announce.important`	Mark Horton	`mark@stargate.com`
`news.announce.conferences`	Dennis Page	`denny@tekbspa.tss.com`

9.2.2. Newsfeeds

Usenet news is received through "newsfeeds." A Usenet site's newsfeed is handled by news transfer software and Usenet news administrators.

Newsfeed Software

Within the Internet, Usenet news is usually distributed among Usenet hosts by the Network News Transfer Protocol (NNTP). The tens of thousands of Usenet postings which may be received daily in a newsfeed are stored on one computer that thousands of users can access. NNTP on the main newsfeed computer keeps track of the message-ids of articles currently in storage and can selectively retrieve only those articles that are new. Because of this selectivity and screening, NNTP also allows an Internet Usenet site to have dozens of Usenet newsfeeds. Since Usenet articles can come from all over the world, this means that newsfeeds can propagate in a web-like fashion.

Usenet was originally developed within the UUCP network using the Unix to Unix CoPy protocol suite for communications instead of TCP/IP. In contrast to the multi-directional distribution flow of Usenet articles in the Internet, UUCP based sites receive articles from an "upstream" site. If that upstream site did not receive certain newsgroups or articles then neither would your site.

A given Usenet article might bounce around between UUCP and NNTP propagation as it makes its way around the world to your site.

The News-Admin

Each site that receives Usenet news has a news-administrator (or "news-admin") who is ultimately responsible for what newsgroups a site receives and how the newsfeed is operated. Depending upon the particular situation, the news-administrator may make independent decisions about what newsgroups to display or they may only execute the policies of an institutional board. Usenet sites may choose to restrict the flow of news to a trickle of carefully selected newsgroups, or may choose to let their Usenet users "drink from the firehose" and receive every conceivable (and some inconceivable) newsgroups.

9.2.3. Newsreader Software

Just like you use an electronic mail software program to read your personal e-mail messages in your electronic mailbox, you use newsreader programs to read Usenet articles. However, the big difference between the two is that a newsgroup is like a mailbox which anyone with newsreader software and a Usenet newsfeed can contribute to or read from. You might read a posting by someone from South Africa responding to a previous posting by someone in Saskatoon and your reply to their exchange may well be read by people in Stockholm, Singapore, and Sao Paulo.

Locating Newsreader Software at Your Internet Host

Before diving into Usenet, find out what newsreader software, if any, is available at your Internet host. There are many newsreader packages for both mainframes and personal computers. If you're not sure of the name or even the existence of newsreader software on your computer, ask your local user services staff or computer support staff for help.

9.3. Sample Usenet Session with "rn"

This sample Usenet session uses "rn," a basic but widespread newsreader for Unix computers. Currently, this is a "lowest common denominator," workhorse newsreader—one that just about everyone with a Unix account can probably access. Even if you can use a spiffier, workstation-based newsreader with windows and widgets, working through this rn example with your newsreader should give you a feeling for what a typical Usenet session involves.

Regardless of the newsreader software you use, a typical Usenet session often involves the following steps:

Step 1	Start the newsreader software.
Step 2	Select or subscribe to a newsgroup.
Step 3	Scan the titles of articles in that newsgroup.
Step 4	Read, save, or print articles you find particularly interesting.
Step 5	Send e-mail to another Usenet user or post an article to the newsgroup.
Step 6	Clear all remaining articles in the newsgroup so they won't appear in your next Usenet session.
Step 7	Select or subscribe to another newsgroup.
Step 8	Repeat steps 3 through 8 as desired.
Step 9	End your Usenet session.

9.3.1. Starting a Newsreader

To start the rn newsreading software, simply type "rn". (If your newsreader is on a personal computer or workstation with a graphical user interface, like the Mac or PC's with Windows, you might launch your newsreader by double clicking on an icon.)

Here's what happens when you issue the rn command in Unix.

```
rn

Trying to set up a ".newsrc" file--running newsetup...
Creating .newsrc
Done.

If you have never used the news system before, you may find
the articles in news.announce.newusers to be helpful. There
is also a manual entry for rn.

To get rid of newsgroups you aren't interested in, use the
'u' command. Type h for help at any time while running rn.

(Revising soft pointers--be patient.)
```

Since the newsreader is asking us to be patient, let's look at what's happened so far.

If this is the first time you are running a Usenet newsreader, a news resources file may be constructed for you from the master list of newsgroups subscribed to by your site. In the case of rn, this resource file is called ".newsrc."

This news resource file will be used by your newsreader in future sessions to keep track of which newsgroups you want to read, and which articles you have already read thus preventing duplicated efforts in future Usenet sessions.

Most newsreaders will respond with a series of informative messages and a list of a few basic commands including how to get online help. Depending upon your newsreader, this ranges from a simple list that appears when you start the software, to on-screen menus and icons. For rn, "h" will get you help.

After a short while, you should see something like the following on your screen:

```
Unread news in news.announce.newusers          35 articles
Unread news in news.newusers.questions         85 articles

 ...etc.

35 articles in news.announce.newusers--read now? [ynq]
```

We are now entering the newsgroup selection level.

9.3.2. Selecting and Subscribing to Newsgroups

Depending upon what newsreader you are using, you may be presented with lists of newsgroups from which you can choose or you may be asked to "subscribe" to newsgroups you want to read.

The term "subscription" refers to the fact that your newsreader will keep a record of the newsgroups in which you are interested and which articles in those newsgroups have been read. Note that when using newsreaders that maintain a subscription file, you would need to "unsubscribe" to newsgroups you no longer want to read.

Because this is our first time using rn, we have been presented with a newsgroup that all new Usenet users should read: "news.announce.newusers."

```
35 articles in news.announce.newusers--read now? [ynq]
```

The last line in the startup screen is asking if we want to read articles in the newsgroup "news.announce.newusers." As a newuser, reading these articles would probably be advisable. Note that in rn, selecting the newsgroup is equivalent to subscribing.

The "[ynq]" at the end of the line indicates that we can type "y" for "yes, I want to read this newsgroup," "n" for "no," and "q" for "I want to quit the newsgroup selection level."

(Note that other newsreader software may not start you at this particular newsgroup. You can work with whatever newsgroup happens to pop up on your screen and much of the rest of this session will probably still be relevant.)

Help at the Newsgroup Selection Level

By typing "h", we can see what commands are available at the newsgroup selection level. Using these commands would allow us to jump to other newsgroups in which we might be interested.

```
35 articles in news.announce.newusers--read now? [ynq] h

y,SP      Do this newsgroup now.
.cmd      Do this newsgroup, executing cmd as first command.
=         Start this newsgroup, list subjects before reading
          articles.
u         Unsubscribe from this newsgroup.
c         Catch up (mark this newsgroup all read).
n         Go to the next newsgroup with unread news.
N         Go to the next newsgroup.
p         Go to the previous newsgroup with unread news.
P         Go to the previous newsgroup.
-         Go to the previously displayed newsgroup.
1         Go to the first newsgroup.
^         Go to the first newsgroup with unread news.
$         Go to the last newsgroup.
g name    Go to the named newsgroup. Subscribe to new
          newsgroups this way too.
/pat      Search forward for newsgroup matching pattern.
?pat      Search backward for newsgroup matching pattern.
          (Use * and ? style patterns. Append r to include
          read newsgroups.)
l pat     List unsubscribed newsgroups containing pattern.
m name    Move named newsgroup elsewhere (no name moves
          current newsgroup).

[Type space to continue]
```

9.3.3. Scanning Articles within a Newsgroup

Displaying Article Subject Lines

In rn and many other newsreaders, we can use the "=" command at the newsgroup selection level to display the subjects of articles in the current newsgroup. This is much more efficient than reading through the contents of every message in order.

```
437 Regional Newsgroup Hierarchies, Part II
438 Regional Newsgroup Hierarchies, Part III
440 Regional Newsgroup Hierarchies, Part I
448 How to become a USENET site
449 Publicly Accessible Mailing Lists, Part I
450 Publicly Accessible Mailing Lists, Part II
451 Publicly Accessible Mailing Lists, Part III
452 Introduction to news.announce
453 Rules for posting to Usenet
454 What is Usenet?
455 A Primer on How to Work With the Usenet Community
456 Answers to Frequently Asked Questions
457 USENET Software: History and Sources
458 Hints on writing style for Usenet
459 Emily Postnews Answers Your Questions on Netiquette
460 List of Active Newsgroups, Part I
461 List of Active Newsgroups, Part II
462 Alternative Newsgroup Hierarchies, Part I
463 List of Moderators for Usenet
464 How to Get Information about Networks
465 Alternative Newsgroup Hierarchies, Part II
466 How to Create a New Usenet Newsgroup
467 A Guide to Social Newsgroups and Mailing Lists

[Type space to continue]
```

Whoever has been posting these messages really seems to know how to make informative subject lines! In fact, the articles in news.announce.newusers are written by folks who have been using Usenet almost since it was born, back in 1979. As you can see, just about everything that has been discussed in this chapter can be researched in more detail simply by reading the messages in "news.announce.newusers."

Selecting an Article You Want to Read

The numbers in the left column of the previous screen show the article numbers. To read an article whose title interests you, simply type the article's number instead of pressing the space bar.

```
rn> What next? [^Nnpq]
456
```

9.3.4. Reading a Usenet Article

The Structure of a Usenet Article: "It's Just Like an E-mail Message!"

A Usenet article begins with a header much like a standard e-mail header: there are the familiar, "From," "Subject," and "Date" lines, and the "Newsgroups" and "Followup-To" lines are analogous to the "To" and "Reply-To" lines of e-mail headers. The remaining Usenet header lines are peculiar to Usenet articles. In rn, even more header information can be displayed by typing "v", for "verbose header."

```
Article 456 (34 more) in news.announce.newusers (moderated):

From:          spaf@cs.purdue.EDU
Newsgroups:    news.announce.newusers,news.answers
Subject:       Answers to Frequently Asked Questions
Date:          4 Sep 92 03:52:07 GMT
Followup-To:   news.newusers.questions
Organization:  Dept. of Computer Sciences, Purdue Univ.
Lines:         786
Supersedes:    <spaf-questions_711614923@cs.purdue.edu>

Archive-name: usenet-faq/part1
Original-author: jerry@eagle.UUCP
Last-change: 19 Jul 1992 by mvac23!thomas@udel.edu


                Frequently Submitted Items

This document discusses some questions and topics that occur
repeatedly on USENET. They frequently are submitted by new
users, and result in many followups, sometimes swamping
groups for weeks. The purpose of this note is to head off
these annoying events by...
--MORE--(3%)
```

Also, just like e-mail messages, the actual message is contained in the body.

The article has now filled up the screen. If you wanted to see the next screen, you would press the space key. To display the next article, type "n", or use "q" to exit from the article.

Help while Viewing Articles

In most all newsreaders, you should be able to get help for commands that can be used when viewing articles. In rn and many other newsreaders, just type "h".

9.3.5. Finding Newsgroups You REALLY Want to Read

You're probably just itching to dive right into those exciting, exotic, and educational newsgroups that you've heard about. Here's how to find the newsgroups you want to read.

Listing All Available Newsgroups' Names

This is a good strategy if you're just starting to use Usenet and you aren't yet sure what's available, or how newsgroups are named. Some newsreaders show you all the newsgroup names right away, while in other newsreaders, you have to explicitly ask for a complete list of available newsgroups. In rn, you would use the "l" command (list) when at the newsgroup selection level.

```
l

Completely unsubscribed newsgroups:
alt.znet.fnet
alt.znet.pc
[Type return to continue]

Unsubscribed but mentioned in .newsrc:
alt.3d
alt.activism
alt.alien.visitors
alt.amateur-comp
alt.angst
alt.aquaria
alt.archery
alt.astrology
alt.atheism
alt.bbs
alt.bbs.internet
alt.bbs.lists
alt.beer
alt.books.technical
alt.boomerang
alt.brother-jed
alt.callahans
alt.cd-rom
alt.censorship
alt.child-support
alt.chinese.text
alt.co-ops
--More--
```

Searching Newsgroups' Names for Keywords

You may be able to use your newsreader to search through the newsgroups' names for a particular word which you think might be in the names of groups you'd like to read.

In rn, one could search for all the newsgroups whose names contained the word "mac," using the "/" command followed by the word "mac" in order to identify newsgroups dealing with Apple Macintosh Computers.

```
/mac

bit.mailserv.word-mac
comp.binaries.mac
comp.emacs
comp.lang.forth.mac
comp.os.mach
comp.sources.mac
comp.sys.mac
comp.sys.mac.announce

...  (many more "comp.sys.mac" groups)

gnu.emacs.announce

...  (many more "gnu.emacs" groups)
```

If you use this method to search for newsgroups, try to use the shortest likely abbreviation for a topic (like "bio" instead of "biology") and/or scan the master list of newsgroups to get an idea what a likely abbreviation might be. However, some abbreviations may be redundant and refer to two or even multiple discussion groups. In this example, the word "mac" is also contained in newsgroup names which have nothing to do with Macintosh computers, like "comp.os.mach," and newsgroups dealing with the "emacs" editor.

9.4. Suggestions for First Time Usenet Readers

Usenet is a huge, sprawling collection of thousands of newsgroups containing megabytes of articles and used by millions of people worldwide. If you dive into Usenet carelessly, it's easy to get overwhelmed and frustrated. But if you follow a few simple rules you can learn to love Usenet without having to attend the college of hard knocks.

9.4.1. Start Simply!

As was mentioned in the introduction, each Usenet site may subscribe to thousands of newsgroups. There are a number of steps you can take to make your introduction to Usenet encouraging instead of intimidating. Most importantly:

Start simply. Don't try to read everything. Be selective.

First, issue a newsreader command which gives the names of all newsgroups available at your site in a list format. You can then start exploring Usenet by subscribing to one or a small number of groups that look really interesting to you.

Try reading a few articles to become familiar with the folkways of each newsgroup. These can vary from polite, deferential discussion to contentious free-for-alls.

9.4.2. Read Periodic Postings and Frequently Asked Questions (FAQs)

Newsgroups often feature periodic postings that contain useful information for new and intermediate readers. Such postings usually appear once a month.

Periodic postings include:

- Frequently Asked Questions (FAQs)—these are questions which newcomers to a particular newsgroup often ask and which are better answered in periodic postings than in repeated individual answers;

- things to keep in mind before posting articles to that particular newsgroup;

- and suggestions about where to find commonly needed information about the Internet generally, or Usenet specifically.

You'll get a lot more out of Usenet if you make a point of reading the periodic postings of the newsgroups to which you subscribe.

Periodic Postings from FTP Archives

You can also obtain periodic postings from an FTP archive of FAQs at MIT. The main archives are in the "pub/usenet" directory, in subdirectories named for each of the newsgroups. For example, the subdirectory "news.announce.newusers" contains a file "Answers_to_Frequently_Asked_Questions". Note that not all newsgroups' FAQs have this filename!

FTP host:	`pit-manager.mit.edu`
directory:	`pub/usenet/news.announce.newusers`
file:	`Answers_to_Frequently_Asked_Questions`

If you want to explore these FAQ archives, just cd to the pub/usenet directory, and examine the names of the subdirectories, then cd to the directory of a newsgroup whose FAQs you would like to obtain.

If you do not have access to FTP, you can also access the archive via electronic mail. When accessing these FAQs by e-mail, you simply include the parts of the directory path and filename to the right of "pub/", as in the following example:

```
mail:    mail-server@pit-manager.mit.edu
subject: (none needed)
message: (include the following text exactly as it appears)

send usenet/news.announce.newusers/Answers_to_Frequently_Asked_Questions
```

You can also use the send command in your e-mail messages to this mail server to obtain help about how to use the service. For example, the following request strings will solicit help and index information:

```
send help
send index
send usenet/index
send usenet/news.announce.newusers/index
```

9.4.3. Read Introductory Newsgroups

There are several newsgroups which every new user should read.

news.announce.newusers

This newsgroup contains informative articles which are posted every month to help explain the workings of Usenet.

news.newusers.questions

As the name suggests, this is a question and answer forum for new Usenet users. If you read this newsgroup for several months, most basic questions you have about Usenet that are not answered by this chapter will be asked by new users and answered by Usenet experts.

news.newusers.answers

FAQ files from many Usenet groups are collected into this newsgroup.

news.announce.important

This newsgroup contains announcements about Usenet which are likely to be of interest to all Usenet users. This newsgroup is *not* for political, commercial, or other non-Usenet related announcements, no matter how important you think they may be!

news.announce.newsgroups

If you become an active Usenet reader, you should read this newsgroup to keep up-to-date on announcements of the creation of new Usenet newsgroups.

9.4.4. Selective Reading within Newsgroups

Following Threads of Discussion

You will often find that there may be only a subset of articles you want to read in each newsgroup. Many newsreaders support an automated process for following "threads" of discussion. Threads are articles on the same topic; they can be located either by scanning the subjects, the articles, or even the contents of the articles. (Refer to the help files in your newsreader on how to use thread feature.)

Catching Up

When you first enter the Usenet world, you may encounter a backlog of hundreds of articles which you may not have time to read. Most newsreaders include commands which will erase these backlogged articles. Usually a command such as "catch-up," "clear," or "mark all read," will leave you with a clean and manageable slate with which to start. And don't worry, there will be plenty more articles poring in to take the place of the cleared materials!

Kill Files

Say you are reading "talk.environment" and you are interested in everything discussed except postings about nuclear waste. You can avoid articles that have "nuclear waste" in the subject line by creating a "kill file." Similarly, if you are consistently annoyed by the postings of a user "space-alien@alpha.centuri.gov", the kill file prevents the display of articles coming from this e-mail address.

Strings upon which you want your kills to be based can often be entered from within your newsreader, or you can manually edit a kill file. For more information about kill files, refer to your newsreader's documentation.

9.5. Suggestions for First Time Usenet Posters

The most important thing to keep in mind when sending messages to Usenet is that your message may be sent to tens of thousands of machines and read by hundreds of thousands of people. This translates to a significant quantity of computer resources and a substantial accumulation of person hours.

All of the principles of e-mail etiquette discussed in Chapter 4 apply equally well to Usenet. You are strongly encouraged to review that chapter and the following information before you become an active part of the Usenet community.

9.5.1. Learn Usenet's Folkways

Try not to post until you've become familiar with the folkways of Usenet. Making a premature posting to Usenet is an extraordinarily efficient way to embarrass yourself (and perhaps your organization) in front of tens of thousands of people at the stroke of a single key!

9.5.2. Learn How to Respond

If you are responding to someone else's posting, it is often more appropriate to reply directly to that person with an e-mail message. Use your newsreader's command (often called "reply") that sends mail *directly* to that user and not to the newsgroup. If your newsreader doesn't have such a feature, identify the person's userid and e-mail address on the "From" line of their message or in the information at the end of their posting. You can then use your computer's mail software to send them a message directly without sending the message to the many readers of the newsgroup.

9.5.3. Get the FAQs First

Before you post a question, try your local resources including reference books and manuals, local User Service staff, and friends. If you think your question might be a "Frequently Asked Question," check either news.newusers.answers, or the newsgroup's FAQ posting, if available.

9.5.4. How to Followup

If you want to send a "followup" to a posting (i.e., an article responding to an existing article), scan the rest of the submitted articles in the newsgroup before sending mail or posting. You will often find that one posting may elicit a large number of followups and duplicate answers in a few days or even hours! After you have read the thread of discussion which the original posting prompted, you may find that what you wanted to say has already been said, or that the discussion has wandered off to another point. Of course, if your followup is different or if you believe you have something valuable to contribute, go ahead and send the followup.

9.5.5. Provide Context

If you are responding to someone else's posting, whether by e-mail or in a Usenet posting, include enough of their original message to provide a context for your response. Most newsreaders and e-mail programs provide a feature to automate such "quoting." However, try to include only that part of their posting needed to get their point across.

9.5.6. Send Your Message No Further than Necessary

No matter what you're posting, be sure you have specified an appropriate "distribution."

Distribution refers to how widely your posting is propagated. For example, distributions available at the University of Washington include "world," "na" for North America, "pnw" for the Pacific Northwest, "seattle," and "uw" for the University of Washington. If your posting is only of local interest, only post it locally. For more information about distributions, read the FAQ article "Frequently Submitted Items" in news.announce.newusers.

9.5.7. Crosspost Only if Necessary

Sometimes it may be appropriate to post a message to more than one newsgroup. If you are trying to locate economics simulation software for your Atari ST, you could include the names of an economics newsgroup and an Atari newsgroup in the "Newsgroups" field of a single message. This is known as "crossposting."

If you do crosspost, it is considered good network etiquette to include a newsgroup in the "Followup-to" field of the header. This is the newsgroup to which replies will be sent, regardless from which newsgroup they had been submitted. You can also put "poster" in the "Followup-to" field, in which case the messages will be sent to your mailbox, and not to any of the newsgroups. If you've used the poster option, send a summary of the answers you have received if you feel that it would be of interest to the newsgroups. Sharing is a two way street!

Sometimes, a message to which you are responding has been crossposted inappropriately to many newsgroups. For example, someone may have posted a question about how to keep raccoons out of their orchard to "misc.rural," "comp.protocols.tcp-ip," "alt.fan.monty-python," and "sci.space." Whenever you submit a followup, examine the newsgroups named in the "Newsgroups" field in the header of your response and trim it down to those you feel are most appropriate. In this case, "misc.rural" and maybe "alt.fan.monty-python."

9.5.8. Specifically Prohibited Usenet Activities

Although the Usenet community may best be described as a semi-anarchic democracy, there are two explicitly prohibited activities in most newsgroups:

Usenet Is Not for Commercial Communication

This does not mean that you can't discuss commercial products on Usenet. In fact, objective descriptions and comparisons of commercial computer products is a very useful Usenet activity. But, if you represent a company, don't even think of posting commercial advertisements on Usenet. At the very least, you will probably be flooded with complaints from outraged Usenet users.

Do Not Violate Copyright or Any Other U.S. or International Laws

Feel free to reproduce short extracts of a copyrighted work for critical purposes in your postings, but reproduction of copyrighted works in whole or substantial part is forbidden by U.S. and international copyright law. Respect the hard work of copyrighted authors. Similarly, engaging in or communicating about illegal activities on Usenet is forbidden and could endanger your site's Usenet feed.

9.6. What to Do if Something Goes Wrong

There are three common problems you may encounter when using Usenet: you might make a mistake, someone else might submit rude or insulting postings, or newsreader software might mess up distribution of Usenet articles. Here's what to do in each case.

9.6.1. Cancelling a Posting

Suppose you've just submitted a posting but realize you've just made a big mistake: "Oh no, I've sent my question about Nepali culture to rec.sport.football by mistake!"

Luckily, most newsreaders allow you to cancel a submission. Make sure you know your newsreader's command for cancellation before you post. Your submission might still get to a few sites, but you can usually squelch a mistaken submission if you act quickly. In general, it's not a good idea to post a second message retracting or apologizing for a posting unless you sincerely feel you've made a most grievous mistake.

9.6.2. Dealing with Flame Wars

If someone posts an article that obviously violates Usenet etiquette, it's usually best not to get involved. There are plenty of Usenet old-timers that can deal with the situation in a sagacious way.

Unfortunately, there are also a few hot-headed individuals who sometimes turn such situations into "flame wars," which is Usenet slang for a rude, disputatious, and inappropriate argument that shouldn't be carried out in a newsgroup.

Always resist the temptation to get involved in or start flame wars; there are no winners. And, in the very unlikely event that someone attacks you personally in a posting, simply ignore it; they'll usually stop. Even the most obnoxious flamers will usually desist when they feel that no one is paying attention. And if you keep your peace, it will be apparent to anyone reading such a posting that it is the flamer, and not you, who is of dubious character.

9.6.3. Dealing with Usenet Malfunctions

If you think that your local newsreader or your Usenet feed is malfunctioning, contact your local user services staff. If something is genuinely wrong, they will pass the information on to the news-admin at your site. Unless you are a Usenet administrator you shouldn't post messages about your local Usenet problems.

9.7. Conclusion

The Usenet world is inhabited by people from all walks of life, from many cultures, and with wildly varying temperaments. You will at turns be charmed, annoyed, or uplifted by what you read in newsgroups.

You may opt never to post to a newsgroup. Some people quietly lurk in newsgroups, reading the collective wisdom and folly of people throughout the world. Or you may find yourself becoming an active and vocal participant in one or more newsgroups.

However you choose to use Usenet, you will probably find numerous newsgroups which become essential resources for your research, work, or amusement.

Like the world at large, Usenet has something for everyone. Enjoy!

9.8. For More Information

The best source of information about Usenet is Usenet itself. Be sure to follow the suggestions for first time Usenet users in this chapter!

9.8.1. Bibliography

Quarterman, J.S. *The Matrix: Computer Networks and Conferencing Systems Worldwide.* (Especially Chapter 10.) Bedford, MA: Digital Press, 1990.

Todino, G. and D. Dougherty. *Using UUCP and Usenet.* Sebastopol, CA: O'Reilly and Associates, 1991.

@ 10 @

LISTSERV

If you have an apple and I have an apple and we exchange these apples, then you and I will still each have one apple. But if you have an idea and I have an idea and we exchange these ideas, then each of us will have two ideas.

attributed to George Bernard Shaw

―――――――――――

LISTSERV, a BITNET service, provides discussion forums and database management covering a huge variety of topics. To give you a taste of what's available through LISTSERV, here are 10 of the more than 3,000 currently active LISTSERV discussion lists:

Subject	List Name and Address
Albert Einstein's Writings	`EPP-L@BUACCA`
Apple-II Computer	`APPLE2-L@BROWNVM`
Ecology and the Biosphere	`BIOSPH-L@UBVM`
Fly Fishing	`FLYFISH@UMAB`
Folklore Discussion	`FOLKLORE@TAMVM1`
Gaelic Language	`GAELIC-L@IRLEARN`
Hospital Computer Networking	`HSPNET-L@ALBNYDH2`
Human Genome Mapping	`HGML-L@YALEVM`
Ocean Drilling	`ODP-L@TAMVM1`
Turkish Electronic Mail	`TEL@USCVM`

You might be the only person in your city who would want to read a newspaper or carry on a conversation every day about ocean drilling or fly fishing. But there are many people around the world interested in these topics. Thanks to LISTSERV discussion lists, they can share their interests by communicating electronically.

After you have subscribed to a discussion list, LISTSERV sends news and articles from the list to your electronic mailbox. As a subscriber to a discussion list, you usually can contribute messages which will be distributed to other subscribers.

The LISTSERV application described in this chapter operates primarily on BITNET connected hosts. Be aware that not all commands work for all LISTSERVs. Also note that some of the information provided in this chapter may not apply to the "listserv" service which offers many of the same functions as BITNET LISTSERV. This other "listserv" service is found mostly on UNIX systems; the command structure and syntax, and the services available, will be different than those for LISTSERV.

10.1. Essential Points about LISTSERV

10.1.1. List Managers and LISTSERV Software

Every LISTSERV list has a manager in charge of the list, but day to day list operations are managed by the LISTSERV software program. This software handles subscription and unsubscription requests, and related "official" list management business. Because it is a computer program, it only understands certain precise commands. A table of the most common of these commands is provided later in this chapter.

10.1.2. LISTSERV Addresses

The discussion list and the LISTSERV program that manages it will usually be at the same network address but will have different mailbox names. The mailbox name of the LISTSERV program is usually "LISTSERV@address," and the discussion list itself will have the name "listname@address," where "listname" is a descriptive name, eight or fewer characters in length, and "address" can mean one of several things.

Within the BITNET network, "address" simply refers to the name of the BITNET host machine, so LISTSERVers and discussions lists have addresses of the format "LISTSERV@host" and "listname@host".

For some Internet users, "address" may be replaced by "host.bitnet". The format host.bitnet is a pseudo domain format that your Internet host may understand. If your Internet host does not understand the host.bitnet pseudo domain, you must use the format "listname%host.bitnet@an.interbit.gateway", where "an.interbit.gateway" is replaced by one of the following interbit gateways:

```
cornellc.cit.cornell.edu
cunyvm.cuny.edu
mitvma.mit.edu
vm1.nodak.edu
```

For example, if the pseudo domain format "listname@BITNIC.BITNET" did not work from your host, the format "listname%bitnic.bitnet@cunyvm.cuny.edu" might.

10.1.3. LISTSERVers on Internet Hosts

A growing number of LISTSERVers are on hosts connected to both BITNET and the Internet. In such cases, you can send messages to a LISTSERVer's Internet address directly without having to go through a gateway. For example, the LISTSERVer at the University of Washington, which is known in the BITNET world as "LISTSERV@UWAVM," is also on the Internet where it is known as "LISTSERV@uwavm.u.washington.edu."

10.1.4. Moderated and Unmoderated Groups

Some LISTSERV discussion groups are managed by a moderator. In moderated lists, all material contributed to the LISTSERV is reviewed for appropriateness before being distributed to the group subscribers. Moderators sometimes provide the additional service of organizing submitted materials so that all related discussions are packaged into a few mail messages before distribution. In contrast, messages submitted to unmoderated groups are automatically distributed to all subscribers.

Depending on what you want from your LISTSERV subscription and how much time you have to read the mail from the list (some produce hundreds of messages each week), moderated vs. unmoderated may be an important criterion when selecting the groups to which you will subscribe.

10.2. What Discussion Lists Are Available?

10.2.1. Getting the Global List

You might have encountered references to specific LISTSERV lists in other chapters of *The Internet Passport* or in other network documentation. But if you want a comprehensive list of all lists, you should consult the LISTSERV "global list." You can obtain the global list from a LISTSERVer, or you can use online Internet resources such as WAIS. (See Chapter 18.)

Via LISTSERV

Using LISTSERV, just send the following simple e-mail request to any LISTSERVer. This example is addressed to a BITNET host (BITNIC) via the mail gateway at cunyvm.cuny.edu using the syntax described earlier.

```
mail:     listserv%bitnic.bitnet@cunyvm.cuny.edu
subject:  (none needed)
message:  list global
```

In a few minutes, the LISTSERVer will acknowledge your request and send a copy of the global list.

Understanding the Global List

Each line in the global list has a list's name, the BITNET address of the LISTSERVer which manages that list, and a brief description of the topics discussed in that list. Here are five lines from a global list:

Listname	Address	Brief Description
AGRIC-L	AGRIC-L@UGA	Agriculture Discussion
ALF-L	ALF-L@YORKVM1	Academic Librarian's Forum
ALLMUSIC	ALLMUSIC@AUVM	Discussions on Music
ALTLEARN	ALTLEARN@SJUVM	Approaches to Learning
APPLE2-L	APPLE2-L@BROWNVM	Apple II List

Searching the Global List for Particular Topics

If you want to search the global list for discussion groups on a particular subject, you can add the option "/<topic>" to the list global command, where <topic> is one or more words describing the subject in which you are interested. Since this involves a computer search, this is a good opportunity to think about search strategies.

Say you wanted to retrieve the information for discussion groups about Latin America. You might think that using the search string "Latin America" would be just right. However, many LISTSERV discussion groups are multilingual, so there might be groups whose descriptions contain non-English words or phrases, like "Latinoamericano." Try "Latin" instead.

```
mail:      listserv%bitnic.bitnet@cunyvm.cuny.edu
subject:   (none needed)
message:   list global /Latin
```

Notice that in the sample below, there are a few discussion groups dealing with Latin, but also a few that the string "Latin America" would not have retrieved.

```
Excerpt from the LISTSERV lists known to LISTSERV@BITNIC

Search string: LATIN

Network-
wide ID   Full address      List title
--------  ---------------   ------------------------------------

CANALC-D  CANALC-D@YORKVM1   Latin American and Caribbean Diges+
CLASSICS  CLASSICS@UWAVM     Classical Greek and Latin Discussi+
CH-LADB   CH-LADB@UNMVMA     Latin America Data Base
CREAD     CREAD@YORKVM1      Latin American and Caribbean Elect+
LALA-L    LALA-L@UGA         Latin Americanist Librarians' Anno+
LATAMMUS  LATAMMUS@ASUACAD   Discussion of all aspects of music
MEXNEXT   MEXNEXT@TECMTYVM   Lista para Mexico y Am. Latina: Ne+
OLADE-L   OLADE-L@UNALCOL    Organizacion Latinoamericana de En+
REDALC    REDALC@FRMOP11     Reseau Amerique Latine et Caraibes+
TML-L     TML-L@IUBVM        Thesaurus Musicarum Latinarum Data
```

10.2.2. Many LISTSERV Groups Are Available through Usenet

A growing number of lists are available through Usenet in the hierarchy "bit.listserv." For example, the LISTSERV group "POLITICS" is distributed to Usenet as "bit.listserv.politics."

One advantage of accessing lists through Usenet is that you can read many LISTSERV groups without having the messages clog up your mailbox. However, when you post a message to the "bit.listserv" newsgroup, the message may not be distributed to folks who subscribe to the list via a LISTSERVer. This is of course a real problem if you are responding to a message from someone whose message was posted to the group from LISTSERV!

For more on Usenet, refer to Chapter 9.

10.3. Using LISTSERV to Subscribe to Discussion Lists

Subscribing to LISTSERV discussion lists is very simple:

- to subscribe, unsubscribe, or perform other official business, you send messages to the e-mail address of a LISTSERVer (LISTSERV@address);

- to participate with the discussion list, you send messages to the e-mail address of the discussion list (listname@address).

To make this clear, think about newspapers. You send subscription requests to the subscription department, never to the people who read the newspaper. Imagine how upset newspaper readers would be if half the articles in the daily paper were letters saying "I would like to subscribe..." or "I would like to cancel my subscription."

10.3.1. LISTSERV Etiquette

All of the issues of e-mail and Usenet etiquette discussed in Chapters 4 and 9 apply equally well in the culture of LISTSERV lists. If you have forgotten the main points, please review those passages before entering the LISTSERV world. Take special care that the messages you send to the LISTSERV are appropriate to the topic and the group. As always, personal messages should remain so: send these to the individual for whom they are intended, not to the group. Be especially careful when using your e-mail's automatic reply function so that you don't accidentally send a personal message to the entire group.

10.3.2. Example LISTSERV Subscription Process

Send Your Subscription Request to the LISTSERVer

If you wanted to subscribe to the ALLMUSIC discussion list, you would send the following e-mail message to the LISTSERVer at node AUVM which happens to be at the American University:

```
mail:    listserv@auvm.bitnet
subject: (none needed)
message: subscribe allmusic <your name>
```

Or, if you need to use the full interbit gateway format, send the message as follows:

```
mail:    listserv%auvm.bitnet@cunyvm.cuny.edu
subject: (none needed)
message: subscribe allmusic <your name>
```

In a short while, you should receive an acknowledgment of you subscription from the LISTSERVer by e-mail. Please take the time to read this subscription notice and save it for future reference! It will contain useful information to help you make the most of your subscription to the discussion list, including instructions on how to unsubscribe.

You may receive a notice saying that "subscription to this list is not automatic." In such cases, a list manager reviews the subscription requests which have been received by the LISTSERV program and then manually adds names to the subscription list.

Send Only Discussion Messages to the Discussion List

Once you are subscribed to a LISTSERV list, you can send messages to the list. Messages which you want to be read by list subscribers must be sent to listname@ address not to LISTSERV@ address!

Some LISTSERV acknowledgments request that you introduce yourself to the list when you have subscribed. If ALLMUSIC requested such an introduction (in fact, it doesn't), you might send a mail message like the following:

```
mail:    allmusic%auvm.bitnet@cunyvm.cuny.edu
subject: Introduction from a new ALLMUSIC subscriber

Greetings! I have just subscribed to the ALLMUSIC discussion
list and would like to introduce myself. My name is <your
name>, and I am particularly interested in the influences of
Gregorian chants and Balinese Gamelan in the post-punk
aesthetic of Dutch underground music...(etc.)

<your contact information>
```

LISTSERV Subscriptions Can Become Overwhelming

Unlike a newspaper that is usually only delivered once a day, with all the articles in a neat, single package, most lists are distributed as individual messages. Some lists are very active and can send 10's if not 100's of messages to your electronic mailbox every day.

If you've ever subscribed to two or more newspapers, you know how quickly last week's and last month's issues can pile up. Now imagine that instead of a single issue of each newspaper each day, you had to separately handle every single article from every newspaper every day!

This is one of the main drawbacks to the LISTSERV system. If you're subscribed to several LISTSERV lists and don't check you electronic mailbox for a couple of days, you might find several hundred mail files from LISTSERVers waiting for you when you return. Reading all of these files, or even deleting them all, can take hours of your time. If you are using a small computer system, the impact on your computing and disk resources could be substantial.

Cancel a Subscription by Sending a Message to the LISTSERVer

When you want to cancel a subscription to a discussion list, send your request to the LISTSERV, not to the discussion list. Sending cancellation requests directly to a discussion list is a major faux pas in the LISTSERV world.

For example, suppose you accidentally subscribed to AXOLOT-L@AMPHBIAN and are receiving hundreds of messages about paedomorphic Mexican salamanders which you really don't want to read.

Simply send your cancellation to LISTSERV@AMPHBIAN, and the barrage of messages should desist.

```
mail:     listserv@amphbian.bitnet
subject:  (none needed)
message:  signoff axolot-l
```

10.4. Using LISTSERV as an Information Server

As you will see from the table of LISTSERV commands in 10.5, in addition to handling subscription and unsubscription requests to discussion lists, LISTSERV is also a very powerful software tool for retrieving files and searching LISTSERV file archives, much like the mail servers described in Chapter 3.

You usually don't have to be subscribed to a LISTSERV discussion list to use the information services of the hundreds of LISTSERVers around the world.

10.4.1. Retrieving Files from a LISTSERVer

Many discussion lists have archives of previous discussions which you can retrieve from the LISTSERVers. These discussion list archives frequently have the filename format of "listname logYYMM," where "YY" is a year and "MM" is a month. For example "axolot-l log9209" would be the log of discussions which took place in AXOLOT-L in September, 1992. Note that LISTSERV filenames are comprised of two words (the filename and the filetype) with a space between them.

10.4.2. Searching LISTSERV Databases with LISTDB

LISTDB is a program within the LISTSERV software that allows you to search through files in a LISTSERVer's archives. To use LISTDB effectively, you should have a copy of the global list-of-lists handy so you know which LISTSERV and which lists you might want to search.

For example, suppose you wanted to know how to send e-mail messages to your little sister in Antarctica. The LISTSERV list INFONETS@UGA specializes in questions and answers concerning e-mail to obscure places, so let's give it a shot!

A LISTDB request should be in a precise format. The following message should serve as a useful template for most LISTDB requests; simply change the destination LISTSERV address, the keyword after the word "SEARCH," the name of the database (INFONETS), and how far back into the database you want LISTDB to search (92/01/01):

```
mail:      listserv%uga.bitnet@cunyvm.cuny.edu
subject:  (none needed)
message:

//
DATABASE SEARCH DD=RULES
//RULES DD *
SEARCH Antarctica IN INFONETS SINCE 92/01/01
INDEX
/*
```

In a short while, you would receive an e-mail message with the results from your search request.

```
--> SEARCH Antarctica IN INFONETS SINCE 92/01/01
--> Database INFONETS, 4 hits.

-------   ----   ----  ----   -------
002268 92/04/29 21:11   22    E-mail from Antarctica?
002271 92/04/30 06:58   12    Antarctica
002282 92/05/01 09:52   29    Re: Antarctica
002295 92/05/04 22:25   21    Re: Antarctica
```

To actually retrieve any of these items, you would send the following request. It is almost exactly like the original, except that you change the last line from "INDEX" to "PRINT", followed by the item numbers from the left column of the response.

```
mail:     listserv%uga.bitnet@cunyvm.cuny.edu
subject: (none needed)
message:

//
DATABASE SEARCH DD=RULES
//RULES DD *
SEARCH Antarctica IN INFONETS SINCE 92/01/01
PRINT 2268 2271 2282 2295
/*
```

LISTDB will then send you via e-mail the requested articles from the INFONETS discussion list .

For more information about the database features of LISTSERV, send the request "info database" to any LISTSERVer.

10.5. Basic LISTSERV Commands

LISTSERV is a computer program so it only understands certain commands. Everything you send to a LISTSERVer must fit a precise syntax if you expect meaningful responses. (Avoid including a signature file on the messages sent to the LISTSERV program as it will attempt to process these "commands" and then report to you that it was unable to fill your request.)

You can put multiple requests in a single e-mail message, but they must each be on a separate line. The LISTSERVer sends a response to you by e-mail.

Here's a summary of some of the most useful commands that you can send to a LISTSERVer in an e-mail message.

List Subscription Commands	Result
`subscribe <listname> <your-name>`	Subscribes you to a list
`set <listname> nomail`	Suspends mailing of materials from that list (Very useful if you don't want hundreds of files accumulating in your mailbox while you're on vacation.)
`set <listname> mail`	Resumes mailing of materials to your account after a "nomail" request
`signoff <listname>` or	Cancels your subscription to a list
`unsub <listname>`	

General Purpose LISTSERV Commands	Result
`help`	Receive a brief list of LISTSERV commands
`info`	Receive a catalog of available topics
`info <topic>`	Receive a particular file from the list of info topics (For example, "info refcard" retrieves the LISTSERV "reference card" summarizing all LISTSERV commands.)
`list global`	Receive a list-of-lists that is available from all LISTSERVers
`list global /<topic>`	Receive a list of only those discussion groups which have the specified topic word(s) in their name or description

LISTSERV Information Server Commands	Results
`index <listname>`	Receive an index of the files which have been archived for a particular list
`get <filename filetype>`	Receive a particular file named in the index list (The files' names have two parts in this format—filename filetype.)
`info filelist`	Receive a list of all LISTSERV files on that LISTSERVer that contain LISTSERV help. (Note that you can use the "info" command for each of the files reported by the "info filelist" request.)
`info database`	Receive information about the LISTDB program which can be used to search LISTSERV log files for information

10.6. More about LISTSERV

10.6.1. LISTSERV Is a BITNET Service

LISTSERV is one of the notable services of BITNET, a network devoted to networking of educational institutions. Even though BITNET is not based upon the IP protocol like the Internet, LISTSERV is available to Internet users thanks to interbit gateways that allow e-mail messages to pass between the two networks.

As with other freely available resources on the Internet, use of a LISTSERVer should be viewed as a special privilege, not a right.

10.7. Conclusion

Many Internet users only know about LISTSERV groups by way of those that are gatewayed to the "bit.listserv" hierarchy in Usenet. As this chapter hopefully demonstrates, LISTSERV is a valuable service both as a discussion group service and a database. It merits appreciative use by Internet users.

10.8. For More Information

The best information about LISTSERV is from LISTSERVers. Use the commands in the "LISTSERV COMMANDS" table earlier in this chapter to explore LISTSERV's help files. You can also post general questions to LISTSERV lists to which you are subscribed and perhaps some other generous subscriber will help you out.

For general information about LISTSERV you can subscribe to LSTSRV-L@uga.cc.uga.edu or use the archives of this discussion for LISTDB requests. For informative discussion about LISTDB, subscribe to LDBASE-L%kanvm.bitnet@ndsuvm1.nodak.edu.

@ 11 @

Internet Mailing Lists

Self-expression must pass into communication for its fulfillment.

Pearl S. Buck

Internet mailing lists (also known as Internet interest groups) create forums for people to exchange electronic mail messages on topics of common interest. Mailing lists cover a dizzying variety of subjects: from comic books to works by James Joyce, from hang gliding to spelunking, from viral biology to cosmology. Mailing lists are an easy way to exercise your curiosity and share knowledge.

A mailing list performs two main tasks: it stores a list of the e-mail addresses of people who share an interest in a topic and distributes messages among these individuals quickly and easily. In this way it is like LISTSERV (described in Chapter 10).

Because mailing lists are distributed by e-mail, these services are available to users of other networks that maintain mail gateways to the Internet.

While you're subscribed to a mailing list, messages sent to that list will be forwarded directly to your electronic mailbox. Similarly, messages you send to the list will be distributed to all the other subscribers. You don't need to know their individual e-mail addresses because the mailing list takes care of this for you.

A mailing list transforms e-mail from a one-to-one exchange of messages, to a community in which you can ask questions, give answers, or simply sit back and learn from the conversations that are passed to you through the network. Mailing lists help network users become part of a community defined by interests, not location.

11.1. Using Internet Mailing Lists

11.1.1. Mailing List Names and Addresses

By convention, an Internet mailing list is usually assigned two e-mail addresses. A mailing list with the e-mail address

`listname@an.internet.address`

would typically have a companion address for subscription or cancellation requests called

`listname-request@an.internet.address`

Messages sent to "listname" are distributed to all subscribers of the list while messages sent to "listname-request" are received only by the list manager.

Unlike LISTSERV listnames, mailing list names are often long and informative. It's not unusual to encounter names like "indo-malaysian.archaeology."

11.1.2. Subscribing to Mailing Lists

Here's an example of a subscription request to a hypothetical mailing list, musica-neuva, for discussion of contemporary Brazilian music.

```
mail:      musica-nueva-request@venera.brasilia.br
subject:   subscription request
message:   Please subscribe me to musica-nueva. Thanks!

           Kristina Sadia
           ksadia@a.network.address
           (additional gateway information if needed)
```

Notice that the subscriber included her name and network address in the message text. This is very useful for the list manager if you are subscribing from a network outside of the Internet or if the header of your subscription request happened to be corrupted en route.

Sometimes subscription or cancellation requests are sent to the e-mail address of the person who maintains the list, for example, "sarah@an.internet.address." And subscriptions to some lists may be performed by a software package that expects requests in a precise syntax (much like LISTSERV lists). When in doubt, consult one of the lists-of-lists referred to at the end of this chapter for more information. The comprehensive lists-of-lists gives information and correct subscription addresses for hundreds of lists.

After you have submitted your subscription request, you will usually receive an acknowledgment from the list manager containing useful information about the group, such as how to quit the list, or how to obtain related files such as archives of the list's previous discussions. Save such information for future reference so you can get the most out of your membership!

Some lists have a collegial approach to their membership and the list manager may ask you to submit a brief introduction of yourself to the list.

Once your e-mail address has been added to a subscription list, you will begin receiving copies of all messages mailed to the list.

11.1.3. Kinds of Mailing Lists

Mailing lists can be set up and run in a variety of ways. They range in size, from a few individuals within an organization to thousands of people worldwide; in topic, from the highly specialized to the mundane; in activity, from a message once every couple of weeks to volumes of messages daily; and in tone of discussion, from a polite and deferential English tea to a rough and tumble free-for-all.

Moderated and Unmoderated Lists

Unmoderated lists accept and transfer all submissions. Other lists have a moderator who selects and/or edits the messages before distribution to the subscribers. Moderation helps reduce the number of messages that list subscribers don't want to read, (e.g., requests to unsubscribe, which are often erroneously sent to "listname" instead of "listname-request").

Digests

Some list maintainers will collect submitted messages into a single file, or digest. Instead of receiving separate files, you receive these digests on a periodic basis. This creates work for the list maintainer but makes mail management easier for list subscribers.

Private and Public Lists

Although most Internet mailing lists are public and can be subscribed to by anyone, other lists are private and intended for restricted distribution. The restriction might be due to limits on the amount of time and computer resources of a list manager, or it might be that the list manager and its subscribers want a restricted community. Unlike Usenet newsgroups, it is easy to set up a private list, if so desired.

Specialization of Mailing Lists

Internet mailing lists often deal with highly specialized, cutting-edge, or sensitive topics which may not be appropriate now, or ever, for the more general Usenet newsgroups.

Autonomy of Mailing Lists

Unlike LISTSERV discussion groups that require the willing participation of a BITNET site or Usenet newsgroups that require discussion and voting by the Usenet community, Internet mailing lists do not necessarily require local or network-wide approval to be started. This means that Internet mailing lists can have whatever properties their managers and participants want them to have.

11.2. Finding Mailing Lists

11.2.1. Lists of Mailing Lists

There are several catalogs, or lists-of-lists, which are essential references for helping you track down mailing lists of interest.

> *Dartmouth Special Interest Groups List of Lists*
> *Directory of Scholarly Electronic Conferences*
> *Publicly Accessible Mailing Lists*
> *SRI International List of Lists*

Each of these catalogs has a slightly different emphasis. They provide you with some or all of the following information about mailing lists and other types of discussion groups: name and e-mail address; a brief description of the topics discussed; whether the list is considered private or public; information about the folkways of the group; the mechanism of distribution (will you receive individual files, or periodic digests?); the location, and organization of archives of past discussions contact names and e-mail addresses of group owners/managers; and most importantly, the particular syntax used to subscribe or unsubscribe.

Information on how to access these lists-of-lists can be found in the section "For More Information about Internet Mailing Lists" at the end of this chapter.

11.2.2. Network "Word of Mouth"

If all else fails, you might be able to locate mailing lists of interest by posting a request to related Usenet or LISTSERV discussion groups. Sometimes the information about such lists will be included in a discussion group's FAQ (Frequently Asked Questions) file.

11.3. Mailing List Etiquette and Ethics

Of course, all issues of etiquette and ethics which apply to e-mail and Usenet also apply to mailing lists. (See Chapter 4 for a detailed discussion of these general issues.) If you think of a mailing list as an electronic version of a few good friends in a living room, talking passionately about some topic near and dear to their hearts, you'll pretty much understand the issues of etiquette and ethics that pertain to such lists.

Get to Know the People in the Group

It's generally a good idea to sit back and read a mailing list for awhile before you submit messages, just as you would listen to a conversation before chiming in. Turnover in mailing lists is often much lower than in typical newsgroups which tend to have a constant parade of visitors just popping in for a brief look. Also keep in mind that mailing lists can be heavily influenced by the personalities of a few key subscribers.

Address Your Messages to the Appropriate Destination!

Is the message you're mailing of interest to all the list subscribers? Then by all means, send it to the list. To only a single list subscriber? Then send e-mail directly to that subscriber. Is it a request to subscribe to or quit the group? Then please send it to "listname-request" or the list manager, as appropriate. (Sending unsubscription requests to the group is like constantly interrupting a conversation by asking, "Hey guys, can you let me out the room? I can't open the door!")

Avoid sending the same message to multiple lists. Never send a message to all mailing lists! Such actions are inconsiderate—the initial and response mail volume can overwhelm networks.

Handle Rejection of a Subscription Request Gracefully

You might encounter a list which, for one reason or another, does not accept your subscription request. In such a case, there's no point in making a fuss; mailing lists can be restricted by a list manager and its subscribers in any way they see fit, just like you have the right to decide who to invite into your home for a chat.

Respect a Group's Request for Privacy

Although it is technically true that anything sent via e-mail is public information, some mailing lists would prefer that you not redistribute discussions from the group to the global electronic village.

11.4. Starting an Internet Mailing List

Although setting up a mailing list is not difficult, maintenance and management can be a real time consumer. So think before you leap and do some preliminary research to avoid duplicating others' efforts. Talk with your system administrator or the network support group at your site to get advice and help.

Suppose you wanted to start a mailing list about the use of solar ovens in rural areas.

Is there already a mailing list or newsgroup that covers the topic in part or in whole? Examine the lists-of-lists described at the end of this chapter. You can also ask around the net by posting a query to the LISTSERV discussion group "new-list@vm1.nodak.edu". This group publishes list searches in digest form every few weeks. You might also try topically related Usenet, LISTSERV, mailing lists, or BBSs.

If a search of available resources doesn't uncover an existing forum for an in-depth discussion of solar ovens, you may decide to become a list manager. Consider this carefully, as it could become a serious commitment.

If you have already been exchanging e-mail with others about solar ovens and related topics, you have the first part of a mailing list: a list of potential subscribers. When you send out messages to all of these people about your shared interest, you would then have a one-way mailing list, which is sometimes referred to as a "distribution list." To make multiple mailings easier, most mail software packages allow you to use an "alias" or "nickname" for two or more e-mail addresses. You might set up the nickname "solar-ovens" for the e-mail addresses of this set of people.

To turn this private distribution list into a mailing list to which others on the Internet can subscribe and send mail for redistribution, ask your system administrator to set up two new mailboxes—one named "solar-ovens" and the other "solar-ovens-request." The mailbox solar-ovens would be an alias for the list of your subscribers' e-mail addresses. Mail sent to solar-ovens would automatically be distributed to all persons on this list. The mailbox solar-ovens-request would be an alias pointing to your e-mail address. Mail sent to solar-ovens-request would come to your personal mailbox and you would need to handle these administrative requests (e.g., to subscribe and unsubscribe) when you receive them.

If you wish to moderate the discussion and review all submitted messages before they are sent to the group, then the solar-ovens mailbox should be aliased only to your personal account. All mail sent to solar-ovens would come to your mailbox. In this case, you would also need to maintain a separate list of subscribers' e-mail addresses which would be aliased to a third e-mail address such as "solar-ovens-send." Any message you approve will be distributed to the group when you send it to solar-ovens-send.

If you don't wish to handle messages and subscriptions, you may want to ask other list managers for recommendations about software to handle some or all of the administrative duties of the list. Alternatively, a group that already handles mailing lists, or is otherwise related to or interested in the proposed topic, might consider setting up and managing your list.

If you want to broadly announce your mailing list, you should advertise its existence to the LISTSERV discussion group new-list@vm1.nodak.edu, to the maintainers of the lists-of-lists, and to related forums.

11.5. For More Information

11.5.1. Lists-of-Lists

No one of these lists-of-lists is complete, but together, they contain useful information about most public Internet mailing lists and LISTSERV discussion groups. In addition, these references often include information about functionally similar services such as COMSERVE, MAILSERVE, and MAILBASE.

Dartmouth List-of-Lists

This general purpose list contains a fair number of mailing lists and many LISTSERV lists. It is maintained by David Avery of Dartmouth University. Get the READ.ME file first! This list-of-lists is a huge file which is most easily used with the software programs designed to help you format, display, and search these files on Unix, Macintosh, VMS, and CMS computers.

FTP host:	`dartcms1.dartmouth.edu`
directory:	`SIGLISTS`
filename:	`READ.ME`

Directory of Scholarly Electronic Conferences

An academically oriented list of nearly 800 Internet mailing lists, LISTSERV discussion groups, and other kinds of topically oriented lists, this directory is maintained by Diane Kovacs of Kent University and organized by academic discipline.

FTP host:	`ra.msstate.edu`
directory:	`pub/docs/words-1/Net-Stuff`
filenames:	`acadlist.readme`
	`acadlist.file1`
	`acadlist.file2`
	`acadlist.file3`
	`acadlist.file4`
	`acadlist.file5`
	`acadlist.file6`
	`acadlist.file7`

Publicly Accessible Mailing Lists

A general purpose list of Internet mailing lists is maintained by Gene Spafford of Purdue University. This list is organized alphabetically by list name. Updated versions are posted periodically to several newsgroups (news.lists, news.answers, and news.announce.newusers).

SRI International List-of-Lists

This is a general purpose list-of-lists maintained by Steven Bjork of the Network Information Systems Center at SRI International and it is organized alphabetically by list name.

FTP host:	`ftp.nisc.sri.com`
directory:	`netinfo`
filenames:	`interest-groups`

Lists-of-Lists in WAIS Databases

Ed Vielmetti of MSEN, Inc. is currently maintaining WAIS versions of some of these lists and associated materials in the WAIS server at "wais.cic.net".

WAIS server:	`wais.cic.net`
databases:	`list`
	`mailing-lists`

To get up-to-date information about the current status of these and other lists-of-lists WAIS databases, try a WAIS search for the keyword "list" in the WAIS directory of servers. (For more on WAIS, see Chapter 18.)

11.5.2. Other Sources of Mailing List Information

Usenet Newsgroups

Periodic updates of *Publicly Accessible Mailing Lists*, and many other useful lists-of-lists for other Internet resources, are posted to the following newsgroups:

```
news.announce.newusers
news.answers
news.lists
```

For more on Usenet, see Chapter 9.

Mailing List about Mailing Lists

Updates and general information about the SRI lists-of-lists can be received by subscribing to the mailing list about a mailing list, interest-groups@nisc.sri.com.

To subscribe, send a message to interest-groups-request@nisc.sri.com.

LISTSERV List about Mailing Lists

When new lists are created, new-list@vm1.nodak.edu is one of the main forums in which they are announced. (For more on using LISTSERV, see Chapter 10.) To subscribe to new-list, send e-mail as follows:

```
mail:      listserv@vm1.nodak.edu
subject:   (none needed)
message:   sub new-list <your-full-name>
```

Section IV

Texts and Data

@ 12 @

Electronic Journals and Newsletters

"You can't quit! This isn't a magazine—it's a Movement!"

Harold Ross to E.B. White, quoted in
James Thurbur, *The Years With Ross*

Electronic journals and newsletters are the computer network equivalent of their printed counter parts. Both submission of articles and distribution of the final product are done over the network.

Some electronic journals and newsletters are also distributed in hardcopy. For example, NorthWestNet produces a newsletter called "NodeNews" that is available in both printed and electronic forms.

The content of electronic journals and newsletters ranges from the mainstream to the esoteric. Most electronic journals focus on topics of academic interest and many are really indistinguishable from formal, scholarly, printed journals. These journals are published only after the articles have undergone rigorous peer review with an emphasis on the leading concerns of established academic disciplines. Other electronic journals are considerably more informal.

The articles comprising an electronic newsletter are usually shorter than journal articles and the topics typically focus on news and announcements.

12.1. Using Electronic Journals and Newsletters

12.1.1. Locating Electronic Journals and Newsletters of Interest

The documents listed in the "For More Information" section provide comprehensive and up-to-date listings of the available electronic journals and newsletters.

It is also possible to use information resources such as WAIS, Gopher, CWISs, and World Wide Web to locate electronic journals.

12.1.2. Subscribing to Electronic Journals and Newsletters

To get regular printed magazines, you can subscribe and have each issue sent to you by mail or you can go to a newsstand to pick up each issue individually. Obtaining electronic journals works in essentially the same way, except everything is done from a computer on the Internet.

- You send a subscription request and receive each issue via electronic mail

- or, you obtain current or old issues via FTP, LISTSERVers, mail servers, Gopher, WAIS, or World Wide Web.

Here's an example of how to subscribe to an electronic journal known as "The Electronic Journal of Communication/La Revue Electronique de Communication," a bilingual, quarterly journal devoted to communication theory, research, practice, and policy.

Compose an e-mail message as follows:

```
mail:    comserve@vm.ecs.rpi.edu
subject: (none needed)
message: join ejcrec <your name>
```

To cancel a subscription to this particular e-journal, send the following:

```
mail:    comserve@vm.ecs.rpi.edu
subject: (none needed)
message: dropout ejcrec
```

These requests, as with many subscription requests, will be processed by a mail server—a computer program that only understands a limited and specific set of commands. To learn about this particular mail server, you would send an e-mail message with "help" in the body of the message. For a more detailed description of using mail servers generally, refer to Chapter 3.

Note: The exact syntax used to subscribe or unsubscribe to various e-journals will differ. The information you will need to subscribe to or obtain back issues of specific electronic journals is provided in the lists of electronic journals and newsletters described below.

12.1.3. Electronic Journal and Newsletter Etiquette

It is sometimes possible to subscribe others to an electronic journal. This of course should be done only with that other person's permission.

12.2. For More Information

The Gopher server at the University of North Texas contains archives of, and information about, a wide variety of electronic journals and newsletters. All of this material is currently located in "Newsletters and Journals" found in the root directory. For more on using Gopher, see Chapter 17.

12.2.1. Lists of Electronic Journals and Newsletters

If you want to subscribe to electronic journals or newsletters, you should get a copy of the document titled "Directory of Electronic Journals, Newsletters, and Scholarly Discussion Lists," maintained by Michael Strangelove. This directory currently catalogs over 500 scholarly lists, about 30 journals, over 60 newsletters, and 15 other titles including some newsletter-digests, along with specific instructions for obtaining each publication by mail or FTP.

From LISTSERVs

Electronic copies of this directory are currently available from the following LISTSERV. (Note carefully the spellings of the filenames!)

```
mail:      listserv@acadvm1.uottawa.ca
subject:  (none needed)
message:  get ejournl1 directry
          get ejournl2 directry
```

Electronic Journal List via FTP

Typically, when the directory of e-journals is placed on FTP hosts, the name is rendered more intuitive since most FTP hosts are Unix based and do not have the same filename restrictions as VM/CMS hosts on which most LISTSERVers reside.

Consequently, you should use archie (described in Chapter 16) to search for the string "e-journals" (or other variants of this term) to locate the most up-to-date, FTP'able version of this file.

Electronic Journal List in Print

If you want to purchase a bound book of this information, contact:

> Office of Scientific and Academic Publishing
> Association of Research Libraries
> 1527 New Hampshire Avenue, NW
> Washington, DC 20036 USA
>
> e-mail: **arlhq%umdc.bitnet@cunyvm.cuny.edu**
> phone: (202) 232-2466 or (202) 462-7849

LISTSERV List

The following LISTSERV list is devoted to discussion about electronic journals, including announcements of new journals and the relationship of electronic journals to traditional publication:

> **VPIEJ-L%vtvm1.bitnet@cunyvm.cuny.edu**

12.2.2. Bibliography

Because electronic journals and newsletters cannot be kept in or accessed from a library collection in the same manner as their printed counterparts, librarians and academics have engaged in a lively debate about their future and their utility. The following articles should give you a taste of the many issues that have been raised:

Alexander, A.W. and J. S. Alexander. "Intellectual Property Rights and the 'Sacred Engine': Scholarly Publishing in the Electronic Age." *Advances in Library Resource Sharing* 1 (1990): 176-192.

Gardner, W. "The Electronic Archive: Scientific Publishing for the 1990s." *Psychological Science* 1 (1990): 333-341.

Harnad, S. "Scholarly Skywriting and the Prepublication Continuum of Scientific Inquiry." *Psychological Science* 1 (1990): 342-344.

Litchfield, C. "Local Storage and Retrieval of Electronic Journals: Training Issues for Technical Services Personnel." *Serials Review* 17 (4)(1991): 83-84.

Lucier, R.E. "Knowledge Management: Refining Roles in Scientific Communication." *EDUCOM Review 25* (Fall 1990): 21-27.

McMillan, G. "Embracing the Electronic Journal: One Library's Plan." *The Serials Librarian* 21 no. 2/3 (1991): 97-108.

McMillan, G. "Technical Services for Electronic Journals Today." *Serials Review* 17 no. 4 (1991): 84-86.

Metz, P. "Electronic Journals from a Collection Manager's Point of View." *Serials Review* 17 no. 4 (1991): 82-83.

Metz, P. and P.M. Gherman. "Serials Pricing and the Role of the Electronic Journal." *College and Research Libraries* 52 (July 1991): 315-327.

Neavill, G.B. "Electronic Publishing, Libraries, and the Survival of Information." *Library Resources and Technical Services* 28 (January/March 1984): 76-89.

Okerson, A. "With Feathers: Effects of Copyright and Ownership on Scholarly Publishing." *College and Research Libraries* 52 (September 1991): 425-438.

Piternick, A.B. "Electronic Serials: Realistic or Unrealistic Solution to the Journal 'Crisis'?" *The Serials Librarian* 21 no. 2/3 (1991): 15-31.

@ 13 @

Electronic Books

During the Han Dynasty, Confucian scholars were honored, and the classics were cut in stone...if the classics could be revised and thus cut in wood and published, it would be a very great boon to the study of literature.

Feng Tao, in an official memorandum written to the Chinese National Academy in 932 A.D.

In the broadest sense, an electronic book is any document which is lengthy enough to be considered a book and is stored on diskette, hard drive, magnetic tape, or compact disk (CD). You can read electronic books at your computer screen, print them out in plain text or, if you have access to the right hardware and software, print them out in elegant formats on a laser printer. Note that electronic books are also sometimes referred to as "e-texts."

By this definition, the many computer-related manuals which are available by FTP can also be thought of as electronic books. However this chapter will focus on a special class of electronic books that include classical texts of world literature such as *The Declaration of Independence*, *The Great Gatsby*, the *Bible*, the *Koran*, the *Oxford English Dictionary*, and even *Hikayat Indraputra*, the notable Malay romance.

13.1. Obtaining Electronic Books

In general, you can access electronic books via FTP or by downloading them from Bulletin Board Services (BBSs). You may also order electronic books on diskettes or other storage media from electronic book providers. Not all electronic books are free and costs vary depending on the provider.

Many of the services described throughout *The Internet Passport* allow you to search through the text of books. In particular, Gopher, WAIS, CWISs, BBSs, and World Wide Web, allow access to some of the texts described in this chapter, though it is generally less efficient to obtain entire book-length documents from these services than by FTP.

13.2. Electronic Book Providers

There are currently hundreds of sources of electronic books, and the number of providers and texts will probably continue to grow significantly for years to come. This chapter introduces you to the main Internet providers of electronic books and provides instructions on how to use a catalog service for finding electronic books. The entries in this section are listed alphabetically by name.

13.2.1. Freedom Shrine

The Freedom Shrine project concentrates on e-texts of short documents which have been of crucial importance in the history of democracy, primarily in the U.S.

All Constitutional Amendments	*German Surrender Documents*
Annapolis Convention	*Gettysburg Address*
Articles of Confederation	*Japanese Surrender Documents*
Bill of Rights	*Jefferson's First Inaugural Address*
Charlotte Town Resolves	*Lincoln's Second Inaugural Address*
Constitution of the Iroquois Nations	*M.L. King's: "I Have a Dream" Speech*
Constitution of the United States	*Magna Carta*
Constitutional Transmittal Letter	*Mayflower Compact*
Declaration and Resolves of the 1st	*Monroe Doctrine*
Continental Congress	
Declaration of Independence	*Northwest Ordinance of 1787*
Declaration of the Causes and Necessity of	*Paris Peace Treaty, 1783*
Taking up Arms	
Emancipation Proclamation	*Proclamation of Neutrality*
First Thanksgiving Proclamation	*Treaty of Greenville*
French Declaration of Rights	*Virginia Declaration of Rights*
Fundamental Orders of 1639	*Washington's Farewell Address*

The authoritative site for Freedom Shrine documents is the Cleveland Free-Net BBS. Telnet to one of the following hosts and login as a visitor or apply for an account:

```
freenet-in-a.cwru.edu
freenet-in-b.cwru.edu
freenet-in-c.cwru.edu
```

Once you have read the Free-Net introductory materials, select "The Library" from the main menu to access the Freedom Shrine and other electronic book holdings of the Cleveland Free-Net.

13.2.2. Online Book Initiative

The Online Book Initiative is a project of The World, a commercial Internet services provider. It contains an interesting variety of e-texts including classics of English literature, political science, archives of electronic journals, and standard computer-related materials such as operating system documentation.

A Christmas Caroll	Nerd Humor archives
BSD Unix Documentation	NREN documents
Civil Disobedience	*Seven Voyages of Sinbad*
DOD *Orange Book*	Shakespeare's Complete Works
Five Orange Pips	SunFlash documents
Flatland	Supreme Court Decisions
Grimm's Fairy Tales	Usenet Cookbook
Japanese Technical Reports	William Butler Yeats's Poetry
New Hacker's Dictionary	*Wuthering Heights*

The authoritative site for Online Book Initiative documents is the following:

FTP host:	`world.std.com`
directory:	`obi`
filenames:	(many or all)

13.2.3. Oxford Text Archives

The Oxford Text Archives (OTA) is oriented towards e-texts in many different languages of special interest to literary scholars. Many of the e-texts contained in OTA either have to be purchased or have restrictions on their distribution and use.

Here is a very brief excerpt from OTA's large holdings to give you a feel for the wealth and variety of materials available from this source.

A la Recherche du Temps Perdu	*Hamlet*
Arabic Prose Samples	*Hikayat Indraputra* (a Malay Romance)
Aristotle, Complete Works (in Greek)	*Homer, Complete Works* (in Greek)
Beowulf	*Hyckerscorner, Wynkyn de Worde*
Blues Lyric Poetry: An Anthology	*Il paradiso, Il purgatorio, L'Inferno*
British Columbian Indian Myths	*Llyr gwyn Rhydderch: Ronabwy*
Chinese Telegraphic Code Character Set	*MRC Psycholinguistic Database*
Das Nibelungenlied	*Orwell's "1984"* (in Croatian)
Etymological Dictionary of Gaelic Language	*Plato, Collected Works* (in Greek)
Genji Monogatari	*The Origin of Species*

Another service of OTA is a database of information about e-texts available from other archives around the world.

Accessing the Oxford Text Archives

Direct network access to OTA is currently only possible from within England via the JANET Network. The FTP host is uk.ac.ox.vax and the file is"[archive].snapshot.lis."

Access from the Internet in the U.S. via the Internet-Janet Gateway (by Telnet to sun.nsf-relay.ac.uk) may be possible by the time you read this guide. For more up-to-date information on this gateway service, send an e-mail message with the following two lines of text in the body of your message:

```
mail:      info-server@nsfnet-relay.ac.uk
subject:  (none needed)
message:  Request:  janetpad
          Topic:   userguide
```

For More Information about the Oxford Text Archives

You can get more detailed information about OTA from the following FTP host:

FTP host: `ra.msstate.edu`
directory: `pub/docs/history/e-documents`
filenames: `oxford.text.archives`   (general description)
                          `oxford.text.order.form`   (how to get OTA e-texts)

You can also contact OTA by postal mail or e-mail.

Oxford Text Archive
Oxford University Computing Service
13 Banbury Road, Oxford OX2 6NN UK

e-mail: `archive@vax.ox.ac.uk` (Internet)

13.2.4. Project Gutenberg

Project Gutenberg is a not-for-profit organization whose goal is to prepare electronic editions of more than 10,000 English language books by the year 2001. All documents are available as text-only files, but many can be obtained in PostScript or troff formats.

As of September 1992, the following e-texts were distributed by Project Gutenberg:

1990 U.S. Census Information	*King James Bible*
Aesop's Fables	*Moby Dick*
Alice in Wonderland	*Night Before Christmas*
As You Like It	*Oedipus Trilogy*
Book of Mormon	*Peter Pan*
CIA World Fact Book	*Roget's Thesaurus*
Declaration of Independence	*Scarlet Letter*
Far From the Madding Crowd	*Song of Hiawatha*
Federalist Papers	*Through the Looking Glass*
Frederick Douglass	*Time Machine*
Her Land	*U.S. Constitution*
Holy Koran	*War of the Worlds*
Hunting of the Snark	*Zen and the Art of the Internet*

Obtaining Project Gutenberg E-Texts

Electronic books from Project Gutenberg can be obtained most easily by FTP or mail server. If you don't have access to the Internet, you can purchase floppy disk versions by postal mail. Please note that because of copyright restrictions some of the texts are only available for U.S. citizens.

FTP Hosts for Project Gutenberg E-Texts

As of September 1992, Project Gutenberg files could be retrieved from the following authoritative FTP hosts:

FTP host:	`quake.think.com`
directories:	`pub/etext/1991`
	`pub/etext/1992`
	`pub/etext/usonly`
filenames:	(many or all)
FTP host:	`mrcnext.cso.uiuc.edu`
directories:	`etext/etext91`
	`etext/etext92`
	`etext/usonly`
filenames:	(many or all)
FTP host:	`oes.orst.edu`
directory:	`pub/almanac/etext`
filenames:	(many or all)

For More Information about Project Gutenberg

Project Gutenberg is a not-for-profit effort that relies on volunteers to submit and proof electronic texts and research copyrights. For more information, contact:

> Michael S. Hart, Director Project Gutenberg
> 405 West Elm St.
> Urbana, IL 61801 USA
> hart@vmd.cso.uiuc.edu

13.3. Catalogs of Electronic Book Providers

13.3.1. American Philosophical Association Subcommittee on Electronic Texts in Philosophy

A catalog of e-texts of interest to philosophers is maintained in the bulletin board system of the American Philosophical Association.

> Telnet: `atl.calstate.edu`
> login: `apa`

For more information about the APA "Electronic Agora," see Chapter 15 in the subsection "Grants and Awards."

13.3.2. CPET: Catalogue of Projects in Electronic Text

The Center for Text and Technology (CTT) in collaboration with the Academic Computer Center at Georgetown University compiles a catalog of electronic text projects of interest to researchers in the humanities. The focus is on projects producing electronic versions of primary texts and does not currently include information about encyclopedias, dictionaries, or concordances.

For each project in the catalog, CTT attempts to compile the following information:

- identifying acronym or short reference;
- name and affiliation of operation;
- references to any published descriptions;
- contact person and/or vendor with addresses;
- primary disciplinary focus (and secondary interests);
- focus of the materials—time period, geographical area, or individual;
- language(s) of texts;
- intended use(s) and size (number of works, or entries, or citations);
- file format(s);
- mode(s) of access (online, tape, diskette, CD-ROM, etc.);
- source(s) of the archival holdings—encoded in-house, or obtained from elsewhere.

As of September 1992, the catalog contained information on more than 300 e-text projects in 27 33countries.

Accessing CPET

The CPET catalog is accessible via Telnet or modem calls and features an interactive front end that allows you to locate information on texts of interest.

Telnet:	**guvax3.georgetown.edu**
username:	**CPET**
modem:	(202) 687-2616
connect:	**Esc +**
dial:	**guvax**
local>	**connect guvax3**
username:	**CPET**

To use this service effectively by modem, you may need to obtain a customized version of Kermit from the following FTP host:

FTP host:	**guvax.georgetown.edu**	
directory:	**cpet**	
filenames:	**ibm-kermit.exe**	(for DOS)
	mac-kermit.sit	(for Macintosh)

For More Information about CPET

An illustrated *User's Guide to the Catalogue of Projects in Electronic Text* is available free of charge through surface mail.

Margaret Friedman, Project Assistant
The Center for Text and Technology
Academic Computer Center
238 Reiss Science Building
Georgetown University
Washington, DC 20057 USA

e-mail: **mfriedman@guvax.georgetown.edu**
voice: (202) 687-6096

13.4. For More Information

This is a rapidly growing area. By the time you read this, there may be additional providers of electronic books other than those discussed in this document.

13.4.1 Discussion Groups

The following discussion group focuses mostly on Project Gutenberg, but it is also a forum for discussion about many issues (legal, pedagogical, etc.) concerning e-texts.

To subscribe to the LISTSERV discussion group:

```
mail:    listserv%uiucvmd.bitnet@cunyvm.cuny.edu
subject: (none needed)
message: subscribe gutnberg <your name>
```

The LISTSERV discussion is also gatewayed to the following Usenet newsgroup:

```
bit.listserv.gutnberg
```

13.4.2 Bibliography

Collis, B.A. "The Evaluation of Electronic Books, Educational and Training." *Technology International.* 28(4)(1991):355-63.

Gabriel, M.R. *A Guide to the Literature of Electronic Publishing.* Greenwich, CT: Joi Press. 1989.

Lowry, C.B. "Converging Information Technologies: How Will Libraries Adapt." *CAUSE/EFFECT* 13(3)(1990):35-42.

Seiler, L.H. "The Concept of Book in the Age of the Digital Electronic Medium." *Library Software Review* 11(1)(1992):19-29.

@ 14 @

Libraries on the Internet: Online Public Access Catalogs (OPACs)

The library was laid out on a plan which has remained obscure...only the librarian has received the secret, and he communicates it, while still alive, to the assistant librarian...only the librarian has, in addition to that knowledge, the right to move through the labyrinth of the books, he alone knows where to find them and where to replace them... The other monks may know the list of the volumes that the library houses; only the librarian knows, from the collocation of the volume, from its degree of inaccessibility, what secrets, what truths or falsehoods, the volume contains...a spiritual labyrinth, it is also a terrestrial labyrinth...

Umberto Eco
The Name of the Rose

═══════════════

Over the past decade, many libraries throughout the world have begun to transfer their card catalogs into computer databases called "online public access catalogs," or "OPACs." Many of these libraries in turn have made their OPACs accessible to anyone using the Internet.

Using an OPAC over the Internet is essentially like using a card catalog. The main difference is that instead of going to the library, pulling drawers, and riffling through cards, you access the OPAC from a computer terminal. From your home, school, or office, information about millions of books and articles from around the world is now at your fingertips.

14.1. What Can Be Done with OPACs?

The primary use of today's OPACs is to obtain the kinds of information stored in the traditional card catalog. Because the number of OPAC software packages and implementations is substantial, you will be required to learn commands specific to these systems. Online help is usually available to get you started.

14.1.1. Searching for References by Subject, Author, and Title

From a patron's perspective, the primary use of a traditional card catalog is to search for documents by subject, author, and title. And although some of us old fashioned academic types get an ineffable enjoyment from the physical rhythm of working with a card catalog, this process takes significant time. The movement of directed swarms of electrons through computers and networks is substantially faster than the most skilled bibliophile's hand. In short, a search that would take hours with a regular card catalog can take seconds with an OPAC.

In addition to author, title, and subject searches, a growing number of OPACs include searches based on call numbers, keyword, year of publication, language, ISSN and ISBN numbers, media type, and organizational information. Such additional search fields can be a blessing when doing a highly specialized search. For example, I just searched an OPAC and requested all books that were written in Hindi, published since 1985, and dealt with education. The search retrieved 75 documents. (Not that I can actually *read* Hindi, but if I could, this would be handy indeed.)

14.1.2. Obtaining Detailed Bibliographic Information

The amount of information contained on the typical card in a card catalog is often limited, in part by the physical size of a card, and by the amount of person power required to prepare and update the cards. An individual entry in an OPAC is usually not as restricted in the amount of information it can contain, and it's far easier for librarians to locate, update, annotate, or add fields to entries contained in an OPAC.

14.1.3. Browsing

Many an academic has wandered through library stacks and serendipitously stumbled upon a book or section that proved to be a gold mine for their research. While an OPAC can't show you what's between the covers of the books, some will let you browse. For example, a number of OPAC software packages let you wander forwards and backwards through, authors, subjects, titles, or call numbers, which is almost like browsing in the stacks.

14.1.4. Saving Search Results

Recording information from a regular card catalog can be time consuming and frustrating. (Remember wrestling with a drawer of cards with one hand while trying to transcribe information with the other?) If your goal is to assemble a bibliography, you may then have to go through the extra step of entering the information into a word processor.

In contrast, you can usually save the results of OPAC searches to your own computer with a few keystrokes. Some OPACs feature a built-in service that will send the results of your search via e-mail. Even when using OPACs that do not have this capability, you can almost always capture your session into a local file. For example, the "script" command in Unix will save what appears as screen output to a file. Similar commands or programs exist for most operating systems and communications software packages.

14.1.5. Catalogs of Special Collections

A growing number of OPACs include videos, movies, photographs, maps, microfilm, phonographs, CDs, and other non-book materials. These references may be fully incorporated into the main databases or you may have to specifically request a database of these items once connected to an OPAC service.

14.1.6. Materials Available for Circulation or Interlibrary Loan

Most OPACs are tied into the databases that handle circulation, so you might find out immediately if an item is available for checkout. If the book is already checked out there will usually be an indication of the date it is due back at the library. Some libraries even let you submit requests for materials electronically, either through an OPAC feature or e-mail. Thus you may be able to search for a title, request it, and receive it at your office without ever going to the library itself.

OPACs are often used by librarians and patrons to identify potential sources for interlibrary loans. Some library systems have even linked their entire interlibrary loan systems to the Internet so that paperwork is transmitted electronically instead of being sent by postal mail. Of course, most interlibrary loan materials are still sent by postal mail or fax, but who knows what the future holds!

14.2. What Can't Be Done with OPACs (Yet)

Opportunities to read library books from your computer are practically nonexistent due to technical and legal complications. Manual entry of text into computers is extremely time consuming. Many features of printed materials, such as pictures, tables, charts, or even the number and variety of fonts, challenge today's best scanning equipment and software. Furthermore, there are many copyright issues centering on electronic distribution of texts that must be hashed out by legal experts, publishing companies, and authors. It is not likely that OPAC services will grow to supplant physical access to libraries in the very near future.

Chapters 12 and 13 describe a number of sources for electronic books and electronic journals respectively. Although the number of available electronic texts is expanding, it will probably be some time before they equal the number and diversity of materials held in a typical small college library.

14.3. Effective Use of OPACs

As the previous sections pointed out, OPACs are more than card catalogs, but they aren't full service libraries either. So your approach to selecting and using an OPAC will be different than the approach you take when selecting and using a traditional library.

14.3.1. Selecting the Right OPAC

Every OPAC has unique strengths and weaknesses. This is due to inherent differences in the quality, depth, and breadth of the collections they serve; disparities in the capabilities of the many OPAC software platforms; and varying goals of the administrations and library staffs at these institutions. So finding the OPAC that suits your needs merits careful study.

Internet users often select the biggest, nearest, most prestigious, most exotic, or most familiar OPAC. Here are some general hints on how to pick the right OPAC for the right job.

Essential Guides for Using OPACs

There a number of high quality, frequently updated lists of OPACs, some of which are geographically or topically oriented. These lists also include information on the particular strengths of each OPACs' holdings or helpful instructions about the peculiarities of using or accessing each. Online sources for the major lists of OPACs are provided at the end of this chapter under "For More Information on OPACs."

Define Your Quest

If you're looking for the Holy Grail, then maybe you do want an OPAC with tens of millions of entries. But for most people most of the time, an OPAC with (a "mere") 100,000 titles may be appropriate—especially if that OPAC has a specialized collection included, such as contemporary Latin American poetry.

Ask Your Local Librarians and Peers

For general advice on selecting OPACs, consult the librarians at your Internet site. You might also ask your Internet-savvy peers. If your OPAC needs are for a specialized class of library holdings, you could post a note to an appropriate Usenet newsgroup, LISTSERV list, or Internet mailing list to find out which OPACs are best for searches in particular topics. (For more on Usenet, LISTSERV, and mailing lists, refer to Chapters 9, 10, and 11 respectively.)

WAIS Databases

If you are looking for a library with especially strong holdings in a particular area, you might also try doing a keyword search in the WAIS database versions of the St. George-Larsen and Barron OPAC lists, which are known as "online-libraries-st-george" and "online-libraries" respectively. For example, searching in these WAIS databases for "entomology" revealed that Cornell and the University of California both have particularly strong holdings in this topic. This is no surprise to professional bug hunters, but may not be apparent to the larval researcher.) For more on WAIS, refer to Chapter 18.

14.3.2. How to Think Like an OPAC

Dealing with an Embarrassment of Riches

If you've never used an OPAC before, you're in for a big surprise. OPAC searches can yield hundreds or even thousands of citations if you didn't select your search terms carefully. Most of us are capable of separating the wheat from the chaff when handling actual texts, but even experienced library users sometimes suffer a sense of vertigo when faced with an OPAC screen that announces "7,546 Titles Were Found."

Searches for individual authors tend to yield manageable results, but keyword or subject searches may spew screen-fulls of information to your terminal. I just typed "education" as a keyword search at the University of Washington OPAC, and was told in a matter of seconds that there were 53,216 items in the catalog with that keyword!

Dealing with an Implicit Structure

On the other hand, searches on keywords may lead to a puzzling dearth of results. Most OPACs use Library of Congress Subject Headings or other precise and highly structured classifications system. Subject headings which are intuitively sensible to *you* may not yield any search results, if they do not correspond precisely to an entry in the OPAC's list of subject headings. For example, "learning" seems synonymous with "education," but when searching for the keyword "learn" in the same OPAC, and only 502 citations were reported—a mere 1% of the documents retrieved with the keyword "education."

Although some OPACs will display subject classifications on your terminal, it can be useful to consult your local reference librarian before beginning a large scale OPAC search. Reference books on the Library of Congress subject headings or specialized medical subject headings may also be valuable.

Precision Searches with Boolean, Adjacency, and Other Operators

Many OPACs allow you to use special operators when you do your searches. Boolean operators such as "and," "or," "nand" ("not and"), and "nor" ("not or") are particularly widespread.

Another class of operators are called "adjacency operators." For example, you can sometimes specify that two search terms be immediately adjacent to each other, in the same search field, or in one or more search fields in order to be counted as a valid item.

If you use such operators, be sure you understand how they work and how they interact. They may have varying priority (one operator in a string is acted upon before others), non-transitivity (the order in which operators are placed affects how they are acted on), or other special rules of use. Versions of "not" (such as "not" and "nand") are particularly slippery.

Special Characters or Parts of Speech in Search Terms

If terms you are searching for contain special symbols such as hyphens, apostrophes, commas, numbers, or scientific symbols, understand how the OPAC handles them before including them in a search. They may be forbidden or require special syntaxes to be recognized by the OPAC. Also be aware that certain parts of speech such as prepositions may be ignored or problematic when used in keyword or subject searches and are usually best left out except in title searches.

Wildcards: Truncation, Stems, and Reverse Stems

"Wildcard" operators allow you to specify any words containing a certain string. Similar operators called "stem" and "reverse stem" allow one to search for prefixes and suffixes. For example, in OPACs using BRS software, "map$" would search for all citations containing any words beginning with "map."

Such operators are extremely useful when used intelligently. As an extreme example of an ill-conceived use of wildcards, suppose you wanted to do a search for the discovery of the principles of genetics. Possibly interesting forms of the word "genetics" might include "gene," "genetics," "genetical," "pangenesis," and so forth. In a rush to be clever, the person who earnestly specifies a search for "disc$ and gene$" is likely to retrieve as many citations about "discourses on Genesis" and "the disco generation" as it is to retrieve citations about Mendel and DNA.

Displaying a History of Your Search Requests

Most OPACs allow you to view a list of the search requests you have made during your session. This can be extraordinarily useful for combining distinct searches into one. For example, on reviewing your history of searches, you may find that search query #17 built up from six tedious steps, and search query #29 created by another eight steps, can be combined for exactly the search you need by typing "17 and 29".

Recording Successful Searches as a Search Strategy

Suppose that you need to do exactly the same literature search every several months, and that it requires many steps to achieve the desired result. A few advanced OPACs allow you to record a search strategy that you can later recall by issuing a single command. However, this service is not likely to be available if you are a guest user of an OPAC.

Tailoring the Display of Search Results

Almost all OPACs allow you to tailor the type and amount of information shown when the results of a search are displayed, ranging from a single line per document, to full bibliographic citations each taking up one or two screens. Take advantage of this flexibility! For quick scans of results, use some form of short or review display. To uncover possible terms that will refine your search, pull up every bit of detail you can from relevant documents.

Summary

By keeping these points in mind, your OPACs experience should be remarkably rewarding. If you spend some time improvising, you'll likely hit upon unique strategies that work well for you.

14.4. Accessing OPACs

Since OPACs are among the most popular services of the Internet, it's not surprising that there are probably more paths to OPACs than most any other Internet service. Each access method has its peculiar advantages or target audiences.

If you are at a college, university, or other institution with a local OPAC, you may be able to enter a command from your Internet host that will connect you directly to that OPAC. Consult your online documentation or ask your local user services staff for help.

Most OPACs on the Internet can be accessed using Telnet, or if they are run on an IBM mainframe, with tn3270. You can get their Internet addresses from the catalogs of OPACs listed at the end of this Chapter or from online lists of OPACs like Catalist or Hytelnet (described below).

14.4.1 Internet Front Ends

Gopher

Gopher is a front end to online documents and services including OPACs. For a thorough overview of using Gopher, refer to Chapter 18.

WAIS

A number of specialized libraries have been put into WAIS database format, such as the Columbia University Law Library general catalog and Spanish Law collections, and several French libraries. The number of libraries accessible through WAIS is likely to grow in the coming years, especially as library software incorporating the Z39.50 protocol upon which WAIS is based becomes more widespread.

Other Internet Front Ends

Several other Internet front ends can be used to access OPACs. For example, you can get to many OPACs by telnetting to the following multipurpose services:

Internet Address	Access
bbs.oit.unc.edu	login as "bbs", supply requested information
liberty.uc.wlu.edu	login as "lawlib"
wugate.wustl.edu	login as "services"

14.4.2. OPAC Access Software

Hytelnet

Hytelnet is a very easy to use and customize software package developed at the University of Saskatchewan. It contains a list of many Telnet accessible resources and when installed on an Internet host can automate logins to these sites. Hytelnet includes a great selection of OPACs from around the world as well as exceptionally thorough coverage of CWISs and BBSs.

If you want to try out the Hytelnet software, check with your local computer support services to see if it's installed at your local site. Or if you're feeling adventurous, you can obtain a copy of Hytelnet for your local computer. It is moderately difficult to install and may prove too challenging for the novice network user. There are currently versions of Hytelnet which will work under the VMS, DOS, Mac, Amiga, and most Unix operating systems. You can get Hytelnet (and instructions on installation and customization) via FTP from:

FTP host:	`access.usask.ca`
directories:	`pub/hytelnet/amiga`
	`pub/hytelnet/mac`
	`pub/hytelnet/pc`
	`pub/hytelnet/unix`
	`pub/hytelnet/vms`
filenames:	(many or all)

Libtel

Libtel is an OPAC access program. If you want to try Libtel, it is accessible through the University of North Carolina's CWIS, bbs.oit.unc.edu (login "bbs"). The source code for Libtel is available via FTP.

FTP host:	`ftp.unt.edu`
directory:	`pub/library`
filenames:	`libtel-unix.escape`
	`libtel-unix.noescape`
	`libtel.com`

Catalist

Catalist is an OPAC catalog program for MS Windows. You can have Catalist running in one window displaying OPAC access information and a terminal emulation program running in another. Catalist does not automate Telnet sessions like the other services in this list. It is available via FTP from:

FTP host:	`ftp.unt.edu`
directory:	`pub/library`
filenames:	(many or all)

14.4.3. A Starter Kit for OPAC Exploration

Here is a sample of Internet accessible OPACs throughout the world to get you started.

Internet Address	Institutional Affiliation	Login name
`library.anu.edu.au`	Australian National University	`library`
`melvyl.ucop.edu`	University of California, USA	none
`pac.carl.org`	Colorado Alliance of Research Libraries, USA	none
`ram2.huji.ac.il`	Hebrew University, Israel (features multilingual user interface!)	`aleph`

There are hundreds of other OPACs on the Internet, so don't make these your default sites! If you decide to make extensive use of OPACs, be sure to get one of the catalogs listed at the end of this chapter so you can choose those OPACs which most nearly suit your needs.

14.5. Sample OPAC Session

14.5.1. The Diversity of OPAC Software

OPACs run on a wide variety of platforms. More than 20 OPAC software packages are commonly used and each has different syntaxes and capabilities. To further complicate matters, some of the most widely used packages can be modified heavily once implemented at a site. Some sites rely on home grown packages that may have very peculiar features and behaviors, especially when used from remote locations via Telnet.

However, there are enough similarities between OPACs that a sample session from one robust site should give you a fair indication of what using most other OPACs is like.

14.5.2. About this Sample Session

This section presents a session using the University of California's MELVYL system. Note that the on-screen displays have been edited slightly to make it easier to read in this text.

This sample session is somewhat long and convoluted; this is by design. It would have been simple to present a quick and easy session which immediately produced references to thousands of citations. But as you probably know from your experience with regular card catalogs, effective use of a library often requires careful consideration and reconsideration of how you define your literature search. This OPAC session is meant to reflect this reality. The first search in this example yields no results, but by modifying the search slightly and by following suggestions from MELVYL a very similar search yields more than 600 citations!

14.5.3. Access an OPAC

You should be able to use any one of the access methods described in "Accessing OPACs." But, to make this example as generic as possible, we'll enter MELVYL using a standard Telnet command.

```
telnet melvyl.ucop.edu

Trying...
Connected to melvyl.ucop.edu.
Escape character is '^]'.
```

14.5.4. Identify Your Terminal Type

You will be prompted to provide some information about your computer's terminal emulation.

```
DLA LINE 121 (TELNET) 01:04:24 08/26/92   (MELVYL.UCOP.EDU)
Please Enter Your Terminal Type Code or Type ? for a List
of Codes.
```

As with many Internet services, you will usually have the option of asking what terminal types are available. In MELVYL, type "?" for this information.

```
TERMINAL? ?
Please enter the Terminal Type Code for your terminal.
Supported Terminal Types and their character codes are:

TERMINAL   TERMINAL                     TERMINAL   TERMINAL
CODE                                    CODE


TTY33      Teletype 33 (TTY)            BANTAM     Perkin Elmer Bant
ESPRIT     Hazeltine Esprit             ADM3A      ADM 3a
PE1100     Perkin Elmer 1100            HAZ1500    Hazeltine 1500
HARDCOPY   Decwriter/Gencom             HAZ2000    Hazeltine 2000
VT100      IBM PC (VT100)               VT100      Apple MAC (VT100)
HEATH      Heathkit H19                 VT100      Dec VT100
ACT5A      Microterm Act5a              ADDS       ADDS/NCR
HP2621     Hewlett Packard HP2621       BITGRAPH   BBN Bitgraph
TI700      TI Silent 700                TTY40      Teletype 40 (TTY)
TELE920    Televideo 910, 912, 920 DISPLAY     IBM Displaywriter
TANDEM     Tandem 635X                  OTHER      All Others


Please Enter Your Terminal Type Code or Type ? for a List
of Codes.

TERMINAL? vt100
```

VT100 is a commonly used terminal emulation. If selecting VT100 produces gibberish on your screen, try to logout of the session. If you can't logout, type "^]" (control right bracket), or whatever command gets you to the "telnet>" prompt, then type "quit".

14.5.5. Welcome to the OPAC!

Assuming all is well with your terminal emulation, MELVYL will display an introductory screen with system news and a brief orientation to the system.

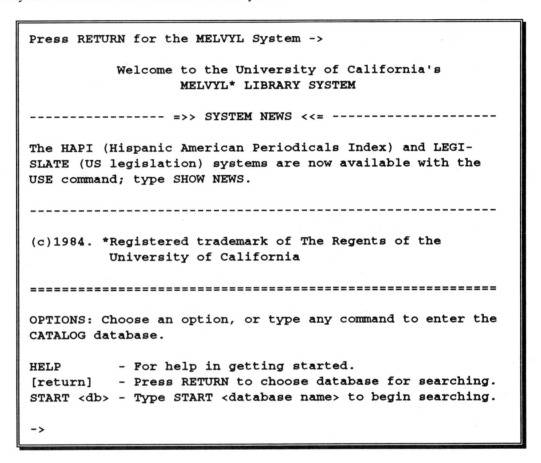

```
Press RETURN for the MELVYL System ->

          Welcome to the University of California's
                    MELVYL* LIBRARY SYSTEM

---------------- =>> SYSTEM NEWS <<= --------------------

The HAPI (Hispanic American Periodicals Index) and LEGI-
SLATE (US legislation) systems are now available with the
USE command; type SHOW NEWS.

-----------------------------------------------------------

(c)1984. *Registered trademark of The Regents of the
            University of California

============================================================

OPTIONS: Choose an option, or type any command to enter the
CATALOG database.

HELP        - For help in getting started.
[return]    - Press RETURN to choose database for searching.
START <db>  - Type START <database name> to begin searching.

->
```

The "->" prompt at the bottom left corner of the screen above, is where we type our commands to MELVYL.

In case you want to exit MELVYL before completing this exercise, here's what you need to do. From any prompt type "end". This command moves you to a simple "->" prompt. Following the instructions at the top of your screen, type "logoff". This will terminate your MELVYL session.

14.5.6. Request a Listing of Available Services

Many OPACs contain more than one kind of service. In MELVYL, pressing the return key at the welcome screen displays the first of two pages of services, some of which are restricted for use by the University of California community.

```
                    MELVYL SYSTEM DATABASES

Library databases:

TEN     Ten-Year MELVYL Catalog - For faster searches type
                                   TEN; material published
                                   from 1982-1992
CAT     Full MELVYL Catalog      - UC libraries and the
                                   California State Library
PE      Periodical Titles        - Cal Academic Lib. List of
                                   Serials

Indexes to recent articles: (for UC users only; password
needed)

MAGS    Magazine & Journal       - 1,000 magazines and journals
NEWS    Newspaper Articles       - five major U.S. newspapers
CC      Current Contents         - 6,500 scholarly journals
CCT     Current Contents         - tables of contents of 6,500
                                   scholarly journals
MED     MELVYL MEDLINE           - 4,000 medical and life
                                   sciences journals
COMP    Computer Articles        - 200 computer magazines and
                                   journals
                                   (continued on next screen)
-------------------------------------------------------------
Type the code for an option (for example TEN),  HELP, or any
command. Press RETURN for more databases.

-> TEN
```

14.5.7. Selecting a Database within the OPAC

For this session, we've selected the MELVYL Ten-Year database which only includes materials published in the last 10 years. Even for this brief period, MELVYL's holdings include more than 1.6 million distinct titles!

```
        Welcome to the MELVYL TEN-YEAR Catalog Database

Contents: As of 8/26/92, approximately 1,639,770 titles
          representing 3,627,100 holdings for materials in
          the University of California libraries, and the
          California State Library,

Coverage: Publication dates 1982 through 1992.

              --=>> NEWS <<=--

The TAGS display for downloading, now available in
Experimental mode.

          Type SHOW EXP 51 for more information.
     For information on Lookup mode, type SHOW DLA 1 NEWS.
--------------------------------------------------------------
OPTIONS:   Type an option and press RETURN, or type any
           command.

 HELP    - For help in getting started.
 E GUIDE - For a brief guide to using the Ten-Year database.
 START   - To start over or change databases.
 END     - To end your session.

TEN-> help
```

14.5.8. Investigate the Online Help

It's always a good idea to investigate online help when using a new Internet service. Typing "help" in the previous screen displays a list of the basic commands in the TEN database of MELVYL.

```
You are in COMMAND Mode in the TEN-YEAR Catalog database.

To do a basic search for books or periodicals, use the
FIND command

For Books:
  Personal Author        FIND PA STEINBECK, JOHN
  Title Word             FIND TW CUCKOO'S NEST
  Exact Title            FIND XT OLD MAN AND THE SEA
  Subject               FIND SU JOB STRESS
  Exact Subject         FIND XS EVIDENCE EXPERT

For Periodicals:
  Periodical Title       FIND PE JOURNAL SOCIOLOGY
  Exact Periodical Title FIND XPE BERKELEY JOURNAL OF
                         SOCIOLOGY

To display the results of your search, type  DISPLAY, or D.

Your results will be displayed using the SHORT display
option which includes library locations and call numbers.

For more information on searching the MELVYL catalog, type:

EXPLAIN FIND     EXPL INDEXES    EXP BROWSE     E COMMANDS
EXPLAIN DISPLAY  EXPL EXACT      EXP COMBINE    E GLOSSARY

TEN->
```

14.5.9. Starting a Search

Now we can try a catalog search. Let's do a subject search on the topic "extinction of species" which we'll abbreviate as "species extinction." (Recall that articles and prepositions are usually not worth including in search terms unless one is doing a title search.)

```
TEN-> find su species extinction

 Search request: FIND SU SPECIES EXTINCTION
 Search result: 0 records in the TEN-YEAR Catalog database

 You may get results by redoing your search in the Title
 Word index, i.e., F TW <search words>. Type HELP for more
 information.

TEN->
```

14.5.10. No Search Results!? Time to Think!

No books were found using "species extinction" as our subject. But don't give up yet! MELVYL now allows the option of doing another search by several other fields, including a title word search (TW). Let's try digging up books that have both the words "species" and "extinction" in their titles.

```
TEN-> find tw species extinction

 Search request: FIND TW SPECIES EXTINCTION
 Search result: 16 records in the TEN-YEAR Catalog database

 Type D to display results, or type HELP.
```

14.5.11. Obtaining Help for Specific OPAC Options

The search string "species extinction," which did not find anything during a subject search, locates 16 titles with a title word search. We've entered "help" to obtain a brief list of display options.

```
TEN-> help

Your search
   FIND TW SPECIES EXTINCTION
retrieved 16 records for items at all libraries.

Type NS to see the Next Screen of display. You can also use
any of the following specifications. Type EXPLAIN DISPLAY
for more information.

To display a record number or group of records   D 3 6 8-10
To display with another option (REVIEW SHORT LONG)  D LONG
To display every nth record                      D BY 3
To display certain fields in the record          D TI SU
To display a combination of the above            D 10- REV

You can also:

Type SHOW SEARCH to see other current results available for
     display.
Type SHOW HISTORY to see your search history.
Type EXPLAIN ADD ON to find out how to broaden or narrow
     your search result.
Type EXPLAIN COMMANDS to find out what other commands you
     can use.
Type END to end your session.
```

14.5.12. Displaying a Successful Search: Abbreviated Mode

We can review all of the titles retrieved by a search request. When we type "rev", the display looks like this:

```
TEN -> rev

Search request: FIND TW SPECIES EXTINCTION
Search result: 16 records in the TEN-YEAR Catalog database

Type HELP for other display options.

 1. AUSTRALIA. Endangered Species Advisory Committee of ...
 2. Australia's endangered species : the extinction ... 1990
 3. Australia's endangered species : the extinction ... 1990
 4. Balancing on the brink of extinction : the Endangere ...
 5. COHN, Jeffrey P.        The politics of exti ... 1990
 6. DELGADO-MENDOZA, Suzzette. Extinction in the en ... 1990
 7. EHRLICH, Paul R.        Extinction : the cas.... 1983
 8. ELDREDGE, Niles.        Fossils : the evolut.... 1991
 9. ERICKSON, Jon, 1948-    Dying planet : the    ... 1991
10. Extinction in paradise : protecting our Hawaiia ... 1989
11. KELLY, Donald M.        Near extinction : C. ... 1990
12. LABASTILLE, Anne.       Mama Poc : an ecolog ....1990
13. MYERS, Norman.          Tackling mass extinctions ...
14. The Road to extinction : problems of categorization  ...
15. The Road to extinction : problems of categoriztyion  ...

Press RETURN to see the next screen.
```

14.5.13. Displaying a Successful Search: Expanded Mode

Now let's ask for a "LONG" display of item number 1 and see if it provides any clues about how to refine the search.

```
TEN-> long

Search request: FIND TW SPECIES EXTINCTION
Search result: 16 records in the TEN-YEAR Catalog database

Type HELP for other display options.

1.
Author:       Australia. Endangered Species Advisory
                Committee.
Title:        An Australian national strategy for the
                conservation of species and habitats
                threatened with extinction. [Canberra, ACT]:
                Australian National Parks and Wildlife
                Service,  c1989.
Description:  28 p. : col. ill. ; 30 cm.
Notes:        "Draft for public comment."
Subjects:     Wildlife conservation -- Government policy --
                Australia. Nature conservation -- Government
                policy -- Australia. Endangered species --
                Australia.
Other entries: Australian National Parks and Wildlife
                Service.
Call numbers: CAS   Mailliard QH77.A8 A85 1989 Biodiv

TEN->
```

As you can see by looking at the subject line, this book is cataloged under a number of subjects, of which "endangered species" seems to be the closest fit.

14.5.14. Refining a Search Based on a Partially Successful Search

So judging by the other titles associated with this particular document, it appears that a subject search for "endangered species" will very likely be fruitful.

```
TEN-> find subject endangered species

 Search request: FIND SUBJECT ENDANGERED SPECIES
 Search result: 624 records in the TEN-YEAR Catalog database
 Type D to display results, or type HELP.

TEN-> D
```

14.5.15. Hitting Pay Dirt...

MELVYL responded with 624 titles!

```
Search request: FIND SUBJECT ENDANGERED SPECIES
Search result: 624 records in the TEN-YEAR Catalog database

Type HELP for other display options.

 1. The 5 sea turtle species of the Atlantic and Gulf Co ...
 2. 1000 points of life, every species counts : threaten ...
 3. 1986 IUCN red list of threatened animals. 1986
 4. 1988 IUCN red list of threatened animals. 1988
 5. 1990 IUCN red list of threatened animals. 1990
 6. AAZPA manual of Federal wildlife regulations. 1985
 7. Action plan for African primate conservation: 1986-90.
 8. Action plan for Asian primate conservation, 1987-91. ...
 9. ADAMS, Douglas, 1952-         Last chance to see. 1991
10. Alaska wildlife week unit : wildlife for the future. ...
11. ALLEN, William B. 1928-        State lists of endan ...
12. ALMENDINGER, John C. Natural communities and rare sp ...
13. ALTENBURG, Wibe.              Etude ornithologique ...
14. Amended listing of endangered wildlife of New Mexico.
15. ANCONA, George.              Turtle watch. 1987

Press RETURN to see the next screen.
TEN->
```

14.5.16. ...Is Just the Beginning of Effective OPAC Use!

This is where the real power of using an OPAC starts. Now that you've established a profitable search strategy, you can easily branch off to other related subject or title searches.

14.5.17. Ending an OPAC Session

To leave the database, type "end" followed by "logoff" to terminate your Telnet connection.

```
TEN -> end

Thanks for using the MELVYL Online Catalog.
Type LOGOFF and press RETURN to terminate your TELNET
session. Press RETURN for the MELVYL catalog.

logoff

ELAPSED TIME = 0:11:53
END OF SESSION
Connection closed by foreign host.
```

14.6. For More Information

14.6.1. Worldwide Lists of OPACs

The following lists provide worldwide coverage of OPACs. Although there is considerable overlap between the lists, they have different formats and emphases, so you might want to obtain all three and determine which most nearly suits your needs.

"Internet Accessible Library Catalogs and Databases" by Art St. George and Ron Larsen.

FTP host:	`ariel.unm.edu`	
directory:	`library`	
filenames:	`internet.library`	(text-only)
	`library.apple`	(Apple PostScript)
	`library.ps`	(generic PostScript)

"Internet Libraries," by Dana Noonan.

FTP host:	`ftp.unt.edu`
directory:	`pub/library`
filename:	`metlib2.txt`

"University of North Texas' Accessing Online Bibliographic Databases," by Billy Barron.

FTP host:	`ftp.unt.edu`	
directory:	`pub/library`	(contains many other useful files on OPACs as well)
filenames:	`libraries.ps`	(PostScript version)
	`libraries.txt`	(ASCII, text-only version)
	`libraries.wp5`	(Word Perfect 5.0 version)

14.6.2. Regional Lists of OPACs

Australia and New Zealand

"AARNet Access to Australian and New Zealand OPACs," by Deidre E. Stanton. Available via FTP from:

FTP host:	`ftp.unt.edu`
directory:	`pub/library`
filename:	`aarnet.library`

United States

"NNSC Internet Resource Guide—Chapter 2: Library Catalogs."

As of September 1992, about 25 libraries and library systems have been described. Although these entries are largely rendered obsolete by the Barron and St. George/Larsen catalogs, they are still useful if you need supplemental information.

Getting Chapter 2 via FTP:

FTP host:	`nnsc.nsf.net`	
directory:	`resource-guide`	
filenames:	`chapter2-ps.tar.Z`	(compressed and tarred PostScript)
	`chapter2-txt.tar.Z`	(compressed and tarred ASCII text)

To obtain individual sections of Chapter 2, first FTP the Chapter 2 table of contents, and then FTP individual sections as desired.

FTP host:	`nnsc.nsf.net`	
directory:	`resource-guide/chapter.2`	
filename:	`intro2.ps`	(PostScript table of contents)
	`intro2.txt`	(ASCII text table of contents)
	`section2-1.ps`	(PostScript of section 2.1)
	`section2-1.txt`	(ASCII text of section 2.1)
	(etc.)	(etc.)

The following book provides good coverage of OPACs in the central United States:

CICNet Resource Guide. Edited by Holbrook, J.P. and C.S. Pruess. Ann Arbor, MI: CICNet, Inc.

14.6.3. Topically Oriented Lists of OPACs

Agriculture

"Not Just Cows: A Guide to Internet/Bitnet Resources in Agriculture and Related Sciences," by Willfred Drew. Contains a list of OPACs with particularly strong holdings in agricultural topics and many non-OPAC resources of interest to agricultural researchers. Available via FTP from:

FTP host:	`ftp.unt.edu`	
directory:	`pub/library`	
filenames:	`agguide.dos`	(DOS Text Format)
	`agguide.wp`	(Word Perfect Format)

14.6.4. FTP Archives Specializing in OPAC Related Materials

The following FTP sites have a wealth of archived materials about OPACs. Although there is some overlap in their contents, it is worthwhile becoming familiar with each of these resources if you are an active user of OPACs.

FTP host:	`hydra.uwo.ca`
directory:	`libsoft`
filenames:	(many or all)

FTP host:	`ftp.unt.edu`
directory:	`pub/library`
filenames:	(many or all)

14.6.5. Online Discussion Groups and Lists via FTP

There are many online discussion groups dealing with OPACs and library information sciences. They range in coverage from discussion on a specific site's OPAC installation to general discussion of present and future OPAC technology. The main forum for general discussion of OPACs is PACS-L, which can be accessed via LISTSERV or as a Usenet newsgroup. The PACS-L archives are also available for searching as a WAIS database.

LISTSERV:	`LIBPACS@UHUBVM1`
WAIS database:	`bitnet.listserv.pacs-1`
Usenet newsgroup:	`bitnet.listserv.pacs-1`

A comprehensive and up-to-date list of most OPAC related groups is included in the "Directory of Scholarly Electronic Conferences," by Diane K. Kovacs of Kent State University. It is available via FTP from many sites throughout the Internet including the following:

FTP host:	`ra.msstate.edu`
directory:	`pub/docs/words-l/Net-Stuff`
filenames:	`acadlist.readme`
	`acadlist.file1`
	`acadlist.file2`
	`acadlist.file3`
	`acadlist.file4`
	`acadlist.file5`
	`acadlist.file6`
	`acadlist.file7`

As of August 1992, the "Libraries and Information Sciences" entries of the list can be found in the file "acadlist.file2." However, you might want to get all of these files. This is a tremendous resource that pieces together information from many sources and makes it available in one easy to use document.

14.6.7. Bibliography

Rather than duplicate the efforts of others, you are encouraged to obtain a copy of one of the following references, which contain very useful bibliographies on OPACs.

Stanton, D.E. "Libraries and Information Resources Networks: A Bibliography." 1991.
Available via FTP from:

FTP host:	`ftp.unt.edu`
directory:	`pub/library`
filename:	`stanton.bib`

"Library Resources on the Internet: Strategies for Selection and Use"

FTP host:	`dla.ucop.edu`
directory:	`pub/internet`
filename:	`libcat-guide`

@ 15 @

Databases and Bibliographies

Nature laughs at a miser. He is like a squirrel who buries his nuts and refrains from digging them up again.

> Henry George
> *Progress and Poverty*

[The] ultimate goal of public policy in every country should be to encourage custodians to disseminate data and researchers to use it.

> D.H. Flaherty
> *Privacy and Government Data Banks: An International Perspective*

A database is a collection of information that is structured to allow easy searching and retrieval of particular items.

One of the tasks at which computers excel is the storage and retrieval of vast quantities of information such as research databases. Until recently, access to computer databases was limited. Now that a growing number of the world's computers are accessible on the Internet, a wide variety of databases are available to anyone using the Internet.

15.1. Database Access

The resources described in this chapter range from relatively small, specialized datasets that you can copy to your own computer by e-mail or FTP, to huge databases with gigabytes of data that must be accessed with sophisticated database software during a Telnet session. A few databases are easily accessible and contain information of interest to the average Internet user, while others are likely to interest only trained specialists.

A few repositories of databases have been included which are not yet on the Internet. They are described either because they are likely to be accessible though the Internet soon, or because their wealth of holdings are too extraordinary to ignore. But in many such cases, you can make inquiries about their data holdings by e-mail through the Internet and may then order CD or magnetic tape copies of the datasets of interest.

15.2. Online Bibliographies? Why Not Just Use an OPAC?

This chapter also includes pointers to bibliographic databases containing extensive literature citations. These bibliographies are often the product of a labor of love on the part of someone who genuinely cares about and intimately knows the literature in a particular field. Such experts have an ability to separate the wheat from the chaff and may also know about citations that would never show up in a purely mechanical search. So if there is already an authoritative, freely-available bibliography compiled by a world expert, it would be silly to spend your own money and time recreating the wheel.

15.3. Database Etiquette

Although these are all publicly accessible resources, you should not use them trivially. Many scholars count on these services for research activities, and excessive use for random or meaningless searches done purely "for kicks" would place a strain on the computational resources of the host computers.

15.4. Related Resources

There are many more databases on the Internet than are described in this chapter!

- Many Online Public Access Catalogs of libraries, described in Chapter 14, allow access to the kinds of databases described in this chapter.

- The archie program maintains a catalog of many of the world's anonymous FTP sites (which can themselves be thought of as databases), and is described in Chapter 16.

- Gopher (Chapter 17), WAIS (Chapter 18), CWISs (Chapter 19), and World Wide Web (Chapter 20) offer access to databases, including many that are described in this chapter.

- Databases of e-mail and other addresses are described in Chapter 21.

Only a few commercial database services are included in this chapter. However, the bibliography at the end of this chapter gives many citations to references describing such services.

15.5. General Interest "Databases"

About These "Databases"

The following three resources are not databases, strictly speaking. However, they contain a great deal of organized information that is of interest to many current and potential Internet users. If you haven't used databases before, these resources are a good starting point. They give you an accessible and immediately rewarding preview of the immense quantities of information you will encounter when using Internet databases.

Free-Nets

Contents: Many informative files and discussion groups on health, education, politics, recreation, technology, and other topics of general interest.

Comments: Free-Net is best described as an "open access community electronic information system" which, for registered users, also allows easy access to discussion groups including Usenet. Free-Net uses a novel interface in which the user wanders through an "electronic city." Files are in "buildings," so for example, to get information on politics and government, one would enter City Hall. This is a rather extraordinary open access system which could be set up at other sites at very little cost. Many Free-Net sites are being established around the world as part of a not-for-profit cooperative network called "The National Public Telecommunications Network" (NPTN).

Access: Several Telnet accessible sites. When you first log in, you will be asked if you want to visit or register. Follow the instructions. As a visitor, your privileges in Free-Net are restricted. If you register, you will be sent a registration packet through the mail which you must fill out and return.

Telnet to one of the following:

```
freenet-in-a.cwru.edu            (Cleveland)
freenet-in-b.cwru.edu
freenet-in-c.cwru.edu
freenet.lorain.oberlin.edu       (Oberlin, OH; login as "guest")
yfn.ysu.edu                      (Youngstown, OH; login as "visitor")
tso.uc.edu                       (Cincinnati, OH; login as "visitor")
heartland.bradley.edu            (Peoria, IL; login as "visitor")
```

Contact: e-mail: aa001@cleveland.freenet.edu

T.M. Grundner, Ed.D
President, NPTN
Box 1987
Cleveland, Ohio 44106 USA

voice: (216) 368-2733

INFO: University of Maryland Database

Contents: Data and files on the following topics: computers, economics, literature, political science, meteorology, area studies, and electronic journals.

Comments: Files can be viewed online while using a menu driven Telnet session, or they can be transferred for local use.

Access: Telnet: `info.umd.edu`
               login: `INFO`

               FTP host: `info.umd.edu`
               directory: `info`
               filenames: (many or all)

WUARCHIVE (Washington University Public Domain Archives)

Contents: An immense quantity of documents, Graphical Interchange Files (GIFs), and public domain and shareware software for the Amiga, Apple II, Atari, CP/M, DOS, GNU, Macintosh, Sun, TeX, Unix, VAX/VMS, and X Windows operating environments. This server "mirrors" a number of other FTP hosts around the world. When mirrored archives receive new information, it is sent also to wuarchive. The archive also contains files besides computer software, but software is its main strength.

Comments: This is a gargantuan archive. A simple listing of just the *filenames* contained in wuarchive is over 15 megabytes in size! To use this resource effectively, it is crucial that you get the README files for each directory whose contents you want to explore. We recommend that you follow the suggestions provided in these README files.

Access: FTP host: `wuarchive.wustl.edu`
               directories: (hundreds!)

Contact: e-mail: `archives@wugate.wustl.edu`

               Washington University
               Office of the Network Coordinator
               One Brookings Drive
               Campus Box 1048
               St. Louis, MO 63130-4899 USA

               voice: (314) 935-7390

15.6. Aeronautics

NOAA Aeronautical Charting Data Sampler II

Contents: Data files used for learning about aeronautical navigation. Specific holdings include the following:

1. Aeronautical Chart Automation Section (ACAS) data files, containing data on 17,000 airports, 21,000 runways, 46,000 obstructions to air navigation, navigational aid data, and ARTCC data for low and high air routes;
2. COMPSYS Distance and Bearing Software used by National Airspace System for computing reporting points, intersections, and other fixes;
3. Special Use Airspace Data Files used to inform pilots of restricted and prohibited airspace; and
4. Advanced Automation System (AAS) Data.

Comments: For learning only: NOT TO BE USED FOR ACTUAL NAVIGATION! MS/DOS databases and programs, requiring at least 120 Mb of free space on a hard drive. These data and the associated programs are from a CD-ROM. If you have a CD-ROM reader, you are probably better off obtaining the CD than using the FTP'able data.

Access: FTP host: `hobbes.ksu.ksu.edu`
               directory: `pub/noaa`
               filenames: `install.bat`   (a batch file for installation)
                                `data/*.*.z`   (data directory contains 10Mb compressed, 62Mb uncompressed)
                                `noaa/*.*.z`   (noaa directory contains 12Mb compressed, 36Mb uncompressed)
                                `instal/*.*`   (instal directory contains 1Mb)
                                `readme.doc`

Contact: You can obtain the CD-ROM version of these data from:

               CD-ROM Project Director, Requirements and Technology Staff
               NOAA, National Ocean Service
               6010 Executive Blvd., Room 1022, N/CG3x22
               Rockville, MD 20852 USA

15.7. Agriculture

PENpages

Contents: Online articles and brochures on agriculture, careers, health, consumer issues, weather, and other topics from the Pennsylvania State Department of Agriculture, Pennsylvania State University College of Agriculture, and Rutgers University.

Comments: Very accessible, general information of interest to almost anyone; vt100 terminal emulation recommended.

Access: Telnet: **psupen.psu.edu**
                login: <your state's 2 letter code>   (from within USA)
                               world   (from outside USA)

Contact: e-mail: **ppmenu@psupen.psu.edu**

                PENpages Coordinator
                405 Agricultural Administration Building
                The Pennsylvania State University
                University Park, PA 16802 USA

                voice: (814) 863-3449

More Info: PENpages *User Guide* available online or by request from above address.

QUERRI (Questions on University Extension Regional Resource)

Contents: A bibliographic database and catalog of information on more than 12,000 agricultural publications, abstracts, and catalogs of audio-visual materials. The North Central Region Educational Materials Project (NCREMP) does not produce or distribute the resources, but you can get full ordering instructions.

Comments: The information in this database is primarily of relevance to the north central U.S.

Access: Telnet: **isn.rdns.iastate.edu**
                dial: **querri**

Contact: e-mail: **j2.ncr@isumvs.iastate.edu**

                North Central Region Educational Materials Project
                B-10 Curtiss Hall
                Iowa State University
                Ames, IA 50011 USA

                voice: (515) 294-8802
                fax: (515) 294-4517

15.8. Area Studies

INFO-SOUTH Latin American Information System

Contents: Extensive listings of citations and abstracts on a wide variety of Latin America issues.

Access: You may order hardcopy or CD versions of the datasets; to access online (via Telnet or DIALOG), you must establish an account.

Contact: e-mail: **msgctr@sabio.ir.miami.edu**

INFO-SOUTH
North-South Center
1500 Monza, P.O. Box 248014
Coral Gables, FL 33124-3027 USA

voice: (305) 284-4442 or (800) 752-9567
fax: (305) 284-5089

More Info: NNSC Internet Resources Guide, Section 3.22

LADB (Latin American Data Base)

Contents: More than 10,000 articles from 1987 to the present organized under the following titles: "Chronicle of Latin American Economic Affairs," "Central America Update," and "SOURCEMEX—Economic News and Analysis on Mexico." Hundreds of articles are added each month, mostly current information originating directly from Latin America.

Comments: You must contact LADB to arrange access.

Access: After contacting LADB, access is via the Internet or by a modem call to an 800 number.

Contact: To establish access, contact:

e-mail: **ladbad@bootes.unm.edu**

Roma Arellano
Latin American Institute
University of New Mexico
801 Yale NE
Albuquerque, NM 87131-1016 USA

voice: (505) 277-6839

More Info: NNSC Internet Resources Guide, Section 3.26.

There is also a LISTSERV list devoted to discussion about this database.

ch-ladb%unmvma.bitnet@vm1.nodak.edu

15.9. Artificial Intelligence

Bibliographic Mail Server for Artificial Intelligence Literature

Contents: Bibliography of more than 26,000 references in artificial intelligence.

Comments: Most appropriate for researchers already very familiar with artificial intelligence.

Access: Via a mail server. To get a basic orientation to this service, send the following e-mail message. You can specify that the output should be sent to you in English, as shown below:

```
mail:     lido@cs.uni-sb.de
subject:  lidosearch info englis
message:  (none needed)
```

Contact: e-mail: bib-1@cs.uni-sb.de

Dr. Alfred Kobsa
Department of Information Science
University of Konstanz
D-W-7750 Konstanz 1 Germany

voice: + 49 75 31 88 1

University of California at Irvine Repository Of Machine Learning Databases and Domain Theories

Contents: Databases and domain theories useful for evaluating learning algorithms.

Comments: The dataset files come in pairs: <filename>.data contains raw data and <filename>.names contains documentation about the dataset file. Some of the files in the archive are not datasets, but in fact are used to generate datasets. If you have datasets of possible interest, you are encouraged to submit them!

Access: By FTP or mail server:

FTP host: `ics.uci.edu`
directory: `pub/machine-learning-databases`
filenames: (many or all)

```
mail:     archive-server@ics.uci.edu
subject:  (none needed)
message:  help
```

Contact: e-mail: `ml-repository@ics.uci.edu`
                          or
                `aha@insight.cs.jhu.edu`

Patrick M. Murphy
Department of Information and Computer Science
University of California, Irvine
Irvine, CA 92717-3425 USA

voice: (714) 856-5011

15.10. Astronomy / Space Science

Lunar and Planetary Institute Gazetteer of Planetary Features and Planetary Bibliography

Contents: Information about most major physiographic features of the planets and satellites of our solar system, and references to maps on which they may be located. If you've ever wanted to know about a particular crater on the backside of Titan, this is the database for you.

Comments: Part of a larger information system run by LPI which also contains an online catalog of monographs, documents, and journals with over 28,000 references.

Access: Telnet: `lpi.jsc.nasa.gov`
                 login: `lpi`

Contact: Lunar and Planetary Institute
                 3600 Bay Area Boulevard
                 Houston, TX 77058-1113 USA

NED (NASA / IPAC Extragalactic Database)

Contents: Extensive information on over 200,000 extragalactic objects (galaxies, quasars, infrared and radio sources) and database software to search raw data, associated bibliographies, and literature abstracts. Much of the software and some of the data are available from the FTP host for copying. Includes online tutorial.

Access: Telnet: `ned.ipac.caltech.edu`
                 login: `ned`

Contact: e-mail: `ned@ipac.caltech.edu`

                 NED c/o IPAC
                 MS 100-22
                 California Institute of Technology
                 Pasadena, CA 91125 USA
                 voice: (818) 397-9503

More Info: FTP host: `ipac.caltech.edu`
                 directories: `ipac-docs`
                                `ipac-sw`
                                `ned`

NSSDC (National Space Science Data Center)

Contents: Official clearinghouse for NASA data; contains a directory of publicly available data. Datasets referenced by this service include: global change datasets; Nimbus-7 GRID TOMS data; Interplanetary Medium Data (OMNI); Geophysical Models; International Ultraviolet Explorer Data; Astronomical Data Center; Voyager and other planetary images; Earth observation data; and star catalogs. The Telnet front end also allows access to the Standards and Technology Information System, back issues of CANOPUS newsletters, etc.

Comments: The data can be purchased in CD-ROM, diskette, or magnetic tape formats. You can set up an official account with user-id and password if you plan to use NODIS regularly.

Access: Telnet: `nssdca.gsfc.nasa.gov`
                 login: `NSSDC` or `NODIS`

Contact: e-mail: `request@nssdca.gsfc.nasa.gov`

                 National Space Science Data Center
                 Request Coordination Office
                 NASA Goddard Space Flight Center
                 Code 633
                 Greenbelt, MD 20771 USA

                 voice: (301) 286-6695

SDDAS (Southwest Research Data Display and Analysis System)

Contents: Space, magnetosphere, and atmospheric data collected from a number of satellites—currently, Dynamic Explorers 1 and 2, UARS Partial Environment Monitor, and TSS-1 ROPE.

Comments: This service can only be accessed through an X-windows terminal. Although you can "take it for a spin" without establishing an account, substantial use requires authorization from the contact person listed below. The service is menu driven, easy to use, and provides extraordinary visual display of the datasets.

Access: Telnet: **espsun.space.swri.edu 10000**   (X-windows only!)

Contact: e-mail: **sddas-help@pemrac.space.swri.edu**

                 Dr. J. D. Winningham
                 Southwest Research Institute
                 Division of Instrumentation and Space Sciences
                 P.O. Drawer 28510
                 San Antonio, TX 78228-0510 USA

                 voice: (512) 522-3259

More Info: *User's Guide* mailed to authorized users; detailed listing of data holdings can be requested from sddas-help@pemrac.space.swri.edu

SIMBAD (Set of Identifications, Measurements, and Bibliography for Astronomical Data)

Contents: Data and bibliographic entries for stars and subsets of non-stellar objects.

Comments: Currently, this service is for use by astronomers with NASA or NSF funding. This service may become available via a mail server in the future.

Access: Accessible through Telnet, but one must have an account.

Contact: e-mail: **simbad@cfa.harvard.edu**

                 SIMBAD c/o Computation Facility
                 Smithsonian Astrophysical Laboratory
                 60 Garden St., MS 39
                 Cambridge, MA 02138 USA

                 voice: (617) 495-7301

More Info: NNSC Internet Resources Guide, Section 3.5

Spacelink

Contents: General purpose databases and interactive system containing information about NASA and NASA activities. A large number of possible curricular activities for elementary and secondary science classes.

Comments: A tremendously valuable resource for elementary and secondary science teachers. Very easy to use (but sometimes slow!). In your first Telnet session, you will be prompted to create a unique user-id and password for subsequent sessions. Files of interest can be downloaded during an interactive Telnet session.

Access: Telnet: **spacelink.msfc.nasa.gov** or **xsl.msfc.nasa.gov**
               login: **newuser**
               password: **newuser**

               FTP host: **ames.arc.nasa.gov**
               directory: **pub/SPACE**

Contact: Spacelink Administrator
               Mail Code CA-21
               Public Affairs Office
               Marshall Space Flight Center
               Huntsville, AL 35812 USA

               voice: (205) 544-0038

Yale Bright Star Catalog

Contents: Machine-readable version of the 4th Edition of the Yale Bright Star Catalog including
               such variables as photoelectric magnitudes, MK spectral types, parallaxed and radial
               velocity, comments (indication and identification of spectroscopic and occulation
               binaries), projected rotational velocities, variability, spectral characteristics, duplicity,
               and group membership.

Access: By FTP:

               MS-DOS version:

                   FTP host: **pomona.claremont.edu**
                   directory: **yale_bsc**
                   filenames: (many or all)

               UNIX version:

                   FTP host: **uxc.cso.uiuc.edu**
                   directory: **pub/star-data/yale**
                   filenames: (all files in all subdirectories)

Contact: e-mail: **jdishaw@hmcvax.claremont.edu**

More Info: FTP host: **pomona.claremont.edu**
               directory: **yale_bsc**
               filenames: **read.me**
                                yaleread.me

15.11. Botany

Herbarium Mail Data Server

Contents: Currently, three datasets: 1) type specimens of the mint family from the Harvard Herbaria, comprising 1100 records; 2) complete herbarium catalog of the Kellogg Biological Station Herbarium, consisting of 6000 specimen records; 3) the Flora of Mt. Kinabalu specimen database of 16,300 specimen records of all known vascular plant collections from the mountain. Key word queries can be based on family, genus, species, locality, dates, and collector's names.

Access: By mail servers, to separate sites for the three datasets:

Harvard Mint Types   `herbdata@huh.harvard.edu`
Kellogg Herbarium   `herbdata%kbs.decnet@clvax1.cl.msu.edu`
Mt. Kinabalu Flora   `herbdata@herbarium.bpp.msu.edu`

To get started, send the following message to one of the three mail servers above.

```
mail:      <mail-server-address>
subject:   (none needed)
message:   help
           replyaddress=<your.internet.address>
```

E-mail addresses for sending corrections and annotations to the specimens:

Harvard: David Boufford
            `boufford@huh.harvard.edu`
Kellogg: Steve Tonsor
            `tonsor%kbs.decnet@clvax1.cl.msu.edu`
Kinabalu: John Beaman
            `beaman@ibm.cl.msu.edu`

Contact: e-mail: `beach@huh.harvard.edu`

James H. Beach
Data Administrator
MCZ, Herbaria, Arnold Arboretum
22 Divinity Avenue
Cambridge, MA 02138 USA

voice: (617) 495-1912
fax: (617) 495-9484

More Info: FTP host: `huh.harvard.edu`
            directory: `pub`
            filenames: (all files in the directory deal with ongoing taxonomic database projects)

LISTSERV list: taxacom%msu.bitnet@cunyvm.cuny.edu

15.12. Chemistry

IuBIO (Indiana University Archive for Molecular and General Biology)

Contents: Molecular biology and chemistry software for DOS, MAC, etc.

Comments: Although this is not a database strictly speaking, it contains many software tools useful for working with chemistry and biology databases. Getting the document "Archive.doc" via FTP will make it easier for you to use this service.

Access: FTP host: `ftp.bio.indiana.edu`
                 directory: `chemistry`

Contact: e-mail: `archive@bio.indiana.edu`

                 Don Gilbert
                 BioComputing Office
                 Biology Department
                 Indiana University
                 Bloomington, IN 47405 USA

More Info: NNSC Internet Resources Guide, Section 3.13.

                 FTP host: `ftp.bio.indiana.edu`
                 filename: `Archive.doc`

15.13. Computer Software

General Information about Computer Software Databases

There are countless archives of computer software available through the Internet. This section is not meant to be a comprehensive listing, just a sampling. In particular, you should examine the contents of WUARCHIVE, described in section 15.5 of this chapter.

COSMIC

Contents: A huge collection of computer software for a wide variety of applications and operating systems created under projects funded by NASA. The COSMIC staff can also perform searches through the COSMIC database to locate programs appropriate to your interests and needs.

Comments: Most of the software must be purchased. The intended users are U.S. citizens.

Access: FTP access to the catalog. The catalog is 5 megabytes in size. You might want to consider getting information via the e-mail contact before retrieving this file.

FTP host:	`cossack.cosmic.uga.edu`
directory:	`catalog`
filenames:	(in separate directories for domestic and international users)

Contact: e-mail: `service@cossack.cosmic.uga.edu`

COSMIC
The University of Georgia
382 East Broad Street
Athens, GA 30602 USA

voice: (404) 542-3265

SUPERSFT (IBM Supercomputing Program Database)

Contents: Catalog of programs suitable for use on IBM supercomputers using vector or parallel processing. The actual programs are not available through this service. If you have written such programs, you can submit information for inclusion in the catalog.

Access: Via a LISTSERVer. Example:

```
mail:    listserv@uicvm.cc.uic.edu
subject: (none needed)
message: (sample messages shown below)

get supersft help       (to get supersft help)
get supersft index      (for an index of files)
get filename filetype   (to obtain a particular file of
                         interest from the supersft index
                         list)
```

Contact: e-mail: **supersft@uicvm.cc.uic.edu**

Supercomputing Support Office
University of Illinois at Chicago
Computer Center (mail code 135)
Box 6998
Chicago, IL 60680 USA

voice: (312) 996-2981

VxWorks Users Group Archives

Contents: VxWorks operating environment programs and information.

Access: Via FTP:

FTP host: **thor.atd.ucar.edu**
directories: **pub/vx**
                 pub/unix

By mail server:

```
mail:    vxworks_archive@ncar.ucar.edu
subject: (none needed)
message: send index
```

Contact: e-mail: **thor@thor.atd.ucar.edu**

Richard Neitzel
National Center for Atmospheric Research
Box 3000
Marshall Field Site
Boulder, CO 80307-3000 USA

voice: (303) 497-2057 or (303) 497-2060

15.14. Ecology and Environment

General Information about Ecological and Environmental Databases

A printed periodical called "The Green Library Journal: Environmental Topics in the Information World" aims to disseminate information about environmental databases and international environmental information centers. For more information about "The Green Library Journal," contact:

e-mail: **anna@idui1.csrv.uidaho.edu**

Maria Jankowska, Editor
Green Library Journal
University of Idaho Library
Moscow, Idaho 83843-4198 USA

voice: (208) 885-6260
fax: (208) 885-6817

CEAM (Center for Exposure Assessment Modeling)

Contents: Environmental simulation models for urban and rural non-point sources, conventional and toxic pollution of streams, lakes and estuaries, tidal hydrodynamics, geochemical equilibrium, and aquatic food chain bioaccumulation.

Comments: CEAM is not on the Internet yet, but might be by time you read this. All materials are in the public domain.

Access: Modem calls to CEAM Bulletin Board Service: (706) 546-3402.

Contact: Catherine Green
                Center for Exposure Assessment Modeling
                Environmental Research Laboratories
                U.S. Environmental Protection Agency
                Athens, GA 30605 USA

                voice: (706) 546-3549

Environmental Exchange

Contents: Archive of files on environmental issues including air and water quality, land-use, energy, waste, wildlife and environmental education programs.

Comments: ECIX is supported by the Joyce Mertz-Gilmore Foundation and the Energy Foundation.

Access: FTP host: `igc.org`
                 directories: `pub/ECIX`
                                    `pub/ECIXfiles`

                 Contact Environmental Exchange for more information.

Contact: e-mail: `tgray@igc.org`

                 Tom Gray
                 The Environmental Exchange
                 1930 18th St. NW
                 Suite 24,
                 Washington, DC 20009 USA

                 voice: (202) 387-2182

15.15. Education

MOLIS (Minority Online Information Service)

Contents: Up-to-date information on Black and Hispanic colleges and universities, fellowships and scholarships, and other announcements and information of interest. Institutional information includes contact information, data on faculty and students, and granting opportunities. Also see FEDIX in the Grants section of this chapter.

Comments: First time users will be asked to enter contact information.

Access: Telnet: `fedix.fie.com`
           login: `molis`
           user-id: `new`

           modem: (800) 626-6547
                      (301) 975-0103

                      settings: data=8, parity=N, stop=1

Contact: e-mail: `comments@fedix.fie.com`

           Federal Information Exchange
           Gaithersburg, MD 20878 USA

           help line: (301) 975-0103

Online Database for Distance Education

Contents: Information about distance education courses run by institutions in the Commonwealth, a worldwide directory of distance teaching institutions and a bibliographic database of literature about distance education. Courses and literature database offers a hierarchical subject classification for searching as well as keyword entry. Institutions are searchable by world regions and countries. Online access or CD versions of the datasets available for a fee; users from lesser developed nations may arrange for free access.

Comments: Access the service as described below to receive up-to-date information about costs.

Access: Telnet: **open.ac.uk**
                 login: **ICDL**
                 account code: **NEW**

                 Should this fail there is an alternative route via the Janet/Internet gateway as follows:

                 Telnet: **sun.nsf.ac.uk**
                 login: **janet**
                 host name: **uk.ac.open.acs.vax**
                 username: **ICDL**
                 account code: **NEW**

Contact: e-mail: **n.ismail@open.ac.uk**   (Internet)
                 e-mail: **n.ismail@uk.ac.open**   (Janet)

                 International Centre for Distance Learning (ICDL)
                 c/o The Open University, Walton Hall
                 Milton Keynes, MK7 6AA United Kingdom

                 voice: + 44 908 653537
                 fax: + 44 908 654173

15.16. Genetics and Molecular Biology

General Information about Genetics and Molecular Biology Databases

If you intend to use any of the Genetics and Molecular Biology databases listed in this section, you are advised to get the Listing of Molecular Biology Databases (LiMB) for an overview of what is available. Most, but not all, of the databases in this section are described in LiMB which is updated very frequently.

You should also make a point of exploring the FTP archives of the National Center for Biotechnology Information (NCBI) described in this section, which might be characterized as the "wuarchive" of the molecular biology world.

LiMB (Listing of Molecular Biology Databases)

Contents: A comprehensive listing of molecular biology and related databases.

Comments: The *essential* resource for anyone using or thinking of using genetics and molecular biology databases. If you are creating such a database, these are the people to notify to be sure of broad notification in the molecular biology community.

Access: The preferred method of obtaining this document is by sending an e-mail request to a mail server. You will receive the LiMB database by e-mail in several parts.

```
mail      bioserve@life.lanl.gov
subject: (none needed)
message: limb-data
```

Contact: e-mail: **limb@life.lanl.gov**

LiMB
Theoretical Biology and Biophysics Group
T-10, Mail Stop K710
Los Alamos National Laboratory
Los Alamos, NM 87545 USA

voice: (505) 667-7510

Bibliography of Theoretical Population Genetics

Contents: A comprehensive bibliographic listing of articles on theoretical population genetics up to
                   1980; a must for any serious population geneticist.

Comments: The two letters at ends of filenames, as in "bible.ac", indicate the range of primary
                   author's last names in citations contained in each file.

Access: FTP host: **evolution.genetics.washington.edu**
                   directory: **bible**
                   filenames: (many or all)

Contact: e-mail: **joe@genetics.washington.edu**

                   Joe Felsenstein
                   Department of Genetics SK-50
                   University of Washington
                   Seattle, WA 98195 USA

                   voice: (206) 543-0150
                   fax: (206) 543-0754

ENZYME

Contents: Dictionary of 3072 enzymes; contains nomenclature, information about catalytic activity, co-factors, and diseases associated with each enzyme.

Access: Accessible through FTP and mail server.

FTP host:	`ncbi.nlm.nih.gov`
directory:	`repository/enzyme`
filenames:	`enzyme.asn`
	`enzyme.dat` (the data set)
	`enzuser.txt` (user's guide)
	`enzclass.txt` (enzyme classification)

To get started with the mail server, send the following message:

```
mail:    netserv@embl-heidelberg.de
subject: (none needed)
message: help
```

Contact: e-mail: `bairoch@cmu.unige.ch`

Amos Bairoch
Medical Biochemistry Department
Centre Medical Universitaire
1211 Geneva 4 Switzerland

voice: + 41 22 61 84 92

Gene-Server

Contents: Repository of several databases including GenBank; PIR protein sequences; R. Roberts
                 Restriction Enzyme Database; and Matrix of Biological Knowledge Archive Server files;
                 also a huge number of software programs for molecular biologists and geneticists.

Access: By mail server send the following message for an introduction:

```
mail:     gene-server@bchs.uh.edu
subject:  (none needed)
message:  send help
```

Contact: e-mail: davison@uh.edu

                 Dan Davison
                 BCHS - 5500
                 Dept. of Biochemical and Biophysical Sciences
                 University of Houston
                 4800 Calhoun
                 Houston, TX 77204-5500 USA

                 voice: (713) 743-8366

More Info: NNSC Internet Resources Guide, Section 3.1.

IuBIO (Indiana University Archive for Molecular and General Biology)

Contents: Although this is primarily an archive of molecular biology and chemistry software, this
                 site also contains some useful datasets, particularly for *Drosophila* genetics.

Comments: Get the document "Archive.doc" via FTP for up-to date information on using this site.

Access: FTP host: ftp.bio.indiana.edu
                 filename: Archive.doc

Contact: e-mail: archive@bio.indiana.edu

                 Don Gilbert
                 BioComputing Office
                 Biology Department
                 Indiana University
                 Bloomington, IN 47405 USA

More Info: FTP host: ftp.bio.indiana.edu
                 filename: Archive.doc

Johns Hopkins Genetic Databases

Contents: Online data from "Mendelian Inheritance in Man."

Comments: You must register first with GDB/OMIM for a user-id and password.

Access: Telnet: **welch.jhu.edu**

Contact: e-mail: **help@welch.jhu.edu**

GDB/OMIM User Support
William H. Welch Medical Library
1830 E. Monument St. Third Floor
Baltimore, MD 21205 USA

voice: (301) 955-7058

MBCRR (Molecular Biology Computer Research Resource)

Contents: Source code and documentation for DNA and protein sequence analysis software for Unix
systems.

Access: FTP host: **mbcrr.harvard.edu**
                     directory: **MBCRR-Package**
                     filenames: (many or all)

Contact: e-mail: **tsmith@mbcrr.harvard.edu**

MBCRR, LG-S127
44 Binney St.,
Boston, MA 02115 USA

voice: (617) 732-3746

More Info: NNSC Internet Resources Guide, Section 3.20.

                     FTP host: **mbcrr.harvard.edu**
                     directory: **MBCRR-Package**
                     filename: **README**

NCBI (National Center for Biotechnology Information)

Contents: Voluminous FTP archives of databases and software tools for biotechnology. Specific databases currently stored include Transcription Factors, Normalized Gene Designations, Eukaryotic Promoters, REBASE, SWISS-PROT , Enzyme Data Bank, SEQANALREF, tables of contents of molecular biology journals, *Drosophila* Genetics (FlyBase), *Caenorhabditis elegans* Database, Expressed Sequence Tags, ECO2DBASE, pkinase, and The Reference Library DataBase.

Comments: The National Center for Biotechnology Information (NCBI) was created by an act of the U.S. Congress to support the development of biotechnology and medicine in the U.S. As mandated by this act, NCBI shall:

1) create automated systems for knowledge about molecular biology, biochemistry, and genetics;

2) perform research into advanced methods of analyzing and interpreting molecular biology data;

3) enable biotechnology researchers and medical care personnel to use the systems and methods developed; and

4) coordinate efforts to gather biotechnology information worldwide.

Access: FTP host: `ncbi.nlm.nih.gov`
                 directory: `repository`
                 files: (many or all)

Most of the databases are in the repository directory. Be sure to obtain the README file for a current overview of its contents. There are many other directories of interest in this host many useful software tools for practicing biotechnologists. For a complete overview, examine the ls-lR file in the root directory.

Contact: e-mail: `repository@ncbi.nlm.nih.gov`

National Center for Biotechnology Information
National Library of Medicine
Bldg 38A, NIH
8600 Rockville Pike
Bethesda, MD 20894 USA

voice: (301) 496-2475

PROSITE

Contents: Dictionary of protein sites and patterns.

Access: FTP hosts: `ncbi.nlm.nih.gov`
                 directory: `repository/prosite`
                 filename: `prosite.dat`

Contact: e-mail: `bairoch@cmu.unige.ch`

                 Amos Bairoch
                 Medical Biochemistry Department
                 Centre Medical Universitaire
                 1211 Geneva 4 Switzerland

                 voice: + 41 22 61 84 92

More Info: Bairoch, A. "PROSITE: A dictionary of sites and patterns proteins." Nucleic Acids
                 Research 20 (1992):2013-2018.

                 Handbook and user's manual:

                 FTP hosts: `ncbi.nlm.nih.gov`
                 directory: `repository/prosite`
                 filenames: `prosite.txt`   (user's manual)
                                   `prosite.doc`   (handbook)

SEQANALREF

Contents: DNA sequence analysis bibliography containing 1657 references.

Access: FTP hosts: `ncbi.nlm.nih.gov`
                 directory: `repository/seqanalref`
                 filenames: `seqanalr.dat`   (the bibliography)
                                   `seqanalr.txt`   (a help file)

Contact: e-mail: `bairoch@cmu.unige.ch`

                 Amos Bairoch
                 Medical Biochemistry Department
                 Centre Medical Universitaire
                 1211 Geneva 4 Switzerland

                 voice: + 41 22 61 84 92

More Info: Bairoch, A. "SEQANALREF: a sequence analysis bibliographic reference data bank."
                 CABIOS 7 (1991): 268.

SWISS-PROT

Contents: Protein sequence data bank containing 21,795 sequences and 21,773 references.

Comments: Frequent updates

Access: FTP hosts: `ncbi.nlm.nih.gov`
                     directory: `repository/swiss-prot`
                     filename: `userman.txt`   (user's manual)

Contact: e-mail: `bairoch@cmu.unige.ch`

                     Amos Bairoch
                     Medical Biochemistry Department
                     Centre Medical Universitaire
                     1211 Geneva 4   Switzerland

                     voice: + 41 22 61 84 92

More Info: Bairoch, A., and B. Boeckmann. "The SWISS-PROTT protein sequence databank."
                     Nucleic Acids Research 20 (1991): 2019-2022.

15.17. Geography and Geology

General Information about Geography and Geology Databases

Bill Thoen (bthoen@csn.org) maintains an up-to-date listing of Internet resources in geography and geology, including databases. It is posted periodically to the newsgroup sci.geo.geology and is also available via FTP.

FTP host: `csn.org`
directory: `COGS`
filename: `internet.resources.earth.sci`

Geographic Name Server

Contents: Currently contains geographic information for U.S. cities, counties, states, some natural features taken from the U.S. Geodetic Survey, and the U.S. Postal Service. There are plans for worldwide coverage. Variables stored include names, elevation, latitude, longitude, population, telephone area code and ZIP codes where appropriate; many other variables are in the works.

Comments: Please enter "help" and "info" before using this service, for instructions, recent changes, and answers to commonly asked questions. The output from this program is most easily used as input for other software packages.

Access: Telnet: `martini.eecs.umich.edu 3000`   (Don't forget port 3000!)

Contact: e-mail: `libert@citi.umich.edu` (Tom Libert)

             voice: (313) 936-0827

GLIS (Global Land Information System)

Contents   A database of information about earth science datasets, containing online samples for evaluation.

Comments: Online requests can be made for datasets of interest.

Access: Telnet: `glis.cr.usgs.gov`

Contact: e-mail: `glis@glis.cr.usgs.gov`

            voice: (800) 252-GLIS

15.18. Grants and Awards

American Philosophical Association

Contents: Grants, fellowships and academic positions, primarily of interest to philosophers, but also many of interest to scholars in the humanities generally. Sources of funding described include NEH, NSF, ACLS, listing of academic and non-academic jobs, and stipends for summer institutes.

Many other resources of interest, besides funding and jobs, are in this bulletin board.

Comments: Although some of this information is available elsewhere, this is a convenient central source for humanities scholars.

Access: Telnet: `atl.calstate.edu`
               login: `apa`

Contact: e-mail: `traiger@oxy.edu`

Saul Traiger
Department of Philosophy
Cognitive Science Program
Occidental College
Los Angeles, CA 90041 USA

voice: (213) 259-2901

FEDIX (Federal Information Exchange)

Contents: Information on Federal education and research programs (including descriptions, eligibility, funding, deadlines); scholarships, fellowships, and grants; used government research equipment; new funding for specific research and education activities from the "Commerce Business Daily," "Federal Register," and other sources; and minority assistance research and education programs.

Comments: Comprehensive education and research related agency information comes from the Department of Energy, Office of Naval Research, National Aeronautics and Space Administration, Air Force Office of Scientific Research, and Federal Aviation Administration. The National Science Foundation, Department of Housing and Urban Development, Department of Commerce, Department of Education, and National Security Agency are providing minority assistance information exclusively.

Access: Telnet: `fedix.fie.com`
               login: `molis` or `fedix`
               user-id: `new`

               modem: (800) 232-4879
                            (301) 258-0953

                            settings: data=8, parity=N, stop=1

Contact: e-mail: `comments@fedix.fie.com`

               Federal Information Exchange
               Gaithersburg, MD 20878 USA

More Info: help line: (301) 975-0103 (M-F, 8:30 - 4:30 EST)

SPIN (Sponsored Programs Information Network)

Contents: Database of funding opportunities from corporate, Federal, and other sources for educational researchers and institutions.

Access: Via tn3270. Account requried.

Contact: Sponsored Programs Information Network
               Research Foundation of the State University of New York
               Box 9
               Albany, NY 12201-009 USA

               voice: (518) 434-7150

STIS (Science and Technology Information System)

Contents: National Science Foundation publications, including NSF Bulletin, Guide to NSF Programs, grants booklet including application forms, grants program announcements, press releases, NSF telephone book, reports of National Science Board, abstracts and descriptions of research projects currently funded by NSF, and analytical reports and news from the International Programs division.

Comments: The Telnet and modem front end is very good (even fun!), and features prompts and full screen menus, online viewing of documents, database search utilities, provisions for downloading, and tutorials. it is well worth your while to work through the "30-Second User's Guide" offered in the help menu.

Access: STIS can be accessed through WAIS, Gopher, Telnet, FTP, or modem calls:

WAIS databases: **nsf-awards** and **nsf-pubs**

Gopher: The STIS Gopher is typically available in the "Other Gopher Servers" menu with the name "National Science Foundation Gopher (STIS)/".

Telnet:	**stis.nsf.gov**
login:	**public**
FTP host:	**stis.nsf.gov**
directories:	(all directories)
filenames:	(all subdirectories and files)
modem:	(202) 357-0359
	(202) 357-0360

Contact: e-mail: **stis@nsf.gov**

Dr. STIS
National Science Foundation
Office of Information Systems,
Room 401
1800 G. Street, NW
Washington, D.C. 20550 USA

voice: (202) 357-7555
fax: (202) 357-7745

15.19. History

General Information about History Databases

The FTP host ra.msstate.edu is a great source to check periodically if you want to keep abreast of developments in history databases. The directory listed below also contains many online archives, articles, bibliographies, and other electronic documents. The archives are maintained by Don Mabry of Mississippi State University.

FTP host: `ra.msstate.edu`
directory: `pub/docs/history`

MEMDB (Medieval and Early Modern Data Bank)

Contents: Data on western Europe between 800-1800 A.D. Information includes wages, prices, housing, mortality, property, charity, nutrition, etc.

Comments: One must pay subscription fees to RLIN.

Access: Through Research Libraries Group, Inc.

Contacts: MEMDB:The Medieval and Early Modern Data Bank
Department of History CN 5059
Rutgers, The State University of New Jersey
New Brunswick, NJ 08903 USA

voice: (201) 932-8335

RLIN Information Center
Research Libraries Group, Inc.
1200 Villa St.
Mountain View, CA 94041-1100 USA

More Info: NNSC Internet Resources Guide, Section 3.3 (MEMDB)
NNSC Internet Resources Guide, Section 2.4 (RLIN)

Military History Databases

Contents: Databases of the U.S. Army Military History Institute and the U.S. Army War College.

Comments: If you are a frequent user of this service, you are encouraged to download the pertinent table of contents files semi-annually.

Access: Use the mail server to get started with this database. Try the following messages:

```
mail:      info-request@carlisle-emh2.army.mil
subject: index
message: (none needed)
```

To view what is available from the U.S. Army War College:

```
mail:      info-request@carlisle-emh2.army.mil
subject: USAWC
message: (none needed)
```

To view what is available from the U.S. Army Military History Institute:

```
mail:      info-request@carlisle-emh2.army.mil
subject: USAMHI
message: (none needed)
```

Contact: e-mail: vetockd@carlisle-emh2.army.mil

                 voice: (717) 245-3611

15.20. Library Sciences

FAXON

Contents: Comprehensive databases of serials publications for use by libraries and academics for ordering and cataloging.

Comments: FAXON also provides e-mail services to its subscribers.

Access: Telnet, once an account is established.

Contact: The Faxon Company
              15 Southwood Park
              Westwood, MA 02090 USA

              voice: (617) 329-3350
              fax: (617) 329-9875

Library of Congress Cataloging Records

Contents: Entries from the Library of Congress databases searchable by subject, keyword, author, title, ISBN (International Standard Book Number), ISSN (International Standard Series Number), LCCN (Library of Congress Card Number), and other fields.

Comments: Full use requires establishing an account with Data Research Associates. Only 2 guest logins are allowed at a time, with restricted searching capability.

Access: Telnet for guest services:

              Telnet: **dra.com**

Contact: Data Research Associates
              Sales Department
              1276 North Warson Road
              St. Louis, MO 63105 USA

OCLC (Online Computer Library Center, Inc.)

Contents: Bibliographic databases containing more than 20 million records; databases include Library of Congress, Dissertation Abstracts, ERIC, and many others.

Access: By Telnet. Account required.

Contact: Online Computer Library Center, Inc.
              6565 Frantz Road
              Dublin, OH 43017-3395 USA

              voice: (800) 848-5878

15.21. Literature

ARTFL (American and French Research on the Treasury of the French Language)

Contents: A textual database of nearly 2,000 French language texts, written from the 17th to 20th centuries, containing about 150 million words. Includes a sophisticated but easy to use full text retrieval system designed for single word and contextual searches. There are several related philological analysis programs available for use with ARTFL.

Comments: A cooperative project of the Centre National de la Recherche Scientifique and the University of Chicago.

Access: Telnet or modem; payment of a small fee by an institution allows all scholars and students access to ARTFL. CD version of the dataset may be available by late 1992.

                There is a guest account *for evaluation purposes only*:

                Telnet: `artfl.uchicago.edu`
                login: `guest`
                password: `suggest`   (The password for the guest account is changed periodically.)

Contact: e-mail: `mark@gide.uchicago.edu`

                American and French Research on the Treasury of the French Language
                Department of Romance Languages and Literatures
                University of Chicago
                1050 East 59th Street
                Chicago, IL 60637 USA

                voice: (812) 702-8488

More Info: FTP host: `ra.msstate.edu`
                directory: `pub/docs/history/databases`
                filename: `database.ARTFL`   (user's guide)

Dartmouth Dante Project

Contents: A database containing the text of Dante's *Divina Commedia* and full texts of 600 years of scholarly commentary on the work. The database uses the BRS/Search program. .

Comments: Note that many of the commentaries are copyrighted, so the database itself cannot be distributed. Available 24 hours a day, except for Mondays, 4:15-6:30am Eastern Time.

Access: Telnet: **library.dartmouth.edu**

                 At the "->" prompt, enter "connect dante".

                 modem: (603) 643-6300   (300 and 1200 baud)
                                  (603) 643-6310   (> 1200 baud)

                 At the "-> " prompt, enter "connect dante".

Contact: e-mail: **dante@dartmouth.edu**

                 Dartmouth Dante Project
                 1 Reed Hall
                 HB 6087
                 Dartmouth College
                 Hanover, NH 03755 USA

                 voice: (603) 646-2633

More Info: Online help and printed user's manual for $4.00 are available.

15.22. Mathematics

---

e-MATH (American Mathematical Society)

Contents: Database of reviews and abstract in nearly 100 topics, including applied mathematics in fields such as astronomy, economics, biology and other natural sciences. The SWAIS database contains preprint abstracts from Duke University, Los Alamos Laboratory, Kyoto, Mathematical Reviews Abstracts, Current Mathematical Publications Citations, University of Nebraska Press Catalog, and the American Mathematical Society Catalog.

Access: Telnet:

    Telnet: `e-math.ams.com`
    login: `e-math`
    password: `e-math`

    WAIS:

    Telnet: `e-math.ams.com`
    login: `waisdemo`
    password: `waisdemo`

Contact: e-mail: `support@e-math.ams.com`

Instant Math Preprints

Contents: A fully searchable database of preprint abstracts, and instructions on how to access to the full texts via FTP.

Access: tn3270   `yalevm.ycc.yale.edu`
    user-id: `Math1` (or `Math2`, `3`, `4`, or `5`)
    password: `Math1` (or `Math2`, `3`, `4`, or `5`)
    operator ID: `Math1` (or `Math2`, `3`, `4`, or `5`)

Contact: e-mail: `victor@jezebel.wustl.edu` (Victor Wickerhauser)

Maple FTP Archives

Contents: Tools for Maple software.

Access: FTP hosts: `neptune.eth2.edu`   (neptune) ETH Zurich, Switzerland
                             `daisy.waterloo.edu`   University of Waterloo, Canada
    directory: `maple`
    filenames: (many or all)

MATLAB User Group Archive

Contents: Functions and utilities for the MATLAB numeric computation system.

Comments: These MATLAB files are also accessible from NETLIB. (See NETLIB entry). If you
                choose not to use NETLIB, you are encouraged to subscribe to the MATLAB users digest
                by sending a subscription request, including your e-mail user-id and address, to
                matlab-users-request@mcs.anl.gov.

Access: Via mail server:

```
mail:    netlib@ornl.gov
subject: (none needed)
message: send index from matlab
```

Contact: e-mail: **bischof@mcs.anl.gov**

                Christian Bischoff
                Math and Computer Sciences Division
                Argonne National Labs
                Argonne, IL 60439 USA

                voice: (708) 972-8875

More Info: NNSC Internet Resources Guide, Section 3.18.

                To subscribe to the MATLAB user's digest, send a request (including your user-id and
                e-mail address) to the following:

                matlab-users-request@mcs.anl.gov

Mathematica FTP Archives

Contents: Tools for Mathematica software.

Comments: Mathematica is a remarkable software system for symbolic mathematics, featuring
                high-quality graphical displays of functions as graphs, surfaces, and three dimensional
                objects. Mathematica software is available for operating systems from Macintoshes to
                Crays.

Access: Several anonymous FTP sites store files pertinent to Mathematica.

                FTP hosts: **mathsource.wri.com**
                                  otter.stanford.edu
                                  siam.unibe.ch
                                  vax.eedsp.gatech.edu

More Info: For advanced discussions of symbolic math and symbolic math software packages,
                including Mathematica, refer to the following:

                newsgroup: **sci.math.symbolic**

NETLIB Mathematical Software Distribution System

Contents: A huge variety of mathematical software and algorithms.

Comments: A tremendously valuable resource. The AT&T site also features a menu driven service called "walk" which allows one to home-in on literature citations for the algorithm appropriate for a particular purpose.

Access: Accessible through FTP, mail server, Telnet, and modem. Please use the site nearest you!

FTP hosts: `research.att.com`   (U.S.)
               `draci.cs.uow.edu.au`   (Australia)
directory: `netlib`

Mail server Access:

`netlib@ornl.gov`   (North America)
`netlib@research.att.com`   (North America)
`netlib@ukc.ac.uk`   (United Kingdom)
`netlib@nac.no`   (Europe)
`netlib@draci.cs.uow.edu.au`   (Australia)

```
mail:    <mail-server of your choice>
subject: (none needed)
message: send index
```

Telnet: `research.att.com`
login: `walk`

modem: (908) 582-1238
login: `walk`

Contact: e-mail: `ehg@research.att.com` (Eric Grosse)

AT&T Bell Labs 2t-504
Murray Hill, NJ 07974 USA

voice: (908) 582-5828

15.23. Medical

General Information about Medical Databases

Medical related databases may also be found in this chapter in the Genetics and Molecular Biology section. PENpages, included in the Agriculture section, also has a substantial amount of medical and health related information.

The following file contains up-to-date information about online medical databases and many other Internet resources of interest to medical professionals.

FTP host:	`ftp.sura.net`
directory:	`pub/nic`
filename:	`medical.resources.10-9` (this filename changes with updates)

Alcoholism Research Database

Contents: A database and bibliography on alcoholism and substance abuse.

Access: Telnet: `lib.dartmouth.edu`

At the "->" prompt, enter "`select file cork`".

Contact: e-mail: `Project.Cork@dartmouth.edu`

Project Cork Resource Center
Butler Building
Dartmouth College
Hanover, NH 03755 USA

voice: (603) 650-1122

CancerNet

Contents: Cancer treatment information from the National Cancer Institute's (NCI) Physician Data Query (PDQ) database.

Access: To get started with this service, send the following e-mail message and you will receive up-to-date CancerNet instructions and the contents list:

```
mail:      cancernet@icicb.nci.nih.gov
subject:   (none needed)
message:   help
```

Contact: e-mail: minht@icicb.nci.nih.gov

               voice: (301) 496-8880.

SEFAIN (Southeast Florida AIDS Information Network)

Contents: A database of AIDS and related research activities in southeastern Florida.

Comments: Support for this database service has been provided by the National Library of Medicine.

Access: Telnet: callcat.med.miami.edu
               login: library
               main menu: select "L"
               next menu: select "1"

15.24. Meteorology

General Information about Meteorology Databases

Ilana Stern (ilana@ncar.ucar.edu) maintains an up-to-date listing of Internet resources in meteorology, including databases, which is posted twice monthly to the newsgroups "sci.geo.meteorology" and "news.answers". The file is also available via FTP from:

FTP host:	`pit-manager.mit.edu`
directory:	`pub/usenet/sci.geo.meteorology`
filename:	`Sources_of_Meteorological_Data_FAQ`

University of Michigan Weather Underground

Contents: Weather information for U.S. and Canada. Specific information includes current conditions, forecasts, ski conditions, long range regional forecasts, earthquake reports, severe weather summaries (including floods, tornados, and severe thunderstorms), hurricane advisories, and national weather summaries.

Comments: For educational purposes only. Potential commercial users should contact Zephyr Weather Information Service (508-898-3511), the providers of the data feed to the Weather Underground.

Access: Telnet: `downwind.sprl.umich.edu 3000`   (Don't forget port 3000!)

Contact: e-mail: `sdm@madlab.sprl.umich.edu`

College of Engineering
University of Michigan
Ann Arbor
Michigan 48109-2143 USA

15.25. Music

Music and Lyrics Archives

Contents: Lyrics and tablature for thousands of songs, discographies, and commentary on the classical music repertoire, and a growing number of other music related files.

Comments: There is a directory, pub/tmp/incoming, to receive contributions to the archive.

Access: FTP host: `vacs.uwp.edu`
                 directory: `pub/music/lyrics`
                 filename: `files.directory`

Contact: e-mail: `datta@vacs.uwp.edu`

NetJam

Contents: MIDI sequences deposited and redistributed for collaborative compositions by Internet users.

Comments: A system for real time music performance and improvisation over the Internet is now being developed.

Access: Information and repositories of sequences by FTP:

                 FTP host: `xcf.berkeley.edu`
                 directory: `misc/netjam`
                 filenames: (many or all)

                 Much of the information in the archives can also be obtained via mail server. Refer to misc/netjam/docs/guide for more information.

Contact: e-mail: `latta@xcf.berkeley.edu` (Craig Latta)

More Info: Mailing list: netjam-users@xcf.berkeley.edu. Please send subscription requests to netjam-request@xcf.berkeley.edu.

15.26. Oceanography

OCEANIC (The Ocean Information Center)

Contents: Information about oceanography research activities throughout the world (particularly the activities of the World Ocean Circulation Experiment (WOCE) This database contains descriptions of oceanographic and climatological datasets and ordering information, directory of oceanographers, and related materials.

Comments: It is possible to view some graphical displays of oceanographic data with Tektronics 4010 terminal emulation.

Access: Telnet: `delocn.udel.edu`
              directory: `INFO`

Contact: OCEANIC
              University of Delaware
              College of Marine Studies
              Lewes, DE USA

15.27. Physics

PINET (Physics Information Network)

Contents: SPIN and General Physics Advanced Abstracts, bibliographic databases, job announcements, AIP meetings, news releases, announcements, and facility for ordering of AIP publications.

Comments: This is a for-fee service which requires an initial registration fee and hourly connect charges.

Access: Telnet: `pinet.aip.org`

15.28. Political Science

U.S. Senate Bibliographies

Contents: Bibliographies of U.S. Senate Committee hearings and publications for the 99th-102nd
               Congresses.

Comments: Filenames in the database have a precise format whose meanings you should understand
               before using the database. Explanations of filename formats are provided in the readme
               file.

Access: FTP host: `ncsuvm.cc.ncsu.edu`
               directory: `senate`
               filename: `readme.*`   (basic information file; the
                                                             last four numbers represent
                                                             year and month of file
                                                             version)

Contact: e-mail: `Jack_McGeachy@ncsu.edu`

               John A. McGeachy
               Documents Department
               D.H. Hill Library,
               North Carolina State University
               Raleigh, NC 27695-7111 USA

               voice: (919) 515-3280

15.29. Social Sciences

BIRON Archive System

Contents: A database of more than 3,000 datasets covering most areas of social and economic life in the United Kingdom, searchable by names of persons or organizations associated with particular datasets, titles or part-titles, dates, and geographical areas of data collection.

Access: Telnet: `solb1.essex.ac.uk`
              login: `biron`
              password: `norib`

Contact: e-mail: `millk@solb1.essex.ack.uk`

Coombspapers Databank

Contents: Intended to be the world's leading depository of social science and humanities research papers and documents, including offprints, specialist bibliographies, directories, thesis abstracts, and datasets. Areas of primary focus are South and NorthEastern Asia.

Comments: Scholars are encouraged to send documents and datasets to the Databank. A special directory in the FTP host, coombspapers/inboundpapers, has been set up to receive such files in ASCII format.

Access: FTP host: `coombs.anu.edu.au`
              directory: `coombspapers`
              filenames: `INDEX`
                             (all other files and subdirectories)

              WAIS databases: `ANU-Asian-Religions`
                             `ANU-Pacific-Linguistics`
                             `ANU-Pacific-Manuscripts`
                             `ANU-SocSci-Netlore`
                             `ANU-SSDA-Catalogues`
                             `ANU-Thai-Yunnan`

              W3:   Other Subjects, Social Sciences, Coombs Paper Archives

Contact: e-mail: `coombspapers@coombs.anu.edu.au`

              Dr. T. Matthew Ciolek,
              Coombspapers Administrator,
              Coombs Computing Unit, RSPacS/RSSS,
              Australian National University,
              Canberra Australia

              voice: + 61 6 249 2214

CULDAT (Canadian Union List of Machine Readable Data Files)

Contents: Bibliographic and descriptive information about computer readable data files held by Canadian academic and governmental data libraries and archives. There are currently about 2,000 databases accessible. Sources of databases searched in a CULDAT session include:

CUSSDA:	Carleton University, Social Science Data Archive
ICPSR:	Inter-University Consortium for Political and Social Research
NAC:	National Archives of Canada
STC:	Statistics Canada
UADL:	University of Alberta, Data Library
UBCDL:	University of British Columbia, Data Library
UMISE:	University of Manitoba, Institute for Social and Economic Research
UWOSS:	University of Western Ontario, Social Science Computing Lab
WATLS:	University of Waterloo, Leisure Studies Data Bank
YUISR:	York University, Institute for Social Research

Access: Via a mail server which accepts Remote Spires (RMSPIRES) commands. To get started, try the following message:

```
mail:     rmspires@vm.ucs.ualberta.ca
subject:  (none needed)
message:  explain culdat
```

Contact: e-mail: abombak@vm.ucs.ualberta.ca

Anna Bombak, Data Librarian
4-15 Cameron Library
352 General Services Building
University of Alberta
Edmonton, Alberta T6G 258 Canada

voice: (403) 492-5212

ICPSR (Inter-University Consortium for Political and Social Research)

Contents: An immense array of datasets for research and instruction in the social sciences.

Comments: ICPSR members can work with datasets remotely or have materials transferred directly over the Internet by e-mail. The Consortium Data Network (CDNet—not to be confused with the Canadian Research and Education Network whose abbreviation is also CDNet) is used for direct access to ICPSR datasets and services by way of the Internet.

Access: Through the Internet or CDNet once you establish an account.

Contact: e-mail: **icpsr_netmail@um.cc.umich.edu**

                 Member Services
                 ICPSR
                 Box 1248
                 Ann Arbor, MI 48106 USA

                 voice: (301) 763-5010

IRSS (The Institute for Research in the Social Sciences)

Contents: Extensive archives of social science data, including IRSS datasets, and public opinion polls (Louis Harris, Atlanta Journal Constitution, Carolina Poll, USA Today). IRSS datasets come from a wide variety of sources; poll databases can be searched for poll questions containing specific words, study dates, or study numbers.

Comments: You must access this service with tn3270 or use Telnet from a VM/CMS mainframe. If you're not used to the CMS operating system, expect to be lost and confused at times. (In particular, note that "PF#" commands never mean "P-F-#" literally. Usually "esc3" or "F3" will do the job of "PF3". Once you learn to get around beginning problems, this is a very good resource.

Access: tn3270:   **uncvm1.oit.unc.edu**   (or telnet from a VM/CMS host)
                 login: **irss1** through **irss7**
                 password: **irss**

Contact: e-mail: **uirdss@uncvm1.oit.unc.edu**

                 David Sheaves
                 Institute for Research in the Social Sciences
                 University of North Carolina
                 Chapel Hill, NC 27599 USA

                 voice: (919) 966-3348
                 fax: (919) 962-4777

National Archives Center for Electronic Records

Contents: An archive of more than 14,000 datasets, with an emphasis on U.S. Federal government information. Very strong in the areas of health, demography, and social sciences.

Access: Currently, one must order copies of datasets of interest on magnetic tape (9 track reels or 3480 cartridges).

Contact: For more information, or a free list of over 4,400 title list of holdings, contact the following:

              e-mail: `tif%nihcu.bitnet@cunyvm.cuny.edu.`

              Theodore J. Hull
              Archives Specialist
              Archival Service Branch
              Center for Electronic Records
              National Archives and Records Administration
              Washington, DC 20408 USA

              voice: (202) 501-5579

More Info: There are two LISTSERV discussion groups of relevance to this and related government holdings: "Federal Electronic Data Special Interest Group" and "Government Documents."

                        `fedsig-l%wvnvm.bitnet@cunyvm.cuny.edu`
                        `govdoc-l%psuvm.bitnet@cunyvm.cuny.edu`

RAPID-ESRC Database of Research Abstracts and Products

Contents: A database in Scotland of the research results of the Economic and Social Research Council.

Access:
Telnet: `ercvax.ed.ac.uk`
username: `rapid`
password: `rapid`

SSDA (Aleph/Hebrew University Social Science Data Archive Catalog)

Contents: A catalog of a very wide variety of social science datasets about Israel. You can search by author, title, subject, and variable names. Cataloged datasets cover the following topics: agriculture, attitudes, census, commerce, crime and violence, culture, demography, drugs, education, elderly, elections, environmental quality, finance, foreign countries, government, health, household behavior, housing, immigration and absorption, incomes and wages, industry, international accounting, Jerusalem, Jewish Diaspora, kibbutz, labour, leisure, local authorities, migration, national accounting, national economy, political behavior, political attitudes, quality of life, religion, savings, social mobility, social stratification, social structure, technology, transportation, welfare, women, and youth.

Access:
Telnet   `har1.huji.ac.il`
username: `SSDA`
             Select 2 from the first menu.

Contact: Datasets of interest can be ordered from:

e-mail: `magar1%hujibvms.bitnet@cunyvm.cuny.edu`

voice: (972) 2-883181
fax: (972) 2-322545

15.30. Statistics

Statlib Statistical Software and Data Distribution System

Contents: Datasets of special interest to statisticians for their historical or theoretical importance, statistical software and algorithms, and a directory of statisticians.

Access: Statlib is accessible via FTP and mail server. Note that for the FTP host, you use the login name "statlib", not "anonymous"!

>   FTP host: `lib.stat.cmu.edu`
>   login: `statlib`
>   password: `<your-e-mail-address>`
>   directories: (many or all)

Mail server:

```
mail:    statlib@lib.stat.cmu.edu
subject: (none needed)
message: send index
```

Statlib will send a file containing information about the contents of the archives and more detailed instructions on how to use the mail server.

Contact: e-mail: `mikem@stat.cmu.edu` (Michael Meyer)

Department of Statistics
Carnegie Mellon University
Pittsburgh, PA 15213 USA

voice: (412) 268-3108

15.31. For More Information

15.31.1. Fellow Internet Users and Peers

If you are interested in particular types of databases, you are advised to subscribe to some of the more quantitatively-oriented Internet discussion groups to keep up-to-date on what databases are available to researchers in your field. Refer to Chapters 9 and 10 for more information on using Usenet and LISTSERV respectively and on selecting the groups most appropriate for your needs.

15.31.2. Database Maintainers

If there are databases in this chapter of special interest to you, try communicating with the listed contact person(s) to see if other related databases exist or are being planned. In many cases, the databases listed in this chapter contain pointers to other related databases. For example, the history archives at Mississippi State University provide information on history-specific sources throughout the world.

15.31.3. Other Online Compendia of Internet Databases

Online information about databases within particular disciplines was provided at the beginning of several of the topical entries throughout this chapter. In general, these will be the most up-to-date and comprehensive sources of information about databases in those topics.

The "SURAnet Guide to Selected Internet Resources" is a thorough and constantly updated source of information about online databases.

FTP host:	`ftp.sura.net`
directory:	`pub/nic`
filename:	`infoguide.dd-mm.txt` (where "dd-mm" is the day and month of the most recent version)

Chapter 2 of the NNSC Internet Resource Guide contains information about online databases and bibliographies updated by the database maintainers themselves.

NSF Network Service Center. Internet Resource Guide. NSF Network Service Center, Cambridge, MA. 1988 - Present.

FTP host:	`nnsc.nsf.net`
directory:	`resource-guide`
filenames:	`chapter2-ps.tar.Z` (compressed and archived PostScript version of Chapter 2)
	`chapter2.txt.tar.Z` (compressed and archived ASCII version of Chapter 2)

15.31.4. Bibliography of Commercial Online Databases

The following bibliography emphasizes commercial databases in several fields that are currently under-represented in freely available Internet databases: Law, K-12, Engineering, and Journalism. The Gale Research Company book is particularly comprehensive. Some of the databases described in these references may be available through your local institution or library.

Atkinson, S.D., and J. Hudson (eds.). *Women Online: Research in Women's Studies Using Online Databases.* New York: Haworth Press, 1990.

Aumente, J. *New Electronic Pathways: Videotex, Teletext, and Online Databases.* Newbury Park, CA: Sage Publications, 1987.

Bjelland, H. *Using Online Scientific and Engineering Databases.* Blue Ridge Summit, PA: Windcrest, 1992.

Chan, L.M., and. R. Pollard. *Thesauri Used in Online Databases: An Analytical Guide.* New York: Greenwood Press, 1988.

Gale Research Company. *Encyclopedia of Information Systems and Services.* Ann Arbor, Mich: Edwards Bros, 1971-1992.

Kinsock, J.E. *Legal Databases Online: LEXIS and WESTLAW.* Littleton, CO: Libraries Unlimited, 1985.

Koch, T. *Journalism for the 21st Century: Online Information, Electronic Databases, and the News.* New York: Greenwood Press, 1991.

Lathrop, A. (ed.). *Online and CD-ROM Databases in School Libraries: Readings.* Englewood, CO: Libraries Unlimited, 1989.

Parisi, L. and V.L. Jones. *Directory of Online Databases and CD-ROM Resources for High Schools.* Santa Barbara, CA: ABC-Clio, 1988.

Pfaffenberger, B. *Democratizing Information: Online Databases and the Rise of End-user Searching.* Boston, MA: G.K. Hall, 1990.

@ Section V @

Resource Discovery and Retrieval Tools

@ 16 @

Archie: The FTP Archive Guru

*Every cloud
has its silver
lining but it is
sometimes a little
difficult to get it to
the mint...*

Don Marquis
"certain maxims of archy,"
from *archy and mehitabel*

Once you've learned how to use FTP to obtain files from archives on the Internet, you're faced with some challenging tasks. How do you find out which FTP site has the file you're looking for? For that matter, how can you find the FTP site with the most up-to-date version of the file? Until recently, to keep track of such resources, you either had to be an FTP archive guru who stayed awake all night prowling through the Internet, or else be lucky enough to know one.

A program called "archie" is an anonymous FTP guru for everyone on the Internet, and is ready and able to help you find what you are looking for. Archie maintains a constantly updated catalog of many of the world's anonymous FTP archives. Currently, it keeps track of more than 2,000,000 files in about 1,200 FTP hosts totaling nearly 100 Gigabytes of information. So if you want to make the most of anonymous FTP, it's well worth your while to learn how to use this service.

16.1 How Does Archie Do It?

Each month, the archie program does an anonymous FTP to all sites contained in its master list. From each site, archie collects a complete directory listing of anonymous FTP holdings (using the recursive directory listing command, "ls-lR") and adds this information to the central archie database.

The part of archie you will use is designed to let you search through this master catalog of FTP files just like you might use a library catalog for a title word search.

Archie's search output includes the Internet domain name of the FTP host and the directory in which a file is located, the size of the file in bytes, and the date on which the file was placed in that FTP host. Once you've gotten this list of sources from archie, you can FTP to a site that has what you are looking for and copy the file to your own computer.

16.2. What Kinds of Questions Can Archie Answer?

Archie is currently designed to answer the following questions:

- Is there a file or directory with a certain name or a certain set of characters? This will be referred to as a "name search."

- What files are about <topic x>? This will be referred to as a "file description search."

- What FTP hosts are currently monitored by archie, where are they located, and what files does a particular FTP host contain? This will be referred to as a "site search."

16.2.1. Name Searches

The most common use of archie is to determine if there is a file or directory containing a particular set of characters in its name on an FTP host. Say you wanted to find a copy of the spiffy new shareware program called "gecko-graf". You could ask archie where in the world of anonymous FTP archives a file with the characters "gecko-graf" might be located.

16.2.2. File Description Searches

You can also search through archie's "Public Domain Software Description Database." This database contains descriptive information about the actual contents of some FTP'able files.

It's a good thing that archie is set up to perform file description searches. You'd be amazed at the obscurity of the names that some people give their programs, files, or directories. Just as a hypothetical example, you might think that a "Computer Aided Design" program would have the letters "CAD" somewhere in its name; but more often than you'd like, a CAD program might have a name like "TLZWYQXP.DTU". In such a case, you just have to hope that the author(s) of this program had the foresight to send a message to the archie folks saying that "TLZWWQXP" was a CAD program.

But be forewarned that only a small percentage of files from FTP hosts have been cataloged into the software description database. In general, file description searches will work best for retrieving information about RFCs, technical Internet documents, and Unix utilities.

16.2.3. Site Searches

Archie also allows you to get information about the FTP hosts which it monitors. You can even search for FTP hosts based on parts of their Internet addresses, so you could search for FTP hosts in a particular geographic region (e.g., FTP hosts in Sweden, whose addresses end with "se"), or you could request a copy of the catalog of files from a particular FTP host.

16.3. Using Archie

You can access archie in a number of ways: from client software installed on your local Internet host; by e-mail requests to remote archie servers; by a Telnet connection to a remote archie server; or by using Gopher (Chapter 17). More information about the first three access methods will be presented later in this chapter. But first, let's go over the basic commands that you'll need to your archie session.

16.3.1. Basic Archie Syntax

Name Searches: Prog

The basic archie search command for a name search is "prog <textstring>", where <textstring> is a set of characters you think would be in a file or directory you are seeking.

Before starting an archie search, you should specify what kind of search you want archie to do by issuing the "set search" command, followed by one of four options:

set search exact	Precise searches ("prog Pine" would find only files and directories named "Pine", not "pine.2.2.tar.Z", "Pineapples", or any other variant or extension.)
set search subcase	Case sensitive substring searches ("prog Pine" would find "Pine" and "Chicken.Pineapple", but not "pineapple.chicken.gumbo".)
set search sub	Case insensitive substring searches ("prog pine" would find anything with the string "pine", including "ALPINE.doc", "pursuit.of.happiness", and so forth.)
set search regex	Searches done with "regular expressions" (This is a very sophisticated technique that allows you to use wildcards, specify whether the string is at the beginning or end of the name, and many other nifty tricks. For a thorough description of regex, use "help regex".)

As a general rule, if you know the exact name of a file you're looking for, then use "set search exact". If you're on a fishing expedition, sub or regex may be most appropriate. For example, if you wanted to find information about the poet William Butler Yeats, you would probably want to do a case insensitive substring search.

```
set search sub
prog yeats
```

In response to this command, archie will present a list containing the names and locations of files and directories containing the string "yeats", regardless of case or the location of "yeats" in the name.

```
Search request for 'yeats'

Host ocf.berkeley.edu    (128.32.184.254)
Last updated 00:17  8 Nov 1992

Location: /pub/Library/Poetry
  FILE rw-rw-r--   702 Nov 8 1989 yeats.Lake_Isle_of_Innisfree
  FILE rw-rw-r--  1271 Nov 8 1989 yeats.Sailing_To_Byzantium
  FILE rw-rw-r--   542 Feb 2 1990 yeats.Sorrow_of_Love

Host ftp.uu.net    (137.39.1.9)
Last updated 06:27 30 Nov 1992

 Location: /doc/literary/obi
 DIRECTORY rwxr-xr-x  512 Jul 27 17:55 William.Butler.Yeats
```

These results from archie tell you the FTP host at which the information is located (e.g., "Host ocf.berkeley.edu"), the date when archie obtained this information (e.g., "Last Updated 00:17 8 Nov 1992"), the directory path in the FTP host (e.g., "/pub/Library/Poetry"), and the name of the file or directory containing the character string you have specified in your prog request (e.g., the file "yeats.Lake_Isle_of_Innisfree"). To get a copy of the poem, "To a Lake Isle of Innisfree," you would need to FTP to ocf.berkeley.edu. and cd to pub/Library/Poetry.

Note that this sample archie result also includes information about a directory whose name contains "yeats".

There are many other ways to tailor your archie name searches, some of which are described later in this chapter. Before using archie for real searches, be sure to use the "help" command and read the most current archie documentation.

File Description Searches: Whatis

Now let's examine a typical file description search. Just type "whatis" followed by any word. Let's try looking for calendar software:

```
whatis calendar

cal              Print calendar
cal-entries      Long list of entries for input to calendar
calen            Calendar program
calend-remind    A souped-up version of UNIX calendar(1)
calendar         Calendar program
calgen           Calendar generation program
do               A calendar-like utility
month            Visual calendar program
monthtool        Monthly apointment calendar, for Suns
pcal             Calendar program, 1 month per page
perpetual        The Last Perpetual Calendar
xcal             A calendar program (X11)
xcalendar        A personal schedule maintainer in X11
xdiary           X11 based calendar and diary
xkal             X11 appointment calendar
```

All lines in the PD Software Description Database containing the word "calendar" have been displayed. Notice that whatis does not tell where any one of these files are located, and not all of these descriptions indicate what operating system the files are for. So submit a prog search for the file of interest, say the "perpetual calendar." (A perpetual calendar would allow you to make a date book for March 1654, BC or AD, if you were so inclined.)

```
set search sub
prog perpetual
```

Site Searches

There are two main commands involved with site searches: "list" and "site".

The list command by itself will produce a list of all FTP hosts currently monitored by archie. You can also follow the list command with "regular expressions" using wildcards, anchors, and other useful features. For example, "list \.tw$" would display all FTP hosts in archie's catalog which end with ".tw", the top level domain for Taiwan. For more on how to use regular expressions, use "help regex".

The site command will give you a listing of all files known to archie from a particular FTP host. But this command should be used sparingly as an FTP host may have thousands or tens of thousands of files!

16.3.2. Locations of Archie Servers

Now that you understand the basic commands, you need to know how to access archie. Regardless of which access method you use, your questions will be handled by an archie server. Always try to use the server nearest you.

From North or South America, you should access one of the following servers:

`archie.ans.net`	(New York, USA)
`archie.rutgers.edu`	(New Jersey, USA)
`archie.sura.net`	(Maryland, USA)
`archie.unl.edu`	(Nebraska, USA)

From Eurasia or Africa, try:

`archie.doc.ic.ac.uk`	(United Kingdom)
`archie.funet.fi`	(Finland)

And from Australia, East Asia, New Zealand, Oceania (or Antarctica!) try:

`archie.au`	(Australia)
`archie.ncu.edu.tw`	(Taiwan)
`archie.nz`	(New Zealand)

16.3.3. Archie from a Local Client

The best way to use archie is from a locally installed archie client. Using a client is faster for you and puts less of a load on the archie servers. You'll be delighted to find that archie client software has been developed for most major operating systems.

There may already be client software installed on your Internet host. Ask your local computer support staff or check the online help. If there isn't an archie client installed at your Internet host, you are strongly encouraged to obtain the software by FTP from any of the archie servers, usually located in the directory "archie/clients" or "pub/archie/clients". You can also use the Telnet access method described below, and the welcome screen may provide instructions about where you can find client software via FTP.

16.3.4. Archie by E-mail

You can also access archie by e-mail. First time users are encouraged to request a help file with the following message:

```
mail:    archie@<an.archie.server.address>
subject: help
message: (none needed)
```

Asking for help is especially important because not all archie commands are available through the e-mail interface. When you access archie by e-mail, you can put archie search requests, one per line, in your message; archie can also read requests placed in the subject line. Note that commands in the message body must begin in the first column to be understood by archie. For example, sending the following e-mail message to an archie server will search for files or directories containing the characters "Yeats" and "Shelley" in their names, and the results will be sent to you in an e-mail message.

```
mail:    archie@<an.archie.server.address>
subject: set search sub
message:

prog Yeats
prog Shelley
```

16.3.5. Archie by Telnet

Finally, you can access archie via Telnet to the nearest archie server. Use the login name "archie". No password is required. You might see a short help screen giving some basic explanation on how to use the system, information about recent changes to archie, and an e-mail (e.g., archie-admin@archie.unl.edu) address for questions concerning the use of that particular archie server. If you are looking for archie client software, this screen may also tell you the location of a nearby FTP host from which it can be obtained.

You can get additional help about archie at any time during an archie session. Typing "help" will give you a list of help files and currently valid commands. To obtain help on a particular command on list, type "help" followed by the command name. For example, to get help on the "prog" command, type the following:

```
help prog
```

Now you're ready to do a name search for all materials in the archie file catalog. Let's look for any document containing the text string "medical" in its name, regardless of whether the name is upper case, lower case, or any mixture of upper and lower case. First set your search to "sub", and then type "prog medical".

```
set search sub
prog medical

# matches / % database searched:     18 / 36%
```

While archie is searching, it will display the percentage of the archie catalog it has searched and the number of occurrences of the string "medical" it has found in file or directory names. In this screenshot, archie has already found 18 matches after having searched through 36% of the catalog.

If a search seems to be taking a very long time or possibly resulting in many spurious occurrences or "hits," you can stop archie by pressing "control c". (Simultaneously press the control key, usually labeled "ctrl", and the "c" key.)

Once an archie search is done and displayed, it may take you awhile to determine which of the files from the search results you actually want to FTP. Or, you may need to think carefully about whether your search needs to be respecified, either by changing the search string or by setting a different search type. If you want to e-mail a copy of the results of this search back to your own Internet host so you can examine archie's output at your leisure, just type:

```
mail <you>@<your-internet-host>
```

This is an especially good idea since it means you can logout of archie as soon as you're done. Remember, like most Internet resources, archie can only serve a finite number of users at once! The more quickly and efficiently you use it, the more other people can use it too. Besides, by mailing search results to your computer account, you will now have a copy to refer to later without having to invoke archie again.

To end an archie Telnet session, simply type "quit".

Any search results you mailed during your Telnet session should arrive in your mailbox within a few minutes.

16.4. Customizing Archie Sessions with Set Commands

Depending upon how you access archie, you may be able to customize many aspects of your archie session by specifying certain variables with the "set" command.

autologout	The number of minutes archie will tolerate inactivity before it logs you out (Telnet access only)
mailto	E-mail address to which output should be automatically mailed
maxhits	Number of specified matches after which "prog" will stop its search (A maxhits value of 100 is often about right for most searches.)
pager	Display search results one page at a time ("unset pager" lets output scroll continuously.) (Telnet access only)
search	Specifies how "prog" searches the database (Options include "exact", "sub", "subcase", and "regex".)
sortby	Specifies how "prog" output is sorted (Options include "hostname", "time", "size", "filename", and "none" Each of these can be preceded by an "r" for reversal, such as "rtime" for reverse time.)
status	Display search progress, or don't display ("unset status") (Telnet access only)
term	Describes your terminal type, e.g., "vt100" (Telnet access only)

For example, to specify that archie should stop searching its catalog after finding 50 matches from one of your prog requests, you would enter "set maxhits 50" before issuing your prog request. For more information about these set variables, type "help set" or "help set <command>", where <command> is one of the commands listed above. To determine what your set variables are while using archie, type "show".

16.5. For More Information

Anything written about archie (or any other Internet resource) may be out-of-date a few days after it is written. When you telnet to archie and before you start your search, read the news messages that appear on your screen. The developers of archie may have implemented a new feature in their program that will make it even easier to use.

Best of all, archie may change in response to your suggestions. Once you've used archie, its developers would appreciate your feedback and comments so they can make archie even more useful. Send comments, bug reports, contributions to the database file, reports of anonymous FTP sites that archie doesn't seem to maintain, or even much deserved notes of appreciation to the following:

> `archie-updates@bunyip.com`

The archie program was written and is maintained by Alan Emtage and Bill Heelan. Ideas and inspiration were (and still are!) provided by Peter Deutsch.

16.5.1. Definitive Archie Documents

Definitive archie documentation can be gotten by FTP from most all archie servers:

FTP host:	`<any.archie.server>`
directories:	`pub/archie/doc` or `archie/doc`
filenames:	`archie.man.txt` (ASCII archie manual)
	`whatis.archie` (brief overview)
	(and many other files!)

16.5.2. Bibliography

Deutsch, P. and A. Emtage. "Archie: An Internet Electronic Directory Service."
ConneXions—The Interoperability Report. (Advanced Computing Environments, Mountain View, CA.) 6(2) (1992):2-9.

@ 17 @

Gopher and Veronica: The Internet on Your Desktop and Your Desktop on the Internet

Crossing the hall, they passed down one of the principal tunnels, and the waving light of the lantern gave glimpses on either side of rooms both large and small, some mere cupboards, others nearly as broad and as imposing as Toad's dining hall. A narrow passage at right angles led them into another corridor, and here the same thing was repeated. The Mole was staggered at the size, the extent, the ramifications of it all..."How on earth, Badger," he said at last, "did you ever find the time and strength to do all this? It's astonishing!"

Kenneth Grahame
The Wind in the Willows

With hundreds of thousands of connected computers and millions of users worldwide, the Internet presents challenges to Internet users looking for information and to the folks who provide the information.

The typical Internet user wonders, "How and where can I find the resources I need? How can I keep track of files whose names and locations are constantly changing? Why do I have to learn how to use so many kinds of services to answer even the simplest questions?"

Information providers struggle with the same kinds of questions, from a different, but complimentary perspective: "What's the most efficient way of ensuring that Internet users can locate our resources? What's the most appropriate vehicle for storing and distributing our information? If the Internet is based on standards, why does information need to be put into so many different formats and services?"

To meet the needs of both the average Internet user and Internet information providers, a team of inspired programmers at the University of Minnesota created "The Internet Gopher."

To the Internet user, Gopher is a very easy to use resource discovery tool. It provides a user friendly Internet front end for a large number of varied resources located throughout the Internet and presents them in a single directory system.

For the Internet information provider, Gopher is a powerful tool to present, organize, and distribute many services from a single platform. It provides a convenient method for "publishing" files or resources on the network.

The name "Gopher" is strikingly appropriate in several ways. Just as a real world Gopher knows how to get around its hidden burrows beneath the prairie, the Internet Gopher can tunnel through the invisible and twisty paths of the Internet and find the information you want. "Go-fer" is also American slang for someone who fetches things or provides services for other people. And by happy coincidence, the Golden Gopher is the school mascot of the University of Minnesota. (It's a good thing for the Internet that their mascot isn't one of the other characteristically Minnesotan animals, the mosquito or the lutefisk. :-)

17.1. What Do Gophers Have in Their Burrows?

Although Gopher was originally developed in April 1991 for use as a local campus wide information system (or "CWIS"), it has proven so powerful that there are already hundreds of "Gopher holes" throughout the world interconnected to form what is fondly referred to as "gopherspace."

What is in gopherspace? You name it!

RESOURCE TYPE	SPECIFIC EXAMPLES
Text and files:	Electronic books Archives of Usenet newsgroups, LISTSERV lists, and other mailing lists Files from FTP archives
Telnet resources:	Online library catalogs (OPACs) Directories of telephone numbers and e-mail addresses Campus wide information systems (CWIS)
Database searches:	Full-text searches of files stored in Gopher Searches of the archie FTP archive database WAIS
Miscellaneous:	Digitized sounds, graphics

Gopher allows you to see all of this information throughout the Internet as if it were in a single set of directories and menus on your computer. You don't need to know where the information is physically located or how to get there from here, because Gopher does most of the hard work for you behind the scenes. Furthermore, Gopher is intentionally designed to easily accommodate new kinds of resources and computers as they evolve, so expect this list to keep growing over the coming years.

Like no previous application, Gopher brings information from the Internet to your desktop—and it also allows you to put information from your desktop on the Internet!

17.2. Accessing Gopher

Gopher can be accessed in three main ways: from a local client installed on a personal computer, workstation, or mainframe; through CWISs or similar services; and by Telnet.

Regardless of how you access Gopher, it is a client-server application. Because the client and server software are separate, developers find that it's easy to change the appearance and features of the client without affecting the server software. Gopher client and server software for many Internet applications has been written for most major personal computer and mainframe operating systems.

In addition, Gopher uses what is called "stateless" communication. The client you use sends a single question to the server ("Could you please display the menu of campus directories?"), the server responds with the requested information, and the connection is closed. This happens almost instantaneously and is more economical and speedy than dedicated connections. A computer wrestling with a handful of simultaneous dedicated sessions in an hour might be able to support thousands of stateless requests in the same time period. This is good for you and for the overall productivity of the Internet.

17.2.1. Gopher via Client Software

Gopher client software may already be installed on your local computer system. If you are using a Unix, VMS, DOS, or VM/CMS computer, you may be able to type "Gopher" to launch this service. If you have access to X-windows services, try "xgopher". And if you're using a Mac or a NeXT, there may be a Gopher icon which you can double click and launch. Ask your computer support staff for help locating your local Gopher services.

If there are no Gophers at your site yet, Gopher client software is available via FTP.

FTP host:	`boombox.micro.umn.edu`
directory:	`pub/gopher`
filenames:	(many or all)

17.2.2. Gopher via Other Internet Front Ends

There are a number of other services which allow you to access Gopher, including many CWISs and World Wide Web. (See Chapters 19 and 20.)

17.2.3. Gopher via Telnet

If a Gopher client is not installed on your Internet host computer, you can try one of the following Internet accessible Gopher clients via Telnet:

Hostname	Login	Location
consultant.micro.umn.edu	gopher	Minnesota, USA
gopher.uiuc.edu	gopher	Illinois, USA
gopher.uwp.edu	gopher	Wisconsin, USA
panda.uiowa.edu	panda	Iowa, USA
info.anu.edu.au	info	Australia
gdunix.gd.chalmers.se	gopher	Sweden
tolten.puc.cl	gopher	Chile
ecnet.ec	gopher	Ecuador

Each of these sites is set up differently and has its own personality. In particular, Panda at the University of Iowa is a modified version of Gopher with different commands and a significantly different look and feel than standard Gopher clients.

17.3. Sample Gopher Session: Putting the Internet on Your Desktop

This sample session demonstrates the use of the text-only, Unix Curses client available to anyone using the Internet. The examples are based on the University of Minnesota client, but many of the files and menus shown here will be available on other Gophers as well, though their exact positions in the menus will be different.

Although you might initially learn how to use Gopher via Telnet, you really should consider installing and using Gopher client software on your local Internet host. You'll be richly rewarded in terms of speed, efficiency, and compliance with your normal operating system's features.

17.3.1. Accessing a Gopher Client

Either start a Gopher client from your host, or Telnet to one of the clients listed above. For example:

```
telnet consultant.micro.umn.edu
```

You will see a connection being established and then be asked to login (type "gopher") and to enter your terminal emulation (if in doubt, try vt100).

```
Trying...
Connected to hafnhaf.micro.umn.edu.
Escape character is '^]'.

Login as "gopher" to use the Gopher system

IBM AIX Version 3 for RISC System/6000
(C) Copyrights by IBM and by others 1982, 1991.
login: gopher
TERM = (vt100) vt100

Erase is Ctrl-H
Kill is Ctrl-U
Interrupt is Ctrl-C
I think you're on a vt100 terminal
```

17.3.2. Gopher Menus

Once you have entered a Gopher client, you'll see a list of menu options.

```
                    Root gopher server: gopher.micro.umn.edu

     -->    1. Information About Gopher/
            2. Computer Information/
            3. FTP Searches/
            4. Fun & Games/
            5. Libraries/
            6. Mailing Lists/
            7. News/
            8. Other Gopher and Information Servers/
            9. Phone Books/
            10. Search lots of places at the U of M <?>
            11. UofM Campus Information/


   Press ? for Help, q to Quit, u to go up a menu      Page: 1/1
```

Notice that although you are logged in to a Gopher client, the information, including directory menus, is stored on the "root gopher server" named at the top; in this case, it's "gopher.micro.umn.edu."

The Pointer

The numbered list in the middle of the page is the root directory of files and services offered by this Gopher client. The "--->" in the left column is called the pointer, and indicates which item would be selected if you pressed the return key.

The Command Line

The bottom of a Gopher screen will usually show a few available commands. The specific commands displayed will change depending upon where you are in the they type of screen being displayed. The "1/1" at the far right of this line indicates that this is the first page of a menu which has only 1 page.

Types of Gopher Menu Items

At the end of each menu item is a symbol that tells you what sort of information or service you'll get when you select that line. Here are the primary supported Gopher services and the symbols that appear in a Gopher menu:

.   a text file

/   a directory

?   a searchable index which will prompt you for a keyword when selected (Gopher will do a "full text" search—every word in every document is treated as a keyword—of the documents linked to the index and a list of retrieved documents will be shown on your screen.)

<tel>   an item that automatically launches a Telnet (or tn3270) session to the indicated resource

<CSO>   a directory search service which displays names, phone numbers, e-mail, and physical addresses

<Bin>   a file which is in binary code (You cannot actually retrieve or view these documents while in Gopher.)

<)   a digitized sound (Not all clients can handle this sort of information. The symbol, "<)", is meant to look like a speaker.)

17.3.3. Asking Gopher for Help

You can usually type "?" to request a display of Gopher client commands. Here are the basic commands for getting around in a Gopher server menu and selecting items in a menu.

```
The following commands are available in the browsing mode.

<Return> or <Right>   View current item
0-9                   Move to a line #
k, ctl-p,or <Up>      Move pointer up
j, ctl-n, or <Down>   Move pointer down
u, or <Left>          Go up a level
m                     Go to the first screen
q                     Exit Internet Gopher
>                     Next Page
<                     Previous Page
=                     Display Tech. info. about current item
o                     change options
?                     This help screen

(followed by a brief definition of Gopher menu items...)

Press <RETURN> to continue, <m> mail, <s> save, <p> print
```

<Right>, <Left>, <Up>, and <Down> refer to the arrow keys which you may have on your keyboard.

Because this help file is a document, the command line at the bottom now displays commands for document handling. If you press the "m" key, you will be asked for your e-mail address and the Gopher server will send the document to you by e-mail. The "s" and "p" commands are only available if you are using a client installed on your local Internet host. To leave this or any other Gopher document, simply press the return key and your screen will return to the directory from which you came.

17.3.4. Moving Around within a Menu

Once you have pressed the return key, you should be back in the main menu. Try moving the pointer up and down the menu by using the pointer movement keys described in the help file. You may find that some don't work from your terminal. You can also type the number of a menu item (it will appear on the command line), press return, and the pointer will jump to that item.

17.3.5. Selecting a Directory

Well, now we're ready to do some browsing through the Gopher hole. The first step is to learn how to select a directory. All you have to do is move the pointer to a menu item and press the return key. Let's try the "News" directory.

```
             Internet Gopher Information Client v1.00

                          Root Directory

          1.  Information About Gopher/
          2.  Computer Information/
          3.  FTP Searches/
          4.  Fun & Games/
          5.  Libraries/
          6.  Mailing Lists/
   -->    7.  News/
          8.  Other Gopher and Information Servers/
          9.  Phone Books/
          10. Search lots of places at the U of M  <?>
          11. University of Minnesota Campus Information/

 Press ? for Help, q to Quit, u to go up          Page: 1/1
```

17.3.6. Selecting and Viewing Documents

The News directory contains university newspapers, Usenet news, UPI news (not accessible to remote users), weather forecasts for the U.S. and Canada, and—*EARTHQUAKES!*?? (Maybe Minnesota has shaken up the Internet by developing Gopher, but it's not known as a hotbed of earthquake activity.) This item ends with a period, so it's a document. What the heck, let's select "4" and find out what this is all about.

```
┌──────────────────────────────────────────────────────────────────┐
│              Internet Gopher Information Client v1.00               │
│                                                                    │
│                               News                                 │
│                                                                    │
│           1. Daily Texan (University of Texas, Austin)/            │
│           2. Minnesota Daily/                                      │
│           3. National Weather Service Forecasts/                   │
│      --->  4. Recent Earthquakes.                                  │
│           5. SOUND, News and Arts Newspaper (Omaha Nebraska)/      │
│           6. Technolog (Institute of Technology, U. of Minn/       │
│           7. UPI News/                                             │
│           8. USENET News (from Michigan State)/                    │
│                                                                    │
│      Press ? for Help, q to Quit, u to go up          Page: 1/1    │
└──────────────────────────────────────────────────────────────────┘
```

When you select this item, the Gopher client retrieves the information from a remote computer; but this happens behind the scenes, and all you see is a document that has been retrieved. No muss, no fuss. (If your screen displays the same text as shown below, you've slipped into a time warp. Consult a local sci-fi writer for help.)

```
┌──────────────────────────────────────────────────────────────────┐
│ Recent events reported by the USGS Nat'l Earthquake Info. Center   │
│                                                                    │
│  DATE-TIME (UT)   LAT    LON    DEP   MAG        LOCATION AREA      │
│  92/08/09 19:49   4.0N  126.6E   33   5.7    TALAUD IS., INDONESIA  │
│  92/08/10 06:09  11.3N   87.2W   33   5.4    NR. COAST OF NICARAGUA │
│  92/08/11 15:14  32.8N  141.8E   33   6.2    S. OF HONSHU, JAPAN    │
│  92/08/12 06:36  32.4N  142.1E   70   5.6    S. OF HONSHU, JAPAN    │
│  92/08/13 20:43   5.8S  149.3E   50   5.9    NEW BRITAIN, P.N.G.    │
│                                                                    │
│ Recent earthquakes in the Northwest located by U. Wash.(Mag > 2.0) │
│                                                                    │
│ DATE-TIME (UT)  LAT(N) LON(W)   DEP  MAG N-STA                     │
│                                                                    │
│ 92/07/29 01:43  47.01  122.00  14.5  2.0  35   20 km    S Enumclaw │
│ 92/07/30 05:10  46.58  120.48   8.5  2.6  33    1 km    E Yakima   │
│ 92/07/31 10:23  48.73  121.78  16.3  2.1   6    4 km  SSE Mt Baker │
│ 92/08/04 07:26  48.83  119.48   0.0  2.1   8   53 km    N Okanogan │
│ 92/08/06 08:00  46.00  118.40   0.0  2.8  19    9 km   SW Walla Walla│
│ 92/08/07 17:23  45.85  119.58   0.6  3.9  29   40 km  SSE Prosser  │
│                                                                    │
│ Press <RETURN> to continue, <m> to mail, <s> to save, <p> to print:│
└──────────────────────────────────────────────────────────────────┘
```

Well, no quakes reported from Minnesota, but there is information about earthquakes here in Washington, NorthWestNet's home office state—six in a two day period! Back at the News menu (if you aren't there already, hit return), pressing "=" next to the earthquakes item reveals that in fact the remote server from which Gopher obtained this information is "geophys.washington.edu," a computer about a mile from my house. I hadn't planned to retrieve information from a local computer host through a Gopher server halfway across the continent, but that's part of the beauty of the Gopher system.

17.3.7. Launching Telnet Sessions from Gopher

Gopher also serves as a launching pad to Telnet accessible services throughout the world. Here is a typical directory, the first of three pages of library catalogs.

```
              Internet Gopher Information Client v1.00

                      Library Catalogs via Telnet

      --->  1. Advanced Tech. Info. Network CSU Fresno <TEL>
            2. Air Force Institute of Technology <TEL>
            3. Arizona State University <TEL>
            4. Athabasca University <TEL>
            5. Australian Defence Force Academy <TEL>

               (etc.)

  Press ? for Help, q to Quit, u to go up           Page: 1/3
```

As usual, you should move the pointer to the service you want and press the return key. You will see a screen that may contain useful instructions for accessing and quitting the remote Telnet service you have selected.

```
        Warning!!!!!, you are about to leave the Internet
          Gopher program and connect to another host.
      If you get stuck press the control key and the ] key,
                     and then type quit

        Now connecting to <the service you requested>

      (Gopher will often display required login information,
      such as userid, password, and preferred terminal types)

                   Press return to connect:
```

Now that you've read what access codes are needed to use the service you've requested, press the return key, and you will see the entry screen for that service.

You may be prompted for access information, so enter the information that Gopher has so thoughtfully supplied in the previous screen. During this session, you will be using commands native to the Telnet service.

When you finally return to the Gopher from which you started, you will recognize the directory as the one where you began.

17.3.8. Searchable Databases

Note that "?" has two meanings on a Gopher screen: as a line command for getting help (?), and as a symbol at the end of a menu item indicating that it is a searchable database (<?>).

Most information stored in Gopher databases is indexed using a program called gindex. This index is accessible by search engines such as WAIS and NeXT Librarian.

Gopher also supports WAIS and archie database searches of non-gindexed materials at remote hosts, but if you plan to use those services a great deal, direct access is sometimes preferable to going through Gopher. (See chapters 16 and 18 for more on archie and WAIS.)

Similarly, you can access Usenet newsgroups through Gopher. However, you will find it more efficient to use a Usenet news reader.

Before you start a search, you should understand what sorts of information are contained in the index you are using. To help you out, many directories with searchable indexes will contain an informative file, usually with a name like "About <topic>" or something similar. Read these files so you can make the most effective use of the particular search index.

When you select a menu item ending with <?>, you will be prompted for the word(s) for which you want to search, and Gopher will send a search request to the server where the indexed materials are stored. I've selected the "Search Electronic Books" index, located in the Libraries directory from the root directory, and have entered "emancipation proclamation" as the index words.

```
           Internet Gopher Information Client v1.00

                      Electronic Books

       1. By Author/
       2. By Call Letter/
       3. By Title/
  -->  4. Search Electronic Books (new) <?>

Index word(s) to search for: emancipation proclamation
```

Gopher will then retrieve files containing these words in their titles or text, and you can retrieve Abraham Lincoln's "Proclamation of Emancipation" by pressing the return key.

```
+----------------------------------------------------------------+
|              Internet Gopher Information Client v1.00           |
|                                                                |
|     Search Electronic Books (new): emancipation proclamation   |
|                                                                |
|   --> 1. emancipation /Gutenberg/Histdocs/.                    |
|       2. emancipation /Gutenberg/Histdocs/.cap/.               |
|       3. first-thanksgiving-proclamation/Gutenberg/Histdocs/.  |
|       4. proclamation-of-neutrality /Gutenberg/Histdocs/.      |
|                                                                |
|          . . .                                                 |
|                                                                |
|      18. The Vain JackDaw  /Gutenberg/aesop/.                  |
|                                                                |
| Press ? for Help, q to Quit, u to go up a menu    Page: 1/3    |
+----------------------------------------------------------------+
```

17.3.9. Searching <CSO> Directories ("Phone Books")

A growing number of campus directory services are accessible through Gopher. Here's a typical menu of directory selections.

```
+----------------------------------------------------------------+
|              Internet Gopher Information Client v1.00           |
|                                                                |
|                         Phone Books                            |
|                                                                |
|     1. Internet-wide e-mail address searches/                  |
|     2. University of Arizona <CSO>                             |
|     3. WHOIS Searches/                                         |
|     4. University of Minnesota (maintained by AIS) <CSO>       |
|     5. Brown University <CSO>                                  |
|     6. University of Utah <CSO>                                |
|                                                                |
|         (etc.)                                                 |
|                                                                |
| Press ? for Help, q to Quit, u to go up        Page: 1/2      |
+----------------------------------------------------------------+
```

After selecting the phone book of your choice, you will be presented with the following screen:

```
┌──────────────────────────────────────────────────────────────────┐
│            Internet Gopher Information Client v1.00                │
│                                                                    │
│                     University of Arizona                          │
│                                                                    │
│      1.  Name    :                                                 │
│      2.  Phone   :                                                 │
│      3.  E-Mail  :                                                 │
│      4.  Address :                                                 │
│                                                                    │
│                                                                    │
│    Press 1-4 to change field, Return to accept and continue        │
│                                                                    │
│    Press ? for Help, q to Quit, u to go up    <RETURN> to exit     │
│                                                                    │
└──────────────────────────────────────────────────────────────────┘
```

Typically, you would type "1", enter the person's name, press return twice, and then see a listing of contact information for people with that name at the site whose directory you have selected. You can also search for information by providing a phone number or e-mail address.

17.4. Field Guide to the Gophers of the World

From the main menu of most Gopher servers, you have the option of locating "Other Gopher and Information Servers."

```
┌──────────────────────────────────────────────────────────────────┐
│            Internet Gopher Information Client v1.00                │
│                                                                    │
│              Other Gopher and Information Servers                  │
│                                                                    │
│    -->       1. All the Gopher Servers in the World/              │
│              2. Europe/                                            │
│              3. Middle East/                                       │
│              4. North America/                                     │
│              5. Pacific/                                           │
│              6. Terminal Based Information/                        │
│              7. WAIS Based Information/                            │
│                                                                    │
│  Press ? for Help, q to Quit, u to go up          Page: 1/1       │
└──────────────────────────────────────────────────────────────────┘
```

Selecting "1" from the menu above retrieves a directory of Gopher servers throughout the world. Now your gopherspace travels can take you to Gopher clients in the United Kingdom, Australia, Switzerland—and maybe even your own backyard!

```
           Internet Gopher Information Client v1.00

              All the Gopher Servers in the World

   -->   1. Appalachian State University (experimental gopher)
         2. Arabidopsis Res. Companion Mass Gen. Hosp./Harvard
         3. Aston University, UK/
         4. Australian Defence Force Acad. (Canberra Australia
         5. Australian National University/
         6. BIOFTP EMBnet Switzerland/
         7. CICNET gopher server (under construction)/
         8. CONCERT Network - Research Triangle Park, NC, USA/
         9. Carnegie Mellon Univ. AC&M Gopher (Experimental)
        10. Centre for Scientific Computing (Finland)/
        11. Chalmers University of Technology, Sweden/
        12. Cleveland State University Law Library Gopher/
        13. Columbia University Experimental Gopher/
        14. Cornell Info. Techologies Gopher (experimental)/
        15. Cornell Law School (experimental)/
        16. Electromagnetic Wave Res. Inst. (Florence Italy)/
        17. Georgia Tech Gopher (experimental)/

 Press ? for Help, q to Quit, u to go up               Page: 1/7
```

This seven page listing only shows the main burrows of gopherspace. Each of these servers may be representing many other Gopher servers at that site, each of which is maintained by information providers who have used the Gopher protocol to put their desktops on the Internet. Again, the beauty of the Gopher protocol is that you don't need to know where the servers are to use them.

17.5. Veronica: Searching through Gopherspace

Now that you've had a chance to work with Gopher a bit, you may be wondering, "where's the catalog?" How do you figure out where in gopherspace a particular kind of resource might be hiding? Well, just like archie serves as a catalog for the names of files in anonymous FTP hosts, a new service called "veronica" is for searching through the names of items in the menus of gopherspace.

Veronica is used from within Gopher, so you don't need to learn another set of commands or a strange new interface. In addition, veronica presents the results of its search in the form of a Gopher menu, so you can immediately examine files, work with searchable indexes, and dive into menus, using whatever Gopher software you know and love.

So what does the name veronica mean? Well, yes, it's true, a character named Veronica is a buddy of the comic strip character Archie, but like almost everything on the Internet, the name is also an acronym. Are you ready? It stands for "Very Easy Rodent Oriented Netwide Index to Computerized Archives." Remembering this full name is about the only difficult aspect of using this service!

17.5.1. Working with Veronica

From most Gopher servers, you can currently get to veronica through one of the main directories, for example "All the Gophers in the World" or "Other Gopher and Information Servers." Once you reach a menu in which veronica is available, you might see a screen like the following:

```
            Internet Gopher Information Client v1.03

                     Other Gopher Servers

   -->  1.   Search Gopherspace using veronica/
        2.   ACM SIGGRAPH/
        3.   Appalachian State University (experimental gopher)/
        4.   Apple Computer Higher Education gopher server/


             . . .

   Press ? for Help, q to Quit, u to go up a menu     Page: 1/15
```

Select veronica, and you will see one or more Gopher searchable database prompts:

```
            Internet Gopher Information Client v1.03

                 Search Gopherspace using veronica

   1. About veronica.
   2. Experimental Reduced-redundancy veronica Search  <?>
   3. Search many Internet gopher menus by SINGLE keyword <?>
   4. Proposals for veronica Development.

   Press ? for Help, q to Quit, u to go up a menu     Page: 1/1
```

Simply select the search index you want and enter a keyword. In a short while, veronica will return a Gopher menu containing items from its catalog of Gopher servers. Your search may potentially retrieve any sort of Gopher resource. Enjoy!

17.5.2. Veronica's (Current) Limitations

As wonderful as veronica is, this service currently has a number of limitations of which you should be aware. Some of these problems are likely to be addressed in the near future, while others may simply be limitations imposed by the nature of gopherspace.

To illustrate, let's go through a search that seems tailor made for veronica. Let's look for all Gopher menu items containing the word "music". Veronica returns the following Gopher menu:

```
            Internet Gopher Information Client v1.03

    Search many Internet gopher menus by single keyword : music

-->    1.  Music/
       2.  The Latest: Grad House Hosts Music Festival.
       3.  MUSIC.
       4.  MUSIC.
       5.  MUSIC.
       6.  MUSIC.
       7.  MUSIC.
       8.  MUSIC.
       9.  MUSIC.
      10.  Music.
      11.  The Ideology of Postmodern Music and Left Politics
      12.  Computer-Assisted Instruction for Music Uniform...
      13.  Music/
      14.  List of Scholarly Elect Conf (Library and Infor...
      15.  Music/
      16.  rec.music.early.src <?>
      17.  indian-classical-music.src <?>
      18.  Archivos de Musica (cs.uwp.edu)/

    Press ? for Help, q to Quit, u to go up a menu      Page: 1/46
```

At first blush, this seems like a mighty haul indeed! Forty six pages of Gopher menus, containing more than 800 items, many of which are themselves directories containing even more items. But as you may recall, Gopher was developed (and is currently widely used) as a CWIS. Consequently, it should come as no surprise that a great deal of this haul is material which is only of interest to folks at a particular institution or even a small department.

So, of these 815 items, more than 500 are descriptions of music courses given at a number of universities. Entries such as "music999: Hegelian Phenomonology of the Oud," listing the time and room number for a course, are probably not what a person doing a search for music wanted.

Well, this still leaves about 300 items. Many are either obvious duplications from multiple Gopher holes (like the 18 entries for the WAIS database "indian-classical-music.src"), or multiple copies of files with different names which, in this case, reduces the number of unique resources to about 150. The veronica developers are currently wrestling with methods to reduce this redundancy.

The next cut is the large number of items that are of interest only to a local community or are outdated announcements. You probably don't want to read that the first floor of Scarab Hall at Coleoptera College will be hosting a Beatles tribute—oops—make that *hosted* a Beatles tribute, last October.

So now that we've separated the wheat from the various sorts of chaff, there are maybe 50 to 100 generally interesting resources in veronica's music menu. Compared to the initial haul of 815, this may not seem like much. But lest we forget, it might take days of crawling through gopherspace to pull out what veronica has found in about a minute.

17.5.3. "Veronica, Where in Gopherspace ARE We??"

One of the values of veronica is that it allows a view of gopherspace by keyword rather than by Gopher server. But suppose there is a particularly rich cluster of Gopher resources in a veronica search result, yet neither the titles nor the contents of the Gopher menu items give clues as to where a particular resource is actually located. After all, you might want to explore the Gopher hole from which those materials came, step-by-step and directory by directory.

To determine where in gopherspace a particular Gopher item is located, use the "=" command. This will display technical information about a Gopher menu item. (Note that this is a Gopher command that you can use for any item on any Gopher menu.) For example, where is the "School of Music" whose Gopher directory is shown in the display below?

```
           Internet Gopher Information Client v1.03

    Search many Internet gopher menus by single keyword : music

        145. Higbie, C., Measure and Music: (Harry C. Barnes).
        146. indian-classical-music.src <?>
--->    147. School of Music/
        148. MUJ Music Jazz Studies /
        149. MUP Music Performance
```

Simply type "=" and you'll find out:

```
Name=School of Music
Type=1
Port=70
Path=1/UofO/Time Schedules/spring92/Music
Host=pith.uoregon.edu
```

Well, "pith.uoregon.edu" is most likely located at the University of Oregon. (Although, as you are probably aware by now, it's not always so easy to figure out an institution's name on the basis of a domain name.) So, in this case, you could select the University of Oregon Gopher from the list of Gophers in the server of your choice or install this technical information into your client software.

17.6. Putting Your Desktop on the Internet

Gopher is an extraordinary tool for information providers: you can put a wide variety of information into a Gopher hole, it's easy to advertise your service to all the other Gophers in the world, and users will be able to access your information from a service providing document retrieval, text searches, Telnet sessions, and more.

The technical details of setting up a Gopher server are beyond the scope of *The Internet Passport*, but here's some general information to help you get started and a few things to keep in mind if you decide to burrow your own Gopher hole.

17.6.1. Getting the Software

Gopher client and server software has been written for a wide variety of operating systems. You can obtain this software for free by FTP from the University of Minnesota and other sites.

FTP host:	`boombox.micro.umn.edu`
directories:	`pub/gopher/Mac-server`
	`pub/gopher/Macintosh-TurboGopher`
	`pub/gopher/NeXT`
	`pub/gopher/PC-client`
	`pub/gopher/PC-server`
	`pub/gopher/Rice_CMS`
	`pub/gopher/Unix`
	`pub/gopher/VMS`
	`pub/gopher/VieGOPHER`
	`pub/gopher/gopher_protocal`
	`pub/gopher/incoming`
	`pub/gopher/mvs`
	`pub/gopher/os2`

17.6.2. How to Care For and Feed Your Gopher

If you choose to start a Gopher server, keep the following points in mind.

Gophers are Highly Social

While a solitary server is useful, you can take full advantage of the Gopher world by letting other users know about your services. Register your server by sending an e-mail message to gopher@boombox.micro.umn.edu.

Gophers Have Ravenous Appetites

A growing number of people are using Gopher to store and retrieve the information they would like to share with other users locally or globally. Because Gopher sets up pointers to remote resources rather than storing the information on your own computer, you can construct menu structures that make sense to you and your users without having to worry about running out of disk space.

Gophers Are Playful

The Gopher protocol is still young and very flexible, and the original authors of Gopher encourage experimentation with and customization of the client software. Many new and exciting applications are being developed by users throughout the world: for example, the "Gopher in A Forest" client developed for the NeXT computers allows the clients, the servers, and directories of gopherspace to be displayed graphically. Such a visual image of the service is useful—and engaging! Experiment with putting novel services on your client, modify the software to work with different operating systems, and in general, feel free to be creative.

17.7. For More Information

Although Gopher has only been in existence since April, 1991, it is already a major Internet service. The diversity of resources which will be added to Gopher and the number of Gopher servers and clients in the world is likely to keep growing. In the week that this chapter was written, an extension of Gopher called Gopher+ has just been released and it promises to provide further extensions to the already remarkably useful Gopher protocol.

17.7.1. From Gopher

If you already have access to Gopher, you can get a great deal of information from within Gopher itself.

1) Most Gopher servers include a directory called "Information About Gopher" in the root directory. This should be your first stop.

2) As an exercise in exploring Gopher and veronica, you might want to see how much of the following reference material you can get from within gopherspace!

17.7.2. Usenet Newsgroup

If you want to keep up with the latest breaking news about Gopher via Usenet, read the following newsgroup:

```
comp.infosystems.gopher
```

17.7.3. Internet Mailing List

To keep track of the evolution of Gopher, you can subscribe to the "gopher-news" mailing list by sending an e-mail subscription request to gopher-news-request@boombox.micro.umn.edu.

17.7.4. FTP Archive

Software for Gopher clients, servers, and some associated documentation can be found in the following FTP archive:

FTP host:	**boombox.micro.umn.edu**
directory:	**pub/gopher**
filenames:	(many or all)

17.7.5. Bibliography

"The Internet Gopher." *ConneXions*, July 1992.

"Exploring Internet Gopher Space." *The Internet Society News* 1(2) (1992).

"The Internet Gopher Protocol." *Proceedings of the Twenty-Third IETF, CNRI*, Section 5.3.

"Internet Gopher." *Proceedings of Canadian Networking '92.*

"Tools Help Internet Users Discover Online Treasures." *Computerworld*, July 20, 1992.

@ 18 @

WAIS (Wide Area Information Server): Easy Access to Internet Databases

Surround yourself with auxiliary wits... It is a singular greatness to use wise people: better than the barbaric taste of Tigranes, who wanted to enslave the kings he conquered. This is a new way of mastering...choose a subject, and let those around you serve quintessential knowledge. If you can't make knowledge your servant, make it your friend.

Baltasar Gracian
Oracula Manual y Arte de Prudencia (15)

The Internet contains a vast amount of information stored in many different formats on computers with many different operating systems. To provide a single port of entry for searching diverse and large databases from a single, easy to use interface, a group of researchers have developed an innovative system called WAIS (the Wide Area Information Server). Although WAIS is used for accessing traditional databases, it is also adept at handling complex textual information, so in some ways it's more like an electronic librarian than a database service. Examples of materials currently accessible through WAIS include the following:

- books
- bibliographies
- network addresses
- traditional databases
- archie databases
- software catalogs
- library catalogs
- Internet information, such as lists of lists of Internet services
- archives of Usenet newsgroups, LISTSERV lists, and mailing lists

18.1. How WAIS Works

WAIS is based on the client-server model. You use a WAIS client that retrieves information from WAIS servers that may be located anywhere on the Internet. After selecting one or more databases (known as "sources" in the WAIS world) from the displayed list, you simply enter one or more keywords. Behind the scenes, WAIS makes connections to the remote servers where the information is actually stored. Materials containing your keywords are returned to your WAIS client and displayed on your screen.

Each retrieved document is assigned a score, ranging from 0 to 1000, for how well the document corresponds to what you want to find, with 1000 being deemed a perfect fit. The score is based on the frequency of the keywords within a document.

Like all information retrieval tools, how well WAIS works for you is largely a function of how well you specify your search. Unlike other database tools with which you may be familiar, WAIS features a novel technique called "relevance feedback." You can select retrieved documents that closely match what you want and these texts will be used by WAIS as keyword sources for further searches.

One of the many exciting possibilities opened up by WAIS and related information servers is that you can create a personal electronic newspaper. You can have WAIS automatically pull all items of interest together into a single document monthly, weekly, or even daily.

18.2. Accessing WAIS

18.2.1. WAIS Client Software

Because WAIS is a client-server application, it is best to use a locally installed WAIS client if you can. There are versions of WAIS available for the Mac, Unix computers, X-window terminals, and VMS. Ask your computer support staff if a local client is available.

If a local WAIS client is not yet installed, WAIS software can be obtained by anonymous FTP from one of the following sites:

FTP host:	`ftp.cnidr.org`
directory:	`wais`
filenames:	(many or all)
FTP host:	`sunsite.unc.edu`
directory:	`pub/wais`
filenames:	(many or all)

18.2.2. Gopher, W3, and CWISs

WAIS is easily accessed from a number of Internet information mediators, including Gopher, World Wide Web (W3), and many CWISs. For more information on using these other services, please refer to Chapters 17, 20, and 19 respectively.

18.2.3. Telnet

You can use Telnet to directly access these WAIS clients which use Simple WAIS, or SWAIS, a basic text-only client available to anyone on the Internet.

`hub.nnsc.nsf.net`	(login as "wais")
`kudzu.cnidr.org`	(login as "wais")
`quake.think.com`	(login as "wais")
`sunsite.unc.edu`	(login as "swais")

18.3. Sample WAIS Session Using SWAIS

Even if you have access to WAIS via a local client or a Gopher, you are encouraged to work through this SWAIS example just to get a basic overview of how WAIS works. But once you have a grasp of the basic concepts, you will find the use of local client versions of WAIS to be much more powerful and satisfying.

18.3.1. Logging in to SWAIS

To get started with SWAIS, just telnet to quake.think.com or hub.nnsc.nsf.net.

```
telnet quake.think.com
```

You will then be asked for a login name (enter "wais"), your e-mail address, and your terminal type. If you are unsure of the latter, try vt100.

```
login: wais

Welcome to swais.
Please type user identifier (user@host): <you>@<your.internet.host>

TERM = (vt100) vt100
```

18.3.2. The Menu of WAIS Sources

In a short while, you should see a menu of WAIS databases, usually referred to as the sources.

```
SWAIS                     Source Selection              Sources: 285

   #           Server              Source                      Cost

001: [              archie.au] aarnet-resource-guide          Free
002: [weeds.mgh.harvard.ed] AAtDB                              Free
003: [      archive.orst.edu] aeronautics                      Free
004: [ bloat.media.mit.edu] Aesop-Fables                       Free
005: [nostromo.oes.orst.ed] agricultural-market-news           Free
006: [      archive.orst.edu] alt.drugs                        Free
007: [      wais.oit.unc.edu] alt.gopher                       Free
008: [sun-wais.oit.unc.edu] alt.sys.sun                        Free
009: [      wais.oit.unc.edu] alt.wais                         Free
010: [         150.203.76.2] ANU-Aboriginal-Studies    $00.00/minute
011: [      coombs.anu.edu.au] ANU-Asian-Religions      $00.00/minute
012: [         150.203.76.2] ANU-Pacific-Linguistics    $00.00/minute
013: [      coombs.anu.edu.au] ANU-Pacific-Manuscripts          Free
014: [      coombs.anu.edu.au] ANU-SocSci-Netlore       $00.00/minute
015: [         150.203.76.2] ANU-SSDA-Catalogues        $00.00/minute
016: [      coombs.anu.edu.au] ANU-Thai-Yunnan                  Free
017: [      quake.think.com] Applications-Navigator            Free
018: [         132.183.190.21] Arabidopsis-BioSci              Free

Keywords:

<space> selects, w for keywords, arrows move, <return> searches
q quits, or ?
```

The column labeled "#" is a line number for the source; "server" is the Internet address of the server where the database is actually located; "source" is a brief description of the contents of the database; and "cost" is the cost to the user. (Currently, all databases in SWAIS are free.) In the upper right hand corner, "sources: 285" indicates that there are 285 sources known to this particular SWAIS client.

Source #1 should appear highlighted in some way on your screen. This indicates where your source selector is currently located.

At the bottom of most SWAIS screens, you will see a small selection of commands that you can use. To get started, let's use the "?" command.

18.3.3. Commands for Working with SWAIS Menus

After you've pressed the "?" key, you should see a list of commands that can be used with SWAIS to work with source menus. Notice that you've got several options for moving around within the menu of sources. So if your arrow keys don't work from your terminal, you can use letter commands, or you can type in a source's number. Just below we display the help file for menu commands, slightly edited to make it clearer:

```
SWAIS                    Source Selection Help              Page: 1



        1. Moving Around in the Source Menu

j, down arrow, ^N       Move Down one source
k, up arrow, ^P         Move Up one source
J, ^V, ^D               Move Down one screen
K, <esc> v, ^U          Move Up one screen
###                     Position to source number ###
/sss                    Search for source sss

        2. Selecting, Unselecting, and Getting Info About Sources

<space>, <period>       Select current source
=                       Deselect all sources
v, <comma>              View current source info

        3. Searching Sources

s                       Select new sources (refresh sources list)
w                       Select new keywords
<ret>                   Perform search

X, -                    Remove current source permanently
o                       Set and show swais options
h, ?                    Show this help display
H                       Get brief information about WAIS
q                       Leave WAIS
```

Press any key, and you will be back at the first page of the source menu.

18.3.4. Moving Around in the Source Menu

Now that you are back at the source menu, try the various commands for moving around in a menu that are listed in section 1 of the previous display. Find out which keys work (up and down arrow keys don't work from all terminal types) or are easiest for you to remember.

18.3.5. Selecting a Source

Now that you know how to move around in the menu, you're ready for the next steps: selecting and then searching a source.

Let's proceed by selecting and searching the ERIC (Educational Resources Information Center) Digests database which contains short reports of interest to educators. To get to this source you can move through the menu with the commands you've just learned, or you can press the "/" key, and then type "eric". This searches through the source names and puts the selector right on a source containing this word.

The part of the menu containing the ERIC sources should now be on your screen, and the line "ERIC archive" should be highlighted. If not, use your movement keys until it is highlighted.

```
110:   [        nic.sura.net]  ERIC-archive              Free
111:   [sun-wais.oit.unc.edu]  eric-digest               Free
112:   [        140.174.7.1]   fidonet-nodelist          Free
```

To select this source, type "." or press the space bar. You should now see an asterisk in front of the number indicating that this source has been selected and is ready to be searched. (Note that you can select as many sources as you want for a keyword search. For this search, you might want to select the eric-digest as well.)

```
110: * [        nic.sura.net]  ERIC-archive              Free
111:   [sun-wais.oit.unc.edu]  eric-digest               Free
112:   [        140.174.7.1]   fidonet-nodelist          Free
```

18.3.6. Searching Selected Sources

Keywords

To search a selected source, type "w", which stands for "keyword." Your cursor will appear in front of the "Keywords:" prompt. Since reform is a perennial topic in education, let's see what the ERIC database has to say on this topic. Type the word "reform" and press return.

```
110: * [        nic.sura.net]  ERIC-archive               Free
111:    [sun-wais.oit.unc.edu]  eric-digest               Free
112:    [       140.174.7.1]  fidonet-nodelist           Free

Keywords: reform

Searching ERIC-archive.src...
```

The SWAIS client is now establishing an Internet connection to the WAIS server at "nic.sura.net" and asking it to search through the ERIC database for any document containing the word "reform." In a few seconds, the search is done and the results are shown on your screen.

```
SWAIS                   Search Results                    Items: 40

  #     Score      Source              Title               Lines

001: [1000] (ERIC-arch) Title: Social Studies Curriculum Reform    284
002: [ 945] (ERIC-arch) Title: Fiscal Policy Issues and School R    264
003: [ 834] (ERIC-arch) Title: The Impact of Educational Reform     254
004: [ 500] (ERIC-arch) Title: Trends and Directions in Career E    267
005: [ 500] (ERIC-arch) Title: The Old College Try. Balancing Ac    220
006: [ 500] (ERIC-arch) Title: The Influence of Reform on Inserv    212
007: [ 444] (ERIC-arch) Title: The 1983 Educational Reform Repor    219
008: [ 444] (ERIC-arch) Title: Education for Tomorrow's Vocation    292
009: [ 389] (ERIC-arch) Title: Restructuring the Schools. ERIC D    245
010: [ 333] (ERIC-arch) Title: At-Risk Students. ERIC Digest Ser    193
011: [ 333] (ERIC-arch) Title: Collaboration between Schools and    252
012: [ 333] (ERIC-arch) Title: Emerging Issues in State-Level Sc    237
013: [ 278] (ERIC-arch) Title: Foreign Language Teacher Educatio    230
014: [ 222] (ERIC-arch) Title: World History in the Secondary Sc    327
015: [ 222] (ERIC-arch) Title: Restructuring American Schools: T    339
016: [ 222] (ERIC-arch) Title: The Role of Business in Education    272
017: [ 222] (ERIC-arch) Title: Trends and Options in the Reorgan    284
018: [ 222] (ERIC-arch) Title: School-to-Work Transition: Its Ro    251

<space> selects, arrows move, w for keywords, s for sources,
? for help
```

SWAIS has retrieved 40 documents, which is the default maximum number of documents that SWAIS will allow. Most WAIS clients allow you to increase or decrease this maximum number of documents.

The "score" column indicates SWAIS's estimate as to how well that article fits your request, with 1000 being considered a "perfect fit" to your search request. This score is based on the number of times that a keyword occurred in the documents.

This "results" menu looks and works like the sources menu. Each document has a number in the left hand column and you can move up and down with position keys. To display a highlighted document, press the return key.

```
Title: Social Studies Curriculum Reform Reports. ERIC Digest.

Personal Author: Patrick, John J.

Clearinghouse Number: SO020890

Publication Date: Apr 90

Accession Number: ED322021

Descriptors: *Curriculum Development; Curriculum Problems;
*Educational Change; Educational Resources; *Elementary School
Curriculum; Elementary Secondary Education; Geography; History;
*Secondary School Curriculum; *Social Studies

Identifiers: 1980s; ERIC Digests

Abstract: The 1980s were years of concern about the curricula in
elementary and secondary schools. Throughout the decade educators in
the social studies, as well as in other fields of knowledge, formed
curriculum study groups to assess the status quo and to recommend
improvements in widely distributed reports. This ERIC Digest
examines:
—More—
```

To leave a document you are viewing and return to the results menu, press the "q" key followed by the return key. To leave the results menu to return to the sources menu, press the "s" key.

Stopwords

When materials are WAIS indexed, certain words may be excluded from the indexing process, and therefore won't work as keywords. By default, any words that occur more than 20,000 times in the material are excluded. For example, a set of software description files containing 24,000 entries, each of which starts with the phrase "software name," would not contain the words "software" and "name" in the WAIS index you search. Similarly, WAIS indexed material will often exclude conjunctions ("but," "and," etc.), prepositions ("in," "around," etc.), articles ("a," "an," etc.), and a number of common verbs ("tell," "is," etc.). Such non-indexed words are called "stopwords."

Some of the words which are not included as WAIS keywords include the Boolean operators such as "not," "or," and "and," which you may be used to using in searches of databases or OPACs. Future versions of WAIS may include Boolean operators, but for the time being, you'll have to do without them.

Although the fact that certain words, including Boolean operators, have not been indexed may be a disadvantage at times, it helps you use "natural language" queries more easily, if you are so inclined. The following two searches might yield exactly the same documents, depending upon the stopwords that had been used in creating the source.

```
keywords:  Tell me where I can get french bread recipes
```

```
keywords:  french bread
```

18.3.7. About Relevance Feedback

Humans take for granted their ability to synthesize many distinct impressions into an overall image, or "Gestalt." We can look at three objects and assert that object A is more like object B than it is like C, without necessarily being able to specify exactly why.

"Relevance feedback" is a feature of WAIS that allows you to involve your Gestalt impressions when searching databases. You can use part or all of a document you have retrieved in one search as input for further searches. This is, in some ways, equivalent to telling WAIS that, "sure enough, all the files you retrieved contain the keyword I have supplied, but this particular file is most like what I am looking for. Find more that are like it!"

As a trivial example, let's suppose that your keyword was "wing," and WAIS retrieved documents about airplane wings, wingtip shoes, and wing-nuts. By selecting one of the airplane wing documents as input for relevance feedback, words like "airplane," "aeronautics," and "fuselage" would become keywords in subsequent searches and should prevent spurious hits on gangster stories and hardware catalogs. As this point should make clear, a careful choice of keywords from the start probably would have worked as well, but the point of relevance feedback is to make database searches easy even for people who don't want to take the time to formulate a carefully specified search.

Using Relevance Feedback

How you invoke relevance feedback depends upon which client you are using. Typically, you select one or more articles from a previous WAIS search as being "relevant" to your question by putting it into a "similar to:" window. In some clients, you can copy portions of retrieved documents and place these passages into the relevance feedback hopper.

However, if you want to try relevance feedback in SWAIS, be forewarned! This feature has only recently been added to the SWAIS interface and does not have the full abilities of other WAIS clients. You cannot use portions of a document as relevance feedback input, and in fact, relevance feedback will frequently crash your SWAIS session. If you are excited about relevance feedback, you should probably try to get WAIS client software installed locally.

18.3.8. Determining Which Sources to Search

If you want to use WAIS to its fullest, you need to know which sources should be searched for a particular question.

Search the Directory of Servers

Say we want to identify which of the WAIS sources have information about agriculture. From the list of servers menu, select the source "directory of servers." (First be sure to unselect any other sources you may have been working with by typing the "=" command!) Start a keyword search and enter the word "agriculture."

```
. . .
098: * [       quake.think.com]  directory-of-servers            Free
. . .
Keywords: agriculture
```

SWAIS will respond with a list of source description files containing this term.

```
001:   [1000] (directory-of-se)  agricultural-market-news       23
002:   [ 834] (directory-of-se)  ANU-Thai-Yunnan                44
003:   [ 834] (directory-of-se)  usda-rrdb                      28
```

If you select one of these documents, you'll see a source description file that begins with technical information used by WAIS client software followed by a brief description of what's in the source. If you select "agricultural-market-news," you will see the following information:

```
(:source
  :version  3
  :ip-address "128.193.124.4"
  :ip-name "nostromo.oes.orst.edu"
  :tcp-port 210
  :database-name "agricultural-market-news"
  :cost 0.00
  :cost-unit :free
  :maintainer "wais@nostromo.oes.orst.edu"
  :subjects "business marketing commodities agriculture agricultural"
  :description "Server created with WAIS release 8 b3.1 on Oct 5
               22:48:47 1991 by wais@nostromo.oes.orst.edu

This server contains the agricultural commodity market reports
compiled by the Agricultural Market News Service of the United
States Department of Agriculture. There are approximately 1200
reports from all over the United States. Most of these reports
are updated daily. Try searching for 'portland grain.'

For more information contact: wais@oes.orst.edu
```

To leave this technical description and return to the sources menu, press the "q" key followed by any other key.

Making Sense of the Source Titles

You could page through the menu of sources and identify likely sources by their names. Most names are fairly descriptive so you can pretty much guess what's in the source.

But how do you figure out what's in sources with names like "AAtDB," "uxc.cso.uiuc.edu," or "meval-bibtex-zenon-inria-fr?" To find out, enter the source number in the command line, press the return key, and enter "v", the view command. This will give you a brief descriptive file written by the person maintaining the source.

18.3.9. Ending an SWAIS Session

To leave SWAIS, simply type "q" from the sources menu.

18.4. For More Information

The FTP host at the Clearinghouse for Networked Information Discovery and Retrieval (CNIDR) contains much of what you need to know to get started using or installing WAIS.

FTP host:	`ftp.cnidr.org`
directory:	`wais`
filenames:	(many or all)

18.4.1. Mailing Lists

There are a number of Internet interest groups devoted to discussions about WAIS.

`wais-discussion@think.com`	moderated mailings every 1 or 2 weeks
`wais-interest@think.com`	major monthly announcements about WAIS
`wais-talk@think.com`	unmoderated and active discussion for WAIS users and implementors

18.4.2. Usenet Newsgroup

`comp.infosystems.wais`

18.4.3. Bibliography

An up-to-date bibliography of written materials and resources is available via FTP.

FTP host:	`ftp.cnidr.org`
directory:	`pub/wais/wais-discussion`
filename:	`bibliography.txt`

WAIS was developed as a joint project between Apple Computer, Dow Jones, KMPG Peat Marwick, and Thinking Machines Corporation. For basic information about WAIS, you can order hardcopies of documents from:

Thinking Machines Corp.
1010 El Camino Real, Suite 310
Menlo Park, CA 94025 USA

voice:	(415) 329-9300
fax:	(415) 329-9329

@ 19 @

Campus Wide Information Systems (CWIS)

Il faut cultiver notre jardins.

Voltaire
Candide

A "campus wide information system" (CWIS) is an online service used as a central source of information at a college, university, institution, or company. The typical CWIS wears many hats: it might provide access to campus directories, newspapers, calendars of events, course descriptions, information about the surrounding community, reports from the local weather service, or potentially anything else that may be of interest to its users.

Typically, a CWIS is maintained on one or a few central computers and accessed from public terminals, networked personal computers, and workstations in people's workplaces, dorm-rooms, off-campus homes—or even by remote users throughout the Internet!

There are hundreds of Internet accessible CWISs installed around the world. Some CWIS services open doors to the Internet and are rapidly converging on what one might call "network wide information systems." The fabric of online information is becoming more and more tightly knit, and CWISs are playing an increasingly important role in distributing local information globally, and global information locally.

19.1. The Benefits of CWISs

Information at Any Time

If you've ever tried to call campus information after working hours, you'll appreciate the value of a service which is alert and available 24 hours a day. A well maintained CWIS doesn't have to sleep.

One-Stop Information Shopping

How many documents would you need on your desk to keep track of campus phone numbers, the time and location of the Thespian Club's weekly meetings, which dining halls are serving sloppy joes ("again?!? yuk!"), and everything else you need to know about your campus? A good CWIS may be able to answer your most pressing (and maybe even some of your most frivolous) questions from the convenience of your personal computer.

Up-to-Date Information

Printed documents like directories, handbooks, and calendars are difficult to update or correct once they've been distributed. The economics of print as a medium means that such sources of information may be out of date for much of the time between reissues. But information on a CWIS may be updated much more frequently and be continuously available to the community.

Information for Remote Users

A CWIS connected to the Internet can enhance the accessibility of an institution. If you're a high school student comparing colleges, you might be able to obtain more information about a college's academics and extracurricular activities from a CWIS than the typical admissions office could fit into an envelope. If you're a nostalgic alumnus, you can stay in touch with your old *alma mater*. And if you're at an institution which does not yet have a CWIS installed, you can try out Internet-accessible CWIS to determine the value of installing a CWIS at your own site.

Community (and Commonsense) in a Distributed (and Complicated) World

Keeping track of what's going on in a large campus can be daunting, especially for commuting students. A CWIS is like an informational student union for anyone at, or interested in, an institution.

Have you ever been unable to locate someone because you didn't know in which cubicle on which floor of which building of which sub-department of which school of which campus they were located? If your institution seems like an alphabet soup of departments and acronyms, a well organized CWIS can help people find who or what they need, quickly and easily.

19.2. A Lighthearted Introduction to CWIS Exploration: ALICE

To illustrate some of the common features of CWISs, consider the main menu (shown below) displayed by a CWIS named "ALICE" at the hypothetical "Wonderland University."

The main menu of a typical CWIS is like a book's table of contents and its index at the same time. You can move to "submenus" by selecting their numbers, and many CWIS also allow you to use a command to search through some or all of the CWIS for a particular word or phrase.

For example, by typing "2" in the main menu of ALICE, the screen would show the menu for the Admissions Office which would probably include information about entrance requirements and related topics. Similarly, by typing "Find Red Queen" from the main menu you might retrieve information on courses she teaches in the Law School, what moves she made in the last Faculty-Student chess competition, or even when and why she declared "Off with their heads!" By selecting "11", ALICE would give you access to other information throughout the Internet. And if you became confused you could type "Help", an option which Alice, the person, would have appreciated in her visit to Wonderland.

```
         Welcome to the Wonderland University CWIS

                           ALICE

         ("A Lighthearted Introduction to CWIS Exploration")

                         Main Menu

      Topic                  Partial Description of Contents
      ------------------     -------------------------------------
   1 About ALICE            Help, How to Answer Riddles

      ADMINISTRATIVE

   2 Admissions             Rabbit Hole, Mirrors; "Who are YOU?"
   3 Consulting             The Mad Hatter's Corner
   4 Courses                Of Course a Catalog, Lessen Plans
   5 Policies               "Off With their Heads!"

      LIFE IN WONDERLAND

   6 Athletics              Croquet, Chess, Cards
   7 Calendar               Coming Events, When Will I Wake Up?
   8 Dining Halls           Eating, Drinking, How to Change Size
   9 Directory              Staff, Students, Animals
  10 Social Events          Lobster Quadrille, Tea Parties

      THROUGH THE LOOKING GLASS

  11 Internet               Resources Throughout the Internet

  Commands: Help, Backup, Find, Main_menu
  Enter # of Menu Choice, or First Letter of Command -->
```

So even the arbitrary and perplexing world on the other side of the Looking Glass might be rendered comprehensible and navigable by a CWIS.

19.3. CWIS Access

If a remote CWIS is connected to the Internet, you can probably access it directly by Telnet, tn3270, or indirectly by going through a service like Gopher or Hytelnet that establishes the connection for you. You may be able to invoke a local CWIS at your institution by typing a simple command when you are connected to the campus network. Please contact your local user services staff for specific information on accessing a local CWIS.

19.3.1. CWIS Access via Telnet (or tn3270)

Most CWISs can be accessed through the Internet by Telnet or tn3270. To access a CWIS by this route, you will need to know the following:

- how to use Telnet or tn3270 (Chapter 6) and

- the Internet address of the CWIS. (See "Sample Table of CWISs" or one of the "Lists of CWISs" named at the end of this chapter.)

In addition, you may also need to know some additional information:

- the login name, password, and possibly other access codes for the CWIS; and

- the type(s) of terminal emulation which can be used (e.g., vt100).

Once you've used CWISs and other Internet information systems for awhile, you can second-guess some of this access information based on subtle clues from the screen or the system's responses. But why waste time guessing! Consult one of the "CWIS Lists" named at the end of this chapter for a compendium of such information.

19.3.2. CWIS Access through "Network Wide Information Systems"

There are several network-wide information systems explicitly designed to automate and facilitate the use of services like CWISs throughout the world. Typically they contain a list of CWIS services and you can poke through the list, select a CWIS, and have a session launched without having to type in a lot of Internet addresses.

Gopher

Gopher was originally designed at the University of Minnesota as a local information system, but it has quickly proven to be a world-class, front end for a variety of Internet resources. Gopher presents lists of documents and services—even though they may be located elsewhere in the world—as menus on your screen. When you select a CWIS from a Gopher menu, Gopher supplies you with a screen containing up-to-date information about login names, passwords, or other quirks about the CWIS, and then launches a session. For more on Gopher, see Chapter 17.

Hytelnet

Hytelnet is an easy to use, customizable software package developed at the University of Saskatchewan. It contains a list of many Telnet accessible resources, and, when installed on an Internet host, it can automate logins to these sites. Hytelnet includes a great selection of CWISs, as well as exceptionally thorough coverage of OPACs, BBSs, and other Internet resources. You can try out the Hytelnet system via any of the Internet front ends described in the next section.

Hytelnet may already be installed at your local site. Try typing "hytelnet" at your system prompt; if this doesn't work, ask your local user services staff for assistance. Or, if you are feeling adventurous, you can obtain a copy of Hytelnet for your local computer. Installation is moderately difficult and may prove too challenging for the novice network user. There are currently versions of Hytelnet available for VMS, DOS, Mac, Amiga, and most Unix operating systems. You can get Hytelnet along with instructions on installation and customization via FTP.

> FTP host: `access.usask.ca`
> directories: `pub/hytelnet/amiga`
>   `pub/hytelnet/mac`
>   `pub/hytelnet/pc`
>   `pub/hytelnet/unix`
>   `pub/hytelnet/vms`

Other Internet Front Ends

Several other Internet front ends can be used to access CWISs. For example, you can get to many CWISs by telnetting to the following multi-purpose services:

Internet Address	Access	Location of CWIS info
`bbs.oit.unc.edu`	login as "`bbs`" and supply requested information	in the libtel menu
`liberty.uc.wlu.edu`	login as "`lawlib`"	main menu
`wugate.wustl.edu`	login as "`services`"	main menu

19.4. CWIS Etiquette

Even if a CWIS is Internet accessible, it may not really be designed to support users from around the world. If messages on the screen indicate that there are restrictions for off-site users, respect those requests. For example, many CWISs feature databases that are licensed to a particular institution and cannot be used by remote users. And if you want to take a remote CWIS for a spin, try to restrict your use to that site's non-peak hours. Anytime after 5pm and before 9am their local time will help prevent undue congestion and degradation of service.

So what is true for all network services is sometimes even more true of CWISs: using or even exploring another institution's CWIS is a privilege, not a right.

19.5. Sample CWIS Session

There are many different kinds of CWISs in operation, so there is no universal user interface. (As someone once sagely noted, "the problem with standards is that there are so many of them.") Furthermore, a single CWIS may be able to present different features depending upon what kind of terminal emulation you are using. For example, you may be able to move around a full screen session with arrow and tab keys when using vt100 terminal emulation, but only access the command line when using dumb terminal emulation.

However, there are enough similarities among CWISs that a sample session to one robust site will be fairly representative. In this example, we will go through step-by-step instructions for using the University of North Carolina's CWIS, called "INFO." You can also try any of the CWISs listed in Gopher, Hytelnet, or one of the CWIS lists.

19.5.1. Accessing a CWIS

If you are using Telnet, type "telnet" followed by the Internet address of the CWIS. (If you are using a service such as Gopher or Hytelnet, the Telnet command may be executed for you.)

```
telnet info.acs.unc.edu
```

When the remote computer receives your connection request, you should see an acknowledgment of the connection, and possibly some useful information about how to exit from the CWIS.

19.5.2. Providing Login Information

Some CWISs may take you directly to a menu of options; others may request that you specify one or more of the following: a) a special username for the CWIS; b) a password; c) your terminal emulation. Screens prompting you for such information will sometimes tell you the magic words you need to get in. But to save yourself time and effort, obtain an up-to-date copy of one the CWIS lists or use Gopher or Hytelnet if they are available to you.

In the case of the University of North Carolina, we only need to supply the username "INFO" to get into the CWIS.

```
                    W E L C O M E    T O
                         U N C
             Office Of Information Technology
                   Computing Systems
                        UNCVX1

Username: INFO
```

19.5.3. CWIS Main Menus

Once you've entered the correct access information, you will usually see a main menu for the CWIS. Such a screen will often contain a "Welcome" message of some sort, a list of topics available in the CWIS, and most importantly, how to get help.

```
Information Center

                    1. About INFO

2. About UNC-Chapel Hill        8. Research

3. Academics                    9. Services and facilities

4. Directories                  10. Sports schedules

5. Events                       11. Student life

6. Human Resources              12. Transportation and parking
      (faculty/staff)

7. Publications                 13. Other Information Systems

  Commands: Help  Quit  Main  Backup  Find
      Enter menu choice number or command:
```

Commands

The basic commands available at a particular level are usually given at the bottom of your screen. When a word begins with an UPPERCASE or **BOLD** character (like "Quit"), it generally means that you can use that single letter as an abbreviation for the whole command.

Selecting Items

In UNC INFO, we can select an item by typing it's number in the "command area" following "command:" on the bottom line. Some CWISs allow you to use your arrow and tab keys to move around the screen and select items if you are using the correct terminal emulation. Those that can be accessed via a client (e.g., Gopher) may allow you to use application specific tools like a mouse or pull-down menus.

19.5.4. Obtaining Help in a CWIS

Be sure to take advantage of any online help. In addition to a concise list of commands at the bottom of the screen, you can usually get a more comprehensive explanation of commands available by typing "Help", "?", or something similar. Here's the first of many pages of expanded help available from UNC INFO.

```
-------------------------------------------------------------------
Type | Command          | Command Description
-------------------------------------------------------------------
 --> | Next Page        | Go to the next page in a document
 <-- | Previous Page    | Go to the previous page in a document
 B   | Backout          | Back out from the current page
 GM  | Go to Mark       | Return to a page where a book mark is
 GP  | Get PM           | Display your personalized menu
 H   | Help             | Display this help file
 L   | Local            | Save or print page or document, etc.
 M   | Main Menu        | Go to the Main Menu
 NC  | Next Choice      | Go to the next page of a menu range
 PC  | Previous Choice  | Go to the previous page of a menu range
 Q   | Quit             | Quit the UNC-CH INFO system
 R   | Reveal           | Display hidden information about a page
 S   | Search           | Search for page using predefined keyword
 SF  | Send Form        | Send a form after form is completed
 SM  | Set Mark         | Set a temporary book mark on a page
 SP  | Set PM           | Set up a personal frequent-use menu

-------------------------------------------------------------------
x                       [HELP page 1 of 11]        Next page -->x
x    Commands:   Backout    Quit info                          x
-------------------------------------------------------------------
     Enter command:
```

To exit from this help screen, type "b".

19.5.5. Exploring a CWIS: Diving into the Menus

Suppose you're a high school student looking for information about student life at UNC. By selecting item 11 from the main menu of this CWIS, you'd get the following menu chock full of valuable information. It's almost like taking a tour of the campus without having to pay for the airfare.

```
Choose from the following topics about student life at UNC:

  1. Academic advising           20. Leadership
  2. Black Cultural Center        21. Legal services
  3. Campus Code                  22. Living/learning
  4. Campus safety                23. Lost and Found
  5. Campus Y                     24. Minority affairs
  6. Career Planning and Placement 25. Noise permits
  7. Carolina Union               26. Orientation
  8. Club Sports                  27. Publications
  9. (University) Counseling Center 28. Regulations, policies
 10. Cultural activities          29. Student Affairs
 11. Extracurricular involvement  30. Student Health Service
 12. Finances/expenses/aid        31. Student judicial gov.
 13. Handbook (The Source): Part 1 (A-I)  32. Student organizations
 14. -------------------- Part 2 (J-Z)    33. Stud. org. recognition
 15. Handicapped student services 34. Tickets (sports)
 16. (The) Honor Code             35. Tutoring
 17. Honorary societies           36. Varsity, J. V. sports
 18. Housing                      37. Veterans affairs
 19. International Center          38. (The) Writing Center

 Commands: Help  Quit  Main  Backup  Find
     Enter menu choice number or command: 7
```

In a big, state school like UNC, the student union is a hub of activities, so we'll select option 7, the Carolina Union.

```
    The Carolina Union participates in several ways to provide
opportunities for cultural enrichment on campus. The Carolina
Union Performing Arts Series offers students the opportunity to
see at minimum cost performances by outstanding artists in musical
theater, classical music, and dance.

    For students seeking a more active role than simply attending
Union-sponsored programs, The Carolina Union provides  "hands on."

(etc.)

                    The Undergraduate Bulletin, 1991-1993
 Commands: Help  Quit  Main  Backup  Find  Next
     Enter command:
```

19.5.6. Exiting a CWIS

Since CWISs vary, so do the commands to end your session. Common exit commands are "Bye", "Quit", "Exit", "End", or "Logout". (Commands like "Let me out of here!" or "Ecrassez l'infame!" usually don't work.) Refer to the online help if you are confused. If all else fails, you may have to terminate your Telnet session "ungracefully" by using the escape code specific to your software. For example, when using Telnet on a Unix system use "^]" (i.e., control right bracket).

19.6. Conclusion

For many people, the essence of the Internet has been the sharing of online information. Similarly, one of the goals of education is the dissemination of knowledge. A CWIS can be the union of these two visions and become an integral part of the give and take that is helping create a truly worldwide, information environment.

If you are interested in starting a CWIS at your site, Appendix C, "Setting Up a CWIS," may be helpful. This overview focuses on the administrative and design issues associated with implementing and running a CWIS.

19.7. For More Information

19.7.1. CWIS Usenet Groups and LISTSERV Mailing Lists

To keep up-to-date about CWISs, or to discuss CWISs with others, you can subscribe to the following LISTSERV mailing list, or read it as a Usenet newsgroup:

`cwis-l@wuvmd.bitnet`	(LISTSERV)
`bit.listserv.cwis-l`	(Usenet, may become comp.infosystems.cwis.)

The archives of CWIS-L can be searched using the WAIS database "bit.listserv.cwis-l," or the LISTSERV LISTDB tool.

There are also several Usenet newsgroups and LISTSERV mailing lists for specific software platforms which can be used as, or as part of, CWIS services.

`comp.infosystems.gopher`	(Usenet)
`comp.infosystems.wais`	(Usenet)
`comp.infosystems.www`	(Usenet)
`vtx-l@ncsuvm.bitnet`	(LISTSERV)

For more information on using Usenet, LISTSERV along with LISTDB, and WAIS, please refer to Chapters 9, 10 and 18.

19.7.2. Master Lists of CWISs

Judy Hallman maintains an up-to-date list of CWISs. This list is periodically updated and posted to the CWIS-L LISTSERV mailing list described above, and is also included in Art. St. George and Ron Larsen's document, "Internet Accessible Library Catalogs and Databases."

Hallman's List:

FTP host:	`sunsite.unc.edu`
directory:	`pub/docs/about-the-net`
filename:	`cwis-l`

St. George-Larsen "Internet Accessible Library Catalogs and Databases":

FTP host:	`ariel.unm.edu`
directory:	`library`
filename:	`internet.library`

The access files used by Hytelnet also provide good coverage of CWIS services. Refer back to the Hytelnet section of this chapter for accessing these files by FTP.

For more information about using FTP, refer to Chapter 7.

19.7.3. Bibliography

The following printed materials either deal with CWISs directly, or provide general information relevant to employing online information services in a campus setting.

Arms, C.R. (ed.). *Campus Strategies for Libraries and Electronic Information.* Bedford, MA: Digital Press, 1990.

Finnegan, G. A. "Wiring Information to a College Campus: A Port for Every Pillow." *Online* 14(2) (1990): 37-40.

Hallman, J. (In press.) "Campus Wide Information Systems." *Advances in Library Automation and Networking.*

Hawkins, B.L. (ed.). *Organizing and Managing Information Resources on Campus.* McKinney, TX.: Academic Computing Publications, 1989.

Heterick, R.C., Jr. *A Single System Image: An Information Systems Strategy.* Professional Paper Series, #1. Maynard, MA: Digital Equipment Corp., 1988.

Kinney, T. "Toward Telecommunications Strategies " in: *Academic and Research Libraries: Ten Case Studies in Decision- Making and Implementation.* Washington, DC: Office of Management Services, 1988.

Waren, M.S. "How Much Paper Do You Need to Support an Electronic Information System?" *Proceedings, ACM SIGUCCS User Services Conference* XVIII, 1990, pp. 355-360. 1990.

@ 20 @

World Wide Web: A Hypertext-Based View of the Internet

In Xanadu, did Kubla Khan
A stately pleasure dome decree,
Where Alph, the sacred river ran,
through caverns measureless to man...

> Samuel Taylor Coleridge
> from "Kubla Khan, or a Vision in a Dream"

I was of three minds,
like a tree
in which there are thirteen blackbirds.

> Wallace Stevens
> from "Thirteen Ways of Looking at a Blackbird"

═══════════════════

World Wide Web—often abbreviated as WWW or W3—is an innovative front end for information throughout the Internet. Like Gopher, it allows a single point of entry to many Internet sources, including WAIS, archie, Telnet accessible services, online databases, and text files.

The basic goal of W3 is (simply!) to make all online knowledge part of one "web" of interconnected documents and services, and to allow you to follow facts or texts in W3 anywhere they might lead, for as many steps as you care to travel. If you were reading this text in W3, you could select a reference in this document—a word, a name, or a network service—and W3 might display definitions, contact information, or establish access to a network service. Each of these results could then be used as a jump-off point to other parts of the W3 universe, and so forth without end.

W3 is significantly different from most Internet services you've probably encountered so far because it uses a method called "hypertext" to organize, search, and present information. The unique approach of W3 is that it uses a combination of hypertext and full-text searching to allow you to view the information universe in any way that you might like. This has advantages, but it also creates unique challenges for the W3 user. So before you use W3, you should have a basic understanding of the hypertext philosophy.

20.1. What Is Hypertext?

Hypertext is text that is accessed or stored, in part or in whole, in a non-hierarchical structure. Each piece of hypertext (or node) is connected to one or more other pieces of hypertext by "links." As more nodes and links are added to the structure, the nodes and links form a web. To help you visualize hypertext, think of something physical with a web-like structure: a piece of lace, or a spider's web glistening in the morning dew. You can get from place to place in the web by following many different paths and you don't have to return to where you started, unless you want to. There are no real ends in a web.

In contrast, directories are branching, hierarchical storage systems. To get to a certain document in a directory system, you start at the root, and then work your way down through a path of directories. Each step down the directory path leads to more and more specific sub-categories, eventually leading you to a file (e.g., "pub/documents/networks/a.file"). There is usually only one path to a particular file, and when you get to the end of a directory tree, your only options are to move backwards or exit.

Compare a bird flying from twig to twig in a tree to an ant climbing on branches and the difference between hypertext and hierarchical information should be clear. The methodical path of the ant represents an adherence to a tree's geometry, and the flights of the bird represent the hypertext links between any and all parts of a tree. Hypertext lets you "fly" from branch to branch (or node to node) in an information universe.

20.1.1. The Printed Word as Fossil Hypertext

The term hypertext sounds alien and futuristic, but in fact, we all use hypertext-like behavior. Consider an example from everyday life.

We usually think of sentences, paragraphs, and books, as linear and hierarchical structures. This chapter has sections and subsections. This sentence had a beginning, and now it has an end. Maybe sometimes you'll jump around in a book, but it's usually to re-read something you've forgotten in the linear presentation of the text, to skip some information that you already know, or maybe to look at the pictures.

But no word, passage, or book exists in isolation. Whenever you go to a dictionary to define an unfamiliar word or refer to a book mentioned in a bibliography, you're using the hypertext model. In fact, there are many hypertext conventions in text, such as footnote numbers which point to text at the bottom of a page. Each footnote points to a citation elsewhere in the literature, a definition from a dictionary, or further explanatory text which would divert from the main expository purpose of the passage. To a specialist, hypertext links to other nodes are often the most valued part of a text. For more on hypertext, see the citations at the end of this chapter. :-)

For example, you've probably seen (or maybe even written) essays which bristle with footnotes after almost every word. Consider a typical passage from a university term paper:

> *In the summer of 1797, Samuel Taylor Coleridge had been prescribed an anodyne [1] by his doctor for an illness [2]. Drowsy from his medicine, he fell into a hypnagogic sleep [3] while reading the book "Purchas's Pilgrimage" [4]. In a dream, he composed a three hundred line poem named "Kubla Khan." Coleridge's friend and mentor, Lord George Byron, later read the poem, and encouraged Coleridge to publish the still incomplete piece. For the past 200 years, this poem, "Kubla Khan," about a mysterious locale, "Xanadu" [5], has inspired a voluminous discussion about the mysterious role of the unconscious in creativity [6]...*

If the essay about Coleridge were in W3, each number would represent a node with a link to another hypertext node. By selecting "4", we might retrieve a citation for "Purchas's Pilgrimage" or possibly the entire document. By selecting "5", we might find out that Xanadu is the name of Ted Nelson's original hypertext system, or that it is a phonetic spelling of the old Chinese name for Beijing. And by selecting "6", we would expect to be led to something about creativity. . .

20.1.2. Hypertext, W3, and the Internet

Hierarchical systems like library catalogs or file directories are very useful for storing and retrieving information that is static and/or easily classified. However they have weaknesses when dealing with information that is dynamic, multidisciplinary, difficult to classify, or chock-full of references to all sorts of seemingly unrelated things. (Sounds suspiciously like much of the Internet, doesn't it?)

The goal of W3 is to combine hypertext and full-text searches so that all information on the Internet can be linked according to a person's needs. This process world converges on a global and dynamic web of information, memory, and imagination.

20.1.3. How Many Texts, Could a Hypertext Text, if a Hypertext Could Text Text?

With a universal hypertext system, a text no longer slumbers between its covers. Any part can leap out and be linked with passages from any other text. With hypertext a reader becomes an author, and this has been proclaimed as one of the great advantages of hypertext. But of course, not every reader is willing or able to take on the time and effort that authorship entails. This is one of the challenges of using hypertext systems.

Quite honestly, using W3 or other hypertext systems is sometimes frustrating. Although our own thoughts may be free-flowing links and associations, we usually count on an easy-to-understand order in our surroundings. When using someone else's W3 server, you might find yourself lost, going in circles through loops of texts, or unable to get to the document or service you're hoping to retrieve. Don't get discouraged! To become an effective, efficient hypertext voyager requires practice and perseverance.

20.2. World Wide Web Access

20.2.1. Client Software

W3 is at it's best when used with locally installed client software. So if you plan to use W3 extensively, find out if there is a W3 client available at your site or ask your local computer support staff if they can help with installing W3 on one of your site's computers.

The "line browser" W3 client is a text-only version suitable for operating systems with character only displays, such as Unix, DOS, or VM/CMS. In W3 line browsers, you track hypertext links by typing their numbers. There are also a variety of W3 clients for operating systems with windowed environments, like X-windows, the NeXT, and the Macintosh. These clients allow you to use the features of your local system that you know and love, such as clicking with your mouse, or playing sounds on your NeXT.

20.2.2. Telnet Access

The following sites can be accessed directly via Telnet and, in cases where you are asked for a user-id, login as "www":

```
info.cern.ch        (128.141.201.74)     (Switzerland)
eies2.njit.edu      (128.235.1.43)       (USA)
vms.huji.ac.il      (128.139.4.3)        (Israel)
```

20.3. Sample Session

In this example, we will access the W3 line browser at CERN in Switzerland.

Because W3 uses a method for storing and displaying files different than you may be used to, this sample session is mainly a lesson in getting used to using the hypertext interface. Please take the time to learn the basic navigational tools before you dive into the web!

The W3 servers at eies2.njit.edu and vms.huji.ac.il allow access to many services which info.cern.ch displays, but won't let you access. However, the purpose of this sample session is to get you oriented with the W3 user interface, so CERN was chosen because it is the "authoritative" W3 site. If you want to use W3 for getting around the Internet, telnet to the eies2.njit.edu or vms.huji.ac.il sites listed in the table of Telnet accessible W3 sites or install a W3 client.

Note: Shortly before this book went to press, the structure of the W3 system at CERN had been changed, and it was not possible to update this sample session to reflect those changes. What is true of the Internet as a whole is especially true of W3: it is a resource that evolves at a rate which is certainly exciting, but definitely challenging to document.

20.3.1. Entering the Web

To connect to the basic line browser at CERN, use Telnet from any Internet host.

```
telnet info.cern.ch
```

The Home Page

The first screen you should see is the "home page" of this W3 browser. The home page gives you an overview of what this W3 site has to offer and the numbers you should enter to get to those items. If you get lost in W3, you can always return to the home page by typing "Home" at the command line.

```
                                          Welcome to CERN (25/24)

CERN is the European Particle Physics Laboratory in Geneva,
Switzerland. Select information by number here, or
elsewhere.

  Help[1]                  About this program

  World Wide Web[2]        About the W3 global information
                           initiative

  CERN information[3]      Information from and about this site

  Particle Physics[4]      Other HEP sites with information
                           servers

  Other Subjects[5]        Catalogue of all online information
                           by subject. Also: by server type[6].

If you use this service frequently, please install a W3
browser on your own machine (see instructions[7] ). You
can configure it to start anywhere in the web. If you have
any problems or suggestions, please mail
www-bug@info.cern.ch.

1-7, Up, Quit, or Help:
```

The screen title information should help you figure out the purpose of any particular screen. The text and numbers in the body of the screen are information about current hypertext nodes and links or the results from searches when using WAIS or other services.

As long as you have not left W3 to access a remote service, you will see a command line at the bottom of the screen. The command line starts with a range of numbers corresponding to the numbers of the hypertext nodes to which you can link, and a subset of commands that are currently available to you from this screen. Finally, the input area at the lower right is where you actually enter your W3 requests.

If you have initiated a remote session from W3, your screen will usually display the normal features of that remote service.

20.3.2. What Resources Are Available in the Web?

To find out what sorts of resources are in W3, select the number for "server types" (6) or "other subjects" (5). This is the display from a request for server types.

```
World Wide Web        See the list of W3 servers[3] . See also:
                      about the WWW initiative[4], and the HTTP
                      protocol[5].

WAIS                  Find WAIS index servers using the
                      directory of servers[6]. See also: about
                      WAIS[7], news archive[8], about the
                      WWW-WAIS gateway[9].

Network News[10]      Now available directly in all www
                      browsers.

Gopher                Campus-wide information systems, etc. See
                      list of sites[11], about Gopher[12], news
                      archive[13].

Telnet access         See list by Scott Yanoff[14], Art St.
                      George's index[15] (yet to be hyperized)
                      etc.

VAX/VMS HELP[16]      Available using the help gateway[17] to
                      WWW.

Anonymous FTP         See the ARCHIE[18] -- An index of most
                      everything available by anonymous FTP.
                      For example of an FTP site, see the
                      uu.net[19] server.

TechInfo              A CWIS system from MIT. Very provisional
                      access through gateway[20] may be turned
                      off at any time. Gateway thanks to Linda
                      Murphy/Upenn. See also more about
                      techninfo[21].

Other protocols       Other forms of online data[22].
```

You could dive further into W3 by entering a bracketed number from the page. For example, entering "6" from the screen above allows you to search through the WAIS directory of servers. But, before you start weaving through the web, you should probably work through the following navigational lessons.

20.3.3. Getting Help

It's *always* a good idea to review the online help for any new Internet service you are exploring, and this is especially true of W3. There are two main kinds of help available in this version of W3: help on the actual underlying mechanics of W3 and help for commands that are available from any given screen.

Help for an Overview of World Wide Web

From the home screen, you can get general help for W3 and much more detailed background information about the W3 project.

```
                 User Guide for the WWW Line Mode Browser

                 WWW LINE MODE BROWSER

The World Wide Web line-mode browser allows you to find
information by following references and/or by using
keywords.

References are numbers in [brackets] after particular
phrases. Type the number and RETURN for more information on
the phrase.

Some documents are indexes. These contain little text, but
allow you to search for information with keywords. Type
"find" or "f" (space) and the keywords. For example, "f
sgml examples" searches the index for items with keywords
SGML and EXAMPLE. You can only use the "find" command when
it is present in the prompt. You can omit the "f" if the
first keyword doesn't conflict with existing commands[1].

See also command line syntax[2], shortcuts[3],
installation[4], customization[5], deeper details[6].

Please send any bugs and suggestions to
www-bug@info.cern.ch.

1-7, Back, <RETURN> for more, Quit, or Help:
```

Help On Commands

Because W3 is a web instead of a tree, you have many ways of getting around. From the help screen above, select link number 1 for "existing commands," and you should get an up-to-date table of W3 commands.

20.3.4. Table of World Wide Web Commands

The following commands are available at the prompt within W3. Some are disabled when not applicable. All commands may be abbreviated. Case is not significant.

```
COMMAND           DESCRIPTION

Help              List available commands

<Return>          Display next page of current document

<number>          Display a document referred to by the number

Find keywords     Search a current index for keywords

Back              Go back to the document you were reading

Home              Go back to the first document

Recall            List documents you have visited
Recall <#>        Select a document from the recall list

List              Display sources of documents
List <#>          Display source for a specified document

Next, Previous    Work through a list of documents, displayed
                  by the  "list" command

Go <address>      Go to the document represented by the given
                  hypertext address

Up, Down          Scroll up or down one page in the current
                  document

Top, Bottom       Go to the top or the bottom of the current
                  document

Verbose           Toggle verbose mode on or off

Quit              Leave W3


Additional Commands for Unix versions of W3

Print             Print the current document
> file            Save or append the current document to a
                  file
| command         Pipe current document to the given command,
                  without the numbered document references.
! command         Execute a shell command without leaving W3
CD (or LCD)       Changes the local working directory
```

20.3.5. The Recall Command

To keep track of where you are and have been in the web, you can use the "recall" command to display the screen names of the files that you have visited during your W3 session.

```
    Documents you have visited:-

R   1)    in Welcome to CERN
R   2)    in User Guide for the WWW Line Mode Browser
R   3)    Commands -- /LineMode

1-3, Back, <RETURN> for more, Quit, or Help:
```

The recall command is really helpful if you've been wandering through the web for awhile and don't quite know where you are and how you got there. It works like a thread that is laid down while exploring—a tactic used by Theseus in the Greek myth of the Minotaur's labyrinth.

You can get back to any one of the displayed documents by entering its number. Pressing the return key from the recall screen will return you to the most recently visited document.

20.3.6. Seeing Hypertext Links in a List

Another useful command when using W3 is "list". This displays the documents that are referenced on a particular screen. The list command also displays the actual locations and filenames of the links from a particular document.

First, be sure you are in the home directory by typing "home". Now type "list" and you should see a screen like the following:

```
      References from this document:-

[1] User Guide for the WWW Line Mode Browser
[2] The World Wide Web project
[3] CERN Entry Point
[4] High-Energy Physics Information
[5] http://info.cern.ch/hypertext/DataSources/bySubject/...
[6] http://info.cern.ch/hypertext/DataSources/ByAccess.html
[7] http://info.cern.ch/hypertext/WWW/LineMode/Defaults/Inst

1-7, Back, Up, Quit, or Help:
```

These are the seven documents linked to the home directory. They are shown in a list format instead of being embedded in text.

You can access any one of these documents directly from the list screen by selecting a document's number. When one of those documents is displayed, you can also work your way through the remaining documents from the list by using the "next" and "previous" commands. These commands allow you to step forward or backwards through the listed documents.

This display also shows where each document is actually located. Most document references have the following standard format:

```
[#] protocol_type://Internet_host_address/directory_path/file_name
```

20.3.7. Using the Web as a Resource Discovery Tool

Now that you've gone through a basic orientation of the intricacies of W3, you are ready to use it as an informational resource. Because CERN restricts outgoing Telnet from W3, you should try the eies2.njit.edu or vms.huji.ac.il sites for more extensive explorations.

Like Gopher, W3 may be used as a resource discovery tool for the rest of the Internet. When you access remote Internet services through W3, your screen will display that remote service's screen and prompts.

To whet your appetite, the next page shows a listing of resources available in W3 organized by academic categories. (You'll find this listing by selecting "other subjects" from the home menu.)

20.3.8. Exiting

From any screen, just type "quit".

```
                    INDEXES OF ACADEMIC INFORMATION

Information categorized by subject. See also by
organization[1], protocol[2], and commercial[3] online data.

  Mail www-request@info.cern.ch if you know of online
  information not in these lists....

Aeronautics            Mailing list archive index[4].
Astronomy,Astrophysics Abstract Indexes[5].
Bio Sciences           See separate list[6].
Computing              See Networking[7], Jargon[8],
                       news[9], Software Technology[10],
                       Languages[11], Algorithms[12].
Geography              CIA World Fact Book[13], India:
                       Misc. information[14], Thai-Yunnan:
                       Davis collection[15]
Libraries              Few libraries currently have servers
                       - you have to log on to them. But you
                       can find out how with Art St.George's
                       list of library systems[16], about
                       "Library" in the internet resource
                       guide[17] and the hytelnet index[18].
Literature             Project Gutenberg[19] : two classic
                       books a month, available by FTP. See
                       their explanations [20], the index
                       and newsletter [21], books published
                       in 1991[22], 1992[23], and reserved
                       for the USA[24].
Humanities             BMCR classical reviews[25],
                       Poetry[26], Scifi reviews[27]. See
                       also electronic journals[28].
Mathematics            CIRM library[29] (french)
Meteorology            US weather[30], state by state. Also
                       WAIS weather[31] (around MIT :-).
Music                  MIDI interfacing[32], Song lyrics[33]
Physics                High Energy Physics[34], Astrophysics
                       abstracts[35].
Politics & Economics   US information[36].
Reference              Roget's Thesaurus[37].
Religion               The Bible[38] (King James version),
                       The Book of Mormon[39], The Holy
                       Qur'an[40]
Social Sciences        Coombs papers archive[41].
```

Note that some displayed resources cannot be accessed when using the CERN W3 via a Telnet session; in such cases, you'll get a message saying something to the effect of "sorry, the service cannot be accessed; please install a W3 client to get full W3 services." If this is a problem, try the "eies2" or "huji" sites mentioned in the list of Telnet accessible W3 sites.

20.4. Working with the World Wide Web Initiative

If you are excited by W3 and what it has to offer, install a local client. Using a local client allows you to construct a web that corresponds to your view of the world online.

Like WAIS and Gopher, the W3 Initiative will work best if there are many servers installed throughout the world. The W3 servers can store and distribute information in a wide variety of formats and have built-in gateways to archie, WAIS, Gopher, and most other kinds of Internet services. The master FTP source is info.cern.ch, directory pub/WWW. Even if you don't install a W3 server, W3 server maintainers might be interested in including any datasets, text, or other machine accessible resources which you would like to share.

All aspects of W3 are still under development. Feel free to send your suggestions, comments, or contributions to www-bugs@info.cern.ch.

20.5. For More Information

20.5.1. Mailing Lists

As of August 1992, there are two mailing lists for W3. Note that these lists are maintained by Unix listserv software, which is not to be confused with BITNET LISTSERV software.

`www-announce@info.cern.ch`	Major announcements of interest to the W3 community (This is intended to be a low volume, high subscription group.)
`www-talk@info.cern.ch`	Discussion among W3 developers (A good place for W3 users to share experiences and ask questions about W3 not addressed in the W3 online information.)

20.5.2. Usenet Newsgroups

By the time you read this, there might be newsgroups called "comp.infosystems.www" and "comp.infosystems.hypertext". The following newsgroup is currently a good forum for discussions about hypertext generally, and sometimes W3 specifically:

`alt.hypertext`

20.5.3. FTP Archives

The authoritative FTP archive for W3 related information and software is at CERN.

FTP host: `info.cern.ch`
directories: `pub/www/bin`   (already compiled W3 binaries)
                `pub/www/doc`   (documentation files for W3)
                `pub/www/src`   (uncompiled source code for W3 in tarred and archived formats)

You may be able to locate other useful W3 FTP archive sites elsewhere in the world by using archie to search for the string "www".

20.5.4. Bibliographies

W3

Berners-Lee, T.J., R. Cailliau, J-F. Groff, and B. Pollermann, "World Wide Web: An Information Infrastructure for High-Energy Physics." Presented at "Artificial Intelligence and Software Engineering for High Energy Physics" in La Londe, France, January 1992. Proceedings to be published by *World Scientific*, Singapore, ed. D Perret-Gallix. 1992.

Berners-Lee, T.J. "Electronic publishing and visions of hypertext." *Physics World* 5(6) 1992.

"The Fruitful, Tangled Trees of Knowledge." *The Economist* June 20, 1992.

Hypertext

Barrett, E. (ed.). *The Society of Text: Hypertext, Hypermedia, and the Social Construction of Information.* Cambridge, MA: MIT Press, 1989.

Bolter, J.D. *The Writing Space: The Computer, Hypertext, and the History of Writing.* Hillsdale, NJ: L. Erlbaum Associates, 1991.

Horn, R.E. *Mapping Hypertext : The Analysis, Organization, and Display of Knowledge for the Next Generation of On-line Text and Graphics.* Lexington, MA: Lexington Institute, 1989.

Horton, W.K. *Designing and Writing Online Documentation: Help Files to Hypertext.* New York: Wiley, 1990.

Nelson, T. *Computer Lib / Dream Machines.* Redmond, WA: Microsoft Press, 1987.

Nielsen, J. *Hypertext and Hypermedia.* Boston: Academic Press, 1990.

@ 21 @

A Big Black Book: Directories of Internet Users and Hosts

When I was a boy, my grandmother's dialless telephone was an object of mystery. It was like a clock without hands or a ladder without rungs - I couldn't fathom the use of it. Then my grandmother demonstrated. She picked up the receiver and said, "Jenny, get me Mrs. Wilson, please. Thank you, dear."

> Brian Hayes
> "The Numbering Crisis in World Zone 1"
> *The Sciences* 32(6) (1992):12

In my house there's this light switch that doesn't do anything. Every so often I would flick it on and off just to check. Yesterday, I got a call from a woman in Germany. She said, "Cut it out."

> Steven Wright

One of the most frequently asked Internet questions is ,"how do I find someone's e-mail address?"

You can usually obtain a person's e-mail information with one or a few well-planned phone calls or postal letters. When you contact them, ask them directly for their e-mail address. But if you can't find a person's Internet address by these traditional methods, or if you are like a growing number of Internet users who want to do everything through the Internet, there are several Internet directory services that you can try. There are also a number of directories which can help you locate Internet services and their addresses, which will also be described in this chapter.

21.1. Challenges to Internet Directory Services

It's easy to get information about telephone numbers: all we have to do is look in a phone book or call directory assistance. To provide analogous services for the Internet, there are many efforts to create resources that provide access to e-mail addresses of individuals and institutions, and contact information for Internet services. By loose analogy to the page colors of published telephone directories in the U.S., such directories of Internet addresses for people and services are often referred to as "white pages" and "yellow pages," respectively.

But making directories of Internet users and services is a challenge for a number of reasons.

21.1.1. Volatility of Computer Information

E-mail addresses change more rapidly than postal addresses or people's names. Your town has probably been in the same state since it was established, the street you live on has probably had the same name for decades, and very few people change their first names. In contrast, the domain name of an Internet computer might change every couple of years, and your user-id(s) can be changed at any time based on decisions made by you or systems administrators.

21.1.2. Local Information Services Are Still Embryonic

In order for an Internet-wide information directory system to be created, it would be useful for local sites to develop and perfect local directories, just like regional telephone companies keep track of phone numbers in their service areas. But unfortunately, many institutions still do not have a master list of local user-id's and services.

21.1.3. Privacy and Security Issues

Many sites are understandably reluctant to publicize some or all addresses or user-ids because of concerns about unauthorized access to sensitive data or costly computer resources, or the privacy of users at those sites.

21.1.4. Competing Paradigms

Standardized Internet protocols have already been established for transmitting data (TCP/IP) and resolving computer names (DNS), but there are still a number of competing approaches for providing Internet white pages and yellow pages services. Very likely, even more will be created in the next few years. On the bright side however, there are several protocols being developed to present a single user interface for querying distinct information databases.

21.2. Strategies for Using Directory Services

As of 1992, there is no single directory service for all of the Internet. Services like Gopher and WAIS are including a growing number of the many bits and pieces of the directory world and may render documents such as this chapter obsolete at some time in the future. But it's still necessary to do a little poking around the net to find the directory service most appropriate for each search.

To find an Internet address, you should choose the directory which is most likely to have the information you are seeking. Before diving into the catalog of directory services, here's a quick review of possible strategies for some general classes of searches.

21.2.1. Finding Addresses of "Average Users"

There are several directory services of special interest in tracking down the average Internet user. Here's the order in which you might try these databases. (Complete information on using these resources is provided later in the chapter.)

When You Don't Know Where They Are...

Most directory services will not be of much help unless you know where the person is located just as you can't get someone's telephone number unless you know what area code to call. However, a few directory services try to collect unique addresses from throughout the Internet.

The Usenet addresses database is a great place to start. It is created from the e-mail addresses in articles posted to Usenet newsgroups and currently contains hundreds of thousands of unique addresses.

Next, you might try the Knowbot Information Server which is a very powerful "one-stop shopping" service providing automatic access to several directory services from one front end.

Gopher and WAIS servers throughout the world are adding access to most of the directory services described in this chapter and may become the preferred interface for working with directory databases. The University of Notre Dame Gopher is particularly strong with more than 100 directory services available as of September 1992.

The Usenet newsgroup "soc.net-people" is specifically for tracking down people with whom you've lost contact. Typically, you would post a message with a subject line containing the person's name, a likely geographical region in which they are located, and a detailed message containing information that may help people figure out who you're talking about. This service should be considered a forum of last resort.

When You Do Know Where They Are...

The command "finger" will often help you find e-mail addresses if you know the name of the Internet host where the person's home account is located. However, this will work only if finger is installed and active both on your Internet host and on the host you are querying.

Netfind is a very powerful directory service with Internet-wide coverage. To use this service effectively, you need to know the person's name and some information about their geographical location and/or institutional affiliation.

21.2.2. Finding Addresses for Administrators

There are a number of directory services that are either intended solely as network administrative directories or are at early stages of development and have started with this restricted and structured set of information. Directions on using these services are provided later in the chapter.

Europe

"Paradise" is mainly an administrative directory service for the COSINE X.500 project in Europe. In the future it may contain a comprehensive directory of general users in Europe as well.

Japan

"whois@nic.ad.jp" is currently an experimental whois service for network administrators in Japan. At some point, it may become a general purpose directory service.

North America

"whois@nic.ddn.mil" is sort of the granddaddy of network directory services. It contains a great deal of contact information for network administrators as well as U.S. military personnel. Some other Internet users are also in this database, but providing a general listing is not its primary focus.

The "PSI White Pages" contain contact information for network administrators and staff of participating institutions. This project might, in the future, become a general purpose directory service.

Worldwide

The section titled "Directories of Computer Addresses" describes databases which are primarily for finding addresses of Internet hosts, but many of these contain contact information for administrators and technical staff at the hosts as well.

21.3. General Purpose Directories of E-mail Addresses

College E-mail

Overview: A very useful document for finding e-mail addresses at North American colleges and universities. Includes hints about which hosts are most likely to be used by certain sets of people, the conventions for the construction of user-ids, and local directory services at each site. Although focusing on students, the information is useful for finding administrators, faculty, and staff as well.

Access: WAIS, FTP, and as a periodic posting to the newsgroups "soc.college", "soc.net-people", and "news.answers".

WAIS database: `college-email`

FTP host:	`pit-manager.mit.edu`
directory:	`pub/usenet/soc.college`
filenames:	`FAQ:_College_Email_Addresses_1_3_[Monthly_posting]`
	`FAQ:_College_Email_Addresses_2_3_[Monthly_posting]`
	`FAQ:_College_Email_Addresses_3_3_[Monthly_posting]`

More Info: e-mail: `mkant@cs.cmu.edu` (Mark Kantrowitz)

E-mail Addresses for the Former Soviet Union

Overview: A list of names, addresses, phone numbers, fax numbers, and some e-mail addresses for most organizations in the former Soviet Union which either have or plan to have e-mail connections.

Access: WAIS database: `cissites`

FTP host:	`impaqt.drexel.edu`
directory:	`pub/suearn/misc`
filename:	`cissites.txt`

More Info: e-mail: `cismap@dm.com`

Finger

Overview: Provides e-mail address, full name, telephone numbers, and other optional information about a particular user at a particular site. Although originally available only for Unix computers, there are now versions of finger for other operating systems as well.

Access: From your Internet host, try "finger <your-userid>". If you get a response containing contact information about yourself, finger is installed locally, and you can use it to obtain userids at remote hosts by typing "finger <userid>@<a.remote.internet.host>". Note that finger must be active and fully enabled at that other host for finger to work!

More Info: On Unix, "man finger", and on other operating systems, "help finger", may give you some information.

Gopher

Overview: A very easy to use interface for finding e-mail addresses—once you find which Gopher and which Gopher directory has the services you are looking for! Directory services from throughout the world can be accessed, including the following:

   • CSO nameservers (so called for the Computing Systems Office at University of Illinois, Champaign-Urbana) for several dozen institutions containing e-mail addresses and other contact information for staff and students;

   • access to many of the directory services listed in this chapter; and

   • X.500 directory services.

   Some Gopher sites are especially strong in directory services. Note that a comprehensive listing of all the world's directory services is being developed on the University of Notre Dame Gopher by Joel P. Cooper (cooper@utopia.cc.nd.edu). As of September, 1992, it is located in the directory "Phone Books—Other Institutions/All the directory servers in the world/" and already contains 132 resources.

Access: Via Gopher. Please read Chapter 17 for more information.

KIS (Knowbot Information Server)

Overview: The "Knowbot Information Server" retrieves e-mail addresses, postal addresses, telephone numbers, and institutional affiliation for users throughout the Internet. Knowbot is a resource that allows you to search through many directories at once. Some of the directory services currently accessible through Knowbot include the following:

```
finger@any.Unix.host
mcimail@nri.reston.va.us
mitwp@mit.edu
profile@gwen.cs.purdue.edu
profile@megaron.arizona.edu
profile@nri.reston.va.us
quipu
whois@nic.ddn.mil
X.500
```

Access: e-mail: `kis@nri.reston.va.us`

Telnet:
```
nri.reston.va.us 185,  or
sol.bucknell.edu 185
```
(no password required, but don't forget the port, 185!)

Example: This is a Telnet session in which we search for our dear hypothetical friend, Sue D. Nimh:

```
telnet nri.reston.va.us 185

Trying 132.151.1.1...
Connected to cnri.reston.va.us.
Escape character is '^]'.
Knowbot Information Service (V1.0). Copyright CNRI 1990.
All Rights Reserved.
Try ? or man for help

> query Sue Nimh
```

Multiple searches can also be done in a single e-mail request as long as each user request is placed on a separate line. Results will be mailed back to you.

More Info:	Online help:	help, ?, and help <command> (e.g., help query)

	FTP host:	nri.reston.va.us
	directory:	rdroms
	filenames:	KIS-id.PS
		KIS-id.txt
	Mailing list:	kis-users-request@nri.reston.va.edu

Comments: KIS can be installed locally and run on computers connected to the Internet using any version of Unix with Berkeley-style sockets. KIS currently has translation programs for whois (nic.ddn.mil), profile, mcimail, QUIPU, and finger. Any sites using these services can be added easily to a locally installed KIS.

JANET Directory

Overview: An online directory of individuals associated with JANET, the British Networking organization.

Access:	Telnet	sun.nsf.ac.uk
	login:	janet
	hostname:	uk.ac.jnt.dir

Netfind

Overview: An Internet-wide directory service which can retrieve e-mail addresses and other contact information based on geographical, institutional, and host names.

Comments: This is a very powerful tool. Expect to have to choose between large numbers of possible domain nameservers and then hosts and be sure you have the ability to scroll backwards on your screen to see all the hosts from which you can choose.

Also, don't be surprised if you receive conflicting information, mainly due to old directory information on a person's previous host. Netfind uses information from Usenet news messages, the Domain Naming System, the Simple Mail Transfer Protocol, and the "finger" protocol. Select the Netfind server nearest you!

Access:	Telnet	bruno.cs.colorado.edu	Colorado
		archie.au	Australia
		malloco.ing.puc.cl	Chile
		mudhoney.micro.umn.edu	Minnesota
		netfind.oc.com	Texas
		redmont.cis.uab.edu	Alabama
		sun.uakom.cs	Czech and Slovak Fed. Repub.
	login:	netfind	

Example: This is a sample session looking for our hypothetical friend, Sue D. Nimh. Let's assume
                  that we have reason to believe that she's a software engineer in Corvallis, Oregon, and
                  show you how to use this information to refine a Netfind search.

```
telnet bruno.cs.colorado.edu

login: netfind

(login messages deleted)

Top level choices:
        1. Help
        2. Search
        3. Seed database lookup
        4. Options
        5. Quit (exit server)
--> 2
Person & keys (blank exits)->nimh oregon corvallis

There are too many domains in the list.
Please select at most 3 of the following:

0. ads.orst.edu (oregon st. university,corvallis, oregon)
1. aes.orst.edu (oregon st. university,corvallis, oregon)
2. als.orst.edu (oregon st. university,corvallis, oregon)

(...many other hosts listed)

40. roguewave.com (rogue wave software, corvallis)
41. sosc.osshe.edu (oregon st. system of higher ed ...)
42. stat.orst.edu (statistics department, oregon st.)
43. statware.com (statware, corvallis, oregon)
```

Let's try one of the listed hosts by entering its number:

```
Enter selection (e.g., 3 1 2) --40


(0) check_name: checking domain roguewave.com. Level = 0
The domain 'roguewave.com' does not run its own name
servers.
        Skipping domain search phase for this domain.
```

This particular host does not have directory services enabled, so let's try another search including the word "computer" to see if we can have a narrower, more likely set of hosts from which to choose.

```
Enter person and keys --> nimh computer corvallis

There are too many domains in the list.

Please select at most 3 of the following:
0. cs.orst.edu (comp. sci. department, oregon state...)
1. ece.orst.edu (electrical and computer engineering...)
2. fenris.com (fenris computer services, inc, corvallis)
3. lynx.cs.orst.edu (comp. sci. department, oregon...)

Enter selection (e.g., 3 1 2) --> 1

( 0) check_name: checking domain ece.orst.edu.  Level = 0

SYSTEM: ece.orst.edu

Login name: sdn                    In real life: Sue D. Nimh
Phone: 555-1958
Directory: /u1/user/sdn            Shell: /usr/local/bin/messg
Last login Tue Sep 29 12:09
No Plan
```

More Info: If Netfind is installed at your site, there may be online help. Try "help netfind" or "man netfind". Software and documentation is available at the following FTP hosts:

Documentation:

FTP host:	`ftp.cs.colorado.edu`
directory:	`pub/cs/techreports/schwartz/ASCII`
filename:	`White.Pages.txt.Z`

Software:

FTP host:	`ftp.cs.colorado.edu`
directory:	`pub/cs/distribs/netfind`
filenames:	(many or all)

Paradise

Overview: E-mail address and telephone numbers of people and organizations participating in the COSINE Pilot Directory Service project.

Access: Telnet to one of two European sites:

United Kingdom:

Telnet: `paradise.ulcc.ac.uk`
login: `dua`

Sweden:

Telnet: `hypatia.umdc.umu.se`
login: `de`

More Info: Extensive online help and documents available via mail server.

```
mail:    info-server@paradise.ulcc.ac.uk
subject: (none needed)
message: PARADISE Project
```

PARADISE Help Desk.

e-mail: `helpdesk@paradise.ulcc.ac.uk`
tel: + 44 71 405 8400 x432
fax: + 44 71 242 1845

PSI White Pages Pilot X.500 Project

Overview: Searches for e-mail addresses and related contact information for administrators and staff
                 of institutions participating in the pilot project of the X.500 Directory Service.

Access   Telnet: `wp.psi.com`   or
                                `wp2.psi.com`
                 login: `fred`   ("**FR**ont **E**nd to the **D**irectory")

More Info: Online help: help, ?, and help <command> (e.g., help query). For more information
                 about X.500 and related topics, try the following anonymous FTP host:

                 FTP host: `ftp.psi.com`
                 directory: `wp`
                 filenames: (many or all)

                 The following newsgroups and mailing lists contain discussion about ISO, of which
                 X.500 is a part:

                 Usenet Newsgroups:

                         `comp.protocols.iso`
                         `comp.protocols.iso.dev-environ`

                 Mailing Lists:

                         `iso-request@nic.ddn.mil`
                         `isode-request@nic.ddn.mil`

soc.net-people (Usenet Newsgroup)

Overview: A newsgroup devoted to helping people find other people.

Access: You need access to Usenet newsreading software to make best use of this service. For
              more on using Usenet, refer to Chapter 9.

Example: When you post to this newsgroup, you should make the "subject" line as concise and
              informative as possible. The message should contain any relevant information that may
              spark the memory of a person reading the newsgroup.

              For example, an intelligent posting to find a hypothetical friend Sue D. Nimh might start
              like this:

```
subject: Oregon, Alaska, W. U.S.: Sue D. Nimh

I am attempting to locate a friend named Sue D. Nimh.

Sue grew up in Juneau Alaska, and studied computer
science at Oregon State University in Corvallis,
Oregon, from 1986-1990...

(Introductory sentence should be followed by other relevant information, possibly
                  including hobbies, physical description, and so forth.)
```

Usenet Addresses

Overview: Searches through a catalog of e-mail addresses of people who have posted messages to
              Usenet newsgroups. This is a very useful service for finding Internet users who may not
              yet be in formal or administrative directories.

Access   WAIS database: `usenet-addresses`

              E-mail: send the following e-mail message, with the person's name or user-id:

```
mail:     mail-server@pit-manager.mit.edu
subject:  (none necessary)
message:  send usenet-addresses/<name>
```

---

whois

Overview: Many domains within the Internet have a "whois server" that provides directory
              information for the hosts within the domain.

Access: On most Unix hosts and some other Internet hosts, whois can often be used as a line
              command.

```
whois <-h server-name> <name>
```

The "<-h server-name>" is an option to specify a particular whois server. If you do not
include the "<-h server-name>", the whois command will default to a whois server, very
frequently, whois@nic.ddn.mil. (See next entry in this chapter.)

Sometimes, whois can be used via Telnet to a whois server through port 43, if this service
has been created for that domain. Enter the person's name once the connection is
established.

```
telnet <whois-server.address> 43
```

More Info: On Unix hosts, "man whois"; on other hosts, "help whois".

              Matt Power (mhpower@athena.mit.edu) maintains a definitive list of whois servers:

              FTP host: **charon.mit.edu**
              directory: **pub/whois**
              filename: **whois-servers.list**

---

whois@nic.ddn.mil

Overview: A database of names, e-mail and postal addresses, telephone numbers and other contact
              information for registered users, hosts, organizations, gateways, and networks throughout
              the Internet. Most persons listed are network administrators or technical staff. This
              service provides especially good coverage of MILNET (formerly ARPANET).

Access: Telnet or via command line query from many Internet hosts.

Examples: As a line command from most Internet hosts, just "whois <name>" will query the whois
              server at nic.ddn.mil, or telnet directly to nic.ddn.mil.

              Telnet: **nic.ddn.mil**
                               no login information necessary

More Info: The Telnet accessible service has extensive online help. For help when using whois as a
              local Unix command, type "man whois"

---

whois@nic.ad.jp

Overview: An experimental whois service for Japanese Internet networks. Responses can be given in English or in Japanese.

Access: As a line command if the whois command is installed.

Example: "whois -h nic.ad.jp <name>/e" for English queries; "whois -h nic.ad.jp <name>/j" responds in Japanese; the default is Japanese.

21.4. Institution Specific Directories of E-mail Addresses

A growing number of institutions are putting their staff and student directories online in publicly accessible formats.

Although many of these are directly accessible via a Telnet connection, a growing number are being incorporated into Gopher and WAIS.

21.5. Discipline-Specific Directories of E-mail Addresses

Review of LISTSERV Subscription Lists

Overview: Many LISTSERV discussion lists keep a record of their subscribers, that can be reviewed by sending a command to the LISTSERVer maintaining that list.

Comments: Keep in mind that not all LISTSERV subscribers realize that their contact information is automatically stored when they subscribe to a LISTSERV.

Example: Suppose you have reason to believe that the person you are trying to contact subscribes to the (hypothetical) LISTSERV group, "AXOLOT-L@AMPHBIAN.BITNET". You would simply send the following e-mail message, and if the subscription list for AXOLOT-L is open to public viewing, you would receive a copy of all subscribers in an e-mail message.

```
mail:     listserv@amphbian.bitnet
subject:  (none needed)
message:  rev axolot-l
```

American Philosophical Association

Overview: Names and e-mail addresses of the membership of the American Philosophical Association.

Comments: There are many other services available when you log in.

Access: Telnet: `atl.calstate.edu`
                login: `apa`

                Once you are logged in, select the menu "E-mail Addresses of the Membership."

Contact: e-mail: `traiger@oxy.edu`

                Saul Traiger
                Department of Philosophy
                Cognitive Science Program
                Occidental College
                Los Angeles, CA 90041 USA

                voice: (213) 259-2901

Army Corps of Engineers

Overview: District phone book for the U.S. Army Corps of Engineers, Sacramento District. Names are stored in UPPER CASE, and an empty or null search will return the catalog, which contains the complete phone book.

Access: WAIS database: `usace-spk-phonebook`

More Info: e-mail: `root@spk41.usace.mil`
                              or
                       `postmaster@usace.mil`

Astronomers

Overview: A listing of the contact information for professional astronomers and astronomical facilities around the world.

Access: E-mail requests for this guide should be sent to: e-mail@srf.ro-greenwich.ac.uk.

Biology and Artificial Intelligence Researchers

Overview: Directory of molecular biologists working in artificial intelligence.

Access: WAIS database: **bionic-ai-researchers**

More Info: e-mail: **wais@nic.funet.fi** (Rob Harper)

CSD (Canadian Studies Electronic Mail Directory)

Overview: Names, institutions, specialty, and e-mail addresses of scholars and teachers in the field
                 of Canadian Studies.

Access: FTP or e-mail requests

                 FTP host: **bss.usl.edu**
                 directory: **pub/canada_studies**
                 files: **scholars_alpha**
                                        scholars_area

More Info: e-mail: **jwf3885@usl.edu**

                 John W. Ferstel
                 Department of English
                 University of Southwestern Louisiana
                 Lafayette, LA 70504 USA

To Register: Request an information entry form from jwf3885@usl.edu.

Consortium for School Networking

Overview: A LISTSERV accessible directory of the full membership of the Consortium for School Networking (CoSN).

Access: E-mail messages to LISTSERV@BITNIC.BITNET.

Example: Send the following e-mail message and you will receive the directory via e-mail:

```
mail:     LISTSERV@BITNIC.BITNET
subject:  (none needed)
message:  send cosnlist text
```

IEEE Directory

Overview: An aliasing directory of active IEEE volunteers, that allows you to search for e-mail addresses by supplying "i.lastname" where "i" is the person's first initial and "lastname" is their full last name. The main purpose of this service is for people to be able to send e-mail messages to IEEE members by their real names even if one doesn't know their e-mail address.

Access: You can obtain a list of all valid aliases in the IEEE.ORG Directory Service by sending e-mail to "directory@ieee.org" with the message "aliases".

Oceanographers

Overview: E-mail and postal addresses, institutional affiliations, and names of oceanographers and related researchers.

Access: Telnet: delocn.udel.edu
               login: INFO

               Once you are logged in, select the menu "Who's Who - electronic and mail addresses."

Plant Taxonomists

Overview: A directory of e-mail addresses and other contact information of plant taxonomists and herbaria. Available via FTP.

Access: FTP host: `huh.harvard.edu`
             directory: `pub/email`
             filename: `pto`

More Info: `beach@huh.harvard.edu`   (Jim. H. Beach)
             `visbms@ubvms.bitnet`   (Richard Zander)

Vulcanologists

Overview: Names, e-mail addresses, institutional affiliations, and specializations of vulcanologists.

Access: E-mail requests to a LISTSERV to retrieve the entire directory.

```
mail:     listserv%asuacad.bitnet@vm1.nodak.edu
subject:  (none needed)
message:  get vlist file
```

More Info: e-mail: `jordi@sc2a.unige.ch`

Steve Jordi
Department of Geophysics
University of Geneva
13, Rue des Maraichers
1211 GENEVA 4 Switzerland

Fax: + 41 22 320-5732

21.6. Directories of Computer Addresses

BITNET / EARN Nodes

Overview: A directory of authoritative information about BITNET and EARN hosts including administrative contacts and configuration of the hosts.

Access: Accessible through WAIS (preferred method of access) and FTP:

               WAIS database: `bitearn.nodes`

               FTP host: `vm.utdallas.edu`
               directory: `bitnet`
               filename: `bitearn.nodes`

British Online Yellow Pages—British Telecom

Overview: A directory of British firms and organizations that can be searched by name of firm, location, and product.

Access: Telnet: `sun.nsf.ac.uk`
               login: `janet`
               hostname: `uk.ac.niss`
               NISS menu: select **U**
               UK menu: select **E**
                               Press the return key.

Domain Organizations

Overview: Database of domain names, organizational acronyms upon which they are based, and a limited amount of administrative contact information. A very useful database for finding a domain name when you know the organization's name or acronym.

Access: WAIS database: `domain-organizations`

More Info: e-mail: `emv@cic.net`

FidoNet Node List

Overview: A listing of the systems within FidoNet; contains FidoNet node number, geographic location, contact name, and title.

Access: WAIS database: `fidonet-nodelist`

More Info: e-mail: `pozar@kumr.lns.com`

Fido Software
Box 77731
San Francisco, CA 94107 USA.

Netinfo

Overview: A multi-purpose service with many commands for finding information about Internet hosts, and some information about BITNET and UUCP as well. Also contains great general online help for many aspects of network addressing. Although the help information has been collected specifically for users at Berkeley, much of the information is of value to any Internet users. For example "help mail net index" gives information on addressing e-mail messages to non-Internet networks.

Access: Telnet: `netinfo.berkeley.edu 117`   (Don't forget the port, 117!)
              Online help: `?`   (use "?" for a quick
                                                             display of available
                                                             commands)

More Info: e-mail: `netinfo@netinfo.berkeley.edu` (Bill Wells)
              voice: (510) 642-9801

nslookup

Overview: A useful Unix command for finding an IP numeric address when you know the Fully Qualified Domain Name of a host. Has many additional features and options when run in interactive mode, such as listing hosts within a domain, using different name-servers, and using finger from within the nslookup session.

Access: From a Unix host enter "nslookup" followed by part or all of a Fully Qualified Domain Name (non-interactive mode). Entering "nslookup" by itself will launch an interactive nslookup session.

More Info: "man nslookup", or during an interactive session type "help" once you are at the ">" prompt.

United Kingdom Name Registration Database

Overview: Contains hostnames and addresses of all hosts in the Janet network.

Access: WAIS database: `uk-name-registration-service`

More Info: e-mail: `sjl@doc.ic.ac.uk`

21.7. Administrative Directory Services

Horton

Overview: A software package for the automatic updating of a site's whois database that operates by periodically fingering each host in a domain. If your company or university doesn't yet have an e-mail directory, Horton can help you get it started.

Access: The Horton source code is available via FTP from many Internet sites. Use archie to find the archive nearest you.

More Info: e-mail: `dank@blacks.jpl.nasa.gov` (Dan Kegel)

Internet Phonebook

Overview: The contents of the WHOIS database, as of late 1990, in WAIS accessible format. Each entry is a 1 line summary for each entry in the Network Managers Phonebook published by the NSF Network Service Center.

Access: WAIS database: `internet-phonebook`

More Info: e-mail: `nnsc@nnsc.nsf.net`

RIPE (Reseaux IP Europeen) Network Management Database

Overview: E-mail and postal addresses, names, and phone numbers of administrators and managers of the RIPE network.

Access: WAIS database: `ripe-database`

              FTP host: `ftp.ripe.net`
              directory: `ripe/dbase`
              filename: `ripe.db`

More Info: e-mail: `marten@ns.ripe.net`

21.8. Internet Directory Services: Where Do We Go from Here?

During 1992 there has been a tremendous change in the number and quality of Internet directory services. It has taken years of development to attain the level of quality we have come to expect from traditional information systems such as telephone directory services, so it should not be surprising that Internet directories are not yet as comprehensive, reliable, or easy to use as they could be.

As the Internet evolves, available services respond to the needs and activities of its users. With strong demand from the user community and rapid response from service providers, more complete and reliable directory services could be at hand before the end of the decade.

21.9. For More Information

Most of the directory services described in this chapter have online help that may include pointers to technical references describing their inner workings.

The following RFCs contain some general discussion about directory services and specific information about the X.500 protocol:

RFC 1107	Plan for Internet directory services
RFC 1202	Directory Assistance service
RFC 1295	User bill of rights for entries and listing in the Public Directory
RFC 1308	Executive introduction to directory services using the X.500 protocol
RFC 1309	Technical overview of directory services using the X.500 protocol

21.9.1. Bibliography

Kille, S.E. *Implementing X.400 and X.500: The PP and QUIPU Systems.* Boston, MA: Artech House, 1991.

Rose, M.T. *The Little Black Book: Mail Bonding With OSI Directory Services.* Englewood Cliffs, NJ: Prentice Hall, 1992.

Section VI

Targeted Interests

@ 22 @

A Schoolhouse for the World: Using the Global Internet in K-12 Education

"Do you know what it is to be alive?"
  "It's when you can do things."
"Is a cat alive?"
  "Yes."
"A table?"
  "No."
"Why not?"
  "It can't move."
"Is a bicycle alive?"
  "Yes."
"Why?"
  "It can go."
"Is a bicycle alive when it isn't moving?"
  "Yes."
"Is the moon alive?"
  "Yes, sometimes it hides behind the mountains."

From a conversation between
Jean Piaget and a seven year old boy
The Child's Conception of the World

Until recently, computer networks have been used almost exclusively in universities, corporations, and governments. But in the past few years, there has been exponential growth in the use of local, national, and even international networks in pre-college, or "K-12," education.

Consider the possibilities: a global, pre-college school would have classrooms spanning continents. Although the plans of this global schoolhouse are still being drawn, its halls are already beginning to ring with the voices and activities of enthusiastic students and teachers.

The aim of this chapter is to provide the information you need to help you use the Internet in a way that is appropriate for you, your students—and your students' futures. You will get a quick tour of this rapidly growing global school. You'll be introduced to its classes, conference rooms, libraries, field trips, and science labs, and given some ideas about how the Internet is currently incorporated into the K-12 curriculum.

22.1. Why Use Global Networks in K-12 Schools?

Computer networks might seem to be just another classroom gadget like film projectors or televisions. At first glance, a networked computer looks like a computer with some wires running into the wall. But the tiny hole in the wall through which those wires pass is actually a window to the world.

The many benefits offered by networked computers can be grouped into three categories: educational opportunities for the students, resource sharing, and in-service training for the teachers.

22.1.1. Educational Opportunities for the Students

For decades, visionaries have talked about how telecommunications could create a global village in which it is as easy to communicate with someone on the other side of the world as it is to visit a next-door neighbor. Computer networks are currently making this abstract global village a reality for students. From a humble classroom computer connected to networks like the Internet, your students can:

- engage in global dialogue with students and instructors using electronic mail;
- practice foreign language writing skills with native speakers in online discussion groups;
- participate in, or even initiate, meaningful projects based on collaboration and cooperation of thousands of students throughout the world;
- obtain supplemental instructions from online tutorials or enroll in distance education courses in your national or even foreign institutions; and
- gain "information literacy," a basic understanding of how to navigate in and take full advantage of the networked world into which they will be graduating.

Unlike outdated filmstrips of life in Hong Kong or Patagonia, a global network allows your students to communicate directly with fellow students from these and many other places.

22.1.2. Resource Sharing

When a school invests in the hardware and software to connect to a full-service, worldwide network like the Internet, it immediately gains access to billions of dollars of resources. Even the smallest and most isolated rural school can use the same services enjoyed by the largest and best endowed urban universities. These resources include:

- the catalogs of hundreds of the world's best libraries;
- free educational software and documents from file archives containing thousands of Megabytes of files;
- databases of real research data containing information from agricultural markets, global climate simulations, or even space missions to other planets; and
- supercomputer training programs which give students access to the world's most powerful computers.

Networks can be a powerful democratizer of educational resources. While not every school will use all of these resources, they are available if needed.

22.1.3. In-Service Education and Teacher Enrichment

The Internet and the global schoolhouse it creates can also address the needs of teachers and other educators. The staff of primary and secondary schools sometimes feel isolated from their peers or have difficulty maintaining contact with the professors and facilities they depended on throughout their training in colleges and universities. By using computer networks, K-12 educators can:

- increase the number and diversity of educational resources they use while teaching;
- participate in continued education by enrolling in universities and colleges that offer distance education programs via networks;
- continue professional contacts formed during their college or university education; and, of course,
- use the extraordinary informational resources of the Internet for any professional or personal development they might desire.

22.2. To What Network Should a K-12 School Connect?

K-12 schools can obtain network connectivity from a wide variety of providers, including government sponsored educational networks, not-for-profit cooperative networks, and commercial networks. How does one choose which network service is best? A wise decision will take, minimally, the following factors into account:

- How much computer experience do your teachers and students already have?
- What sort of computer equipment does your school already have?
- What are the costs of obtaining the hardware and software required for connectivity?
- What sorts of fees must you pay the service provider?
- What services are provided in exchange for the fees paid—technical support? Users support? Training? Documentation? Manuals and guides?
- Are there any legislative restrictions which make certain options difficult?
- How well will a particular option scale as more demands are placed on it by newly enthusiastic students and teachers?

If your school hasn't yet been connected to an external network, you might think that the most basic network services would be adequate. But judging from the experiences of universities and research institutions, it is likely that once you've made a connection to a global network, the use of computer networks by students and teachers at your school will grow rapidly.

Like universities, K-12 schools have many choices for network connectivity, including:

- Internet networks, such as NSF sponsored regional networks in the U.S.;
- statewide or provincial networks;
- not-for-profit cooperative networks; or
- commercial network providers.

22.2.1. Internet Networks

In terms of comprehensive networking capabilities, the Internet has no match. In fact, most every kind of resource that is available through computer networks is available through the Internet.

It should be noted that Internet connectivity does not have to be high-tech nor high investment. Many school districts find that modem dialup access to the Internet initially provides ample service with only a small investment.

National Internet Networks

Of particular interest to K-12 educators in the U.S. is the National Science Foundation Network (NSFNET). This high speed network was created specifically to support the use of computer networks in education and research. Analogous government sponsored networks have been or are being developed in many other nations.

By the time you read this, NSFNET and similar national Internet networks may have been renamed the National Research and Education Network (NREN). In December of 1991, the High Performance Computing Act, authorizing the creation of a permanent NREN, was signed into law. The bill authorized the expenditure of $2.9 billion over the next five years to enhance the U.S.'s high performance computing and communications infrastructure.

Regional Internet Networks

The NSFNET is a framework or "backbone" network currently linking NSF-sponsored regional networks in the U.S. Each regional network serves many sites throughout its specific geographic region.

Some regional networks, such as BARRNet in the San Francisco and Silicon Valley area, service a geographically small but densely computerized portion of a single state. Others help bring large, sparsely populated regions together into the network world. For example, NorthWestNet serves over 29% of the U.S. land mass, including Alaska, Idaho, Montana, North Dakota, Oregon, and Washington.

A growing number of K-12 schools are reaping the many benefits of direct connections to regional Internet networks.

Statewide or Provincial Networks

Another promising source of network connectivity for K-12 schools are statewide or provincial networks. Many of these networks are part of the Internet.

For example, within the U.S. a survey of statewide networks released in April, 1991, reported that most all 50 states either had established or were about to initiate state networks that would include K-12 connectivity as a central goal (Kurshan, 1991). Similar intranational networking is taking place in Canada and European nations.

Every state network is different. The technical sophistication of statewide networks varies tremendously between and within states. In some states, connections from K-12 schools are made through dialup modems, while other states use technologies such as high speed (T1) lines, fiber optics, point-to-point microwave, and satellite links. Some statewide networks feature direct K-12 Internet access. Most statewide networks offer electronic mail, though in some cases this is still restricted to administrative use.

Comprehensive overviews of state networks can be found in Kurshan (1990b, 1991).

22.2.2. Not-for-Profit Cooperative Networks

There are many national and even international not-for-profit, cooperative computer networks which may be appropriate for K-12 educational networking. These networks are particularly valuable for K-12 sites which cannot, or choose not, to connect directly to the Internet or whose state networks are still embryonic.

FidoNet

FidoNet is an international network with more than 10,000 electronic "bulletin board systems" (BBSs) in more than 50 countries. It is a grassroots, decentralized, not-for-profit network operated entirely through volunteer effort.

A FidoNet BBS can be run with minimal hardware and software requirements. All you need is a telephone, a modem, a personal computer, a hard-disk, and free FidoNet software. A good file backup system is a wise investment as well.

K12Net

Another particularly promising and widespread not-for-profit network for K-12 education is K12Net, an offshoot of FidoNet. The goal of K12Net is to create a demand for networking services within the K-12 education community by making it as easy as possible for K-12 schools to start networking. If you have access to a telephone, modem, and computer, you can dial up a FidoNet or K12Net BBS and start exploring the world of K-12 networking immediately. K12Net is an accessible, hands-on, network-based technology simple enough for students to learn and even operate.

K12Net offers the following services:

- global electronic mail, which can be sent to and received from the Internet;
- K-12 discussion groups;
- rich archives of K-12 oriented educational software (currently for MS-DOS computers only), documents, and other information available at 19 major K12Net BBSs.

In many ways the strengths of K12Net and FidoNet are derived from their simplicity, but this is also their limitation. They cannot offer the tremendous range of resources provided by the Internet. Contact information for several K12Net coordinators can be found at the end of this chapter.

National Public Telecommunications Network

The National Public Telecomputing Network (NPTN) is a not-for-profit organization dedicated to establishing and developing free computerized information and communication services for the general public, including the K-12 community. Current NPTN services are based on locally oriented bulletin board systems called Free-Nets. They provide information of interest to the general public, usually concentrating on serving a restricted geographic region. Please see Chapter 15 for more information on accessing Free-Nets.

NPTN sites are operating or are planned in many cities including Buffalo; Chicago; Cleveland; Denver; Lorain County, OH; Los Angeles; Minneapolis/St.Paul; Portland, OR; Philadelphia; Summit, NJ; Washington, D.C.; Helsinki, Finland; Singapore; and Wellington, New Zealand.

22.3. Getting Started with K-12 Networking

Because K-12 networking began in earnest only a few years ago and because the networking world is evolving so rapidly, there are no definitive answers to even some of the most basic questions about how to use the Internet in K-12 education. In fact, there may never be definitive answers, and that may be a good thing!

Unlike many national, federally sponsored networks which have centralized authority and administration, each K-12 school district serves a distinct and unique constituency. This diversity and plurality will be reflected in the strategies adopted by each K-12 school district, from the technical to the pedagogical. No single solution can be right for everyone.

The rest of this chapter will present some specific examples of how the Internet is being used in K-12 education. What you learn in this chapter should help you make informed decisions about which Internet resources are best for your school.

22.3.1. Network Etiquette and Ethics

The current Internet community is mainly comprised of people from universities and research institutions who have developed unspoken rules of conduct in the networked world. Just as we unconsciously internalize standards of etiquette in our everyday behavior, the issue of network etiquette may not be apparent to new users of network services, especially among K-12 students. As Jack Crawford, one of the main forces behind K12Net has written, "the ability to keep our echoes animated, well behaved, and oriented toward K-12 curriculum increasingly depends upon the zealousness, energy, and skill of moderators."

Before starting a K-12 networking project with students, it would be wise to read about network etiquette so you have an appreciation of these rules before you and your students begin Internetworking. Chapter 4 deals with some of the issues of etiquette involved in electronic mail communications.

22.4. Communicating in the Global Schoolhouse

There are several discussion groups which act as the assembly halls and bulletin boards for teachers to announce projects requiring the cooperation of fellow K-12 classes, to share ideas, and in general, shape the future of K-12 use of the Internet.

Online discussion groups can put you in immediate communication with people throughout the world who share any interest you might have. Specific instructions on how to use Usenet, LISTSERV, and mailing lists are given in Chapters 9, 10, and 11 respectively. Just follow the examples in those chapters, and you can probably access any of the groups described below.

22.4.1. Usenet and K-12 Education

Among the thousands of Usenet newsgroups are a number of special interest to K-12 educators.

The "k12" Hierarchy

As described in Chapter 9, there are several top level hierarchies within Usenet. The "k12" hierarchy contains newsgroups distributed to Internet and K12Net users and are geared directly towards K-12 education.

`k12.chat.elementary`	Informal discussion, elementary students, K-5
`k12.chat.junior`	Informal discussion, students in grades 6-8
`k12.chat.senior`	Informal discussion, high school students
`k12.chat.teacher`	Informal discussion, K-12 teachers
`k12.ed.art`	Art curriculum in K-12 education
`k12.ed.business`	Business education curriculum in grades K-12
`k12.ed.comp.literacy`	Teaching computer literacy in grades K-12
`k12.ed.health-pe`	Health and physical education in grades K-12
`k12.ed.life-skills`	Home economics and career education, grades K-12
`k12.ed.math`	Mathematics curriculum in K-12 education
`k12.ed.music`	Music and performing arts curriculum in K-12
`k12.ed.science`	Science curriculum in K-12 education
`k12.ed.soc-studies`	Social studies and history curriculum in K-12
`k12.ed.special`	Education for students with handicaps or special needs
`k12.ed.tag`	Education for talented and gifted students
`k12.ed.tech`	Industrial arts and vocational education in K-12
`k12.lang.art`	Language arts curriculum in K-12 education
`k12.lang.deutsch-eng`	Bilingual German/English with native speakers
`k12.lang.esp-eng`	Bilingual Spanish/English with native speakers
`k12.lang.francais`	Bilingual French/English with native speakers
`k12.lang.russian`	Bilingual Russian/English with native speakers
`k12.library`	Discussion of K-12 library use on the Internet

The "k12.sys" Newsgroups

When you use the k12 Usenet hierarchy, you will notice newsgroups with names beginning "k12.sys." The newsgroup "k12.sys.projects" is for the coordination of activities in the newsgroups "k12.sys.channelX," where "X" is currently a number between 0 and 12. Each of these "channels" may be devoted to the exclusive use of a project for up to two months. For example, someone may announce in "k12.ed.science" or "k12.sys.projects" that they want to set up a project for collecting rainfall data. After participants have been collected, a "k12.sys" channel may be assigned for this project.

For more information about using the "k12.sys" newsgroups, read "k12.sys.projects."

Other Usenet Newsgroups of Potential Interest to K-12

There are many newsgroups which, although not set up specifically for the K-12 community, may nonetheless be of interest to both K-12 educators and students. Here is a small subset of such general interest newsgroups.

bionet.general	misc.writing
comp.dcom.modems	news.announce.newusers
misc.consumers	news.answers
misc.consumers.house	news.newusers.questions
misc.education	news.software.readers
misc.kids	sci.edu
misc.rural	

22.4.2. Mailing Lists

Among the best places for Internet users from the K-12 community to get started are the mailing lists KIDSNET and KIDS.

KIDSNET Mailing List

KIDSNET is an international discussion group used by K-12 educators throughout the world. Note that KIDSNET is not a network; you can think of KIDSNET as an assembly hall for the global K-12 Internet school.

If you want to learn about the latest activities, share your ideas, or find collaborators from throughout the world, KIDSNET is the place for you! Everyone can have a seat in the audience or climb onto the stage to make an announcement. KIDSNET is consistently informative and the mood of the group is positively uplifting. In the best spirit of the Internet, everyone on KIDSNET seems to be genuinely interested in sharing and helping.

Subscribing to KIDSNET

You can subscribe to KIDNSET by sending an e-mail message containing your request as follows:

```
mail:     kidsnet-request@vms.cis.pitt.edu
subject:  (none needed)
message:  <your subscription request>
```

After you have subscribed, copies of all messages that are sent to KIDSNET by subscribers throughout the world will be sent to your electronic mailbox.

KIDSNET is very active, so you should be ready to handle many messages every week. If you do not plan to use your Internet account for an extended period, you should send an unsubscription request to the above e-mail address so that your mailbox does not become flooded with messages!

New KIDSNET subscribers are encouraged to introduce themselves to the list. To send an introduction or any other message to the readers of KIDSNET, send an e-mail message as follows:

```
mail:    kidsnet@vms.cis.pitt.edu
subject: <an informative subject line>
message: <your message>
```

Searching KIDSNET via WAIS

You can also search the archives of the KIDSNET discussion via WAIS. This database is currently named "kidsnet" and is accessible through the WAIS servers as described in Chapter 18.

KIDSNET FTP Archives

If you want to retrieve a whole month's worth of KIDSNET discussion, you can use anonymous FTP to retrieve digests of KIDSNET discussion.

FTP host:	`vulcan.phyast.pitt.edu`
directory:	`pub/kidsnet`
filename:	`kidsnet.YYMM`

For each of the filenames, YY is the year, and MM is the month, for example, kidsnet.8905 is the first KIDSNET archive from May, 1989. The files are very large, in fact some are more than 1 megabyte in size, so be sure you have room on your hard disk or diskette for any file(s) you want to retrieve.

KIDS Mailing List

"KIDS" is a spin-off mailing list of KIDSNET for all pre-college students. You can meet thousands of students your age, from all over the world, just by reading and typing messages on your classroom computer. You may still be too young to travel around the world, but you can start making friends to visit when you do!

Subscribing to KIDS

You subscribe to KIDS by sending an e-mail message to:

`joinkids@vms.cis.pitt.edu`

After you have subscribed, messages sent by other students throughout the world will be sent to your electronic mailbox. Be sure you know how to read and get rid of e-mail messages before subscribing.

To send a message to all the kids subscribed to KIDS, send an e-mail message like the following:

```
mail:      kids@vms.cis.pitt.edu
subject:   <one line telling what your message is about>
message:   <a message you would like to share with other kids
           throughout the world>
```

Cancelling a Subscription to KIDS

Before you go on vacation or if you are getting too many messages, you may want to cancel your subscription to KIDS by sending the following e-mail message:

```
mail:      joinkids@vms.cis.pitt.edu
subject:   cancelling kids subscription
message:   <your request to cancel your KIDS subscription>
```

22.4.3. LISTSERV Discussion Groups and K-12 Education

There are more than 3,000 BITNET LISTSERV discussion groups, so first time users are sometimes overwhelmed by the global list-of-lists. At the end of this chapter is a list of the names and addresses of about 100 discussion groups organized by topic that may be of interest to K-12 users. Here are just two of these groups.

KIDLINK and KIDCAFE

KIDLINK is a LISTSERV discussion group that is designed to act as a structured forum for e-mail exchanges between children aged 10-15. A dialog is set up each year called "KIDS-XX" where "XX" is the current year. Each participating child posts an e-mail message answering the following four questions before they can engage in the dialog:

> 1) Who am I?
> 2) What do I want to be when I grow up?
> 3) How do I want the world to be better when I grow up?
> 4) What can I do to make this happen?

After these answers have been submitted, the child can then participate in the KIDCAFE LISTSERV discussion group.

For more information about KIDLINK and KIDCAFE, subscribe to the groups or send an e-mail message to Odd de Presno (opresno@extern.uio.no).

America 2000 Daily Report Card

This is a daily collection of news items about education. Although it deals specifically with how schools in the U.S. are working towards meeting the goals of the America 2000 Project, it is probably of interest to educators worldwide. To subscribe, send the following e-mail message:

```
mail:      listserv%gwuvm.bitnet@cunyvm.cuny.edu
subject:  (none needed)
message:  sub rptcrd <your-full-name> <your-organizations-name)
```

This report is also available by mail in paper form. For more information contact:

America 2000 Daily Report Card
American Political Network, Inc.
282 N. Washington St.
Falls Church, VA 22046 USA

voice: (703) 237-5130

22.5. Collaborative Projects

One of the most exciting uses of the Internet in K-12 education is for communication and collaboration between and among students and teachers at distant schools. Such collaborative projects have the potential to dramatically reshape the educational process. You will learn about many such activities by subscribing to KIDSNET and the many other Usenet and LISTSERV groups. But to get you started, here's a sampler of some notable projects with which you and your students could become involved.

22.5.1. Disabled Data Link Group and Chatback

DDLG and the Chatback Project for Children currently involves about 100 schools supporting the use of networks by disabled students in an effort to assist those with special needs. For more information, please contact Cliff Jones at the e-mail address Cliff.Jones@f71.n254.z2.fidonet.org.

22.5.2. Earth Kids

Earth Kids is a not-for-profit international organization devoted to using networking to promote hands-on, community based ecological projects among the children of the world. For more information, contact:

Marshall Gilmore

e-mail: **Marshall.Gilmore@f606.n105.z1.fidonet.org**
voice: (503) 363-1896

22.5.3. FrEd Mail Foundation

The FrEdMail Foundation specializes in establishing innovative and educationally rewarding collaborative projects using the Internet for the K-12 community. For more information about FrEdMail generally, please contact:

Al Rogers
FrEdMail Foundation
PO Box 243, Bonita, CA 91908 USA

e-mail: **arogers@bonita.cerf.fred.org**
voice: (619) 475-4852

To give you an idea of the diversity and value of FrEdMail, here is a sampling of some current FrEdMail projects.

Newsday

This is a multi-curricular project in which students in participating schools produce local newspapers that are distributed throughout the network. Students become news gatherers and reporters, editors, layout and graphics artists, and publishers. Participation on a national and international scale leads to understanding of broad issues which transcend local concerns. This project can involve your students in weeks of cross-curricular activity.

> Nancy Sutherland
> FrEdMail Foundation
> PO Box 243, Bonita, CA 91908 USA
>
> e-mail: `newsday@bonita.cerf.fred.org`
> voice: (619) 475-4852

Tele-Fieldtrips

This is a program to share the field trip experiences of students with other students throughout the world. Any sort of locale could be of interest including zoos, museums, aquariums, historical sites, natural wonders, or industries. You announce your trip to Tele-Fieldtrips and students and teachers throughout the world can send questions they want answered during your field trip.

This program gives students experience in writing about their surroundings and their experiences. Tele-Fieldtrip participants have found that these electronically distributed reports tend to reflect an interest and excitement not found in their paper counterparts. The students know that what they prepare will be read by many other interested students.

For more information on how to participate in this program, contact:

> Nancy Sutherland
> FrEdMail Foundation
> Box 243
> Bonita, CA 91908 USA
>
> e-mail: `fieldtrips@bonita.cerf.fred.org`
> voice: (619) 475-4852

22.5.4. I*EARN (International Education and Research Network)

I*EARN is a collaborative project of more than 250 schools in 18 countries including the U.S., the former U.S.S.R., Argentina, Australia, Belgium, Canada, China, Costa Rica, England, Finland, Hungary, Indonesia, Israel, Japan, Korea, Mexico, Netherlands, and Spain. Negotiations are currently underway with educational institutions in Nicaragua, Kenya, and Zimbabwe. Projects in I*EARN are intended to make meaningful contributions to the health and welfare of the planet.

In addition to e-mail messages, I*EARN member schools use low cost video-speaker telephones. Although I*EARN is based on the APC Network (comprised of EcoNet, PeaceNet, GlasNet, and GreenNet), all I*EARN mailboxes are accessible through the Internet.

For more information about I*EARN, contact:

Ed Gragert
Director of Programs
Copen Family Fund
345 Kear St.
Yorktown Heights, NY 10598 USA

e-mail: **ed1@igc.org**
voice: (914) 962-5864
fax: (914) 962-6472

22.5.5. Project IDEALS (International Dimension in Education via Active Learning and Simulation)

This project enables multisite, interactive teleconferences simulating international negotiations. Scenarios may be based on real or hypothetical nations or issues. For example, a treaty governing emissions of CFCs or the uses of the ocean can form the basis of a simulation. There are participating schools in many countries including Canada, Finland, Hong Kong, Japan, Latvia, Peru, the United Kingdom, the U.S., and the former U.S.S.R. For more information, please contact:

Project IDEALS
Morgan Hall
Box 870244
University of Alabama
Tuscaloosa, AL 35487 USA

e-mail: **cfarmer1@ua1vm.ua.edu**
voice: (205) 348-9494
fax: (205) 348-5298

22.5.6. TERC

TERC is a not-for-profit organization that concentrates on establishing and coordinating well-planned and scientifically meaningful network-based collaborative projects in the sciences. A representative TERC project is The Global Laboratory Project, an international, telecommunications based initiative supporting biological, chemical, and physical monitoring of the environment by K-12 students.

TERC
2067 Massachusetts Ave.
Cambridge, MA 02140 USA

e-mail: **ken-mayer@terc.edu**
voice: (617) 547-0430
fax: (617) 349-3535

22.5.7. Independently Developed Projects

A growing number of K-12 teachers and students are developing collaborative activities. This section describes two representative projects that have been started by one or a few individuals and have become effective and useful network wide projects. They are very good examples of the simple but very effective use of e-mail in the K-12 curriculum.

Although you are of course encouraged to participate in these activities, the main point of these examples is to help you realize that you don't need to invest a great deal of money in hardware or software to become a contributing member of the global classroom. Once you are part of the Internet, you can help direct the ways in which it is used for education, not only at your own school, but potentially throughout the world.

Kids WeatherNet

In this project, classes throughout the Internet share local weather and climate information, either from a class weather station or from information taken from local weather bureaus. Each Monday, students send their weather reports to all participating schools. For more information, contact:

> Bill Wallace
> 1801 Central Ave. NW
> Manzana Day School
> Albuquerque, NM 87104-1197 USA
>
> e-mail: `echo@bootes.unm.edu`

Mr. Science

Kurt Grosshans of the Christiansburg High School in Christiansburg, Virginia, has set up a service called Mr. Science. Advanced placement (AP) students at the high school respond to e-mail questions about science sent in by elementary students from throughout the world. To submit a question to Mr. Science, send your question to apscichs@radford.vak12ed.edu. If you want to learn more about the Mr. Science project, send e-mail to kgrossa@radford.vak12ed.edu.

22.6. The Library

Are the libraries in your school or even your community adequate for the needs of your students and educators? If not, you can use worldwide library, electronic journal, and online document resources that are available through the Internet.

22.6.1. Online Public Access Catalogs (OPACs) \r "k12OPAC"

Online library catalogs (more precisely known as "online public access catalogs," or OPACs for short) are electronic versions of library card catalogs. OPACs have been created at hundreds of the world's libraries and are generally free of charge for anyone with an Internet connection. A more complete discussion of OPACs is provided in Chapter 14.

What Can OPACs Offer K-12 Education?

Most OPACs on the Internet are based at the libraries of large research institutions, so you can generally do anything that students or faculty at those institutions can do with their OPAC. In particular, OPACs provide the following services of special interest to K-12 education:

- searches by school librarians to help determine which materials to order for the school library;
- resources for staff doing active research;
- access to online catalogs of the libraries of schools or departments of Education;
- inter-library loan arrangements; and,
- full literature searches for teachers or students.

22.6.2. Electronic Books

A growing number of services are offering books in electronic format, including many texts typically used in high school literature classes, such as Shakespeare or the poems of W.B. Yeats. Many of these electronic books are in pure text format that can be read and printed using most any kind of computer and printer. Many of these text services are described in Chapter 13.

22.6.3. Electronic Journals

Electronic journals are like regular magazines. They feature submitted articles which are reviewed, edited, and placed in an organized format within a computer file. The following table lists a few of the many electronic journals which may be of interest to K-12 educators. For more on electronic journals refer to Chapter 12.

Currents	The use of computing in education. Subscription: send e-mail message to jebell%uncamult.bitnet@vm1.nodak.edu
Distance Education Online Symposium (DEOS)	Distance education; many articles on K-12 issues. Subscription: send e-mail to listserv%psuvm.bitnet@cornellc.cit.cornell.edu. message: SUB DEOS <your-full-name>. To cancel a subscription, send mail to the same address, message: UNSUB DEOS.
EFFector Online	Computer based communication, especially issues of freedom of speech, privacy, censorship, and policy. Subscription: send an e-mail message to eff-request@eff.org.
Ejournal	An electronic journal about electronic journals. Subscription: send e-mail message to listserv%albnyvm1.bitnet@cunyvm.cuny.edu with the message: SUB EJRNL <your-full-name>. To cancel a subscription, e-mail to the same address, message: UNSUB EJRNL.
F.A.S.T. News	Articles, bibliographies, job listings, etc. on fine arts, science, and technology. Subscription: send e-mail message to isast@garnet.berkeley.edu.
Handicap Digest	Issues dealing with the handicapped. Subscription: send e-mail message to wtm@bunker.shelp.isc-br.com. Via modem: Handicap News BBS (203) 337-1607 (300, 1200 and 2400 baud). (Fidonet 1:/141/420) Compuserve 73170,1064.
Impact Online	Social and ethical concerns of information technology; send subscription requests to bcs-ss1@compass.com.

22.7. K-12 Oriented Databases

Through the Internet, K-12 schools have access to databases which previously could only be used at research institutions. Of the many databases described in Chapter 15, there are several of special interest to or designed specifically for K-12 education. In particular, you should refer to the entries for FEDIX, MOLIS, and QUERRI. The PENpages, Spacelink, and ERIC databases are described in this chapter since they are probably of the most interest to the K-12 community.

22.7.1. PENpages

PENpages is a very easy to use, general interest database of articles and brochures on agriculture, careers, consumer issues, health, weather, and other topics from The Pennsylvania State University. The materials are written in simple and straightforward language and should be suitable for use as class materials in most schools.

Access:	Telnet:	`psupen.psu.edu`	
	login:	`<your state's 2 letter code>`	(within USA)
		`world`	(outside USA)

22.7.2. Spacelink

Spacelink contains information about NASA and NASA activities, including a large number of curricular activities for elementary and secondary science classes.

Access:	Telnet:	`128.158.13.250`
	username:	`newuser`
	password:	`newuser`

22.7.3. ERIC (Educational Resources Information Center)

ERIC is a database of short abstracts and information on education-related topics of interest to teachers and administrators. This database is funded by the Office of Educational Research and Improvement (OERI) of the U.S. Department of Education (ED).

Many local network service providers include ERIC in CWISs or other information systems; for example, NorthWestNet members can use ERIC through the UWIN service at the University of Washington. Users throughout the Internet should be able to access ERIC in one of the three following ways.

ERIC at the Colorado Alliance of Research Libraries (CARL)

ERIC is one of many databases and OPACs accessible through the Colorado Alliance of Research Libraries (CARL).

Access: Telnet: `pac.carl.org`

Once you are connected, you will be asked about your terminal emulation. Selecting the menu numbers for "vt100" or "hardcopy" from the list of options should work from your computer. You will have to press the return key several times to get to the main menu, and the word ERIC will probably appear in one of the main menu options. (Try the selection "Current Article Indexes and Access.") To leave CARL, type "//EXIT".

ERIC at the University of Saskatchewan, Canada

The University of Saskatchewan currently provides access to two of the ERIC databases, "Current Index to Journals in Education" and "Resources in Education."

Access: Telnet   `skdevel2.usask.ca` or
                                  `skdevel.usask.ca`
                 request: `sklib`
                 username: `sonia`

Once you are connected, you should select "CIJE and RIE" from the main menu. (By the time you read this, this may have been changed to "ERIC.") The University of Saskatchewan service also features a tutorial for beginning ERIC users. Just type "beginner" after you have accessed ERIC.

ERIC Access by WAIS

ERIC can also be accessed through WAIS. Unless you have WAIS installed on your local computer, you will have to use Telnet to access one of the publicly accessible WAIS clients. A sample session using WAIS and accessing the ERIC database is given in Chapter 18.

22.8. The Supply Room: Teaching Aids and Educational Tools

Another immediately valuable service of the Internet for K-12 education is the diversity of educational software and teaching materials that can be obtained free of charge.

22.8.1. Anonymous FTP Hosts

There are thousands of computers in the world containing file archives whose contents can be transferred for your own use at no charge. These FTP archives contain millions of files including documents, courseware, and software for almost any kind of computer. Overviews of using anonymous FTP archives can be found in Chapters 7 and 8.

22.8.2. K12Net Libraries

File archives useful for K-12 education are maintained in the "K12Net Libraries" located throughout the world. These K12Net Libraries contain thousands of files including:

- educational software;
- course outlines and other material for curricular development; and
- documents relating to education generally, including distance education and government publications.

Document files can be used on most any kind of personal computer. Most of the software currently held in the K12Net Library is for MS DOS based machines, but there are plans to start adding materials for other personal computers such as the Macintosh, Apple IIs, and Amigas.

You can currently access the K12Net Library by modem calls to K12Net sites. To locate the K12Net Library nearest you, get in touch with one of the K12Net contacts listed at the end of this chapter.

22.8.3. Software and Courseware Online Review

This resource is available as a WAIS database called "k-12-software-reviews" and lists software and courseware organized by subject and computer platform.

22.8.4. K-12 Oriented Information Systems

There are a number of Internet online information services that contain BBSs, curriculum guides, training materials, and other files for the K-12 community.

GC EduNET

GC EduNET is an information system set up for educators in Georgia, but may also be of interest to K-12 throughout the world. Access to GC EduNET is currently free, but you will be asked to register when you first log in.

> Telnet: `gcedunet.peachnet.edu`

Technology Resources in Education (TRIE)

The California Technology Project (CTP), in cooperation with the California State University's Telecommunications and Networking Resources group, operates the Technology Resources in Education (TRIE) electronic information service. This service informs educators throughout California about educational technology programs.

> Telnet   `eis.calstate.edu`
> login: `guest`

Briarwood Learning Systems

As described in Chapter 17, Gopher is an easy to use system for accessing information throughout the Internet. A growing number of K-12 schools and districts have been exploring the use of Gopher to access the sets of services of most interest to those users.

A good example of what can be done with Gopher in the K-12 world is the work planned by Briarwood Learning Systems. Beginning in the 1992-1993 academic year, this project will use Gopher and WAIS to distribute children's literature through the Internet. The goal is to provide materials which aid in the teaching of written and spoken language, to instill a taste for quality literature, to increase understanding of the English language, and to promote the individualization of the teaching process.

For more information about this project, contact:

> Dr. Joyce Stone
> Briarwood Learning Systems
> 379 North University Ave.
> Suite # 202
> Provo, UT 84604 USA
>
> e-mail: `joyce_stone@byu.edu`
> voice: (801) 374-2273

22.9. Field Trips without Buses

Of the many resources available via Telnet that have been described throughout *The Internet Passport*, many are of potential interest to the K-12 community. Using these resources can, if handled well, be like electronic field trips to remote sites. The trick is finding which services are appropriate!

22.9.1. Easy to Use Internet Front Ends

"Liberty," "Services," and the University of North Carolina Extended Bulletin Board (UNC EBB) are comprehensive front ends to the Internet that allow you to access a large proportion of the commonly used Telnet sites.

Liberty:	Telnet	`liberty.uc.wlu.edu`
	login:	`lawlib`
Services:	Telnet	`wugate.wustl.edu`
	login:	`services`
	terminal	`VT100`
UNC EBB:	Telnet	`bbs.oit.unc.edu`
	login:	`bbs`

22.10. Supercomputer Training

Several of the NSF-sponsored supercomputer sites have established programs for K-12 students and educators. Typically, these programs feature visits to the supercomputer site or allocation of time and access to the supercomputers. Here are the phone contacts for information on five such programs:

- Cornell National Supercomputer Facility   (607) 254-8686

- National Center for Supercomputer Applications   (217) 244-0644

- National Energy Research Supercomputer Center   (415) 422-1544

- Pittsburgh Supercomputer Center   (412) 286-4960

- San Diego Supercomputer Center   (619) 534-5124

For more detailed information about these and other supercomputer sites, please refer to Chapter 23.

22.11. Distance Education Programs for K-12 Educators

There are numerous opportunities for K-12 educators and students to enroll in courses at other institutions around the world. Such "distance education" programs are the electronic equivalent of correspondence schools, but with a major difference. They often allow real time, interactive contact with instructors and other students via computer networks with electronic mail or two-way video.

Moore and Thomson (1990) and Moore et al. (1990) discuss distance education generally. Information on specific statewide programs for K-12 educators can be found in Kurshan (1990b). There are also a number of LISTSERV discussion groups dealing with distance education, such as deosnews%psuvm.bitnet@cornellc.cit.cornell.edu.

22.12. Conclusion

Used appropriately, the Internet and other computer networks have a great deal to offer K-12 education. But with all the ballyhoo surrounding computers in the modern world, it's crucial to remember that computer networks should be thought of as only a supplement to K-12 education.

The quality of human life on earth ultimately depends upon the nurturing of fundamental interpersonal skills: what we learn as children, we build upon as adults. Computers and computer networks are a blessing only insofar as they promote these skills.

Similarly, the most important assets of schools are skilled, dedicated teachers and parents who have a supportive enthusiasm for their children's education. Computers are a tool or a supplement, but can never be a replacement for the human resources of our schools.

Happily, most applications of computer networks in education are sensitive to these issues. If used intelligently and always with an eye towards students and teachers as people, networks can deliver substantial educational benefits. Every K-12 school should consider the many advantages of joining a computer network and becoming part of the global schoolhouse.

22.13. For More Information

The best information on K-12 networking can be obtained by diving headlong into the active and exciting discussions taking place on computer networks throughout the world. Several of these discussion groups have been described in this chapter. Subscribe to some of the K12Net, Usenet, and LISTSERV groups, and you will be able to keep posted on collaborative projects suited to your particular educational curriculum.

Admittedly, this strategy presents a bit of a "bootstrapping" problem for those of you who do not yet have network access, so here's a list of printed references, journals, and professional societies which are of special interest to K-12 educators.

22.13.1. Bibliography

Beals, D.E. "Computer Mediated Communication among Beginning Teachers." *T.H.E. Journal,* 18(9) (1991):74-77.

Carlitz, R.D. "Common Knowledge: Networks for Kindergarten through College." *Educom Review* 26(2) (1991):25-28.

Clement, J. "Networking for K-12 Education: Bringing Everyone Together." Available from Educom: 1112 16th Street, NW, Suite 600, Washington, D.C. 20036. 1990.

Hunter, B. "Linking for Learning: Computer and Communications Network Support for Nationwide Innovation in Education." *Journal of Science Education and Technology* 1 (1992).

Kurshan, B. "Home Market for Educational OnLine Services: Growth of Market and Strategies for Expansion." Research Report. Educorp Consultants, 4940 Buckhorn Rd., Roanoke, VA. 1990a.

Kurshan, B. "Statewide Telecommunications Networks: An Overview of the Current State and the Growth Potential." Research Report. Educorp Consultants, 4940 Buckhorn Rd., Roanoke, VA. 1990b.

Kurshan, B. "Statewide Education Networks Survey Results." Research Report. Educorp Consultants, 4940 Buckhorn Rd., Roanoke, VA. 1991.

Melmed, A. and F.D. Fisher. "Towards a National Information Infrastructure for Selected Social Sectors and Education." Center for Educational Technology and Economic Productivity. New York: New York University. 1991.

Moore, M.G. and M.M. Thompson. *The Effects of Distance Learning: a Summary of Literature.* University Park, PA: Pennsylvania State University. 1990.

Moore, M.G., P. Cookson, J. Donaldson, and B.A. Quigley. *Contemporary Issues in American Distance Education.* NY: Pergamon Press. 1990.

Newman, D., S.L. Bernstein, and P.A. Reese. Local Infrastructure for School Networking: Current Models and Prospects. *BBN Report 7726.* Cambridge, MA: Bolt Beranek and Newman, Inc. 1992.

Phillips, G.M., G.M. Santoro, and S.A. Kuehn. "The Use of Computer-Mediated Communication in Training Students in Group Problem-Solving and Decision-Making Techniques." *American Journal of Distance Education*, 2(1) (1988): 38-51.

Roberts, N., G. Blakeslee, M. Brown, and C. Lenk. *Integrating Telecommunications into Education*. Englewood Cliffs, NJ: Prentice-Hall. 1990.

St. George, A. "A Voice for K-12 Networking." *Research and Education Networking* 3(1) (1992):10-12.

"Rural America at the Crossroads: Networking for the Future." U.S. Congress Office of Technology Assessment. (S/N 052 003 0122806; available in government document repositories or through your legislator.) April 1991.

22.13.2. Printed Journals

The following printed journals are particularly informative for K-12 educators using computer networks:

American Journal of Distance Education
Classroom Computer Learning
Computing Teacher
Educational Technology
EDUCOM Review
Electronic Learning
Journal of Computers in Mathematics and Science Teaching
Learning Tomorrow
Research and Education Networking
T.H.E.Journal
University Computing Times

22.13.3. Periodic Conferences

CAUSE
Consortium for School Networking
EDUCOM
International Conferences on Technology and Education
International Council for Distance Education Conferences
International Symposia on Telecommunications and Education
NorthWestNet
SHARE
USENIX

22.13.4. Organizations

Consortium for School Networking (CoSN)
1112 16th Street, NW
Suite 600
Washington, DC 20036 USA

EDUCOM
1112 16th Street, NW
Suite 600
Washington, DC 20036 USA

voice:	(202) 872-4200

22.13.5. A Sampler of K-12 Related LISTSERV Discussion Groups

Listname	BITNET Address	Topical Area
		Student Oriented Lists
KIDCAFE	@ NDSUVM1	KIDCAFE youth dialog
KIDS-ACT	@ NDSUVM1	KIDS-ACT What can I do now?
SCOUTS-L	@ NDSUVM1	Youth groups including Boy and Girl Scouts, etc.
SGANET	@ VTVM1	Student government global mail network
		Education Oriented Lists
EDUCOM-W	@ BITNIC	Technology and Education Issues of Interest to Women
KIDLEADR	@ NDSUVM1	KIDLINK Coordination
KIDLINK	@ NDSUVM1	KIDLINK Project List
KIDPLAN	@ NDSUVM1	KIDLINK Planning
KIDPLAN2	@ NDSUVM1	KIDLINK Working Group
KIDPROJ	@ NDSUVM1	Special KIDLINK Projects
KIDS-92	@ NDSUVM1	KIDS-92 Project List
K12STCTE	@ BITNIC	K-12 Steering Committee of CoSN
RESPONSE	@ NDSUVM1	Response to KIDS-92
VT-HSNET	@ VTVM1	VT K-12 School Network
		Hobbies and Recreation
CHESS-L	@ GREARN	Chess discussion and organization of tournaments
DJ-L	@ NDSUVM1	Campus radio DJ's technical discussion
EAT-L	@ VTVM2	Exchange of international recipes
GAMES-L	@ BROWNVM	Computer games of any sort

Subject-Specific Lists Relevant to K12 Education

AQUIFER	@	IBACSATA	Discussion about aquifers
BIOSPH-L	@	UBVM	Anything relevant to planetary ecology
CHEMED-L	@	UWF	Chemistry education
CW-L	@	TTUVM1	Computers and writing
DISARM-L	@	ALBNYVM1	Discussion of global disarmament
FILM-L	@	VMTECMEX	Film; art, entertainment, techniques equipment
HISTORY	@	UBVM	History discussion list
IAPCIRC	@	NDSUVM1	International Arctic Project, student projects
INTERCUL	@	RPIECS	Study of intercultural communication
LITERA-L	@	TECMTYV1	Literature in English and Spanish
LITERARY	@	UCF1VM	Discussions about literature
LLTI	@	DARTCMS1	Language learning and international technology
MARINE-L	@	UOGUELPH	Marine studies, shipboard education
MCLR	@	MSU	Midwest consortium for Latino research
MULTI-L	@	BARILVM	Language and education in multilingual settings
MUSIC-ED	@	UMINN1	Music education
NATIVE-L	@	TAMVM1	Issues pertaining to aboriginal people
PEACE	@	INDYCMS	Peace studies
PHYSHARE	@	PSUVM	Sharing resources for high school physics
RURALDEV	@	KSUVM	Community and rural economic development
SAIS-L	@	UNBVM1	Science awareness and promotion
SCREEN-L	@	UA1VM	Discussion of TV from a pedagogical perspective
SHAKSPER	@	UTORONTO	International electronic Shakespeare conference
SPORTPSY	@	TEMPLEVM	Exercise and sports psychology
TECHED-L	@	PSUVM	Employment, training, and literacy issues
TESL-L	@	CUNYVM	Teaching English as a second language
URBANET	@	TREARN	Urban planning student network

Special Education / Talented and Gifted Education

ABLE-L	@	ASUACAD	Study of academically, artistically, and athletically able
ALTLEARN	@	SJUVM	Alternative learning strategies, physically handicapped
ASLING-L	@	YALEVM	American Sign Language list
AUTISM	@	SJUVM	Autism and developmental disabilities
BEHAVIOR	@	ASUACAD	Behavioral and emotional disorders in children
BLIND-L	@	UAFSYSB	Computer use by and for the blind
BLINDNWS	@	NDSUVM1	Blind News Digest
BRAILLE	@	CSEARN	Discussion group for the blind, in English and Czech
COMMDIS	@	RPIECS	Speech disorders
DEAF-L	@	SIUCVMB	Deaf list
L-HCAP	@	NDSUVM1	Technology for handicapped, funding info, etc.
SPCEDS-L	@	UBVM	SUNY/Buffalo special education (students)
TAG-L	@	NDSUVM1	Talented and gifted education

Teacher Oriented Lists

BIOPI-L	@	KSUVM	Secondary biology teacher enhancement
TEACHEFT	@	WCU	Teaching effectiveness

Educational Uses of Computers and Networks

AACE-L	@	AUVM	Assoc. for Advancement of Computing in Education
CNEDUC-L	@	TAMVM1	Computer networking and education, esp. K-12
CONFER-L	@	NCSUVM	Academic interactive conferencing
COSNDISC	@	BITNIC	Consortium for School Networking
CW-L	@	TTUVM	Use of computers in teaching writing skills
DEOS-L	@	PSUVM	The Distance Education Online Symposium
DEOSNEWS	@	PSUVM	The Distance Education Online Symposium (Periodical)
DISTED	@	UWAVM	Journal of Distance Ed. and Communication
EDPOLYAN	@	ASUACAD	Professional and student discussion of education
EDTECH	@	OHSTVMA	Educational technology
EDUTEL	@	RPIECS	Education and information technologies
GLOBALED	@	UNMVM	Use of computer networks as a global classroom
MEDIA-L	@	BINGVMB	Educational communications for media services
SCIT-L	@	QUCDN	Studies in communication and info. technology

Software for Education

ACSOFT-L	@	WUVMD	Academic software development
PCSERV-L	@	RPIECS	Public domain software servers

Hardware and Operating System Oriented Lists

APPLE2-L	@	BROWNVM	Apple II List
COCO	@	PUCC	Tandy color computer List
COMMODOR	@	UBVM	Commodore computers discussion
I-AMIGA	@	UTORONTO	Info-Amiga List
I-IBMPC	@	UIUCVMD	IBM PC discussions
IBMPC-L	@	UGA	INFO-IBMPC Digest
INFO-APP	@	NDSUVM1	Apple II series user's mailing list
INFO-MAC	@	UIUCVMD	INFO-MAC Digest
MAC-L	@	YALEVM	Macintosh news and information
MACMAIL	@	UTORONTO	MAC Mail
MACPROG	@	WUVMD	Macintosh programming
MACSYSTM	@	DARTCMS1	Advice about Macintosh operating system
NEXT-L	@	BROWNVM	NeXT computer list
PC-EVAL	@	IRLEARN	Personal Computer evaluation
PC-L	@	UFRJ	IBM PC forum
PCSUPT-L	@	YALEVM	Discussion for MS DOS PC technical support staff
PCTECH-L	@	TREARN	MS DOS compatibles support group
PROG-A16	@	UOGUELPH	INFO-ATARI16 programs
SHOPTALK	@	MCGILL1	Microcomputer users' forum
SOFTREVU	@	BROWNVM	Small computing systems software review
SYS7-L	@	UAFSYSB	Macintosh System 7.0
WIN3-L	@	UICVM	Microsoft Windows and related issues
WORD-MAC	@	HVRFORD	Microsoft Word for the Macintosh

22.13.6. Cooperative Not-for-Profit K-12 Network Providers

K12Net

For more information about K12Net, contact any of the following members of the K12Net Council of Coordinators in Australia, Belgium, Canada, or the U.S.:

Gordon Benedict
6733 2nd Ave. N.W.
Calgary, Alberta
CANADA T2N 0E4
Sysop of 1:134/49 (403/283-5261) K12Net Zone 1 Backbone

e-mail: `Gordon.Benedict@f49.n134.z1.fidonet.org`
voice: (403) 283-5214

Jack Crawford, W-FL Teacher Resource Center
3501-K County Rd 20
Stanley, NY 14561 USA
Sysop of 1:260/620 (716/526-6495)
K12Net Zone 1 Backbone
K12Net Echo Moderator Coordinator

e-mail: `jack@k12net.org`
voice: (716) 526-6431

John Feltham
P.O. Box 2047
Townsville, Qld 4810 Australia
Sysop of 3:640/706 (61-77-79-2250)
K12Net Zone 3 Coordinator

e-mail: `lvg@psg.com`
voice: +32 3 455 16 53
fax: +32 3 455 16 55

Janet Murray, Wilson High School
1151 S.W. Vermont St.
Portland, OR 97219 USA
Sysop of 1:105/23 (503/245-4961)
K12Net Zone 1 Backbone

e-mail: `jmurray@psg.com`
voice: (503) 280-5280

Rob Reilly, Lanesboro School
188 Summer St.
Lanesboro, MA 01237 USA
Sysop of 1:321/218 (413/443-6725)
K12Net Zone 1 Backbone
K12Net Files Library

e-mail: **rreilly@athena.mit.edu**
voice: (413) 443-0027

Gleason Sackmann, Coordinator
Technical Operations and Training
SENDIT Project
NDSU Computer Center
Fargo, ND 58105 USA
K12Net Internet Coordinator

e-mail: **sackman@plains.nodak.edu**
voice: (701) 237-8109

Helen Sternheim
K12Net Projects and Channels Coordinator
Sysop of 1:321/110 (413/545-4453)

e-mail: hsternheim@phast.umass.edu

Mort Sternheim, Dept. of Physics and Astronomy
University of Massachusetts
Amherst, MA 01003 USA
Sysop of 1:321/109 (413/256-1037)
K12Net Zone 1 Backbone

e-mail: **sternheim@phast.umass.edu**
voice: (413) 545-1908

Andy Vanduyne, Norwood Elementary School
Norwood, NY 13668 USA
Sysop of 1:2608/75 (315/353-4565)
K12Net Zone 1 Backbone

e-mail: **n2psl@k2cc.sos.clarkson.edu**
voice: (315) 353-6674

Louis VanGeel
Maria Gorettistraat 17
B-2640 Mortsel, Belgium
Sysop of 2:29/777 (32-3-4552073)
K12Net Zone 2 Backbone

e-mail: **lvg@psg.com**
voice: + 32 3 455 16 53
fax: + 32 3 455 16 55

National Public Telecommunications Network (NPTN)

T.M. Grundner, Ed.D.
President, NPTN
Box 1987
Cleveland, OH 44106 USA

e-mail: **aa001@cleveland.freenet.edu**
voice: (216) 368-2733

@ 23 @

Using Supercomputers

A man wanted to know about mind, not in nature, but in his private large computer. He asked it (no doubt in his best Fortran), "Do you compute that you will ever think like a human being?" The machine then set to work to analyze its own computational habits. Finally, the machine printed its answer on a piece of paper, as such machines do. The man ran to get the answer and found, neatly typed, the words:

```
"THAT REMINDS ME OF A STORY"
```

Gregory Bateson
Mind and Nature

One of the original purposes of many parts of the Internet within the U.S. (particularly NSFNet) was to provide researchers easy access to supercomputing resources at a number of centralized supercomputer sites. This chapter provides an introduction to the basic principles of supercomputer use and includes detailed site descriptions for a number of the NSF-sponsored supercomputer facilities accessible through the Internet.

23.1. Supercomputers: Growth and Future

One of the most amazing phenomena of recent times has been the growth of the computer industry from a laboratory curiosity at the end of World War II to a major player in the economies of the world today, followed by rapid penetration into nearly all areas of life. The growth has been accomplished through extraordinary reductions in size and cost, and improvements in speed, reliability, and usability.

Not long ago a new class of computers has emerged: supercomputers. By one definition supercomputers are "At any given time, that class of general-purpose computers that are both faster than their commercial competitors and have sufficient central memory to store the problem sets for which they are designed" [1]. By this definition, it might appear that supercomputers have been with us from the start, and differ only quantitatively from other computers. In fact, supercomputers are qualitatively different in that they employ different architectures which result in major differences in programming and use.

According to the report "A National Computing Initiative" [2] the American research community will require a thousand-fold increase in computational power over the next few years. This growth is propelled by factors which are likely to exist for a long time to come.

One reason is the dramatic change in international economic competition. Since World War II many countries, especially in Eastern Asia, have entered into the economic mainstream armed with a powerful combination of Western technology and indigenous cultural backgrounds. These countries are redefining many economic and industrial roles and are putting severe pressure on the American economy. Technological innovation, especially in leading-edge fields such as computers, is viewed as a major way to help our competitive stature.

Another reason is that computers are assuming new roles. Computation is now recognized as the third mode of science, co-equal with theory and laboratory research [2]. Simulation of complex real world phenomena is increasingly possible and indeed necessary for future advance: investigations of very large (galaxies), very small (electron orbits), very fast, very slow, very complex, dangerous, or highly energetic phenomena are often possible only through simulation. Computers can also provide "impossible views" of objects under conditions which can never be obtained physically.

Finally, human activities are causing changes in the natural world: developments such as pollution, the destruction of rain forests, ozone depletion, and the greenhouse effect, require extensive monitoring and modeling which would be impossible without the computational and data management capabilities of supercomputers.

23.1.1. Supercomputers—Always a Need

The enormous progress in computer hardware will result in a "desk-top-CRAY" in the near future. With such powerful personal computers will we still need supercomputers? The answer appears to be yes. However powerful PC's become, there will always be problems which strain the leading edge of whatever computational powers we develop. The objects of study of disciplines such as mathematics (especially combinatorial problems), and the physical, biological and social sciences are infinitely complex, and computer simulations can never exhaust analytical possibilities. Many simulations today scrape by with the coarsest possible resolution in the hope that important details are not neglected. Increased resolution can come only at great computational cost: for example, a ten-fold increase in spatial resolution in each of 3 dimensions translates into a thousand-fold increase in computational operations. Naturally, many-dimensional problems would require much greater increases. The combined requirements of computational power, data storage, and data flow should insure the continued need for supercomputer sites.

23.1.2. Supercomputer Sites

By their very nature, supercomputers are expensive and require extensive hardware, software, documentation, and personnel support in order to function. Vast computational performance must be matched by massive data storage capacities, large data flows, high resolution output devices, an extensive communications interface, as well as a wealth of software applications, libraries, documentation, and expert consulting.

A number of supercomputer sites are currently promoted as national research centers. They are focal points for the collection and distribution of software, documentation, and extensive sets of examples; for training programs, seminars, and symposiums for high-performance graphics laboratories for visualization; and communication facilities in the form of e-mail, lists, and bulletin boards for specialized user groups.

The wealth of different services available at supercomputer sites implies that you should shop carefully in order to locate a site which best matches your needs. The types of software (editors, languages, packages, and operating systems), hardware (memory size and structure, vector and parallel hardware), and services (graphic output, type of consulting) affect the appropriateness of a site to your intended uses. For example, some systems couple high performance vectorization with somewhat limited memories, others feature very large memories with limited vectorization capabilities, whereas others specialize in massively parallel systems.

23.1.3. The NSF Backbone

Supercomputers were born in the U.S. but were generally unavailable to university scientists because of their high costs. Some American scientists actually went to Europe to obtain time on U.S.-built supercomputers. Recognizing the importance of computing access, the NSF established five supercomputer centers across the nation in 1984. Time on these machines is obtained mainly through several grant mechanisms and is otherwise free of charge.

The NSF also helped establish a communications network, called the NSF backbone, which connects these centers and links them to regional networks.

Originally, the centers were deliberately designed to differ from one another in order to make more options available to researchers, and to test out a variety of novel machine architectures, operating systems, and support strategies under real-life conditions. Recently, however, the systems have converged around several models of CRAY computers and the new massively parallel Connection Machines, mostly running slight variants of Unix.

23.2. Supercomputer Hardware

Supercomputers are not just big, fast machines that use state-of the-art hardware; they also feature special architectures. While these architectures can greatly boost performance, their full power can only be exploited under certain conditions and often require that the program and/or problem itself be restructured by someone who understands how these architectures function.

The most common supercomputer architectures include special memory organization, such as independent memory banks in the CRAYs, vector hardware (also called pipeline hardware) present in nearly all supercomputers, and parallel hardware, usually in the form of multiple processors. All of these features have recently started to appear on non-supercomputers, but their implementation and support are especially well developed on supercomputers.

23.2.1. Cache Memories

For a given price, memory can either be big and slow or small and fast. A cache is a small and very fast memory which serves as a buffer to a large slow memory; therefore, cache memories can, under certain conditions, improve overall performance by reducing the time to access main memory. When an operand is fetched from main memory, both it and a number of its nearest neighbors are placed in the high speed cache. If the next reference is to a neighbor, it will be taken from the cache instead of the main memory. If memory usage in the program tends to be highly clustered, then the program operates mainly out of the cache and performance increases greatly. On the other hand, if memory usage is highly scattered, then the cache memory can actually degrade performance.

23.2.2. Independent Memory Banks

Independent memory banks are another method for speeding memory access and storage. A reference to a given bank of memory cells ties up the bank for a number of machine cycles, and no further access is possible until the bank is free. Some computers arrange memory into a number (64 on the CRAY) of independent banks so that most memory references address different banks and do not interfere with one another.

Typically the banks are arranged so that adjacent words, such as X(1), X(2), X(3), reside in different banks. For example, the loop

```
DO 10 I=1,N
```

runs faster with an independent memory bank architecture since the storage times for X(1), X(2), X(3), X(4) etc., are overlapped. However, array structures or patterns of array access which are discordant with the memory architecture can defeat the architecture and slow execution considerably. For example, on a 64 bank memory the code

```
     DIMENSION X(64,50)
     DO 10 J = 1,50
10 X(1,J) = 0.0
```

would nail the same bank each and every time through the "J" loop, since X(1,1), X(1,2), X(1,3) etc. reside in the same bank. In this case the problem can easily be solved by redimensioning X as X(65,50) in order to change the memory layout.

23.2.3. Vector Hardware

Vector hardware is currently the most widespread and mature of the special architectures found in supercomputers. Vector units consist of CPU components such as add or multiply units which are divided into a number of sequential stages or segments. The units typically accept two vectors of numbers which proceed through the segments and emerge out the other end as a vector of results. As long as the vectors continue to flow, the process is efficient, and speedups by a factor of 5 or 10 are not uncommon, but starting and stopping the units for short vectors can actually increase execution time. Efficient vector operation often requires some restructuring of code by the programmer as well as the use of compiler directives to monitor and control the process. A more complete description of vector operations appears later in this chapter.

23.2.4. Parallel Hardware

Parallel architecture distributes the processing of a single program over a number of different physical processing units. It offers the greatest potential for vast increases in performance of any known architectural layout. For example, a machine with 10,000 processors might solve some problems almost 10,000 times more quickly than a single processor machine. However, most programs cannot be partitioned so completely into independent units, and many difficult hardware and software issues remain unsolved and are the subject of intense research. At present, limited parallelism can be exploited on the CRAYs, and massive parallelism is possible with the Connection Machine. The effort needed to restructure code ranges from about the same as for vectorization to considerably more. A more complete description of parallel operations appears later in this chapter.

23.2.5. Impact on Debugging and Graphics

Supercomputers are so powerful and generate such vast amounts of information that they force major changes in both debugging techniques and in the presentation of output. Ad hoc debugging techniques are woefully inadequate for dealing with, say, an error in the 471,000-th iteration of a 500 variable program operating on 18 million separate values. Special debugging software is required which lets you examine values, restart code at various points, observe the effects of changes in values, run controlled experiments, etc.

Similarly, traditional printed and even standard graphical output is often inadequate to represent the millions or even billions of separate data values that can be provided by a supercomputer run. The term "visualization" is used to describe the sets of advanced graphical techniques which address this problem. Visualization often involves high resolution displays, extensive use of color, 3D representations, and extensive interactive control of the image in order to control the viewing angle, collapse dimensions in a multi-dimensional data set, or perform image processing functions in order to extract or highlight desired information. Existing graphics packages are often insufficient for the task as they emphasize the display of 2- and 3-dimensional XY, XYZ, or contour plots, whereas the representations of complex simulated phenomena require some combination of image processing approaches along with more standard graphic techniques. In addition, graphics rendering, especially when combined with real time interaction, can place severe demands on data transmission paths.

23.2.6. Other Hardware Issues

Other hardware issues include memory size and use of high speed peripherals, such as the Solid State Disk (SSD) available on some CRAYs.

The hardware available at different supercomputer sites should be a major consideration in your selection. For example, a CRAY Y-MP is extremely good for highly optimized vector operations, but is somewhat limited in terms of memory, and a Connection Machine is much superior for highly parallel problems.

23.3. Supercomputer Software

Supercomputer sites are often endowed with a rich collection of applications software in the areas of Chemistry, Physics, Engineering, Mathematics, and Graphics. Computer languages, however, are confined mainly to FORTRAN, Pascal, and C, and FORTRAN is often the only language that is extensively optimized for vector/parallel operations at all sites.

23.3.1. Operating Systems

While the early sites featured a variety of operating systems, most have converted to variants of Unix (UNICOS on the CRAYs and ULTRIX on some front ends).

23.3.2. Workstation Support

Some sites provide extensive support for workstation and PC software to be used in conjunction with the supercomputer or its front end. NCSA at Illinois, for example, provides free downloadable graphics and communications software for PCs, SUNs, and Macintoshes.

Software is probably the single most important consideration in site selection. Unfamiliar languages or editors can greatly increase learning time; programs, data files, and data formats may have to be restructured to move to a particular environment, and future portability must be kept in mind; non-FORTRAN programs may have to be rewritten or run in a non- or sub-optimized mode; and major applications programs, libraries, or graphics libraries may be unavailable or at different revision levels.

23.4. Supercomputer Performance Gains

Despite the many "fringe" benefits of supercomputer sites, such as access to software, training, graphics, and collaborative research, the main purpose in using supercomputers is to exploit their size and speed in order to handle otherwise intractable problems. The performance of supercomputers is due mainly to two factors.

- Supercomputers are generally big, fast machines which employ high performance technology. As a result, all computer programs automatically benefit.

- Hardware architectures, such as cache memory, independent banks, instruction stacks, high speed I/O, vector, and parallel operations which, although not unique to supercomputers, are usually more highly developed. The exploitation of these features is partly automatic but can also benefit significantly from modifications by the programmer.

Vector and parallel architectures are most often emphasized in optimization, but attention to the other architectures mentioned above can bring about major performance gains as well. One should also note that (a) extensive optimization should only be done in conjunction with special timing tools which locate those portions of the program which can benefit most, and (b) optimization should only be carried to a certain degree—smarter compilers in the near future will be able to optimize well structured code much better than the "spaghetti" code that often results from overzealous hand optimization.

23.5. Performance Gains through Specialized Hardware

The most significant performance gains are obtainable through vector processing and parallel processing hardware.

23.5.1. Vector Processing

Vector processing can best be explained through analogy. Imagine a factory that assembles 6-bladed airplane propellers. It has 6 people, p1 through p6, at 6 workstations who attach each blade in turn to the hub. Person p1 receives a tray with the parts and assembles the first blade to the hub. When done, he passes the tray along with his partial assembly to p2. P2 attaches the 2nd blade and when done passes the tray and his partial assembly to p3, and so on.

Of course, when p1 has passed his partial assembly to p2 he does not just quit for the day. Instead he immediately gets a new tray and starts a new assembly. Similarly, p2 no sooner finishes his assembly when he gets the tray and the partial assembly from p1 and begins attaching the second blade.

After 6 time periods, the pipeline is filled with 6 different stages of assembly. The important point to note is that while it still takes 6 time periods to assemble any given propeller, a new finished propeller emerges from the assembly pipeline each and every time period. We have speeded up the assembly process by a factor of 6 by using 6 people in a quasi-parallel manner. Note that even if a product required 10,000 stages to assemble, the products would still emerge at the rate of 1 per time period. In other words, production speed is independent of the complexity or length of the assembly process. On the other hand, if the pipeline is interrupted for any reason, a very long pipeline (or assembly process) will take much longer to restart than a short one.

In supercomputers, the vector or pipeline process is usually applied to arithmetic units, such as add, multiply, or divide units which "assemble" new numbers from the vectors of input numbers.

For example, a multiply unit on the CRAY contains 7 stages. The FORTRAN code

```
      DO 10 I = 1,60
 10 C(I) = A(I)*B(I)
```

is converted to vector instructions which start loading the vectors A(1), A(2),... and B(1), B(2),... into special vector registers. As soon as the first pair is available, A(1) and B(1) enter the multiply unit to begin the first stage of multiplication.

At the end of one clock cycle, the partial multiplication of A(1)*B(1) moves to the 2nd stage in the multiply unit, and A(2), B(2) enter stage 1; at the end of the 2nd cycle, A(1)*B(1) moves to stage 3, A(2)*B(2) moves to stage 2, and A(3), B(3) enter stage 1. This process continues and at cycle 7 all seven stages are being utilized, the fully multiplied value of A(1)*B(1) emerges and is stored in C(1), and A(8), B(8) get ready to enter stage 1. From then on, a new multiply is finished every clock cycle, even though it takes 7 cycles to complete one multiply. We have increased the speed almost by a factor of 7 (except for initiating the pipeline).

Vectorization only applies to explicit DO-loops in FORTRAN and their equivalents in other languages. Only one loop within a nest of loops can be vectorized, but the software automatically selects the loop unless that choice is overridden by directives from the programmer.

There exist many obstacles to vectorization, some of which are easily overcome (for example, changing the order of statements), some which require use of compiler directives to modify the vectorization process, and some which require major restructuring of the code. On high performance vector machines, such as the CRAY, speedups of a factor of 5 or 10 for that portion of the code that can be vectorized are not uncommon.

23.5.2. Parallel Processing

The basic idea of parallel processing is easier to grasp than vector processing, but the usage, implementation, and many of the concepts are more difficult. On the other hand, the rewards may be much greater since the potential speedup is proportional to the number of processors available, whereas vector speedup can never be much more than a factor of 10.

Parallel systems distribute the work of a program or subroutine among a number of processors. In some implementations, such as CRAY Macrotasking, the number and operation of parallel processors must be predetermined; in other implementations, such as CRAY Microtasking, the number, identity, or order of execution of the processors is unknown and variable (this has many consequences which influence the structure of a parallel program and hence the modifications needed to convert an existing program to parallel operation). Most of the following discussion applies to CRAY Microtasking.

Some of the concepts of parallel processing are illustrated by the execution profile of subroutine ABC.

```
SUBROUTINE ABC
        (Block B1)    a block of code executed by one processor
        (Block B2)    another block executed by a processor
        (Block B3)    another block executed by a processor
RETURN
END
```

The subroutine is entered at the top under the control of a single processor, after which control is transferred to one, two, or three other processors for blocks B1, B2, and B3. When all of the blocks are finished, control is returned to a single processor which terminates the subroutine. The execution profile might look like this:

Time	Processor 1	Processor 6	Processor 4
1	Start ABC	x	x
2	Run B2	Run B1	Run B3
3	x	x	Exit ABC

where "x" means the processor is idle or engaged with another program. The profile is generally unpredictable and the actual number and identity of processors depends on many factors. Because of this unpredictability, the parallel operation is often referred to as a "fray."

A DO-loop is a special case of the above structure:

```
          SUBROUTINE ABC
          DO 10 I = 1,3 (the i-th iteration of the loop is block B(i))
   10     CONTINUE
          RETURN
          END
```

in which some iterations of the loop may be handled by different processors.

Some obvious and not-so-obvious consequences derive from such an implementation. The different code blocks must be totally independent of the sequence in which they are processed: Block 3, for example, cannot depend on the results of, say, Block 1. It is less obvious that local variables assigned values inside a block can have no validity outside the block, that values associated with loop iterations must be explicitly tied to the loop index, and that global variables which are not indexed by a loop index must be "guarded" from simultaneous access. Consider the following section of code:

```
          K = 0
          DO 10 I = 1, 1000
          K = K + 1
   10     CONTINUE
```

The operation of the above loop depends on whether K is local or global. Local variables in a parallel block of code are replicated for each processor that joins in the "fray" whereas global variables occupy a single location which is accessed by all processors.

Suppose that K is a local variable and the 1000 iterations of the loop are randomly distributed among, say, 64 processors. Then processor 17 might handle 23 iterations of the loop, processor 39 might handle 11 iterations, and so on. At the end of the loop, if control is assigned solely to processor 17 then K=23, if assigned to processor 39 then K=11, whereas in a non-parallel environment K always equals 1000.

Inside the loop, if K is used as a substitute for the loop index, then its value depends only on how many times that processor has handled the loop and so will generally have little relation to the value of the loop index itself. Thus A(K) rarely is the same as A(I), whereas in a non-parallel environment it is always so.

If K is a global variable then it must be guarded from simultaneous access by more than 1 processor. For example, suppose that K=0 and processors 13 and 19 begin execution of RK=K+1S at slightly different times. If 19 accesses the expression before 13 has finished, then K will be reset to 1 instead of being set to 2 as it should be.

This type of code is called a "critical section" and must be guarded by explicit directives which guarantee that another processor can only enter that section of code when the current processor has finished.

Parallel and vector processing are quite compatible and can be used not only in the same program but often in the same nest of loops. For example, some compilers analyze a DO-loop nest and select one loop for vectorization and another for parallel processing. On the CRAY, a single loop can be partitioned into vectorized and parallelized sections.

23.6. Interaction with Optimizing Compilers

The goal of an optimizing compiler is to speed the execution of a program without changing the results. It scans the user's source code and identifies structures which can utilize the special hardware found in supercomputers. Since the conditions under which these structures can be safely optimized are very limited, it must analyze much of the surrounding code to determine if, and to what degree, the code can be optimized.

The compiler is subject to several important constraints which limit its effectiveness. Since the optimization is done at compile time, it can have no knowledge of the run-time structure of the job. Thus, input data values which may change the flow of execution and the degree of optimization cannot be considered, so the compiler has to assume the worst case and do the least amount of optimization. Another constraint is that optimization is often limited to the scope of a single routine, and interactions between routines which might affect optimization cannot be taken into account. In addition, the technology of optimizing compilers is continually advancing, and any given compiler may be unable to optimize code which later versions can handle.

Because of these limitations it is often necessary for the programmer to supply auxiliary information which eliminates ambiguity and resolves problems which the compiler cannot handle. This is especially important in parallel processing, but is also often required in vectorization. The programmer supplies global directives on the compile statement or embeds local directives in the source code, or both, which guide the optimization process. For example, the following loop would be rejected by any vectorizing FORTRAN because of a "recurrence" relation in the loop:

```
        K = IVAL
        DO 10 I = 1,N
10      A(I) = A(I-K) + 1.0
```

While recurrence and other inhibitors of vectorization are beyond the scope of this report (see [4] and [5] for more information), the above code can be vectorized on a CRAY provided that (a) K is negative, or (b) K is greater than 64. If the programmer knows this he can insert compiler directives which force the compiler to vectorize. Thus the code

```
        CDIR$ IVDEP             ("ignore vector dependency")
        DO 10 I = 1,N
10      A(I) = A(I-K) + 1.0
```

in effect, tells the compiler that "I know more than you, so forget your inhibitions and vectorize anyway."

Parallel optimization usually requires more embedded directives than vectorization. It is frequently necessary to explicitly prevent multiple processors from accessing code until all processors have finished operating on a previous section. For example, the CRAY compiler directives

```
CMIC$ DO GLOBAL
              DO 10 J =        (operation on the J-th column of A)
              1,N
     10       CONTINUE
CMIC$         DO GLOBAL
              DO 20 I =        (operation on the I-th row of A)
              1,M
     20       CONTINUE
```

would distribute the operations of the N columns of A and the M rows of A to different processors, but would assure that all columns were finished before any rows were processed. The directives are signaled by "CMIC$" (for Microtasking) in columns 1-5 and apply to the next DO-loop. Thus the start of the second "CMIC$" terminates the first "CMIC$" and tells the compiler that the two loops are to be processed in sequence.

23.7. Migrating Program to Supercomputers

The main point in using supercomputers is to achieve dramatic increases in processing speeds. The increases are partially due to the fact that supercomputers are simply big and fast computers, but much of the increase comes from the special architectures that supercomputers employ. Achieving a high degree of optimization on supercomputers requires a well thought-out strategy as well as realistic expectations as to what can actually be achieved.

The maximum gains that can be obtained through parallel processing or vectorization are controlled by "Amdahl's" law [1]: $P = 1/(1-X+X/a)$ where P is the performance gain, X is that ratio of the code which can be optimized (vectorized or processed in parallel), and "a" is the speedup ratio for vector or parallel code. The important part of the law is that the performance is much more controlled by X, the proportion of the code that can be optimized, than by "a." For example, suppose that $X = 0.80$, so that 80% of the code can be vectorized or processed in parallel. Then the absolute maximum speedup possible is a factor of 5, even if vector or parallel operations are infinitely fast (that is, even if "a" is infinity, then $P = 1/(1-0.8 + 0.8/infinity) = 1/(0.2) = 5$).

Note that it is rare for X to exceed 0.8 (factor of 5 speedup) for vector processing applications, whereas X may often exceed 0.99 (factor of 100 speedup) for parallel processing applications.

The first step in migrating code to a supercomputer (after making any adjustments to insure that the FORTRAN code will actually compile and run), is to instrument the program in order to identify "hotspots," that is, code which is extremely CPU intensive. A good candidate program for optimization should have an execution profile such that nearly all of the CPU time is spent in just a few percent of the code. (If the execution profile is fairly uniform, then hand optimization may be a waste of time.) Most supercomputer sites provide easily used compiler directives or other tools which will show you a histogram of CPU time spent versus source code.

If the program has identifiable hotspots, the next step is to read and understand the compiler messages which identify obstacles to optimization. Some compilers provide an in depth analysis of each loop, which identifies not only the obstacles to vectorization, but also the results of an "economic" analysis to determine which loop in a nest of loops yields the best results.

At this point you should analyze the loops highlighted by the compiler to see if any can be replaced by routines from existing optimized libraries. Many such routines are coded in assembly language and are optimized to a very high degree. After this, you should attempt to remove inhibitors to optimization by making local modifications to loops. In many cases this can be done simply by reordering statements, splitting loops, or adding compiler directives. For example, the loops on the left will not vectorize, while the loops on the right (which produce exactly the same results) will:

```
        DO 10 I=2,N                        DO 10 I=2,N
        B(I) = A(I-1)                      A(I)=C(I)
10      A(I) = C(I)               10       B(I) = A(I-1)
        DO 10 I=1,N                        DO 10 J=1,N
        DO 10 J=1,N                        DO 10 I=1,N
10      A(I,J)=A(I,J-1)*B(I,J)    10       A(I,J)=A(I,J-1)*B(I,J)
```

In the above examples, a recurrence relation existed which prevented vectorization. In the following example, the recurrence relation could not be avoided for one expression, but by splitting the loop into two parts, one of the two expressions on the right can be vectorized:

```
        DO 10 I=1,60                       DO 10 I=1,60
        A(I)=B(I)*C(I)            10       A(I)=B(I)*C(I)
10      D(I)=D(I-1)*E(I)          20       D(I)=D(I-1)*E(I)
```

When these steps have been taken, further optimization can be achieved by paying careful attention to memory layout or by restructuring the program to obtain the best match between program structure and the architecture of the machine. The latter is, of course, a very time consuming operation and should only be undertaken when the benefits and the costs are fully considered.

23.8. Supercomputer Access

Resources on all of the NSF sites and some of the other sites are mainly allocated on the basis of grants, rather than by money. Three main grant types are commonly available.

- Large allocations which are subject to formal peer review boards which meet at scheduled times during the year. These boards are comprised of personnel which may be from the site, jointly from several sites, or from NSF.

- Small allocations for startup or familiarization purposes. These are usually available at any time throughout a year.

- Block grants awarded to universities. The universities allocate sub-blocks of time through their own review boards.

23.9. Supercomputer References

[1] "Supercomputing: An Informal Glossary of Terms." IEEE Washington Office, 1111 Nineteenth Street, NW, Washington, D.C. 20036. 1987.

[2] H.J. Raveche, D.H. Lawrie, and A. Despain. "A National Computing Initiative—An Agenda for Leadership." Society of Industrial and Applied Mathematics, 1400 Architects Building, 117 So. 17th Street, Philadelphia, PA, 19103-5052. 1987.

[3] N.P. Smith. "Of Supers and Minisupers." *Computer Graphics World*, August 1988.

[4] H.M. Doerr and F. Verdier. "Improving Vector Performance" and "Introduction to Vectorization." Cornell National Supercomputer Facility, Cornell University, Ithaca, New York. September 1987.

[5] D.D. Soll. "Vectorization and Vector Migration Techniques." *IBM Technical Bulletin*, SR20-4966-0.

23.10. Supercomputer Site Descriptions

The remainder of this chapter provides detailed information about a number of supercomputer sites in the U.S. The purpose of these site descriptions is to allow you to do some preliminary comparisons of each site's hardware, software, and training programs so you can select the supercomputer site which would be most appropriate for your particular research needs.

All of these site descriptions were reviewed or contributed to by representatives of each site's user services staff in September 1992. We'd like to thank the following individuals for their participation:

Supercomputer Site	Reviewed By
Cornell National Supercomputer Facility	Ray Kujawski
	Allison Loperfido
National Energy Research Supercomputer Center	Bruce Kelly
Pittsburgh Supercomputer Center	Deb Nigra
National Center for Atmospheric Research	Juliana Rew
National Center for Supercomputer Applications	Virginia David
Ohio Supercomputer Center	Frankie Harris
San Diego Supercomputer Center	Jayne Waggoner

23.11. Cornell National Supercomputer Facility (CNSF)

23.11.1. Hardware

IBM ES/9000-900

- 2.66 Gflops peak aggregate performance
- 9 Gbytes shared memory
- Each user process may access up to 2 Gbytes virtual memory

Kendall Square Research KSR1

- 2 scalable parallel systems with 128 processors
- 1.28 Gflops peak aggregate performance
- 1 Gbyte shared memory
- 1000 Gbyte address space per processor

Scalable RISC Cluster

- Eight model 550 RISCs
- Minimum of 128 Mbytes of memory in each
- Andrew File System (afs)

23.11.2. Software

- AIX operating system
- Software support for vectorization and parallelization
- Interactive and batch modes
- Editors: vi, emacs, aXe, jove
- Text Processor: TeX
- FORTRAN: apf, fvs, xlf
- Other languages: C, C++

Computational Chemistry

ALCHEMY II	AMBER	AMPAC	CAR-PARINELLO
CHARMm	CORNING	DISCOVER	DMOL
GAMESS	GAUSSIAN	HONDO	INSIGHT
MELDF	MOPAC		

Computational Fluid Dynamics

FIDAP

Graphics

AVS	DATA EXPLORER	CONTOUR	DI-3000
DISSPLA	GNUPLOT	IMSL/IDL	SAS/GRAPH
WAVEFRONT			

Numerical Libraries and Mathematics

ACMALG	BSPLINE	EISPACK	ELLPACK
ESSL	FFTPACK	FISHPACK	FUNPACK
IMSL	ITPACKV	LAPACK	LINPACK
LLSQ	NAG	ODEPACK	QUADPACK
RECIPES	SLATEC	SMPAK	SPARSPAK
TOEPLITZ			

Mechanics

ABAQUS	ANSYS

Parallel Tools

PAT	PVM

Simulation

SLAM II

Statistics

EDA	GLIM	NTSYS	SAS
SAS/ETS	SAS/IML	SAS/STAT	

Symbolic Algebra

AXIOM	MAPLE	MATHEMATICA

Utilities

CLOGIN	CMSTAPE	CMSUNF	DIRED
FPDIFF	GOPHER/XGOPHER	ReelLibrarian	VAST2

23.11.3. Training

- Local and remote workshops
- Introduction to systems, access, languages, and optimization tools for new users
- Summer institutes for researchers working on code
- Undergraduate/Faculty workshops
- Workshops on parallel processing and vectorization
- Discipline specific workshops (e.g. computational chemistry)
- Smart Node regional and consultant workshops
- Visualization and remote graphics workshops

SuperQuest

Ambitious and creative high school students and their teachers are immersed in science and supercomputing through SuperQuest, the only national computational competition of its kind, sponsored by the Cornell Theory Center. Sixteen of twenty teams, chosen on a competitive basis, spend several weeks of intensive training during the summer at the Cornell Theory Center or one of four other supercomputing institutes. Their high-performance computing education includes sessions on vectorization, parallel processing, and visualization techniques. The teams begin projects on the supercomputer that are continued at their home school with the use of computer equipment awarded through the competition.

To bridge the gap between high school and undergraduate use of computational resources, the Theory Center also provides training in computational science technique for high school teachers, so they too can move into the future of scientific experimentation. Since early 1990, more than 57 high school teachers from throughout New York State have received supercomputer training at the Center. This helps to increase the number of college-bound students ready to explore modern methods of scientific analysis and discovery.

SPUR

The Supercomputing Program for Undergraduate Research (SPUR) provides talented undergraduates with the opportunity to become an integral part of current computational research by involving them in a 10-week session of intensive training and scientific inquiry using computational tools. Students work with a research advisor on projects in the fields ranging from geology to chemistry and electrical engineering to biology.

23.11.4. Collaborative Research

- User groups and Research Interest Groups (Computational Chemistry and Statistics)
- Interdisciplinary research groups open to all researchers
- Corporate Research Institute

23.11.5. Documentation

- Telnet accessible online help (Telnet to info.tc.cornell.edu and login as "info".)
- Online documentation: CNSFINFO, CUINFO, InfoExplorer
- Newsletter: ForeFronts
- Training notebooks of presentations from classes and lab exercises
- Online instruction Program: TUTOR
- Online help program and man pages

23.11.6. Consulting

- Consulting via e-mail
- Large scale computing consulting
- Computational research associate staff in agricultural and biological engineering, astrophysics, chemistry, engineering, mathematics, operations research, and statistics
- Visualization consulting
- Strategic user program for those using parallel computing in production work
- Corporate research consulting

23.11.7. Graphics Support

- Support for remote X-Windows (including xim with WaveFront), Tektronix 4105, 4010; Versaterm for Mac; GRAF for PC; VT100 emulators; gnuPLOT and a version of xmovie
- An extensive graphics lab with high speed fiber optic links, an image processing system, facilities for videotape production, a digital camera for 35 mm slides, printers for producing camera ready copy, plotters and color PostScript printers, and a number of Unix workstations

23.11.8. Administration

All proposals for time on the Theory Center's resources are subject to peer review through the Theory Center's National Allocations Committee; researchers must submit an application for supercomputer time directly to the Theory Center to allocations coordinator, Pat Colasurdo. Corporations interested in using the Theory Center through the Center's Corporate Research Institute may contact Linda Callahan.

23.11.9. Contact Summaries

Consulting:	(607) 254-8686
	`consult@eagle.tc.cornell.edu`
Visualization:	Bruce Land
	`land@tc.cornell.edu`
	(607) 254-8686
Allocations:	Pat Colasurdo
	`pat@tc.cornell.edu`
	(607) 254-8686
Training:	Susan Mehringer
	`susan@tc.cornell.edu`
	(607) 254-8686
System Status:	(607) 255-7138
Network help:	Network Management Center
	(24 hrs/day, 7 days/week)
	(607) 255-9900
IBM ES/9000:	`eagle.tc.cornell.edu`
RS/6000 cluster:	`cluster.tc.cornell.edu`
KSR1:	`homer.tc.cornell.edu`
KSR1 (batch only):	`yogi.tc.cornell.edu`

23.11.10. Login Script

The following script shows how to connect to the CNSF ES/9000, login, compile, load and run a program, and then logout. It assumes that you connect from some local machine which supports the TCP/IP Telnet program. Prompts are represented by "local>" for your local system prompt, "Eagle" for the ES/9000, and "EagUs" for user commands supplied to the ES/9000. Comments are enclosed in parentheses.

Prompt	Dialog	Comments
local>	telnet eagle.tc.cornell.edu	(Telnet to eagle)
	...	(Telnet messages)
EagUs>	login: <your userid>	
EagUs>	password: <your password>	
Eagle>	...	(Login messages from eagle)
EagUs>	fvs -o hello hello.f	(Compile FORTRAN program)
EagUs>	hello	(Run Program)
Eagle>	HELLO WORLD	
EagUs>	logout	(Log out)

23.12. National Center for Atmospheric Research (NCAR)

23.12.1. Hardware

- CRAY Y-MP8/864 with 8 processors; CRAY Y-MP2D with 2 processors
- 64 Mwords of main memory for the Y-MP8, 16 Mwords for the Y-MP2
- 48 Mword maximum memory per job for batch; 16 Mwords for interactive
- 6.0 ns clock for both CRAYs; a measured peak rate of over 1 Gflops achieved with a multitasked ocean model
- Vector processing hardware for both CRAYs
- 256 million word SSD for Y-MP8 (1000 Mbyte/sec channel), 128 million word SSD for Y-MP2
- 78 gigabytes of local storage for the Y-MP8, 20 Gigabytes of local storage for the Y-MP2
- Unix front end
- NCAR Mass Storage System (MSS): hierarchical file storage system with no limit per user (The MSS has a 120 gigabyte disk farm and over 115,000 tape cartridges. It features a StorageTek 4400 Automated Cartridge System capable of holding 6,000 cartridges, or a terabyte of information. Currently, MSS stores over 29 terabytes of data and offers extremely high data transfer to the CRAYs; is accessible from front end.)
- Connection Machine 2 (8,000 processors and floating point hardware)
- Gateway for NCAR's Internet Remote Job Entry System (IRJE): create and submit CRAY jobs from local hosts connected to the Internet with output automatically shipped back to the remote host

23.12.2. Software

- UNICOS 6.1.6 operating system on CRAY Y-MP8/864; UNICOS 5.1.11 on CRAY Y-MP2D
- FORTRAN: CFT 77 version 5.0
- Other languages: vectorizing C and Pascal compilers

Application Libraries

Application libraries and documentation are available via the Distributed Software Libraries (dsl) utility. To access dsl, telnet to dsl.ucar.edu and login as "dsl". When prompted for the password, type "software".

ALFPACK	AMOSLIB	CRAYFISH	ECMFFT
EDA	EISPACK	EISPKD	FISHPAK
FITPACK	FUNPACK	IMSL	LINPACK
FFTPACK	MINPACK	MUDPACK	NAG
NCARM	NCARO	ODEPACK	SPHERE
SLATEC	SSDLIN	STARPAC	

Graphics

NCAR/GKS Version 3.1.3a

23.12.3. Training

- UNICOS orientation: a one-day class introducing Unix/UNICOS programming tools and the NCAR computing environment
- Unix Basics Class: Two-day introduction to the basics of Unix
- Remote site visits for sites with a significant number of users
- User conference held every two years: updates users on new developments and new directions in computing at NCAR
- Site liaison workshops held biennially: intensive, in-depth presentations on specific aspects of the NCAR computing facility
- NCAR Graphics on and off site workshops and Fortran optimization workshops

23.12.4. Collaborative Research

- User groups
- Real-time computing during field programs
- Classroom grants of computer time

23.12.5. Documentation

- Documentation via anonymous FTP to ftp.ucar.edu in "/docs/README" file
- User Documentation Catalog referencing both the SCD-supported and vendor documentation: online via anonymous FTP to ftp.ucar.edu with the path and filename "/docs/catalog/userdoc.catalog"
- Online documentation for most of the utilities in the supported libraries via the Distributed Software Libraries (dsl) utility
- Scientific Computing Division (SCD) hardcopy documentation (free except for the GKS Graphics manual)
- NCAR UNICOS Primer: basic information to begin computing at NCAR with step by step examples to create, submit, and receive output from the CRAYs
- Daily Bulletin: Online source of up-to-date information on the computing systems
- Monthly newsletter: SCD Computing News (free)
- Annual planning report: "Supercomputing: The View From NCAR"
- NCAR Annual Report
- NCAR Annual Scientific Report

23.12.6. Consulting

- Phone, 8-5 MST weekdays; walk-in consulting for visitors and local users and extended consulting by appointment
- E-mail consulting available from Internet, BITNET, SPAN, and Omnet
- Specialized consulting for software libraries, networking and data communications, optimization, multitasking, CRAY I/O optimization, segmentation (overlaying) of large applications, math algorithms, NCAR Graphics, IBM PC/AT and Macintosh terminal emulations, and Unix and UNICOS operating systems
- Visitor assistance: access 24 hrs/day, 7 days/week; IBM PCs and Macintoshes for terminal or stand-alone use, color graphics terminals; Canon microfilm/fiche reader/printers, community telephone for business use, documentation library (including vendor documentation)

23.12.7. Graphics Support

- Text and graphics system for both on-site and off-site users providing 16mm film, 35mm color slides, 4"x5" color film, microfiche, and videotape (VHS, Umatic-SP)
- Xerox 4050 laser printers for paper graphical output
- Color and black and white hardcopy output available soon
- CGM metafile support
- Remote graphics support with an NCAR graphics translator (ctrans) on the front end
- Output mailings to users at remote sites

23.12.8. Strengths and Limitations

Strengths

- High performance vector processing
- Extensive user support services
- SSD for large I/O applications
- Extensive data archives for atmospheric and oceanographic research
- High volume fast access mass storage system
- Extremely high volume graphics output capabilities
- Video support and 16 mm movie-making
- Remote job entry system

Limitations

- Few applications outside atmospheric sciences
- Limited memory

23.12.9. Administration

- Allocations for university researchers with NSF grants in atmospheric, oceanographic, and related sciences; grant requests reviewed by a peer review board composed of NCAR staff and university researchers
- Allocations for government agencies on a cost recovery basis

23.12.10. Contact Summaries

Consulting:	`consult1@ncar.ucar.edu` (303) 497-1278
Visitor/User Information:	`scdinfo@ncar.ucar.edu` (303) 497-1225
Allocations:	`knudson@ncar.ucar.edu` (303) 497-1207
Documentation Orders:	`docorder@ncar.ucar.edu` (303) 497-1232
IRJE (remote job entry):	`rje@windom.ucar.edu`

23.13. National Center for Supercomputer Applications (NCSA)

23.13.1. Hardware

- CRAY Y-MP4/464 with 4 processors; CRAY-2S/4-128 with 4 processors; Connection Machine Model 2 (CM-2) with 32,000 parallel processors and 64 bit floating point hardware; Connection Machine Model 5 (CM-5) and Convex C3880 are in "friendly user" mode and are not yet production systems
- 64 Mwords of main memory for the Y-MP; 128 Mwords of main memory for the CRAY-2; 1 GByte main memory for CM-2; 4 Gbyte of physical memory for the Convex C3880
- 6.0 ns clock speed for the CRAY Y-MP; 4.1 ns clock speed for the CRAY-2; 7.0 MHZ clock on the CM-2
- Vector, scalar, and parallel processing
- High speed 128 Mword Solid State Disk (SSD) for the CRAY-Y-MP
- 16 Gbytes temporary storage for CRAYs; 30 GByte DataVault for the CM-2
- Common File System (CFS) with 120 GBytes of permanent file storage running on an Amdahl 5860
- Potentially unlimited magnetic tape storage through an IBM 3480
- Plans for significant increases in mass storage capabilities, replacing CFS with UniTree in 1993
- Three IBM RISC System 6000 model 550's (high-end superscalar machines for predominantly scalar applications); a total six of 550's and one RS/6000 model 950 front end / file server scheduled by the end of 1991
- Three Sun 4/490 front ends running SunOS for the CM-2
- Numerous high end machines from Silicon Graphics, Apple, IBM, and SUN in the Numerical Laboratory, accessible over the Internet
- New network hardware and software being installed in a testbed research project (BLANCA) to prepare for the national gigabyte transcontinental network (NREN); 45 Mbit/sec links to Berkeley and Bell labs and to University of Wisconsin are in place; by summer 1993 BLANCA should include a 622 Mbit/sec trunk to University of Wisconsin

23.13.2. Software

- All production systems run a version of Unix
- Multitasking is supported on the CRAYs; dedicated time is available to allow access to all 4 CPUs
- Editors: vi and Emacs on the CRAYs
- FORTRAN: CF77; cdbx is the debugger on both CRAYs
- Other languages: vectorizing C compiler on both CRAYs
- cfs utility to move files between CFS and the CRAYs and many example programs for vectorization and graphics on CFS
- CM-2: CM Fortran (CMF) supports Fortran 90 and FORTRAN77 constructs; C* programming language with data parallel extensions; *Lisp, and extension of common Lisp
- In-house software development applications staff

NCSA Developed Workstation Software

Public domain software for workstations is available via anonymous FTP from ftp.ncsa.uiuc.edu or 141.142.20.50. (Get the file "README.FIRST" for an informative overview of current holdings and FTP instructions. Each directory, including the root, contains a file named "INDEX" which contains a recursive listing of the files of that directory and of all subdirectories within it.)

Software may also be purchased; contact orders@ncsa.uiuc.edu for additional information and a copy of the current Technical Resources Catalog.

For the IBM PC

    NCSA PC Show
    NCSA Telnet PC

For the Macintosh

    NCSA Contours
    NCSA DataScope
    NCSA GelReader
    NCSA HyperCard
    NCSA Image
    NCSA Import2HDF
    NCSA Layout
    NCSA PalEdit
    NCSA Telnet Mac
    NCSA UIFlow

For the Silicon Graphics 4D Series Workstation

    NCSA Height-Color Visualizer
    NCSA Isosurface Visualizer
    NCSA PolyView
    NCSA Tiller

For the Sun Workstation

    NCSA CompositeTool
    NCSA ImageTool

For Unix machines

    NCSA Reformat/XReformat

For the X Window System

    NCSA X DataSlice
    NCSA X Image

For multiple computer systems

    NCSA HDF Calling Interfaces
    NCSA HDF Vset
    NCSA XDIFF/XFIX

23.13.3. Software On the CRAYs

Astronomy

    MIRIAD

Chemical Engineering

    ASPEN PLUS

Chemistry

AMBER	AMPAC	BROOKHAVEN PDb	CADPAC
CHARMm	DISCO	GAMESS	GAUSSIAN92
GPRLSA	MINP	MM2	MOLECULE-SWEDEN
MOPAC	NCSAdisco	RANFOLD	RNAFOLD
RPAC	SYBYL	XPLOR	

Computational Fluid Dynamics

FIDAP	FLOW3D	KIVA II	PHOENICS

Electrical Engineering

CAzM	HSPICE	MSC/EMAS	PISCES
SIGVIEW	SPICE	SUPREM 4	

Graphics

Blaze	GNUPLOT	GPLOT	MPGS
NCAR (GKS)	NCSA Viewit	PVI Contouring	PVI DI-3000
PVI GK-2000	PVI GRAFMAKER	PVI Metafile System	PVI TEXTPRO
Zetavu			

Mathematics and Statistics

ACM Algorithms	ACSL	ALFPACK	BCS
BCSEXT	CALMATH	DASSL	ECMFFT
EDA	EISPACK3	ELLPACK	FFT
FITPACK	GLIM	HSML	IMSL
ITPACK	KMN	LAPACK	LASO2
MARK14	MINOS	MINPACK	MUDPACK
NAG	NUMERICAL RECIPES	ODEPACK	PCGPAK
PCGPAK2	PORT	POSSOL	SCILIB
SLAM II	SLATEC	SMPAK	SPARSE
SPECFUN	SPSS-X	SSDLIN	TOEPLITZ
XLP	XML2	ZOOM	

Solid Mechanics and General Engineering

ABAQUS	ADINA	ADINAT	ADINA-IN
ADINAPLOT	ANSYS	DADS	DYNA2D
DYNA3D	INGRID	MAZE	MSC/NASTRAN
NIKE2D	ORION	TAURUS	TOPAZ2D

Systems and Utilities

AS	BENCHLIB	CDBX	CF77
CFT	CFT77	GNU Emacs	HDF
KAP/Cray	NCSAHDF	NCSA X IMAGE	PASCAL
PCC	SCC		

23.13.4. Training

- Education program featuring supercomputer use for users from kindergarteners to advanced researchers; strong emphasis on incorporating scientific visualization techniques into education
- Academic Affiliates Program with members at more than 100 institutions; features special training and block grants of computer time for members
- Visitor program for faculty, postdoctoral, and student researchers to support working visits to NCSA
- Renaissance Experimental Laboratory for teaching visualization skills and efforts to incorporate scientific visualization into course curricula
- Workshops and seminars on specialized topics in various disciplines
- Summer institutes and workshops
- Many training video tapes: vectorization, CRAY architecture, multi-tasking, etc.

23.13.5. Collaborative Research

- Association with the Beckman Institute, an interdisciplinary program for artists, computer scientists, and researchers in many intellectual disciplines
- NCSA Collage (Collaborative Analysis and Graphics Environment) (Lets researchers conduct real-time collaborative work sessions across a wide variety of hardware platforms. Collage software and documentation are available without charge by downloading from NCSA's anonymous FTP host; see Software.)
- Unix mail on the CRAYs (Users are encouraged to forward mail to their home systems.)

23.13.6. Documentation

- Unix man pages for technical information
- Documentation system (originally from CTSS) ported to UNICOS for access to complete manuals
- NCSA Technical Resources Catalog lists documentation available from NCSA or third parties
- Many documents available through anonymous FTP in the /ncsapubs directory (see Software)
- Innovative video magazine (NCSA RealTime)
- New users provided with an extensive startup kit and kept informed via frequent distribution of online and printed materials
- Many documents free or for purchase
- Online help available through the new information system called "ncsainfo," based on the BNU Texinfo documentation system (An NCSA gopher server is being established as well.)
- Extensive sets of example programs are available on CFS
- Bimonthly technical newsletter: "datalink" (online)
- Quarterly general information newsletter: "access"

23.13.7. Consulting

- Consulting available via e-mail (24 hours a day) and phone (8am to 5pm central time) (See Contact Summaries below.)
- On-line information system (ncsainfo) as well as specific information resources on each system

23.13.8. Graphics Support

- Strong emphasis on local and remote use for scientific visualization
- Workstation tools for graphics analysis
- CGM metafile support
- Support for remote graphics terminals including Tektronix 4014, 4105, 4113, 4115/4125, PostScript, HPGL, Macintosh
- Media facility features video and audio resources, including Silicon Graphics Inc. frame buffers, Abekas digital disk recorders, D1 format digital VCRs, Macintosh-based digital audio recording, Betacam SP format analog VCRs, computer-controlled editing and routing, and over 150 other components. Activities supported include transfer of images from computers to video, audio, hard copy, and film, as well as between the different formats within each of these media; media processing such as video editing, text generation, electronic paintbox, digital effects, and compositing; audio recording and editing to further supplement basic imagery; and video field production for documentary programming and special projects.
- Consulting on media systems ranging from desktop through digital HDTV

23.13.9. Strengths

- Massively parallel processor systems
- High performance vector processing
- Solid State Disk for fast internal I/O
- Scientific visualization
- State-of-the-art graphics laboratories

23.13.10. Administration

- Requests for 100 or more service units of CPU time are reviewed by a joint NCSA/Pittsburgh Peer Review Board quarterly.
- Requests for fewer than 100 service units are processed eight times a year.
- Applications for less than six service units are reviewed internally by NCSA in the Small Allocations Committee.
- Researchers at academic affiliate institutions may apply for start-up grants for 1-5 hours on the CRAY Y-MP4/464 through their campus affiliate representatives.
- Education projects are available on the Cray systems and Connection Machines. Only a limited number of projects can be allocated on the CMs. For additional information on applying for an education account, send e-mail to uadmin@ncsa.uiuc.edu.

(Note: service units are CPU or wall clock hours weighted by different factors for the various computers.)

23.13.11. Contact Summaries

Academic and Industrial Relations: Scott Lathrop
                                      slathrop@ncsa.uiuc.edu
                                      (217) 244-1099

Accounts / Client Administration: Judy Olson
                                      uadmin@ncsa.uiuc.edu
                                      (217) 244-0074

Allocations: Radha Nandkumar
                                      radha@ncsa.uiuc.edu
                                      (207) 244-0650

Applications: Melanie Loots
                                      mloots@ncsa.uiuc.edu
                                      (207) 244-2921

Chemistry Users Group: Melanie Loots (acting)
                                      mloots@ncsa.uiuc.edu
                                      (217) 244-2921

Consulting: **consult@ncsa.uiuc.edu**
                                      (217) 244-1144

Educational Outreach: Scott Lathrop
                                      slathrop@ncsa.uiuc.edu
                                      (217) 244-1099

Faculty Program: Melanie Loots
                                      mloots@ncsa.uiuc.edu
                                      (217) 244-2921

Industrial Program: John Stevenson
                                      (217) 244-0474

Media Relations: Jarrett Cohen
                                      jcohen@ncsa.uiuc.edu
                                      (217) 244-3049

Media Services: Vincent Jurgens
                                      vjurgens@ncsa.uiuc.edu
                                      (217) 244-1543

Orders for Publications and
Multimedia: Debbie Shirley
                                      orders@ncsa.uiuc.edu
                                      (217) 244-4130

Software Tools Technical Support: Jennie File
                                      jfile@ncsa.uiuc.edu
                                      (217) 244-0638

Software Development Group: Joseph Hardin
                                   jhardin@ncsa.uiuc.edu
                                   (217) 244-6095

Training: Alan Craig (information)
                                   acraig@ncsa.uiuc.edu
                                   (217) 244-1988

                                   Deanna Walker (registration)
                                   dwalker@ncsa.uiuc.edu
                                   (217) 244-1996

Visitors Program: Jean Soliday
                                   jsoliday@ncsa.uiuc.edu
                                   (217) 244-1972

Hardware Status: (217) 244-0710

NSFNET Problems: (617) 873-3400

CRAY Operations: (217) 244-0710

CRAY Y-MP address: **uy.ncsa.uiuc.edu**

CRAY-2 address: **u2.ncsa.uiuc.edu**

CM Sun Front Ends: **cmsun1.ncsa.uiuc.edu**
                                   cmsun2.ncsa.uiuc.edu
                                   cmsun3.ncsa.uiuc.edu

Dial-up Access: (217) 244-0664
                                   (217) 244-0662

Anonymous FTP: **ftp.ncsa.uiuc.edu**   **(141.142.20.50)**

23.13.12. Login Script

The following script shows how to Telnet to the NCSA CRAY, list files, compile and run a job, and logout. The script assumes that you connect to the CRAY from a local machine which supports the TCP/IP program Telnet. Prompts are represented by "user>" for you, "CRAY>" for the CRAY, "Teln>" for Telnet, and "CRus>" for CRAY responses followed by user entries on the same line. Most CRAY responses are abbreviated. Comments are enclosed in parentheses.

Prompt	Dialog	Comments
user>	*telnet u2.ncsa.uiuc.edu*	(Telnet to the CRAY-2)
Teln>	...	(Telnet messages)
CRAY>	CRAY-2 UNICOS 5.0.7 (u2)	
CRAY>	National Center for Supercomputing Applications	
CRus>	login: *<your CRAY userid>*	(login to the CRAY)
CRus>	Password:*<your password>*	
CRus>	account:*<your account>*	
CRAY>	...	(CRAY login messages)
CRus>	u2 1% *ls -la*	(ask to list your files)
CRAY>	. .. .cshrc .login .profile hello.f	
CRus>	u2 2% *cft77 hello.f*	(compile program called "hello.f", generate a binary object file called "hello.o")
CRus>	u2 3% *segldr -o hello hello.o*	(load the object file and create an executable file called "hello")
CRus>	u2 4% *hello*	(submit executable file)
CRus>	u2 5% *cat fort.6*	(display contents of output file)
CRAY>	Hello world, goodbye world	
CRus>	u2 6% *logout*	(logoff CRAY and return to local machine)

23.14. National Energy Research Supercomputer Center (NERSC)

23.14.1. Hardware

- One CRAY 2/8, one CRAY 2/4, one CRAY Y-MP C90, and an X-MP 1/8 for High School Supercomputer Honors Program
- Memory sizes are 128 Mwords memory on the CRAY 2's, 256 Mwords on the C90
- Vector and parallel hardware; 2 processors on the CRAY X-MP/24, 8 processors on one of the CRAY 2's, and 4 on the other, and 16 processors on the C90
- Permanent storage on the IBM-based CFS storage system
- 1500 Gbytes total mass storage
- Auxiliary computers: VAXs and other networked computers

23.14.2. Software

- UNICOS 6.1 on the CRAY 2's and the CRAY X-MP 1/8; UNICOS 7.C. on the C90 developed by the Cray Computer Corporation
- Auxiliary VAXs with VMS operating system
- Editors on the CRAYs: vi, EMACS, and standard Unix editors
- FORTRAN compilers: CF77
- Other languages: C, Pascal, and LISP compilers, and CRAY Assembler
- CFS: software for mass storage
- Example sets, sample programs, and extensive documentation available through the online DOCVIEW program

Math

IMSL   NAG   SCILIB

Graphics

DISSPLA	GKS	GRAFLIB	NCARGKS
TV80LIB			

23.14.3. Training

- New user workshops available both on site and for export
- Monthly on-site UNICOS classes
- Classes on supercomputer related topics
- Work in progress developing online tutorial services
- A high school Supercomputing Honors Program each summer

23.14.4. Collaborative Research

- E-mail via MAIL, MAILX
- Bulletin Board Server with rn
- MFENET/ESNET supported by NERSC networks and providing remote logins, e-mail, and file transfers to and from nodes on these networks and the Internet

23.14.5. Documentation

- Monthly newsletter, "The BUFFER"
- On-line packages: document, docview, and man pages

23.14.6. Consulting

- Phone consulting Mondays through Fridays, 8:00-11:45am, 12:45-4:45pm
- Online e-mail consulting via mail to consultants@nersc.gov

23.14.7. Graphics Support

- A DICOMED camera for film, slides, and fiche; available to remote users
- Support for remote graphics terminals including most Tektronix displays and IBM PCs and compatibles
- Output mailings free of charge to users at remote sites
- PostScript output facilities being explored

23.14.8. Strengths

- Highly optimized vector processing
- Large memory machines
- A network connecting energy research sites supporting collaboration and exchange of information between researchers

23.14.9. Administration

- Most allocations made by applying to the Department of Energy (DOE)

23.14.10. Contact Summaries

Consulting:	(510) 422-1544
	(800) 66NERSC
Accounts (passwords and ID's):	(510) 422-2888
Allocations:	(510) 422-1544
Training:	(510) 422-1544
Hardware status:	(510) 422-4283
Network status:	(510) 422-4283
Direct CRAY connection:	`f.nersc.gov`
	`c.nersc.gov`
	`a.nersc.gov`

23.14.11. Login Script

The following script shows how to telnet to the NERSC CRAYs, login, transfer files from a local account to the CRAY using FTP (NERSC currently has a limited number of FTP functions installed), list files, compile/load/execute a program, and then logout. It assumes that you connect to the CRAY from some local machine which supports the TCP/IP Telnet program.

Prompts are represented by "user>" for you, "Teln>" for Telnet, "CRAY>" for the CRAY, and "CRus>" for CRAY responses followed by user entries on the same line. Comments are enclosed in parentheses. Most CRAY responses are abbreviated using the "..." ellipsis notation.

Prompt	Dialog	Comments
user>	*telnet f.nersc.gov*	(Telnet to the CRAY)
Teln>	...	(Telnet messages)
CRus>	ID: *<your usernumber>*	(enter CRAY usernumber)
CRus>	Password: *<your password>*	(enter CRAY password)
CRAY>	...	(CRAY login messages)
user>	*ftp*	(start FTP)
CRus>	FTP> *connect 128.95.137.4*	(make connection with FTP to your local account)
CRAY>	...	(FTP messages)
CRus>	...	(login to your local account)
CRus>	MAX.U.WASHINGTON.EDU> *get hello.for hello.f*	
		(get your program with FTP from your local account and send to the CRAY)
CRAY>	...	(file transfer messages from FTP)
CRus>	MAX.U.WASHINGTON.EDU> *quit*	(quit FTP and return to CRAY session)
CRAY>	...	(more FTP messages)
user>	*ls*	(ask to list your files)
CRAY>	hello.f	
user>	*CF77 hello*	(compile and load your FORTRAN program)
user>	*logout*	(logout from the CRAY)

23.15. Ohio Supercomputer Center (OSC)

23.15.1. Computer Hardware

- CRAY Y-MP8/864
- UNICOS operating system
- Eight CPU processors, six nanosecond cycle time
- 64 million words (512 megabytes) of memory
- 128 Mw Solid-State Device
- 40 gigabytes of primary storage on DS-40 and DD-49 disk drives
- Communications interfaces: VMS, TCP/IP, FDDI, HIPPI
- StorageTek Robotic Tape Silo with terabyte storage capacity (connected to Y-MP8 and EL)
- CRAY Y-MP EL File Server System
- 256 megabytes (32 Mws) of main memory
- 3 CPUs
- UNICOS and Data Migration software
- 40 gigabytes of data on 4 DAS-2 units
- HIPPI interface connection to the Y-MP8 at 100 megabytes/sec
- Ethernet interface
- FDDI interface

23.15.2. Software (on Y-MP8 only)

Chemistry

AMBER	AMPAC	BIGSTRN	CADPAC
CHARM	COORD	DMOL	GAMESS
Gaussian 90	Gaussian 92	HONDO	MOPAC
SYBYL			

Computational Fluid Dynamics

ARC2D	ARC3D	DSMC	EAGLE
FIDAP	FDL3D	FLOW3D	FLUENT
FLUENT/BFC	NASCRIN	NISA	PARC2D
PARC3D			

Graphics

ABAPOST	apE	BAPLOT	DISSPLA
I-3000	NCAR	PLOT3D	

Mathematics and Statistics

BCSLIB	BCSEXT	BNCHLIB	GISPACK
IMSL	ITPACK	LAPACK	LINPACK
MINPACK	NAGhelp	NAGlib	SPARSE

Programming Languages

C	Fortran	LISP	Pascal
PROLOG	PSL	REDUCE	SISAL

Solid Mechanics and General Engineering

ABAQUS	ABAQUS/EXPLICIT	ANSYS	ASTROS
DYNA2D	DYNA3D	INGRID	NASTRAN
NIKE2D	NIKE3D	SPICE2	TAURUS
TOPAZ2D	TOPAZ3D		

Systems and Utilities

ABQNQS	ANSNQS	BNCHUTL	F2C

23.15.3. Training

- Training for beginning and advanced CRAY users
- Special programs for computational mechanics and computational chemistry
- Workshops on UNICOS, Cray Fortran, C programming, vectorization and optimization, performance analysis tools, job control, and network use
- Summer classroom programs for high school and undergraduate students
- Summer internships for high school students

23.15.4. Collaborative Research

- Program for Computational Reactive Mechanics
- Online information archive and mailing list for computational chemistry
- Software porting program providing blocks of time for software developers
- Trollius multicomputer operating system development and distribution
- Visiting collaboration with University of Florida Quantum Theory Project

23.15.5. Documentation

- Quarterly Visions general purpose and SuperBits user newsletters
- Monthly "oscbits" e-mail newsletter for up-to-date user information
- Online mailings: "oscupub" for reporting publications by users; "oscalloc" for reporting allocations of CRAY resources from the Statewide Users Group; "oscprop" for information on grant programs of interest to supercomputer users
- Online e-mail archive for computational chemistry, academic grant application, electronic mailings and newsletters
- Local and CRAY documentation on docview information system
- Documentation directory on CRAY containing software and general publications and user documentation
- OSC Program Book gives "one-stop" source of information for users on programs, account charges, software, etc.
- Local quick-start manual, EZGUIDE to Supercomputing
- UNICOS online manual pages
- Manuals from Cray Research available on order from Kinko's copies in Columbus by U.S. mail or pickup

23.15.6. Consulting

- Resident consulting at Ohio universities and colleges on most aspects of supercomputer use and access
- By e-mail to oschelp@osca.osc.edu anytime
- By telephone (toll-free inside Ohio) M-F, 1-5pm
- Emergencies after hours or network access problems: contact network operations center

23.15.7. Graphics Support

- Ohio Visualization Laboratory with state-of-the-art graphics equipment and output services for computer graphics and animation
- Systems: 7 SparcStations with an aggregate of 7.5 gigabytes of disk space, Macintosh II, Sun 3/60, Sun 3/110 workstations, NeXT 68040 processor, Silicon Graphics Personal Iris (4D/70GT), NeXT Dimension, Stellar GS2000
- Output media: 2 Texas Instruments OmniLaser 2115 Printers, 2 Tektronix 4693D Thermal Transfer Color Printers, Apple Laserwriter II Printer
- Video equipment: Sony 3/4" Video Editing Suite, Ampex 1" Video Editing Suite, Solitare Film Recorder, Slide Scanner, Abekas Still Storer

23.15.8. Strengths

- Vector, parallel processing on CRAY Y-MP8/864
- Computational chemistry and computational mechanics software support
- Strong user group involvement
- Availability of CRAY for university classes

23.15.9. Administration

- Active user group, with committees for allocations, hardware and operations, and software and activities
- Grant applications accepted by e-mail; 10 resource unit (10 CRAY Y-MP hours, approximately) awards available on demand to Ohio academic researchers; 100 resource unit awards depending on committee review; and larger awards depending on peer review
- Dedicated CRAY Y-MP time available for challenging parallel applications
- Availability of CRAY for classroom educational activities
- Industrial program for U.S. companies: CRAY time, consulting, and code development services

23.15.10. Contact Summaries

Accounts/Allocations:	Michele Erlenwein `michele@osc.edu`
Consulting:	M-F 1-5pm, (614) 292-1800 or (800) 686-6472 `oschelp@osca.osc.edu`
CRAY Manuals:	Al Stutz `al@osc.edu`
Industrial Program:	Charlie Bender, Marty Lobdell, and Al Stutz `marty@osc.edu`
Network Administration:	Dan Wintringham `danw@oar.net`
Newsletters:	Barbara Woodall `woodall@osc.edu`
Numerical Analysis Assistance:	Steve Koehl and Moti Mittal
Ohio Visualization Laboratory:	Barb Helfer `barb@ovl.osc.edu`
OSC Documents:	Frankie Harris `frankie@osc.edu`
Service Programs:	Nitta Cofer `nitta@osc.edu`
Visitors:	Elaine Hamilton `elaine@osc.edu`
Workshops:	Leslie Southern `leslie@osc.edu`

23.16. Pittsburgh Supercomputing Center (PSC)

23.16.1. Hardware

Cray Y-MP/832 with 8 processors, 64 million words of memory, and a high speed (156 Mword/second) 128 million word Solid-State Storage Device (SSD)

- A maximum of 54 Mwords per user
- 6.0 ns clock; maximum speed 2.6 gigaflops
- High performance parallel and vector hardware
- Very large temporary storage per user
- Permanent storage in both the Andrew File System (afs) and IBM-based Common File System (CFS) (See later section on afs.)
- Dedicated time available through request

Cray Y-MP/C90 with 16 processors, 256 million words of memory:

> Scheduled to arrive at PSC in October, 1992. It will have access to the 128 MW Solid-State Storage Device (SSD). The PSC is now accepting applications for the use of the C90.

Connection Machine CM-2 with 32,768 processors, 1 gigabyte of memory, and 10 gigabytes of high speed storage on the DataVault:

> The processors work in parallel. Each processor has 32 Kbytes of memory associated with it, for a total of 1 gigabyte for the machine. The CM-2 is driven by two front ends, CMSUNA and CMSUNB. CM applications are executed on the front ends, while those parts of the application which benefit from parallel processing are executed on the CM-2.

- 8K, 16K, or 32K available for simultaneous use
- 1,024 64-bit floating point accelerator chips
- Maximum speed in the gigaflop range
- Temporary space and permanent storage space available on the Andrew File System (afs) through the CM-2's front ends (See later for more information on afs.)
- Driven by CMSUNA and CMSUNB, both SUN 4-470s running Unix
- Dedicated time by request

Connection Machine CM-5 with 256 parallel processing nodes:

> Each node has 16 MB of memory. These nodes are controlled by two machines, CM5A and CM5B, which run an enhanced version of Unix. Each of the control machines accesses 128 of the parallel processing nodes. Users also have access to a third machine, CM5COMP for CM-5 compilations. Doing compilations on CM5COMP leaves CM5A and CM5B free for executing codes.

The CM-5 can also access the 10 gigabyte DataVault. The CM-5 does not yet have vector units for floating-point or integer operations. Because of this, peak performance is at 5 megaflops per processing node, or 1.28 gigaflops for all nodes. When the CM-5 supports vector units, performance will peak at 128 megaflops per node, or 32 gigaflops.

- Two front ends which drive the CM-2 (CMSUNA and CMSUNB)
- Two VAX 6420s (CPWSCA and CPWSCB) running VMS from which you can reach either the Y-MP, CMSUNA, or CMSUNB; 10,000 blocks of permanent storage and a large amount of temporary storage for users
- Two Vaxstation 5100s (PSCUXA and PSCUXB) running ULTRIX from which Y-MP, CMSUNA, or CMSUNB can be reached; these front ends running afs as their file system; 10,000 1024-byte blocks of permanent storage on afs and a limited amount of temporary space for users

23.16.2. System Software

Y-MP

- UNICOS
- Editors include EMACS, vi, ed, and LSEDIT (Language sensitive editor for CFT77)
- FORTRAN: CFT77 and FORGE (an aid to vectorization)
- CF77 compiling system includes CFT77, automatic optimization and autotasking, and loader
- Other languages: C (with vectorization support), Pascal
- Mass storage: Common File System (CFS) with automatic tape storage and retrieval, and afs
- A large examples system: sample jobs, data, and the resulting output available to public
- Downloadable public domain software

C90

- UNICOS
- Editors include EMACS, vi, and ed
- Languages: FORTRAN CF77 compiling system includes CFT77, automatic parallel processing, automatic vectorization and scalar optimization; Cray standard C, with automatic vectorization, scalar optimization, and automatic parallel processing
- Mass storage: Common File System (CFS) and afs

CM-2 and CM-5

- Front ends run Unix
- Editors on front ends include EMACS, vi, and ed
- Languages: FORTRAN (cmf), C, and Lisp
- Mass storage: afs (See below.)
- Examples system: sample jobs, data, and the resulting output available to public

23.16.3. Application Software

The software lists below is not comprehensive. No utilities, benchmarking software, or similar packages have been included.

Biomedical

CLUSTER	CONSORT	CORMA	FIBERDRAW
IB_TO_GB	IRMA	MDPP	PICKEMBL
PICKGEN	SPIDER		

Databases

BROOKHAVEN	CAMBRIDGE	ECD	EMBL
ENZYME	GENBANK	PROSITE	REBASE
NBRF-PIR	SWISS-PROT		

Fluid Dynamics

FACET	FIDAP	FLOW3D	KIVA II
NEKTON			

Gene Sequencing

AMPS	COMPAR	CONSENSUS	DISTAN
GCG	MAXSEGS	MSA	MSC
NWGAP	PROFILE	RNAFOLD	SN
SP	ST		

Molecular Modeling and Quantum Chemistry

AMBER	AMPAC	AMSOL	CADPAC
CHARMM	CHELP	DISCOVER	GAMESS
GAUSSIAN	GROMOS	MOLPRO	MOPAC
SWEDEN			

Structural Analysis

ABAQUS	ANSYS	DYNA2D	DYNA3D
INGRID	MAZE	NIKE2D	NIKE3D
TOPAZ2D	TOPAZ3D		

X-Ray Crystallography

GPRLSA	HKSCAT	PROTIN	XPLOR
XRFORM			

23.16.4. Graphics and Animation Software

ANIMATOR	CODEBOOK	DI3000	DISPLAY-P3D
DISSPLA	DRAW	DRAWCGM	DRAWP3D
GEODATA	GPLOT	GRAPHX	IMAGETOOL
LVR	MACGPLOT	MOVIE	MP3D
NAVIEW	NCARGKS2	ORION	P3D
PDBMODEL	PLOT3D	PLT2	RENDER-P3D
REQUESTAPE	SMONGO	TAURUS	TEXTMAKER
TITLEMAKER	TRACE-SNAPS	TURB3D	

23.16.5. Mathematical and Statistical Software

AMOS	AMOSLIB	APML	APSTAT
AUTO	BAILEY	BANDIT	BCSLIB
BIHAR	BIVAR	BLAS	BORMAT
CALMATH	CGLIB	CM2LIGHTS	CMLIB
CYCLE	DASSL	DRIV	DVERK
ECMFFT	EISPACK	ELLPACK	FFTPACK
FFTPACKT	FISHPACK	FITPACK	FN
GAMS	GBSOL	HARWELL	HBSMC
HSSXEV	IMSL	IMSL IDL	INSITE
ITPACK	LAPACK	LASO	LINPACK
LLSQ	LOCLIB	LOPSI	LSQR
MAPLE	MATLAB	MFFT	MINPACK
MUDPACK	NAG	NAPACK	NETCDF
NMS	NSPCG	ODEPACK	ODRPACK
PDE2D	PDEONE	PITCON	PLTMG
POLYHEDRA	QUADPACK	RANPACK	REDUCE
S	SGEFAC	SLAP	SLATEC
SPARSKIT	SPLPAK	SPARSPAK	SPICE
SPSS	SSDLIN	STARPAC	STEAM
SUBSET	TESTMAT	TOMS	VCFT
VFFTPK	VIEWIT	YSMP	ZERO

23.16.6. Andrew File System

The Andrew File System (afs) is a distributed network file system. PSC plans to make afs available on all of its machines. Users therefore maintain one set of files, accessible from all machines, so it is not necessary to keep multiple copies of files. Automatic daily backups are done. PSC maintains documentation, examples, libraries, executables and source code on afs in a single location which is accessible from all machines. Each user has a quota of 10,000 1024-byte blocks of permanent storage. A limited amount of temporary storage is also available.

23.16.7. The Biomedical Initiative

PSC received a grant from the National Institutes of Health's (NIH) Division of Research Resources Biomedical Research Technology program to provide the biomedical community with supercomputing resources, training, and user support. The staff of the Biomedical Initiative includes four PhD's and two programmers with large-scale computational backgrounds to support the supercomputing activities of the biomedical community.

23.16.8. Distributed High Speed Computing

The Distributed High Speed Computing (DHSC) project at PSC aims to provide an easy to use interface to the HiPPI (High Performance Parallel Interface) link between the Center's Cray Y-MP/832 and the Connection Machines. This HiPPI network link between the Cray and both CMs is capable of transmitting data at rates of up to 100 MBytes/sec. Through the use of distributed high speed computing, users are able to partition applications between the Cray and the CMs, thus choosing the most appropriate type of supercomputer to solve different portions of the application. Because of the vastly different kinds of problems which can be solved on the Cray and the Connection Machines, some applications will see significant speedups in overall execution time via this approach.

The DHSC project is embodied in a set of library routines, callable from CFT77 and Standard C on the Cray, and from CMFortran, C*, and C-Paris on the Connection Machines. These library calls provide a simple interface to transfer data between programs running in parallel on the two machines. Control issues (such as synchronization of flow) and data conversion issues (such as parallel to serial and IEEE to Cray floating point conversions) are handled internally by the libraries, freeing the user from these low level concerns. DNSC also works in conjunction with Parallel Virtual Machine (PVM), a popular message-passing library for distributing applications among groups of workstations. PVM handles job control and data passing via Ethernet.

23.16.9. The High School Initiative

The PSC, with support from the NSF, has developed a High School Initiative program. Now in its second year, the program grants a high-performance workstation and time on the PSC's Cray supercomputer to ten high schools selected nationwide on the basis of a project proposal. The proposal is judged on scientific merit, creativity, effective use of the supercomputer, feasibility of the project, and how well it can be integrated into the curriculum. The size and the aid ratio of the school district are taken into consideration also, as are indications of minority, female, and underserved populations.

Applications and project proposals are due in the spring for the program beginning the following fall. For more information, contact the Secondary Education Outreach Coordinator at (412) 268-4960.

23.16.10. Training

New User Workshops

- Cray Techniques workshop (5 days) including two days of vectorization training which may be attended separately
- Connection Machine Techniques workshop (5 days) including two days of training in either C* for the CM, or CM FORTRAN which may be attended separately
- Summer Institute (2 weeks)

Advanced User Workshops

- Code Optimization (one day)
- Multitasking (one day)
- Visualization (one day)

Discipline-Specific Workshops

- Introduction to Gaussian Theory and Practice (4 days)
- National Institutes of Health Workshops

Through grants from the National Institutes of Health, the PSC offers a series of workshops dedicated to the biomedical research community, including an overview of biomedical software and databases available at PSC. Topics presented have included molecular mechanics/dynamics, nucleic acid and protein sequence analysis, macromolecular structure refinement, fluid dynamics with immersed flexible structures, and image reconstruction from electron microscopy. Topic-specific workshops are provided on an "as needed" basis and new workshops are under continual development (e.g., biomechanics and neural nets).

23.16.11. Documentation

- Many vendor and hundreds of PSC publications online, including policy, allocations, and user guides
- CRAY manuals mailed via UPS
- List of documents available online
- Hot tips and news in BULLETIN and rn on the VMS front ends and the ULTRIX front ends, respectively; also notices posted on 'news' on the Y-MP
- Online help includes man pages on every PSC system
- PSC Users Guide mailed to all users
- Online EXAMPLES system with complete job setups
- An annual report, "Projects in Scientific Computing," highlights the scientific projects completed at PSC

23.16.12. Consulting

- Phone consulting available M-F 9am to 8pm, Saturday 9am to 4pm (Eastern time)
- E-mail consulting via userid REMARKS
- Online man pages
- Discipline-specific consulting
- "Life-cycle" consulting: starting with algorithm selection through data layout, programming, and program optimization for CM users

23.16.13. Graphics Support

- CGM metafile support
- CGM-based video animation system for VHS tape and videodisk
- Support for remote graphics terminals includes many devices (Also PSC is willing to acquire or develop drivers for nearly any modern device on request.)
- VHS tape output mailed to remote users
- On-site graphics labs with Silicon Graphics IRIS, SUN Sparcstation, IBM RS6000, and DECStation 5000
- Capability to make 35mm color slides using Matrix Instruments SlideWriter
- Color output from Cannon CLC-500 color copier/printer (Prints color PostScript files as well as makes color copies.)

23.16.14. Administration

- All proposals to PSC are screened by the Internal Review Committee (IRC) for scientific merit and computational efficiency. The IRC meets on the first and third Mondays of each month and may award up to 99 service units. Larger grant requests are referred by the IRC to an independent Peer Review Board (PRB). The PRB meets quarterly. Final consensus on awards is arrived at by group caucus of all PRB members. Any decision of the IRC or PRB may be appealed in writing. Awards initially last one year, but may be renewed to complete the research project.
- Starter grants are available for any researcher who wishes to explore the use of the PSC.

Contact summaries:	Consulting	(412) 286-4960
	Accounts	(412) 286-4960
	Allocations	Allocations Coordinator `stock@cpwsca.psc.edu` (412)286-4960
	Training	(412) 286-4960
	High School Initiative	(412) 286-4960
	Hardware status	(412) 286-4960
	Network status	(412) 286-4960
Internet Addresses:	Front ends	`a.psc.edu` `b.psc.edu` `pscuxa.psc.edu` `pscuxb.psc.edu`
	CM-2 front ends	`cmsuna.psc.edu` `cmsunb.psc.edu`
	CM-5 front ends	`cm5a.psc.edu` `cm5b.psc.edu`
	Cray Y-MP	`pscymp.psc.edu`

23.16.15. Login Script

The following script shows how to connect to the front end VMS VAX, login, create a job which submits 'hello.f' to the CRAY, and then logout. It assumes that you connect to the front end from some local machine which supports the TCP/IP Telnet program.

Prompts are represented by "user>" for you, "PSC>" for the front end, "Teln>" for Telnet, and "PSCus>" for front end responses followed by user entries on the same line. Most responses are abbreviated. Comments are enclosed in parentheses.

Prompt	**Dialog**	**Comments**
user>	*telnet a.psc.edu*	(telnet to the front end)
Tel>	...	(Telnet messages)
PSCus>	Username: *<your userid>*	
PSCus>	Password: *<your password>*	
PSC>	...	(PSC login messages)
user>	*emacs hello.job*	(create the following job to be submitted to the CRAY)
	#USER=<userid> PW=<password>	
	#QSUB -r hello	(name the job "hello")
	#QSUB -lM 0.8 Mw	(specify 0.8 Mw limit)
	#QSUB -lT 5	(specify 5 second limit)
	ja	(start accounting log)
	date	
	set -x	(echo commands to output)
	cd $TMP	(move to temp space)
	fetch hello.f -t 'usr$root0:[userid]hello.f	(fetch hello.f from CPWSCA)
	cf77 hello.f limsl11	(compile hello.f; include the IMSL library)
	mv a.out hello.exe	(rename the executable "hello.exe")
	hello.exe > results	(run "hello"; store answers in file "results")
	cfs -r5 store results	(store results in CFS)
	rm hello.exe hello.f	(delete code and executable)
	ja -st	(stop accounting and print an accounting record for yourself)

(At this point, you save your job and exit from EMACS.)

user>	*cray*	
PSC>	**The Cray Station is available**	
user>	*csubmit hello.job*	
PSC>	**%CX-S-SUB_OK, Job: Hello queued for submission**	
PSC>	**VAX TO CRAY:%SYSTEM-S-NORMAL, normal successful completion**	
PSC>	**VAX TO CRAY: FILE=HELLO**	
PSC>	**VAX TO CRAY: 1215 BYTES TRANSFERRED**	
PSC>	**CRAY TO VAX: %RMS-S-NORMAL, normal successful completion**	
PSC>	**CRAY TO VAX: FILE = 1DUA102: [USR2.USERID]HELLO.CPR;1**	("hello.cpr" is the log of the Cray job "hello.job")
PSC>	**CRAY TO VAX: 34 BYTES TRANSFERRED**	
user>	*logout*	

23.17. San Diego Supercomputer Center (SDSC)

23.17.1. Hardware

- CRAY Y-MP8/864 running UNICOS
- Up to 32 Mwords main memory per user
- 6 ns clock; a maximum of 2.7 Gflops for the entire system; up to 337 maximum Mflops per CPU
- Vector processing hardware
- 82 Gbytes online temporary storage
- 256 MWord SSD
- Intel iPSC/860, 64 nodes
- 8 MBytes of memory per node totaling 512 MBytes
- Peak speed of 5.1 Gflops (for 32-bit arithmetic)
- nCUBE 2, 128 nodes
- 64 nodes with 16 MByes of memory each
- 64 nodes with 4 Mbytes of memory each
- Total memory 1.3 Gbytes
- Peak speed of 420 Mflops (for 32-bit arithmetic)
- DataTree for file storage on an Amdahl 5860

23.17.2. Software

- UNICOS on the CRAY Y-MP
- Editors: vi, emacs, and standard Unix line editors on the CRAY Y-MP
- FORTRAN: CFT77 vectorizing compiler
- Other languages: Pascal (vectorizing), CC (ANSI C vectorizing compiler), CRAY C, AS (CRAY Assembly language)
- Extensive example programs available

Biology

DRAW	FASTA	GenBank DB	PIR DB
RANFOLD	RNAFOLD	SN	

Chemistry

AMBER	AMPAC	BIGSTRN-3	CADPAC
CAMBGIDGE DB	CHARMm	CHELP	CORMA
DELPHI	DGEOM	DISCOVER	DMOL
ECEPP2	GAMESS	GAUSSIAN 88	GAUSSIAN 90
GROMOS	MARDIGRAS	MM2	MM3
MMTOOLS	MMX	MOPAC	MPLOT
POLYRATE	PROLSQ	PSI77	QCFF/PI
VENUS	X-PLOR		

Electrical

HSPICE	NETSCAT	PRECISE	SPICE
SUPREM	UMSPICE		

Mechanics

ABAQUS	ADINA	ANSYS	CONTINUSYS
CSQ	DYNA2D	DYNA3D	FACET
FIDAP	FLOTRAN	FLOW-3D	FLUENT
FLUENT/BFC	INGRID	INS3D	MARC
MASPAT	MAZE	MOLDFLOW	MPGS
MSC/NASTRAN	NIKE2D	NIKE3D	ORION
STARDYNE	TAURUS	TOPAZ2D	TOPAZ3D
VSAERO			

Math

BCS	BCS-EXT	DASSL	ELLPACK
HARWELL	HOMPACK	IMSLMATH	IMSLSFUN
IMSLSTAT	ITPACKV	LAPACK	LASO
LIBSCI	MATLAB	MINOS	MINPACK
MUDPACK	NAG	NREG77	NSPCG
ODEPACK	OMNI	PLTMG	SLAP
SLATEC	SMPAK	SPARSPAK	SPSS-X
TOEPLITZ	TOMS	VECTFFT	

Graphics

DISSPLA	GKSNCAR	GKSUL	GNUPLOT
HDF	KHOROS	MOVIE.BYU	NCARGRAPHICS
PLOTXY	VOGLE	XDATASLICE	XIMAGE

Nuclear Engineering

DIF3D	DOS	ENDF DB	MCNP
NJOY	REBUS	SABRINA	TRANSX
TWOHEX			

23.17.3. Training

- Two-day workshops for new users at the beginning of each quarter and at remote sites when requested
- Advanced workshops on specialized topics (e.g., vectorization, visualization, and parallel computing); both on-site and for export
- Summer Institute for those with developed code: applications reviewed by an SDSC committee and open to faculty, graduate students, undergraduates, and industry

23.17.4. Education

- SDSC field trip
- HPCC half-day in-service
- SDSC road show

23.17.5. Collaborative Research

- Visiting scientists program
- Research Fellows program for undergrads, postdoctoral, and senior staff

23.17.6. Documentation

- Over 150 complete user documents online for viewing and/or printing
- Over 3,000 man pages online, including over 300 developed locally
- Hot tips and news in NEWS
- The bi-monthly newsletter "Gather/Scatter"
- User's Guide for all users
- Extensive examples and instructions available online
- Annual report, "Science at the San Diego Supercomputer Center 19xx"
- An overview brochure with application for computing resources

23.17.7. Consulting

- Phone consulting 8am-5pm, Monday-Friday (Pacific time)
- Online consulting through MAIL CONSULT@Y1.SDSC.EDU
- Discipline-specific consulting in most applications

23.17.8. Graphics Support

- Canon CLC-500 color laser copier/printer/scanner
- A Management Graphics Solitaire-8 digital film recorder
- Matrix 6264 analog film recorder
- Lasergraphics LFR Macintosh film recorder
- Hewlett-Packard Paintwriter color Macintosh printer
- Complete audio and video post-production facility for animations
- Complete set of image manipulation and conversion software
- Rendering software including Alias, AVS, Explorer, Renderman, and Wavefront
- Output mailings to your site

23.17.9. Strengths

- MIMD parallel computing
- Networking—infrastructure and research
- Visualization
- Large collection of applications and math software
- High performance vectorization

23.17.10. Administration

- Allocations for large blocks of time; reviewed by allocation committee and must be submitted 60 days prior to each quarter
- Small allocations (1-50 hours): submit at any time

23.17.11. Contact Summaries

Consulting:	`consult@y1.sdsc.edu` (619) 534-5100
Accounts:	(619) 534-5100
Allocations:	Dr. Rozeanne Steckler `steckler@sds.sdsc.edu` (619) 534-5120
Training:	Ms. Jayne Keller `jaynek@sds.sdsc.edu` (619) 534-5124
Hardware status:	(619) 534-5100
Network status:	(619) 534-5100
CRAY Internet address:	`y1.sdsc.edu (132.249.10.1)`

23.17.12. Login Script

The following script shows how to telnet to the San Diego CRAY, login, list files, compile and execute a simple FORTRAN program, and then logout.

Prompts are represented by "user>" for you, "Teln>" for Telnet, "CRAY>" for the CRAY, and "CRus>" for CRAY responses followed by user entries on the same line. Comments are enclosed in parentheses. Most CRAY responses are abbreviated using the "..." ellipsis notation. Note that the system prompts on the SDSC CRAY Y-MP currently have the form "y1-n%" where "n" is the line number.

Prompt	Dialog	Comments
user>	telnet y1.sdsc.edu	(telnet to the CRAY)
Teln>	...	(Telnet messages)
CRus>	login: <your CRAY userid>	(login to the CRAY)
CRus>	Password: <your password>	
CRAY>	...	(CRAY login messages)
CRus>	y1-1% ls	(ask to list your files)
CRAY>	hello.f	
CRus>	y1-2% cf77 -o hello hello.f	(compile "hello.f" code and generate executable file called "hello")
CRus>	y1-3% hello	(execute "hello" program)
CRus>	y1-4% logout	(logoff CRAY, return to your local machine)

@ Appendices @

Appendix A: Learning More About the Internet

To a large degree, the Internet is self documented. Pointers to online information specific to particular Internet applications are provided in each of the chapters of *The Internet Passport*. But there are thousands of online documents dealing with both general and technical issues in far more detail than is possible in any introductory Internet book. The purpose of this appendix is to familiarize you with general purpose online or organizational resources not specific to particular Internet applications.

Requests For Comments (RFCs)

Requests For Comments, or "RFCs", are documents created by and distributed among members of the Internet community to help define the nuts and bolts of the Internet. As of September 1992, there were more than 1,300 RFCs containing general information, technical specifications, and occasional general essays of interest to Internet users. In particular, all the components of the TCP/IP protocol suite are specified in many of the RFCs.

RFCs are available as online documents which you can retrieve from many of the services described throughout this book, such as mail servers, anonymous FTP hosts, or information systems such as Gopher, WAIS, campus wide information systems, or World Wide Web.

Here are three of the many current RFC repositories:

FTP host:	`nic.ddn.mil`	
directory:	`rfc`	
filenames:	`rfcxxxx.txt`	(where "xxxx" is the RFC number, e.g., rfc1000.txt or rfc822.txt)

FTP host:	`nis.nsf.net`	
directory:	`internet/documents/rfc`	
filenames:	`rfcxxxx.txt`	(where "xxxx" is the RFC number, e.g., rfc1000.txt or rfc0822.txt)

FTP host:	`src.doc.ic.ac.uc`	
directory:	`rfc`	
filenames:	`rfcxxxx.txt.Z`	(where "xxxx" is the RFC number, e.g., rfc1000.txt.Z or rfc822.txt.Z)

For the most up-to-date information on obtaining RFCs via FTP or e-mail send the following mail message:

```
mail:    rfc-info@isi.edu
subject: (none needed)
message: help: ways_to_get_rfcs
```

In response to this request, you should receive a file named "rfc-retrieval.txt," containing detailed information about all primary and secondary FTP repositories of RFCs.

If you want to receive new RFCs as they are released, you can subscribe to the RFC distribution list by sending a subscription request to rfc-request@nic.ddn.mil. (Note that this is not a discussion list, but rather a list from which you will receive materials.)

Here are some introductory RFCs which are useful as an overview of the Internet:

RFC1087:	Ethics and the Internet
RFC1118:	Hitchhiker's guide to the Internet
RFC1150:	F.Y.I. On F.Y.I.: Introduction to the F.Y.I. notes
RFC1175:	FYI on where to start: A bibliography of Internetworking information
RFC1206:	FYI on questions and answers: Answers to commonly asked "new Internet user" questions
RFC1207:	FYI on questions and answers: Answers to commonly asked "experienced Internet user" questions
RFC1208:	Glossary of networking terms
RFC1290	There's gold in them thar networks! or searching for treasure in all the wrong places
RFC 1359	Connecting to the Internet: What connecting institutions should anticipate

If you do not yet have access to the Internet, many of the RFCs have been collected and organized topically into a multi-volume printed series called *The Internet Technology Handbook*, available from:

SRI International
Network Information Systems Center
333 Ravenswood Ave., Room EJ291
Menlo Park, CA 94015 USA

e-mail: nisc@nisc.sri.com

voice: (415) 859-6387
fax: (415) 859-6028

The FYI (For Your Information) Notes

A subset of the RFC series, called the FYI (For Your Information) notes, is of particular interest to new Internet users. The numbers in the left column are the FYI series numbers.

1	RFC1150:	F.Y.I. on F.Y.I.: Introduction to the F.Y.I. notes
2	RFC1147:	FYI on a network management tool catalog: Tools for monitoring and debugging TCP/IP internets and interconnected devices
3	RFC1175:	FYI on where to start: A bibliography of internetworking information
4	RFC1325:	FYI on questions and answers: Answers to commonly asked "new Internet user" questions
5	RFC1178:	Choosing a name for your computer
6	RFC1198:	FYI on the X window system
7	RFC1207:	FYI on Questions and Answers: Answers to commonly asked "experienced Internet user" questions
8	RFC1244:	Site Security Handbook
9	RFC1336:	Who's who in the Internet: Biographies of IAB, IESG and IRSG members.
10	RFC1290:	There's gold in them thar networks! or searching for treasure in all the wrong places
11	RFC1292:	Catalog of available X.500 implementations
12	RFC1302:	Building a network information services infrastructure
13	RFC1308:	Executive introduction to directory services using the X.500 protocol
14	RFC1309:	Technical overview of directory services using the X.500 protocol
15	RFC1355:	Privacy and accuracy issues in network information center databases
16	RFC1359:	Connecting to the Internet: What connecting institutions should anticipate
17	RFC1391:	The Tao of IETF: A guide for new attendees of the Internet Engineering Task Force

These documents can be obtained by any of the methods described for RFCs; they are also often stored and available with the filenames "fyixx.txt," where "xx" is their number within the FYI series. For a current list of FYIs, look for a file called "fyi-index."

FYIs may also be ordered via e-mail by sending a message to mail-server@nisc.sri.com. In the body of the messaage, write "send fyixx". To obtain the FYI index, your message should read "send fyi-index".

If you do not yet have an Internet connection, you can obtain printed copies of any FYI from SRI, either individually or as part of an RFC subscription. For more information about this service contact nisc@nisc.sri.com or call (415) 859-6387.

Some Organizations and Conferences for Internet Users

As a new or prospective member of the Internet, you may be interested in joining one of the many organizations devoted to the future of Internetworking. Many of these organizations also sponsor periodic meetings or conferences. Although the following list is not comprehensive, it should serve as a good starting point for learning what organizations or conferences may be of interest to you.

Association for Computing Machinery (ACM)

"The Association for Computing Machinery is dedicated to the development of information processing as a discipline, and to the responsible use of computers in an increasing diversity of applications...

"ACM's Special Interest Groups (SIGs), devoted to the technical activities of its members, offer the individual ACM member all the advantages of a homogeneous, narrower-purpose group within a large professional society The SIGs operate as semiautonomous bodies within ACM for the advancement of activities in varying subject areas. ACM members are eligible to join as many special interest groups as they wish...

[Of particular interest to Internet users is SIGCOMM:] "This special interest group is devoted to encouraging and reporting scholarly research and developments in the field of computer communication systems. The scope of SIGCOMM interests include design, analysis, measurement, maintenance, standards, applications, and social impacts of computer networking. Regulatory matters and the transfer of technology into the marketplace are also of great interest."

--From the Communications of the ACM

The Association for Computing Machinery
11 West 42nd Street
New York, NY 10036-8097 USA

e-mail: **acmhelp@acm.org**

voice: (212) 869-7440
fax: (212) 869-0481

FTP host: **acm.org**
directories: many or all   (note that this is a VMS based FTP host,
                                          so refer to chapter 7 if you need help)

Coalition for Networked Information (CNI)

"The mission of the Coalition for Networked Information is to promote the creation of and access to information resources in networked environments in order to enrich scholarship and to enhance intellectual productivity."

--From the CNI mission statement in
the file "cni.prog.oview.txt"
stored on the CNI FTP host

Joan K. Lippincott
Assistant Executive Director
Coalition for Networked Information
1527 New Hampshire Avenue NW
Washington, D.C. 20036 USA

e-mail: **joan@cni.org**

voice: (202) 232-2466
fax: (202) 462-7849

FTP host: **ftp.cni.org**
directory: **CNI**
directories: (many or all)

Computer Professionals for Social Responsibility (CPSR)

"CPSR is a public-interest alliance of computer scientists and others interested in the impact of computer technology on society. We work to influence decisions regarding the development and use of computers because those decisions have far-reaching consequences and reflect basic values and priorities. As technical experts, CPSR members provide the public and policymakers with realistic assessments of the power, promise, and limitations of computer technology. As concerned citizens, we direct public attention to critical choices concerning the applications of computing and how those choices affect society."

--From the file "cpsr brochure" available in
the archives of the LISTSERV discussion
list, CPSR@GWUVM.GWU.EDU

CPSR National Office
Box 717
Palo Alto, CA 94302 USA

e-mail: **cpsr@clsi.stanford.edu**

voice: (415) 322-3778
fax: (415) 322-3798

EDUCOM

"EDUCOM, a nonprofit consortium of higher education institutions founded in 1964, will focus in the 1990s on (1) increasing individual and institutional intellectual productivity through access to and use of information resources and technology and (2) ensuring the creation of an information infrastructure that will meet society's needs into the twenty-first century. EDUCOM's work is done in cooperation and partnership with the broader education and library communities, professional societies and information industries. EDUCOM programs and projects offer critical information for policymakers and planners in higher education. ...[the Educom Annual Fall Conference] is the preeminent international event for anyone concerned with information technology in higher education. "

> --From the file "EDUCOM-what-is-EDUCOM"
> in the FTP host educom.edu

EDUCOM
1112 16th Street, NW
Suite 600
Washington, DC 20036 USA

e-mail: **inquiry@educom.edu**

voice: (202) 872-4200
fax: (202) 872-4318

FTP host: **educom.edu**
directory: **pub**
filenames: (many or all)

Electronic Frontier Foundation (EFF)

The mission of the Electronic Frontier Foundation is to:

"1. Engage in and support educational activities which increase popular understanding of the opportunities and challenges posed by developments in computing and telecommunications.

"2. Develop among policy-makers a better understanding of the issues underlying free and open telecommunications, and support the creation of legal and structural approaches which will ease the assimilation of these new technologies by society.

"3. Raise public awareness about civil liberties issues arising from the rapid advancement in the area of new computer-based communications media. Support litigation in the public interest to preserve, protect, and extend First Amendment rights within the realm of computing and telecommunications technology."

--From the file "mission-statement"
in the FTP host ftp.eff.org

The Electronic Frontier Foundation, Inc.
155 Second St., #1
Cambridge, MA 02141 USA

e-mail: **eff@eff.org**

voice: (617) 864-0665
fax: (617) 864-0866

FTP host: **ftp.eff.org**
directory: **pub/EFF**
filenames: (many or all)

FARNET (Federation of American Research Networks)

"FARNET is a non-profit corporation whose mission is to advance the use of computer networks to improve research and education. ...FARNET offers frequent educational programs for its members; works with other national and international organizations to improve the quality of information and services available to network users; provides information about networking to interested consumers, the media, and decision-makers; negotiates discounts on products and services for its members; provides a forum for the discussion of key technical and policy issues; publishes a monthly online newsletter and regular proceedings of its meetings. ...Membership in FARNET is open to any organization that supports its mission."

--From the file "what-is-farnet"
in the FTP host farnet.org

FARNET
100 Fifth Avenue
Waltham, MA 02154 USA

e-mail: **breeden@farnet.org**

voice: (617) 890-5120
         (800) 723-2763
fax: (617) 890-5117

FTP host: **farnet.org**
directory: **farnet**
filenames: (many or all)

Internet Engineering Task Force (IETF)

"The IETF mission includes: identifying and proposing solutions to pressing operational and technical problems in the Internet; specifying the development (or usage) of protocols and the near-term architecture to solve such technical problems for the Internet; making recommendations to the IAB regarding standardization of protocols and protocol usage in the Internet; facilitating technology transfer from the Internet Research Task Force (IRTF) to the wider Internet community; and providing a forum for the exchange of information within the Internet community between vendors, users, researchers, agency contractors, and network managers."

--From the file "1ietf-description.txt"
in the FTP host cnri.reston.va.us

Corporation for National Research Initiatives
Attn: IETF Secretariat
1895 Preston White Drive
Suite 100
Reston, VA 22091 USA

e-mail: `ietf-info@cnri.reston.va.us`

FTP host: `cnri.reston.va.us`
directory: `ietf`
filenames: (many or all)

Internet Society

The Internet Society is "a non-profit organization and will be operated for academic, educational, charitable and scientific purposes among which are: to facilitate and support the technical evolution of the Internet as a research and education infrastructure and to stimulate involvement of the academic, scientific and engineering communities, among others in the evolution of the Internet; to educate the academic and scientific communities and the public concerning the technology, use and application of the Internet; to promote scientific and educational applications of Internet technology for the benefit of educational institutions at all grade levels, industry and the public at large; to provide a forum for exploration of new Internet applications; and to foster collaboration among organizations in their operation and use of the Internet."

--From the file "isoc-pkg.txt" in
the FTP host cnri.reston.va.us

Internet Society
1895 Preston White Drive
Suite 100
Reston, VA 22091 USA

e-mail: `isoc@isoc.org`

voice: (703) 648-9888
fax: (703) 620-0913

FTP host: `cnri.reston.va.us`
directory: `isoc`
filenames: (many or all)

The National Research and Education Network (NREN)

By time you read this book, much of the Internet in the U.S., including NSFNET and similar national Internet networks, may have been renamed "The National Research and Education Network" (NREN). The High-Performance Computing Act, signed into law in November 1991, authorized the creation of a permanent NREN. The bill allocated $2.9 billion over the next five years to enhance the United States' high-performance computing and communications infrastructure. Additional acts and funding are currently under review.

Information on the NREN is available from the following FTP hosts:

FTP host:	`nis.nsf.net`
directory:	`nsfnet`
filenames:	many or all
FTP host:	`expres.cise.nsf.gov`
directories:	`pub/recompete`
filenames:	many or all
FTP host:	`farnet.org`
directories:	`farnet/nren`
filenames:	many or all

The following mailing lists deal with the NREN, and the commercialization and privatization of the Internet:

Mailing List name:	To subscribe, send e-mail to:
`nren-discuss@psi.com`	`nren-discuss-request@psi.com`
`com-priv@uu.psi.com`	`com-priv-request@uu.psi.com`

Appendix B: Connecting to the Internet

Even if you don't think you have access to the Internet, you might! If you are in school or are employed, your organization may already have Internet access. So before spending a great deal of time and effort examining Internet access options, ask around. If your organization is not connected to the Internet, suggest that they consider the many benefits of the Internet to their activities. Organizations located in Alaska, Idaho, Montana, North Dakota, Oregon, or Washington, are encouraged to call NorthWestNet for information.

If you are certain that your organization lacks Internet connectivity, or if you want a private account, there are a growing number of Internet service providers who would be happy to help you.

In general, there are two classes of Internet connections: connectivity for sites such as schools or companies that will support many users and access for individuals. The former is most often achieved by obtaining "dedicated access," i.e., direct IP connections to the Internet. Individuals usually obtain a "dialup" account which is reached through a modem connected to your personal computer.

There are also varying degrees of Internet service. Your options range from e-mail-only access, to full-service connectivity with optional access to commercial databases thrown in. So be sure to shop around, compare prices, and consider what options are most appropriate to your needs.

The following are directions on how to get frequently updated lists of Internet service providers.

Obtaining Current Lists of U.S. Internet Service Providers

Multi-User Service Providers

Up-to-date lists of organizations that provide Internet access to schools or companies can be obtained from the NSF Network Service Center (NNSC). This "referral list" contains a complete list of Internet service providers in the U.S., and the "limited referral" list contains a list of Internet service providers who provide limited services such as e-mail-only access.

You can contact the NNSC by phone, postal mail, or e-mail.

NSF Network Service Center (NNSC)
BBN Laboratories Inc.
10 Moulton St.
Cambridge, MA 02138 USA

e-mail: `nnsc@nnsc.nsf.net`

voice: (617) 873-3361

You can also obtain these service provider lists by sending a message to the NNSC mail server.

```
mail:     info-server@nnsc.nsf.net
subject:  (none needed)
message:  request nsfnet (follow with one of these two topic
                          requests)

          topic: referral-list      (for a complete list of
                                      Internet service providers
                                      in the U.S.)

          topic: limited-referral   (for service providers
                                      providing limited services
                                      such as e-mail only)

          request: end               (required at the end of
                                      your message)
```

To learn more about the NNSC Info-server and the many other files that it provides, send the following e-mail message:

```
mail:     info-server@nnsc.nsf.net
subject:  (none needed)
message:  request info
          topic: help
          request: end
```

Public-Access Internet Hosts

A growing number of entrepreneurs are providing Internet access from Bulletin Board Systems which you can call from your personal computer via modem.

Peter Kaminski maintains a list of such services, which is distributed as a periodic posting to several Usenet newsgroups ("alt.bbs.lists" and "alt.bbs.internet") and via e-mail requests:

```
mail:     kaminski@netcom.com
subject:  Send PDIAL
message:  (none needed)
```

You can also subscribe to the PDIAL distribution so that you will receive updates as they are released.

```
mail:     kaminski@netcom.com
subject:  Subscribe PDIAL
message:  (none needed)
```

Another list of this sort is known as the "nixpub" (uNIX PUBlic access systems) list. These are typically Unix-based BBSs providing access to Usenet newsgroups and e-mail access to the Internet. Short and long versions of the nixpub list are distributed as a periodic posting to the Usenet newsgroups "comp.misc" and the various "alt.bbs" newsgroups, or you can request a copy by sending one of the following e-mail messages:

```
mail:     nixpub@digex.com
subject:  (none needed)
message:  (none needed)
```

```
mail:     archive-server@cs.widener.edu
subject:  (none needed)
message:  (one of the following messages)

send nixpub long
send nixpub short
send nixpub long short
index nixpub
```

Obtaining Current Lists of Non-U.S. Internet Service Providers

A list of Internet service providers worldwide is currently maintained by SRI, International. In addition to being available in their printed book, *Internet: Getting Started*, this list can be obtained by postal or electronic mail, or from the SRI FTP archives:

SRI International
Network Information Systems Center
333 Ravenswood Avenue, Room EJ291
Menlo Park, CA 94015 USA

e-mail: **nisc@nisc.sri.com**

voice: (415) 859-6387
fax: (415) 859-6028

FTP host: **ftp.nisc.sri.com**
directory: **netinfo**
filename: **internet-access-providers-non-us.txt**

And if you are unsure as to whether there are any Internet services in your country (for example, you don't see your country's name in the list of national domains in chapter 1), you can contact the Network Information Center at Government Systems, Inc., and ask for the contact name of the administrative contact person(s), if any, for your nation's domain.

> Government Systems, Inc.
> Attn: Network Information Center
> 14200 Park Meadow Drive
> Suite 200
> Chantilly, VA 22021 USA
>
> e-mail: `hostmaster@nic.ddn.mil`
>
> voice: (703) 802-4535
> voice: (800) 365-3642 (U.S. only)
> fax: (703) 802-8376

Bibliography

The following printed books are particularly thorough in their coverage of Internet service providers. Frey and Adams, Marine et. al, and Quarterman also provide great coverage of network service providers outside the U.S. However, printed materials about the Internet become outdated very quickly, and you are encouraged to obtain one of the lists mentioned earlier in this appendix for the most up-to-date information.

Frey, D. and R. Adams. *!%@:: A Directory of Electronic Mail Addressing and Networks.* Sebastapol, CA: O'Reilly and Associates, 1990.

LaQuey, T. *The User's Directory of Computer Networks.* Bedford, MA: Digital Press, 1990.

Marine, A., S. Kirkpatrick, V. Neou, and C. Ward. *Internet: Getting Started.* Menlo Park. CA: SRI International, Network Information Systems Center, 1992.

Quarterman, J.S. *The Matrix: Computer Networks and Conferencing Systems Worldwide.* Bedford, MA: Digital Press, 1990.

Appendix C: Setting Up a CWIS

Installing a CWIS could prove valuable for people at your institution and potentially, people throughout the Internet. But setting up a CWIS is not a matter of "plug and play." You should anticipate spending considerable organizational effort to start and maintain a CWIS. The well-planned CWIS reaps the greatest rewards and you'll reduce future maintenance overhauls and overhead.

If your institution is considering starting a CWIS, there are several issues that should be considered:

Who is your audience?
What information will be provided?
How will the information be
structured?
What campus computer would be
used?
What software should be used?
Who will be responsible for installing
and maintaining the information?

Answering these questions will require input from information providers, programming staff, administrators, software providers, and potential users.

Much of the information in this section is derived from Judy Hallman's 1992 CWIS article, cited in the bibliography of chapter 19, and articles posted to the CWIS-L LISTSERV mailing list. You are encouraged to read those sources for a much more thorough discussion of these issues.

Basic Research

Understand the Needs of Your Campus Community

Every organization has a unique set of information needs, so the first step should be understanding what role a CWIS would play.

What sorts of information services currently exist on your campus? Have there been any studies or surveys of the strengths and weaknesses of these services? How would a CWIS interact with existing information services? What is the overall vision for the role of a CWIS within the community?

Examine Available CWIS Software Systems

There are a wide variety of software platforms for CWISs. Explore the various services to see how well they would address the needs of your community.

Some of the "traditional" software platforms for CWISs include VTX and AIE (for VAX computers), PNN (for Unix, VM, VAX, SunOS, and Macs), and MUSIC and CUINFO (for IBM mainframes). A rapidly growing number of sites are using Gopher for their CWISs. WAIS and World Wide Web are also beginning to appear in the CWIS world as well.

While exploring possible CWIS software options you should keep the following questions in mind: will this software run on my system? How much, if anything, does it cost? Who, if anyone, supports it? Is it easy to use—will our users need training? Is it easy to contribute information—will our information providers need training? How easy would it be to customize various features of the software if necessary? And if you don't find CWIS software that meets all of your needs, would the in-house development of a new system or modification of already available software be a cost effective route to consider?

CWIS Security

One should make sure that the CWIS software you install does not have security holes which could be broached by computer crackers. For example, some early CWIS systems allowed a user to "break out" of the CWIS shell and then have anonymous access to your system and perhaps from there to the rest of the Internet. Such a situation could be very embarrassing for your institution. Ask the vendor, developer, and other users of a particular CWIS software package direct questions about what security problems are known or suspected to exist.

Privacy and Sensitive Information

By what criteria should information in a CWIS be considered sensitive or hidden? What sorts of concerns might staff and or students have about online distribution of their contact information? Before putting information about individuals (for example a phone or e-mail directory) online, always contact the group at your site that maintains this information. Discussing your needs and plans with the dean of students, registrar, human resources office, or whichever group is appropriate, can help you to understand the privacy issues involved with making information about individuals publicly available.

Management: Who Will Operate the CWIS?

At different institutions, CWISs are operated by the staff of the computer center, library, administration, or any combination of these and other entities. Which organization(s) at your institution is most willing and able to operate and maintain a CWIS? You might find that portions of the task could be allocated to different departments. For example, CWIS software and hardware maintenance could be the responsibility of computer support staff.

However, the more distributed the handling of a CWIS, the more important it is to delineate roles and responsibilities. For example, if erroneous information is posted, who is responsible? If the system crashes in the middle of the night, who will set things right? If you plan to make your CWIS available to the Internet community at large, who will handle the request for assistance from remote users?

Sources: Who Will Provide Information for Your CWIS?

In the long run, providing and updating information in the CWIS is likely to be the most time intensive and expensive task, especially if your plans include the creation of a comprehensive information resource. The model that allows the most room for expansion is to distribute the information gathering and updating among the actual information providers. If you opt for this model, it would be useful to have well established formats for submitted materials. An additional time saver would be to have software that you can distribute to information providers for translating input directly into an approved format, ready for posting directly to the CWIS.

Contents: What Will Your CWIS Provide?

The primary goal of many CWISs is to provide central access to the kinds of information typically included in handbooks, staff and student guides, campus directories, campus publications, and online services such as library catalogs and databases. However, many CWISs also include features which make using the CWIS more enjoyable, such as local weather reports, or question and answer columns. Such features are incentives to otherwise diffident users to try the CWIS. Once connected, most users begin exploring the full range of services offered.

Screen and Menu Design: The Aesthetics and Psychology of a CWIS

As you probably know from your computing experiences, what you see on a screen has a tremendous effect on how user friendly the software seems. A simple and visually appealing interface will make the information in your CWIS more accessible to the user.

Keep in mind that the look and feel of a CWIS will be implicitly understood by users as representing the philosophy of your institution—just like an e-mail message with a "standard disclaimer" nonetheless reflects on one's organization. If your CWIS is well organized, logical, efficient, up-to-date and maybe even fun, CWIS users will have these impressions of your institution.

Visual Design

Even if the CWIS uses text-only displays, the overall visual design of the CWIS screen is important. To address these aesthetic considerations, some CWIS developers have employed artists and psychologists in their design teams. Intelligent use of upper and lower case characters, spacing, and indentation is helpful. As a general rule, ASCII graphics, verbose descriptions, and cluttered displays make it harder for people to see what is on the screen.

Also, information formatted for paper does not always display well on a screen which may be limited to 80 columns and 24 rows. Already existing documents that are to be incorporated into a CWIS may require extensive reformatting to be usable in an online version.

On-Screen Help

How much on-screen help should be displayed on each screen? To a large degree, this depends on how computer literate the potential users of your CWIS are already. Every screen should minimally display the commands for returning to the main menu, a few of the basic navigational commands, the command for obtaining full online help, and the command for exiting the CWIS. Other commands may be included when and where appropriate. (For example, commands for searching when information is searchable, or commands for routing displayed information to the users' workstations are generally useful.)

Depth of Menus

Because most CWISs are confined to a standard terminal screen size, there is a tradeoff between the amount of information on any one screen, and the number of layers down the menu structure a user must go to retrieve rewarding information. This should not be a problem unless you have an ambitious and/or a large CWIS. One solution is to offer multiple paths of access to information within a CWIS; for example, Cornell's CUINFO provides relatively low density menus which one must step down through, and a high density index for those who want to get right to a particular resource.

Organization

How topics are organized will depend on the audience and how the system will be used. What categories should be included in the main menu? In what order should these items appear? Should the information be divided by administrative categories, or by information type? Should entries be listed alphabetically, or conceptually?

Logical classification of diverse information is an area in which campus librarians have a great deal of expertise; but keep in mind that in addition to the purely informational role of the CWIS organization, there may be political or ideological implications to various setups. Such subtleties as the order in which items appear in the main menu or how many menus down one must go to obtain a certain class of information can have unanticipated consequences that you should try to anticipate in discussions with involved parties and the user community.

Consistency of Design

Establishing and adhering to well thought out conventions for standardized formats for menus, help screens, and documents will help your users feel at home with the service. If many different groups are providing information, you might consider distributing descriptions of these standards, and maybe even software and associated templates which the information providers can use to massage the materials they submit into a standard format.

Although there will inevitably be some tinkering with the organization of a CWIS, try to settle on a consistent design and structure for the main menu relatively early. A highly volatile main menu might confuse your entire audience, whereas volatile submenus will only confuse the subset of people who use that submenu, and so forth.

Access

Interoperability

Some institutions use the "lowest common denominator" model and implement a CWIS that is equally accessible to all connected computers, while another CWIS may adopt a different extreme and interface only with a few select computer types.

In the client-server model, what the user sees on their computer screen can be a function of the software on their own computer. Thus, a Mac or NeXT user could have pull down menus, dialog boxes, and scroll bars on their display, while another person accessing the same CWIS at the same time from a DOS machine, would see a

typical DOS interface that used typical DOS key sequences like PageUp, home, arrow keys, and control keys. And users of dumb terminals would still see a basic, command-line driven screen. Currently, Gopher and World Wide Web are popular client-server options for CWISs, though others are used and still others are under development.

Local versus Global Access

Although the term CWIS suggests a local information service, many institutions have chosen to make their systems available to the Internet at large. If you do opt for worldwide access to your service, be sure that the host computer can handle all local users, as well as the additional load from outside users. And you may also decide that certain sections of your CWIS should not be accessible to non-campus users. If so, what are the most appropriate methods for restricting outside use of parts of a CWIS? What sorts of licensing restrictions might there be on installed services, such as commercial databases, that are accessible through your CWIS?

Appendix D: NorthWestNet Network Operations Center (NOC) Services

Much recent national attention has focused on improving the quality of Internet connectivity services by enhancing "end-to-end" network management. In the three tiered hierarchy of the Internet, high priority has been placed upon the critical role of the midlevel networks in delivering quality connectivity services. "Tempering the Network" has emerged as the phase most often used to describe the portion of this new national initiative. Given the recent consensus regarding the importance of "end-to-end" network connectivity focused on midlevel networks, this brief summary of NorthWestNet's Network Operations Center (NOC) has been included in *The Internet Passport*.

The purpose of this appendix is to identify the services that the Network Operations Center (NOC) will provide to maintain the operational integrity of the network. This appendix is available via anonymous FTP on "ftphost.nwnet.net" in the directory "nwnet/doc/" as the file "uw-nwnet.noc".

Network Monitoring, Repair, and Trouble Tracking

The NOC will provide real-time network monitoring and repair at the layers one (1) through four (4) in the OSI model. The link state of each NorthWestNet circuit will be queried periodically (approximately once a minute) by a Network Management Station (NMS). The NMS will be monitored 24 hours a day, seven days a week. This NMS is expected to provide a real-time view of the entire network and have some rudimentary network diagnosis tools available to operators to identify common or general problems with link layer connectivity.

The level of staffing is expected to vary between primary shifts (approximately 8:00 a.m. to 6:00 p.m. Monday through Friday) and the secondary shifts (the complement of the primary shift hours). The primary shift will have skilled network analysts available and trained in more complex network diagnostic tools. These analysts will be able to assist in problem diagnosis and resolution at the Network and Transport Layers. The secondary shift operators will be expected to recognize simple circuit outages (at the Physical and Link Layers) and initiate work orders with telecommunications providers. Once an outage or problem is identified, it will be tracked with a trouble ticket system to help provide consistency across multiple shifts and to identify reoccurring problems.

Circuit Commissioning and Equipment Installation

The NorthWestNet NOC will configure the equipment necessary to facilitate member connections to the network and deliver it to the member site. If the technical representative of the member institution requires additional support to complete the installation, the NOC will endeavor to assist. The NOC will also assist the public telecommunications providers in specifying and commissioning the required data circuits.

Equipment Maintenance and Upgrade

The NOC will reconfigure and coordinate upgrades of the NorthWestNet-managed equipment as necessary. In case of a hardware failure, the NOC will ship a spare to the member institution's technical representative not later than the next business day following discovery of the problem.

Diagnostic Tools Repository

The NMS will act as a repository for network management tools. Tools in the public domain, developed locally by programming staff, or available to the NOC through licensing agreements, will be stored on and available from the NMS.

NMS Data Collection and Analysis

The NMS periodically (approximately every 15 minutes) will query each router to retrieve a set of Management Information Base (MIB) variables that can be considered useful for diagnosis and analysis. This data will be stored on the NMS and made available for report generation or post-processing analysis. Rudimentary programs will be available to query this database and generate graphs as aids to problem diagnosis and reporting. Simple monthly reports on outages and circuit usage will also be derivable from this data.

Domain Name Service (DNS)

Upon the request of a member, the NOC will provide interim primary or continuing secondary Domain Name Service. Members may request interim primary DNS from the NOC, which implies that all host name additions, changes, or deletions be done by NOC staff. When a member site is able to provide its own primary DNS, the NOC will, if requested, continue to provide secondary DNS. Any correspondence with the NOC regarding DNS should be done through the mailing list "domainmaster@nwnet.net".

Agency Interaction

The NOC will interact with national, regional, and member network agencies, as well as telecommunications providers and equipment vendors, to facilitate transitions in network topology, resolve outages, or provide other operational assistance as required.

Support for Hub Sites

The NOC will assist technical staff at NorthWestNet hub sites in resolving connectivity problems. This assistance will be mainly in the form of consulting by phone and e-mail.

Network Engineering

With consultation from and review by the NorthWestNet Technical Committee, the NOC will provide network engineering services to define and implement a network topology and architecture that will achieve NorthWestNet's connectivity and cost objectives as set forth by the NorthWestNet Management Committee.

Revision 2.2
September, 1992

Appendix E: NorthWestNet Acceptable Use Policies

NorthWestNet Acceptable Use Policy For Research and Education

NorthWestNet is a regional data communications network serving a consortium of universities, colleges, industrial research groups, libraries, hospitals, government agencies, primary and secondary schools and school districts, and commercial enterprises in the northwestern United States. NorthWestNet is wholly owned, managed, and operated by the Northwest Academic Computing Consortium, Inc. (NWACC).

NorthWestNet embraces the mission to promote research, education, and economic development by providing access to network communications, computing, and electronic information systems and services. This document describes certain research and education uses which are consistent with the objectives of NorthWestNet, but does not exhaustively enumerate all such possible acceptable uses.

Membership in NorthWestNet conveys the right to access NorthWestNet facilities and network services for research and educational purposes. A companion document, "NorthWestNet Acceptable Use Policy for Commercial Enterprise," describes access and usage policies for business enterprise.

Some Acceptable Uses of NorthWestNet Facilities:

1. All use of NorthWestNet network services and facilities shall be consistent with the mission of NorthWestNet and NWACC. All use shall be intended to facilitate the exchange of information, intellectual property, and services to promote research, education, and technology diffusion, and otherwise be consistent with the broad objectives of NorthWestNet.

2. Use of NorthWestNet facilities and services for research, education, instruction, and as a vehicle for scholarly communications by member institutions through the provision of a high-speed data communications and computing, and electronic information resources and services is encouraged.

3. Use as a means for members to access remote computing and information resources for the purpose of research, education, or instruction is encouraged. Notable examples of such resources are the NSF supercomputing centers.

4. Use necessary to support other acceptable uses is itself acceptable. For example, administrative communications which are part of the support infrastructure needed for research, education, instruction, and development are acceptable.

5. Use required by agreements with NSF, a primary funding agency for NorthWestNet, is acceptable.

6. Use by member institutions as a laboratory for research and experimentation in computer communications is permitted where such use does not interfere with production usage. However, any experimental use requiring modification to router software or protocol layers below ISO layer 4

requires prior review and approval from the Director of Technical Services.

Some Unacceptable Uses:

7. Use of NorthWestNet facilities and network services for any illegal purpose, or to achieve unauthorized access to systems, software, or data is prohibited.

8. NorthWestNet shall not be used to transmit any communication where the meaning of the message, or its transmission or distribution, is intended to be highly abusive to the recipient or recipients thereof.

9. NorthWestNet is a production communications network on which many users depend. Users of NorthWestNet network services and facilities should promote efficient use of the networks and thereby attempt to minimize and, if possible, avoid unnecessary network traffic which might interfere or otherwise impact negatively with the work of other users of NorthWestNet or connected networks. Uses that significantly interfere with the ability of others to make effective use of the network or which disrupt

NorthWestNet or any connected networks, systems, services, or equipment are prohibited.

10. Use for business or commercial enterprise is prohibited under this policy. However, access to NorthWestNet facilities and network services for commercial use is available as a value-added service to NorthWestNet member organizations for an additional service fee.

Interpretation, application, and modification of this Acceptable Use Policy shall be within the sole discretion of NorthWestNet and NWACC. Questions about any issue related to this Policy should be directed to NorthWestNet by member organizations when an issue first arises.

NorthWestNet and NWACC make no warranty of any kind, expressed or implied, regarding Internet resources or services, or the contents of resources or electronic messages over the Internet, nor shall NorthWestNet or NWACC be liable in any event for incidental or consequential damages, direct or indirect, resulting from the use of either NorthWestNet or the resources and services available through NorthWestNet Internet facilities or network services.

Version 3.1
February 12, 1993

NorthWestNet Acceptable Policy for Commercial Enterprise

NorthWestNet is a regional data communications network serving a consortium of universities, colleges, industrial research groups, libraries, hospitals, government agencies, primary and secondary schools and school districts, and commercial enterprises in the northwestern United States. NorthWestNet is wholly owned, managed, and operated by the Northwest Academic Computing Consortium, Inc. (NWACC).

NorthWestNet embraces the mission to promote research, education, and economic development by providing access to network communications, computing, and electronic information systems and services. This document describes certain commercial enterprise uses which are consistent with the objectives of NorthWestNet, but does not exhaustively enumerate all such possible acceptable uses.

Membership in NorthWestNet conveys the right to access NorthWestNet facilities and network services for research and educational purposes as defined in a companion document, "NorthWestNet Acceptable Use Policy for Research and Education." Access to NorthWestNet facilities and network services for commercial use as described in this Policy is available as a value-added service to NorthWestNet member organizations for an additional service fee.

Some Acceptable Uses of NorthWestNet Facilities:

1. All use of NorthWestNet network services and facilities shall be consistent with the mission of NorthWestNet and NWACC. All use shall be intended to facilitate the exchange of information, intellectual property, and services to promote research, education, technology diffusion, economic development, and commerce and otherwise be consistent with the broad objectives of NorthWestNet.

2. All uses defined as acceptable under the companion policy, "NorthWestNet Acceptable Use Policy for Research and Education" are acceptable.

3. When requested by a user of NorthWestNet or any connected network, transmission of product information and commercial messages is permitted. Discussion of a product's relative advantages and disadvantages by users of the product, and vendors' responses to those who pose questions about their products, is permitted.

Some Unacceptable Uses:

4. Use of NorthWestNet facilities and network services for any illegal purpose, or to achieve unauthorized access to systems, software, or data is prohibited.

5. NorthWestNet shall not be used to transmit any communication where the meaning of the message, or its

transmission or distribution, is intended to be highly offensive to the recipient or recipients thereof.

6. Intrusive or unsolicited advertising (or other commercial information) may not be "broadcast" or be otherwise sent to any user of NorthWestNet or any connected network.

7. NorthWestNet is a production communications network on which many users depend. Users of NorthWestNet network services and facilities should promote efficient use of the networks and thereby attempt to minimize and, if possible, avoid unnecessary network traffic which might interfere or otherwise impact negatively with the work of other users of NorthWestNet or connected networks. Uses that significantly interfere with the ability of others to make effective use of the network or which disrupt NorthWestNet or any connected networks, systems, services, or equipment are prohibited.

Interpretation, application, and modification of this Acceptable Use Policy shall be within the sole discretion of NorthWestNet and NWACC. Questions about any issue related to this Policy should be directed to NorthWestNet by member organizations when an issue first arises.

NorthWestNet and NWACC make no warranty of any kind, expressed or implied, regarding Internet resources or services, or the contents of resources or electronic messages over the Internet, nor shall NorthWestNet or NWACC be liable in any event for incidental or consequential damages, direct or indirect, resulting from the use of either NorthWestNet or the resources and services available through NorthWestNet.

Version 1.1
February 12, 1993

Appendix F: NSFNET Backbone Services Acceptable Use Policy

General Principle

(1) NSFNET Backbone services are provided to support open research and education in and among U.S. research and instructional institutions, plus research arms of for-profit firms when engaged in open scholarly communication and research. Use for other purposes is not acceptable.

Specifically Acceptable Uses:

(2) Communication with foreign researchers and educators in connection with research or instruction, as long as any network that the foreign user employs for such communication provides reciprocal access to U.S. researchers and educators.

(3) Communication and exchange for professional development, to maintain currency, or to debate issues in a field or subfield of knowledge.

(4) Use for disciplinary-society, university-association, government-advisory, or standards activities related to the user's research and instructional activities.

(5) Use in applying for or administering grants or contracts for research or instruction, but not for other fundraising or public relations activities.

(6) Any other administrative communications or activities in direct support of research and instruction.

(7) Announcements of new products or services for use in research or instruction, but not advertising of any kind.

(8) Any traffic originating from a network of another member agency of the Federal Networking Council if the traffic meets the acceptable use policy of that agency.

(9) Communication incidental to otherwise acceptable use, except for illegal or specifically unacceptable use.

Unacceptable Uses:

(10) Use for for-profit activities, unless covered by the General Principle or as a specifically acceptable use.

(11) Extensive use for private or personal business.

This statement applies to use of the NSFNET Backbone only. NSF expects that connecting networks will formulate their own use policies. The NSF Division of Networking and Communications Research and Infrastructure will resolve any questions about this Policy or its interpretation.

June, 1992

Current versions of this file are available via FTP:

FTP host: **nic.merit.edu**
directory: **nsfnet/acceptable.use.policies**
filename: **nsfnet.txt**

Trademarks and Copyrights

SAS is a trademark of SAS Institute, Inc.

Telenet and TELE-MAIL are trademarks of GTE Telenet Communications Corporation.

UNIX is a registered trademark of AT&T Bell Laboratories.

VT100 is a registered trademark of Digital Equipment Corporation.

Word Perfect is a trademark of the Word Perfect Corporation.

Xerox is a registered trademark of Xerox Corporation.

@ Glossary @

Internet Symbols, Terms, and Acronyms

This glossary covers some of the symbols, terms, and acronyms you may need to have defined in your excursions through the Internet. It is a potpourri of standard Internet terminology and a few terms from general telecommunications and computer science meant to complement the materials covered in *The Internet Passport*.

Many of the terms in this glossary have additional meanings outside of the context of the Internet; but the definitions provided here are meant to cover only those meanings relevant to the Internet. In many cases, there are a variety of definitions or shades of meaning for a term even in the context of the Internet. The definitions given are usually for the most frequently encountered uses of the terms.

While using the Internet, you are bound to encounter many terms and acronyms which have not been included in this glossary. For additional materials you may want to obtain the "Glossary of Networking Terms" currently available as RFC1208 (recently updated and soon to be assigned a new RFC number).

Letters and Symbols

C   The programming language of choice in the Unix operating system and much of the Internet.

K   Abbreviation for kilo. "K" is used to denote 1000 (kilogram = 1000 grams, kilometer = 1000 meters, etc.) In the computing vernacular, K often refers to a kilobyte, or 1024 bytes. Why 1024? Because, as with many useful numbers in the computing sciences, 1024 is a power of 2 (2 to the 10th to be exact). To help make K concrete, one K of text is a little less than a standard screen of text.

.Z   Suffix added to the names of files which have been compressed with the Unix compress program; for example, the file "passport.txt.Z" is very likely a compressed version of the file "passport.txt."

:-)   A smiley. Looks like a smiling face when viewed sideways. Used in electronic messages to indicate that the preceding text was meant in a humorous or lighthearted way. There are many variants on the basic smiley to indicate subtleties of tone. See Chapter 4 for a compact bestiary of smileys.

::   Part of the notation typically found in DECNet addresses which separates a userid and a DECNet address (decnet_host::userid).

@   "At." the symbol separating a userid from an Internet host name in a user's e-mail address. Indicates that a given userid is "at" (i.e., has a mailbox at) a certain Internet address; for example, userid@an.internet.address. This symbol is also used in the same role in the addressing syntaxes of many other networks, such as BITNET.

!   "Bang." Part of bang path notation within the UUCP network separating host names along the route a message is to take in UUCP's store and forward delivery paradigm. (See "bang path.")

%   A symbol typically used to make an alien network's addressing syntax pass through the Internet unscathed so it can be processed by an e-mail gateway. For example, an Internet user can send a message to a user on a BITNET host by sending an e-mail message to the e-mail gateway cunyvm.cuny.edu with the following syntax:

                 `userid%host.bitnet@cunyvm.cuny.edu`

                 The gateway at cunyvm converts the "userid%host.bitnet" to "userid@host," and forwards the message onto the BITNET network for delivery. Mixing "%" and "!" in an address should be avoided.

/   In Unix notation the forward slash is a separator between directory, subdirectory, and file names; e.g., "directory/subdirectory/filename". DOS uses "\" (backslash) for the same purpose. By itself, "/" represents the root directory of the Unix system.

*   A wildcard. Many operating systems and software packages allow you to use this symbol to indicate that any possible character(s) or value(s) might be in it's place. For example, in Unix you might use this to move all files beginning with the word "passport" into an appropriate directory:

```
mv passport.* /essential.internet.documents
```

Words and Acronyms

Acceptable Use Policy (AUP)

> Conditions or restrictions that apply to the use of a network. For example, some portions of the Internet explicitly restrict commercial communications, or an institution may prohibit the playing of computer games on an Internet host during certain hours.

acknowledgment

> A message returned to its sender to indicate that data has successfully arrived at a destination; a feature found in some e-mail software packages.

address

> Loosely used to refer to either an e-mail address (see "e-mail address") or an internet address (see "internet address" and "domain name").

address resolution

> The conversion of an Internet address to its corresponding physical address.

alias

> A short and easy to remember name or command that substitutes for a longer, harder to remember name or command. Aliases are often used for e-mail addresses, e.g., "sue" could be an alias for the full e-mail address sra@idacrk.hs.idaho.edu.

Andrew File System (afs)

> A distributed file system developed at Carnegie Mellon University.

anonymous FTP

> An Internet application which allows one to gain access to a remote Internet host through the userid "anonymous" and to copy files from the remote host to one's local computer.

anonymous FTP host

> A computer on the Internet that allows anonymous FTP access for remote file retrieval, and sometimes storage, by remote users. There are more than 1,000 substantial anonymous FTP hosts throughout the world that collectively contain millions of files.

ANSI (American National Standards Institute)

> U.S. organization which, among other things, approves computer communications standards. ANSI is also sometime used, in context, for specific ANSI standards (e.g., ANSI terminal emulation).

application

> A software program designed to perform a specific task for a user.

archie

> A software program developed at McGill University that maintains a frequently updated central catalog of files contained in many of the world's anonymous FTP hosts.

archive

> 1) An organized holding of computer files stored for later retrieval, for example, an anonymous FTP archive, or collections of messages from mailing lists or discussion groups;

> 2) a set of files which are stored as a single file to simplify handling and processing; an archived file must be "unpacked" before it can be used. (See "tar" and "self-extracting archive.")

ARPANET (Advanced Research Projects Agency Network)

> A network sponsored by the Advanced Research Projects Agency which served as a testbed for many of the communications protocols used in today's Internet.

ASCII (American Standard Code for Information Interchange)

> A method of representing the alphabetic, numeric, and control characters used in computer communications and coded in hexadecimal notation. "ASCII file" is used to indicate a file that is stored in clear text (i.e., readable by humans). Also see "EBCDIC."

authentication

> Verification of the "true" identity of an individual or process, usually in the context of systems security and access.

backbone

> A portion of an internet that acts as a main connection for the interconnection of other networks. The top structural level of many internets. In some cases, the backbone of an internet is built with higher capacity lines to accommodate the aggregation of traffic from the other "tributary" networks.

bandwidth

> 1) The amount of digital information that a circuit is capable of transmitting in a given amount of time; e.g., a 56kb circuit can, under optimal conditions, transmit 56 kilobits (56,000 bits) of information per second.

> 2) The specific electromagnetic frequency or range of frequencies (usually measured in hertz) that a given medium is designed to carry.

bang path

A sequential list of the names of computer hosts, each separated by "!", through which a message must be routed for transmission through the UUCP network; for example "next_host!intermediate_host!destination_host". Bang paths may soon be a thing of the past.

baud

A unit of communications speed measured as the number of distinguishable events per second. If each event is a bit, then baud is equivalent to bits per second (BPS). Used most often to describe the speed of modems; e.g., a 9600 baud modem can transmit data 4 times as fast as a 2400 baud modem.

BBS (Bulletin Board System)

A computer and associated software that typically provides electronic messaging services, archives of files, and any other services or activities of interest to the bulletin board system's operator (SYSOP). Although BBSs have traditionally been the domain of hobbyists, an increasing number of BBSs are connected directly to the Internet, and many BBSs are currently operated by government, educational, and research institutions.

binary

Representation of information in the form of "0" and "1" (base 2 notation). In terms of electrical circuits, 0 and 1 correspond to "off" and "on." Humans, having ten fingers, like to use base 10; computers, who don't have fingers, prefer base 2. :-)

binary file

Used to denote a non-ASCII file, often an executable program or a file used by application software.

bit

Abbreviation for "binary element." The smallest possible unit of information: "yes" or "no," "on" or "off," "1" or "0."

BITNET (Because It's Time Network)

1) An e-mail and file sharing network used by a large number of academic and research institutions, based on a proprietary store and forward transport protocol. Now gatewayed in many places to the Internet.

2) The specific BITNET network coordinated by the Corporation for Research and Educational Networks. (See "CREN.")

Boolean search

A method of searching for information, often used in databases and online library catalogs, using the Boolean operators "AND," "OR," "NAND" (not and), and "NOR" (not or).

bounce

> The network equivalent of the famous Elvis Presley song, "Return to Sender, Address Unknown." The return of an e-mail message because of an error in it's addressing or delivery.

bps (bits per second)

> The number of bits of information transmitted per second through a transmission medium.

BTW (By The Way)

> A "three letter acronym" (TLA) frequently used in e-mail messages.

cache

> Area in volatile memory where information is retained for rapid access. In contrast, when information is written to disk, tape or other permanent storage media, access time is longer.

CAUSE (Association for the Management of Information Technology in Higher Education)

> An association for the management of information technology in colleges and universities.

CCIRN (Coordinating Committee for Intercontinental Research Networks)

> An international organization responsible for planning and coordinating the research and implementation of international networking activities.

CCITT (Comite Consultatif International de Telegraphique et Telephonique)

> A branch of the United Nations International Telecommunications Union that makes recommendations about protocols for data communications systems.

checksum

> A value computed from the entire contents of a message before and after transmission. A receiving host compares the transmitted checksum with a calculated checksum; if the two match, it is likely that the message was transmitted without error.

client

> A computer or process that relies on the resources of another computer or process (the server).

CMC (Computer Mediated Communication)

> Systems like e-mail, mailing lists, and discussion groups, that allow people to exchange messages using computers.

CNI (Coalition for Networked Information)

> A working group established jointly by EDUCOM, ARL (Association of Research Libraries) and CAUSE that focuses on implementation of and access to network information services and resources.

compression

> Methods of reducing the amount of storage or bandwidth that information occupies without altering the informational content. Files on anonymous FTP hosts are often stored in various compressed formats. As a trivial example of one compression technique, the many blank spaces that frequently occur at the ends of lines of computer files can be stored as the symbol for blank space plus the number of blank spaces that follow.

connectionless communication

> Networking communications in which information is transmitted without prior establishment of a connection. Each packet of data contains enough information to reach its destination.

cracker

> IMHO, an individual who willfully and sometimes maliciously attempts to breach the integrity and security of other's computer resources and data. Not to be confused with hacker!

CREN (Corporation for Research and Educational Networking)

> An umbrella organization formerly responsible for two national U.S. networks, BITNET and CSNET. Although CSNET is now defunct, BITNET is still a major provider of national educational networking.

crossposting

> Submitting a message to two or more discussion groups or newsgroups.

CWIS (Campus Wide Information System)

> A software system for electronically providing information of interest to the members of a particular community, most frequently a college or university.

cyberpunk

> A popular literature dealing with a (hypothetical?) computer based society or a person who embraces the cyberpunk vision.

cyberspace

> Loosely used to describe the indeterminate location of one's mind when using computer networks; for example, "I had a Telnet connection to Switzerland, from which I launched an FTP session to Singapore, and I forgot where *I* was: I think I was sort of lost in cyberspace." A term coined by William Gibson in his cyberpunk novel *Neuromancer*, to describe a "space," partly visual, partly conceptual, in which human minds and networks meet through brain-computer interfaces.

DARPA (Defense Advanced Research Projects Agency)

An agency of the U.S. Department of Defense which (among other activities) funded the research that led to communications protocols that have in turn made today's Internet possible.

DDN (Defense Data Network)

A network of networks used by the U.S. Department of Defense (DARPANET, MILNET, etc.).

DDN NIC (Defense Data Network Network Information Center)

Currently the authoritative repository of many of the core documents for the Internet (RFCs, FYI's, Internet Drafts, etc.), as well as the central database for Internet IP addresses and domain names. The DDN NIC also provides a server to answer queries about their database based upon the "whois" application.

/dev/null

A place to which information goes, never to be seen again. The term is based on the Unix data sink of the same name and is equivalent to the old fashioned "circular file." As a particularly brutal example that captures the pathos of the slang usage of this term, if you've broken up with your boyfriend via e-mail, you might write in closing, "send any responses to /dev/null."

dialup

Connection between computers via a telephone line, usually by way of a modem. Unlike dedicated connections, dialup connections are established only for the duration of the session.

directory service

A service which may provide network addresses and/or userids of individuals, hosts, and services; also see "yellow pages" and "white pages."

discussion group

A forum for communication about a topic by e-mail. Each discussion group has a network address to which messages are sent and from which messages are distributed to all discussion group members. Examples of discussion groups include LISTSERV and MAILBASE.

distribution

In Usenet, the geographical region to which a message will be sent. Typically, one can choose institutional, local, regional, continental, or global distribution.

distribution list

A list of e-mail addresses for people who receive periodic messages from a person or a software program. Unlike a mailing list, which acts as a "many-to-many" service, a distribution list is primarily a "one-to-many" service.

DNS (Domain Name System)

> The online distributed database that translates human-readable domain names into numeric IP addresses. DNS servers are located throughout the Internet, and no one DNS server contains information for all Internet hosts.

domain name

> The Internet convention of constructing an address by using userid@domain_name. That is, everything to the right of the @ sign is the domain name. Domain names are an administrative tool and a convenience to human beings; they are not a physical description of the network.

dumb terminal

> A terminal which only has the capacity to connect to another computer on which the actual application software and storage reside. Prior to the personal computer revolution, almost all terminals used were dumb terminals connected to mainframe computers at data processing centers. (I still keep a dumb terminal on my desk to boost the morale of my aging Macintosh SE.)

duplex

> Simultaneous transmission of signals in both directions through a transmission medium.

EBCDIC (Extended Binary Coded Decimal Interchange Code)

> A method of representing alphabetic, numeric, and control characters, used by most IBM computers. Also see "ASCII."

EDUCOM

> A not-for-profit consortium of higher education institutions in the USA that facilitates the introduction, use, and management of information resources in the educational and research communities.

EFF (Electronic Frontier Foundation)

> An organization established to serve as a clearing house for open discussion and analysis of the many legal and social implications of the increasing role of computer communications in the world.

e-mail address

> A userid + a domain name (e.g., info@nwnet.net) designating a person or service at a particular network host. By analogy to regular postal mail, an e-mail address contains a "name" and a "location."

emoticon

> A non verbal symbol used to express emotional nuances in electronic communication. "!," "?" and so forth are already well-established, traditional emoticons. In computer mediated communications, symbols such as "*" for *emphasis,* smileys, and other special symbols are also used.

Glossary

encryption

>   The process of translating data into a more or less secret code. Encrypted data requires a "key" to translate the code back to the original state. Encryption is used when storing or transmitting valuable information: for example, files containing passwords should be encrypted, and sensitive or private e-mail messages might be encrypted.

Ethernet

>   A popular local area network technology. Ethernet allows for transmission speeds of 10 Mbps (10 million bits per second), and is typically found running over passive coaxial cable or shielded twisted pair wiring as the transmission medium.

FAQ (Frequently Asked Question)

>   Questions that are often posed to a particular discussion or newsgroup. To keep such questions from overwhelming discussion, these questions along with their answers are compiled and distributed in files called FAQs. Most groups routinely post the FAQ or directions on how to obtain it.

FARNET (Federation of American Research Networks)

>   A not-for-profit organization whose mission is to advance the use of computer networks and to improve research and education. Its members include networks such as ANS, MERIT, CERFnet, PSINet, CICNet, NYSERNet—and NorthWestNet!

FDDI (Fiber Distributed Data Interface)

>   A high-speed networking standard using fiber optics as a transmission medium and a Token Ring topology.

fiber optics

>   Technology that allows high speed data transmission using light though a flexible bundle of glass fibers.

file server

>   A computer that shares its file storage media with other computers; also see "mail server" and "archive."

file transfer

>   Moving a file from one computer to another.

finger

>   A program that displays information about one or more users on a particular Unix host.

flame

An intentionally polemical, inflammatory, or argumentative statement in an electronic message, or to send a message containing such a statement. When two or more people flame each other in a discussion or newsgroup you have a "flame war"— not a good thing to get involved with and an annoyance to everyone subjected to the heat. "Flame bait" is a statement in a posting to a Usenet newsgroup or other discussion group that is meant to provoke others into a flame war. Resist the temptation to take such bait.

FNC (Federal Networking Council)

A group of representatives from U.S. federal agencies who coordinate networking activities of these agencies.

FQDN (Fully Qualified Domain Name)

The complete domain name by which an Internet host is uniquely identified within the Internet. For example, at your site you may be able to login to an Internet host by typing "solaris", but the FQDN might be solaris.brasilia.br.

Free-Net

A site using the "Free-Net" software developed at Case Western Reserve University; designed to provide community based, public access networking services to the general public.

freeware

Software which can be used and copied without charge.

FTP (File Transfer Protocol)

A machine and operating system independent method of transferring files between computers connected to the Internet.

full duplex

A circuit which allows simultaneous, two way transmission of information.

FYI (For Your Information)

A collection of introductory documents for Internet users within the RFC series distributed by the Internet NIC.

gateway

A computer that connects networks using different communications protocols or applications and that can translate the formats in which data are packaged in the different networks. For example, there are several gateways that allow e-mail messages to be transmitted between Internet and BITNET hosts even though these networks use very different formats for addresses.

GIF (Graphical Interchange Format)

A format for encoding high resolution graphics in computer files. Developed originally in the CompuServe network, but now widely used throughout the Internet.

Gopher

A document delivery system that allows information from all over the Internet to be presented to a user in a hierarchically organized front end. A Gopher user can search through remote documents for texts of interest and can retrieve remote documents to their local system.

the great renaming

The day when the current hierarchical, multilevel Usenet naming scheme was developed (comp, misc, sci, etc., with multilevel subnames). Prior to this time, Usenet newsgroup names had the format "net.newsgroupname," but this became unwieldy with the proliferation of Usenet beyond it's originator's wildest dreams.

GOSIP (Government OSI Profile)

A subset of OSI standards which are intended to become the de facto networking standards for U.S. government networking.

GSI (Government System Inc.)

The current manager of the DDN NIC.

GUI (Graphical User Interface)

A type of full screen software that employs on-screen images of any combination of windows, menus, icons, scroll bars, and other images for manipulating information, and uses peripheral devices such as mice, trackballs, wired-gloves, light pens, or eye-trackers to manipulate these on screen images.

hacker

A person who delights in having an intimate understanding of the internal workings of a system, in particular, computers or networks. For hackers, this understanding leads to an obsession with elegant solutions that extend the capabilities and functionality of the system in question. The popular press has used the word "hacker" for people who break into computers and networks, but such individuals should be referred to as "crackers." Confusing the terms "hacker" and "cracker" is bound to raise a hacker's hackles. (For a wonderful tour through the language and culture of hackers, read *The New Hacker's Dictionary*, by Eric Raymond.)

half duplex

A circuit which can transmit data only in one direction at a time.

header

Information at the beginning of an Internet packet, e-mail message, or Usenet article, that contains information about source and destination addresses, and other information useful for ensuring that the data is transmitted through the network.

heterogeneous network

> A network comprised of computers using a variety of operating systems and/or communications protocols.

hexadecimal notation

> Numerical notation in base 16 (a.k.a. "hex"), with the numbers 10 through 15 having the values "A" through "F." Thus, in hex, 16 would be written as "10," and 31 as "1F." Much computer code is stored and represented in hex notation.

hierarchical file system

> A method of storing files in directories and sub-directories in a hierarchical fashion. A hierarchical file system can be represented as a tree, with a root (directory), branches (sub-directories), and branches off of branches. The leaves (or fruits!) at the ends of the branches of this tree are the files.

host

> As used within *The Internet Passport*, a specific computer or computer system connected to the Internet. For example, "YALEVM" refers to an IBM mainframe at Yale University, whose fully qualified domain name is yalevm.ycc.yale.edu.

host name

> The portion of the fully qualified domain name that refers to the host itself. For example, in milton.u.washington.edu, "milton" is a host name within the "u.washington.edu" domain.

hypermedia

> The inclusion of multiple media within a single format. For example, it is now possible to include digitized sounds and images in e-mail messages by using MIME inclusions.

IAB (Internet Activities Board)

> A committee that is responsible for coordinating policy and standards efforts for the Internet community.

IESG (Internet Engineering Steering Group)

> A group of IETF area leaders concerned with facilitating the progress of the IETF working groups.

IETF (Internet Engineering Task Force)

> A volunteer task force consisting of engineers and scientists from academia, government, and industry, which aids in the development, deployment, and maintenance of new Internet technologies. The IETF is subdivided into many working groups, each addressing specific Internet engineering and operating issues.

IMHO (In My Humble Opinion)

A way of indicating that the writer is aware that others may be offended by a controversial statement; e.g., "IMHO, baseball is vastly inferior to chess in exercising the upper arms."

interest group

A forum for the discussion of a topic via e-mail. The term "interest groups" is traditionally used to describe mailing lists on the Internet. There is usually a network address to which messages are sent and from which messages are distributed to all group members.

internet

(with a lower case "i") A set of heterogeneous networks that can intercommunicate by virtue of applications, gateways, routers, and bridges. Note that an "internet" may include networks which do not use TCP/IP. (See "Internet.")

Internet

(with an upper case "I") Historically, the network of networks throughout the world that intercommunicate by virtue of the IP suite of protocols.

Internet address

A numeric address of the format "www.xxx.yyy.zzz" that is assigned to devices on a TCP/IP network: for example, 128.95.112.1 is the Internet address of the Internet host ftphost.nwnet.net, stored internally as four binary "octets" of 8 bits each.

Internet draft

A preliminary version of an RFC distributed within the Internet community for suggestions and feedback.

Internet Society

A not-for-profit organization devoted to furthering the interconnecting of networks into a global communications and information infrastructure.

IP (Internet Protocol)

A protocol specifying how packets of information are sent across a connectionless network. IP (sometimes referred to as TCP/IP) defines a general set of rules for formatting and routing packets from one network device to another.

Kermit

A file transfer and terminal emulation program developed at Columbia University; available for a wide variety of operating systems.

Kilobyte

1,024 bytes of data.

knowbot

> An application that carries a user's request for information to multiple locations on the network. At each service contacted, the user query is implemented in commands specific to that service. All search results are then collected and returned to the user.

LAN (Local Area Network)

> A network connecting computers in a relatively small area, usually within a room, building, or set of buildings. Because of the short distances between computers in a LAN, these are often high-speed networks despite the use of low-cost transmission media such as coaxial cables or twisted pair wiring.

LISTSERV

> A software program for efficient setup and maintenance of discussion groups. Although originally developed for use in the BITNET network, LISTSERV groups can be subscribed to by Internet users and many LISTSERV discussion groups are gatewayed to Usenet newsgroups.

mailbox

> A file or directory on a user's host computer into which incoming e-mail messages are stored.

mail exploder

> Software which allows e-mail sent to one e-mail address to be automatically distributed ("exploded") to many e-mail addresses.

mail gateway

> A host which transfers e-mail messages between distinct networks and performs reformatting of mail addresses and headers needed for successful handling in the destination network.

mailing list

> A list of the e-mail addresses of people interested in a particular topic. Typically, one sends a message to a mailbox associated with the mailing list, and the message will be distributed to all members of the mailing list.

mail server

> A software program that distributes files or information in response to requests sent via e-mail. Internet examples include Almanac and netlib. Mail servers have also been used in BITNET to provide FTP-like services.

MAN (Metropolitan Area Network)

> A network servicing a metropolitan area; in terms of geographic area serviced, midway between a LAN and a WAN.

MIME (Multipurpose Internet Mail Extension)

An extension to Internet e-mail that allows transmission of non-textual data such as graphics, audio, video, and applications data (e.g., spreadsheets and word processing documents).

modem

A device which facilitates transmissions between digital devices (such as computers) over analog circuits (such as voice telephone lines).

name resolution

Conversion of a domain name to a numeric IP address.

NCSA Telnet

A freeware version of the Telnet software developed by the National Center for Supercomputer Applications for a variety of PC operating systems.

netiquette

"Network etiquette" or socially acceptable actions and communications on a network.

network

Two or more devices connected together in such a way that they can exchange data with each other.

newbie

A usually derogatory (but sometimes affectionate) term for someone new to a network and/or specific network services.

newsfeed

The host from which one receives Usenet news.

newsgroup

A topical discussion group within Usenet propagated via newsfeeds to a loosely defined, worldwide network of computers, including many on the Internet. One may submit messages to a newsgroup and read other's messages with newsreader software.

NIC (Network Information Center)

An organization that provides documentation, training, and related services for users of a particular network.

NNTP (Network News Transfer Protocol)

A protocol that allows Usenet news stored on one Internet host to be selectively copied to or read by newsreaders on other Internet hosts.

NOC (Network Operations Center)

> An organization responsible for the day-to-day monitoring, maintenance, and technical trouble-shooting of a particular network.

node

> 1) In the context of the Internet, a particular computer or computer system connected to the Internet.

> 2) In the context of hypertext, an individual piece of text; each node is connected by one or more links to one or more hypertext nodes.

NPTN (National Public Telecommunications Network)

> A not-for-profit U.S. organization dedicated to establishing and developing free computerized information and communication services for the general public. Loosely modeled on the U.S. National Public Broadcasting systems for radio and television.

NREN (National Research and Education Network)

> An emerging national network in the U.S. designed to promote greater collaboration among educational institutions, government, and federal research laboratories, industry, and high-performance computing centers.

NSF (National Science Foundation)

> U.S. government agency that provides funds for research and education in many areas, including computer networking.

NSFNET (National Science Foundation Network)

> A high-speed TCP/IP backbone in the U.S. connecting midlevel networks. Originally created to provide high speed access to NSF sponsored supercomputer sites, NSFNET has broadened its focus to provide general network connectivity to research and education communities throughout the U.S.

NTP (Network Time Protocol)

> An IP protocol that synchronizes clocks on hosts throughout the Internet.

octet

> Generally, a set of eight. In the context of IP addresses, this term refers to the eight digits in binary (base 2) notation needed to represent the possible values from 0 to 255 ("00000000" to "11111111"). In classical music, an ensemble of eight instruments, or a piece of music written for eight instruments (e.g., Stravinsky's "L'Histoire du Soldat," one of my favorite pieces of music).

OPAC (Online Public Access Catalog)

Electronic databases of library holdings often accessible via a network. OPACs facilitate retrieval of information on library holdings by allowing users to search on such variables as author, title, keyword, and subject.

operating system (OS)

Software that controls the operation of a computer, installed software, and communications with attached devices. The operating system handles such tasks as input/output control, assignment of storage locations for data, control of peripheral devices like disk drives, scheduling of events within the computer, and much much much much much more.

packet

A unit of data sent through a packet switching network.

packet switching network

A network which can transmit data as packets in a connectionless mode.

ping (Packet InterNet Groper)

A program used to determine if a remote Internet host is currently reachable from a local host; also used as a verb, e.g., "to ping a host."

poll

To periodically check a remote host for files, e-mail, or other information. Archie is an example of a software program which polls remote hosts.

port

1) Real or virtual access points to a computer, often times with distinct functions.

2) To modify a program so that it will run on a system for which it was not originally designed.

post

1) To send a message to a newsgroup.

2) An individual item in a newsgroup. Also called a "posting" or an "article."

postmaster

A person responsible for the installation, maintenance, and debugging of e-mail software at a given site. Often, but not always, reachable by the userid "postmaster" (or "postmast" on BITNET hosts).

PostScript

> A programming language with powerful graphics and page-markup capabilities developed by Adobe Systems Incorporated. Many Internet documents are distributed in PostScript format and can be printed on PostScript capable laser printers yielding near publication quality output. On the Internet, files in PostScript format conventionally have filenames which end with ".ps", for example, "rfc1125.ps".

protocol

> Like "protocol" in human diplomacy, a set of previously agreed upon rules of communication within a network. Formal specification of the means of formatting, encoding, transmitting, receiving data, and recovering from communications faux pas.

RARE (Reseaux Associes pour la Recherche Europeenne)

> A European association of research networks.

relevance feedback

> A method for finding information in which the contents of a search result is itself used as input for another search. A major feature of WAIS, relevance feedback is an attempt to allow computer searches to use a method that human beings seem to find natural ("this is like what I'm looking for but I can't tell you exactly how") but which is difficult to specify with standard Boolean logic.

resolver

> A software program that provides name resolution services.

RFCs (Request For Comments)

> Formal documents which are created by and distributed among members of the Internet community to help define the nuts and bolts of the Internet. The Internet would not exist without the core documentation contained in RFCs. In the grand Internet tradition, RFCs range from documents proposing, formalizing, or modifying standard Internet protocols which must be used by all computers connected to the Internet (the bolts) to frivolous doggerel for the amusement of Internet users (the nuts).

root

> 1) In operating systems with hierarchical file systems, the directory from which all other directories branch.

> 2) In Unix, a special account set aside for use by the system manager, who has "root privileges," e.g., they can do almost anything.

route

> The path which information takes in its passage through a network.

RTFM

> A mildly sarcastic way of suggesting that someone asking a question should "Read The Friendly Manual" first. Or is it "Read The FAQ, Matey?"

self extracting archive

> An archive of files which will automatically unpack to its component files when executed.

server

> A computer or device which provides a service to other computers or devices in a network. This is a real catch-all term: for example, name servers provide information about Internet hosts; terminal servers allow terminals to access computers, modem pools, or networks; and mail servers distribute files in response to e-mail requests.

shareware

> Software that a person obtains for free with the understanding that if it is found to be of value, some small fee should be paid to the shareware author.

shell

> A program usually accessed immediately upon login to a Unix account that interprets and executes whatever other programs the user requests. From the shell the user can change their password, look at their file listing, or start another program such as an editor. Common Unix shells include the C, Bourne, and Korn shells.

sig, or signature

> The several lines of text which people often add to the end of their outgoing e-mail messages or Usenet postings; it usually includes contact information and, depending on preference, nuggets of personal philosophy, standard disclaimers, or whatever. If you use a signature, keep it short (< 5 lines, ideally).

SLIP (Serial Line Internet Protocol)

> A communications protocol used over serial lines (such as computers connected via modem to dialup phone circuits) to support IP connectivity.

SMTP (Simple Mail Transfer Protocol)

> A protocol used on the Internet that defines the format, packaging, and commands for the transmission and receipt of e-mail messages.

snail mail

> The derogatory term for regular postal mail used by those of us who have become spoiled by the immediacy of e-mail. Still useful for whatever we can't cram into our terminals, like chocolates or care packages.

SNMP (Simple Network Management Protocol)

> The protocol that includes management of an internet, and network entities such as hosts and terminal servers.

standard disclaimer

> A phrase at the end of an electronic message which is supposed to dissociate an individual's statement from the organization with which they are affiliated.

store and forward

> A stepping-stone version of networking used by BITNET, FidoNet, and their related networks. Although the details vary among these networks, the basic method is that a transmitted message is received and held in an intermediate host until a circuit to the destination or other intermediate host becomes available.

systems administrator

> The person(s) responsible for the day-to-day maintenance of an Internet host; sometimes abbreviated as "sysadmin" or "admin." Usually a sysadmin is working for an institution and does not technically "own" the host, but nonetheless is vested with responsibilities and privileges associated with ownership.

SYSOP (Systems Operator)

> The person responsible for the day-to-day maintenance of a BBS (Bulletin Board System). With the notable exceptions of government and corporate BBSs, a sysop is frequently the owner of the BBS.

T1

> Telecommunications at speeds of approximately 1.5 megabytes/second.

T3

> Telecommunications at speeds of approximately 45 megabytes/second.

tar

> 1) A Unix program that combines two or more separate files into one file; often used to simplify the handling and transferring of files.
>
> 2) The suffix conventionally appended to the filename of an archive made by the tar program.

TCP (Transmission Control Protocol)

> A major protocol used over the Internet Protocol (IP) providing reliable, ordered, end-to-end transmission of byte streams.

TCP/IP (Transmission Control Protocol over Internet Protocol)

> A set of protocols which make Telnet, FTP, electronic mail and other services possible among the computers within a heterogeneous network.

TELENET

> Not to be confused with Telnet! A commercial e-mail service packet switched network using the CCITT X.25 protocols.

Telnet

> The Internet standard protocol allowing logins to remote hosts. With Telnet, one has access to the commands, services, and central processing unit of the remote host.

terminal emulation

> A process by which a computer acts like a specific kind of terminal when connected to another computer. This is necessary because of the wide variety of proprietary methods used by different computers for encoding and sending information: for example, IBM developed "3270" terminals, and DEC developed "VT" series terminals (such as VT100) for use with their mainframes. Terminal emulation software typically allows emulation of a variety of terminal types.

thread

> A topic that is being discussed in a successive exchange of messages by two or more participants within a newsgroup or discussion group.

tn3270

> A version of Telnet used for remote logins to IBM mainframes that uses 3270 terminal type emulation.

Unix

> A multi-user, multitasking operating system which includes numerous utilities that can be linked together for greater effect. Developed at Bell Laboratories, modified by the University of California at Berkeley, and used extensively in the early development of the IP protocols, Unix is a common operating system used throughout the Internet. "*nix" refers to the various versions and dialects of Unix that have been developed, including Dynix, Ultrix, and AIX.

Usenet

> A collection of thousands of topically named newsgroups, the set of computers which exchange some or all of these newsgroups, and the community of people who read or submit Usenet news. Not all Internet hosts subscribe to Usenet newsgroups, and Usenet newsgroups may be received by non-Internet hosts.

userid

> User Identification. The name by which one has authorized access to a computer system, and the part of an Internet address by which a person or service is known in an Internet address.

UUCP (Unix to Unix CoPy)

> 1) A method of sending files and e-mail via dialup lines that was originally developed for use between Unix computers.

> 2) A network which currently uses the UUCP program for transmitting Usenet news and e-mail.

uuencode / uudecode

> Unix commands for modifying binary files in order to be sent via Internet e-mail or UUCP.

vaporware

> Software which has been promised (and often described in glowing terms) but which has not yet been (and may never be) released.

VT100

> A common form of terminal emulation using communications protocols developed for the VT100 terminal from Digital Equipment Corporation. Most communications software includes VT100 emulation, and emulation for other members of the VT family (VT52, VT102, etc.).

WAIS (Wide Area Information Server)

> A client-server information system based on the Z39.50 protocol which allows users to search through heterogeneous databases with a single user interface.

WAN (Wide Area Network)

> A network designed to cover large geographic areas.

white pages

> By analogy to telephone directories, a listing of e-mail addresses and other information pertaining to network users and usually available over the network.

whois

> An Internet directory service program that allows users to obtain information about other users, domains, networks, and hosts. Whois is commonly used to query a central database maintained by the DDN NIC, but may also be used to search databases maintained for smaller portions of the Internet.

WWW (World Wide Web)

> A client-server software package which uses hypertext to organize and present information and services throughout the Internet.

X-windows or X11

> A windowed graphical user interface developed at MIT. X-windows allows information from multiple hosts to be displayed in separate windows on a single screen.

X.400

> A CCITT and ISO e-mail standard.

X.500

> A CCITT and ISO standard for directory services.

yellow pages

> By analogy to telephone directories, a listing of Internet services and/or service providers, ideally including the type(s) of service(s) offered and access information.

Z39.50

> An ANSI information searching and retrieval protocol used by WAIS.

Index

D

electronic books, 155-62. *See also* under specific
    topics (e.g., history).
        catalogs of providers
            American Philosophical Association
                (Subcommittee on Electronic
                Texts), 160
            Catalogue of Projects in Electronic
                Texts, 160-61
        from mail servers, 43
        in Gopher, 270
        providers
            Freedom Shrine, 156
            Online Book Initiative, 157
            Oxford Text Archives, 157
            Project Gutenberg, 155-56
Electronic Frontier Foundation (EFF), 443, 476
electronic journals, 149-53
        and K-12 education, 364
        archives
            University of North Texas Gopher, 151
        cancelling subscriptions, 150
        comprehensive directories, 151
        from INFO (University of Maryland), 190
        from the Online Book Initiative, 157
        subscribing to, 150
electronic library catalogs. *See* OPACs.
electronic mail, 23-39
        accessing archie by, 254
        addresses, 11, 26-28, 476
        aliases, 11
        basic introduction, 23-34
        blind carbon copy (BCC), 31
        carbon copy (CC), 31
        daemons, 33
        etiquette, 47-55
        gateways, 57-62, 478
            online list of, 61
            published compendia of, 62
            table of examples, 60
        mail delivery agents, 33
        mail user agents, 28-29
        message header, 30
        retrieving files via, 41-46
        sample session, 33-36
        size limitations, 32
        software, 28-29
        stylistic conventions, 47-53
        technical references, 37
        within an Internet domain, 30
        within an Internet host, 30
electronics
        supercomputer software, 430
elm, 29, 39

Emancipation Proclamation, 156
emoticon, 476. *See also* smileys.
encryption, 477
engineering
        Army Corps of Engineers directory, 336
        IEEE Usenet newsgroups, 109
        supercomputer software, 405, 417
            nuclear engineering, 430
Enzyme Data Bank, 214
ENZYME database, 211
ERIC (Educational Resources Information
        Center), 366
        via CARL, 366
        via OCLC, 223
        via University of Saskatchewan, 366
        via WAIS, 287, 366
ERNET, 17
ESnet (Energy Sciences Network)
        sending e-mail to, 60
ethernet, 477
etiquette
        and CWIS, 299
        and K-12 networking, 353
        electronic journals, 151
        electronic mail, 47-55
        FTP, 79
        LISTSERV, 131
        mailing lists, 142-43
        Telnet, 64
        Usenet, 121
Etymological Dictionary of Gaelic Language, 157
EUnet, 17
Europe
        archie access by Telnet, 253
        directory services, 331
        Usenet newsgroups, 110
European Academic Research Network (EARN),
        16
        sending e-mail to, 59
executable file, 98
Extended Bulletin Board Service (EBBS), 67

F

F.A.S.T. News, 364
FAQs (Frequently Asked Questions), 477
        from mail servers, 43, 119
        in Usenet newsgroups, 119
Far From the Madding Crowd, 159
FARNET (Federation of American Research
        Networks), 444
FAXON database, 223

supercomputers *(continued)*
    programming strategies, 390-91
    site descriptions, 392-433
    software, 393-94, 399-400, 403-6, 412-13,
        416-17, 421-24, 429-30
    training, 395, 400, 406, 413, 417, 425, 430
Supreme Court decisions, 157
Sweden
    domain, 13
    Gopher access by Telnet, 262
SWISS-PROT database, 214, 216
Switzerland
    domain, 13
    World Wide Web line browser, 310
sysadmin, 488
SYSOP (Systems Operator), 488
systems administrator, 488

T

T1, 488
T3, 488
Taiwan
    domain, 13
talk newsgroups, 109
tar (tape archive), 488
    files, 100, 102
    program, 100, 102
TCP (Transmission Control Protocol), 8, 488
TCP/IP, 8, 489
    software, for personal computers, 74
TechInfo (MIT)
    via World Wide Web, 312
Tektronix terminals, 68
Tele-Fieldtrips, 360
TELENET, 489
Telnet, 63-74, 489
    accessible resources
        sample list, 66
        up-to-date list, 73
    and Catalist, 170
    and Hytelnet, 170
    and terminal emulation, 68
    commands, 70
    ending a Telnet session, 70
    etiquette, 64
    ports, 71
    sample sessions
        archie, 254-56
        Campus Wide Information Systems,
            300-304

        electronic library catalogs, 171-82
        Gopher, 262-73
        Netfind directory service, 329-30
        WAIS, 283-91
        World Wide Web, 310-17
    software, for personal computers, 74
    technical references, 73
    troubleshooting, 67
TERC, 361
terminal emulation, 68, 172, 489
Thanksgiving Proclamation, 156
THEnet
    sending e-mail to, 60
thread, 489
    Usenet, 121
Through the Looking Glass, 159
Time Machine, 159
tn3270, 63, 68-69, 489
toadshr program, 102
toaduu program, 102
Toronto
    Usenet newsgroups, 110
Transmission Control Protocol (TCP), 8, 488
Treaty of Greenville, 156
TRIE (Technology Resources in Education), 368
Tunisia
    domain, 13
Turkey
    electronic mail LISTSERV list, 127

U

Ultrix, 489
unarchiving files, 99, 102
uncompress program, 102
uncompressing files, 100, 102
United Kingdom
    and K-12 networking, 360, 361
    archie access by Telnet, 253
    databases
        social sciences (BIRON), 236
    directory of firms
        British Online Yellow Pages—British
            Telecom, 340
    directory of host addresses
        Name Registration Database, 342
    directory services
        Janet directory, 328
    domain, 13
    sample anonymous FTP host, 84

W

WAIS (Wide Area Information Server), 281-93,
 490
  and Boolean operators, 289
  and OPACs, 169
  client software, 283

  databases of directory information
   bitearn.nodes, 340
   college-email, 325
   uk-name-registration-service, 342
   usace-spk-phonebook, 336
   usenet-addresses, 333
  databases of mailing lists
   list, 145
   mailing lists, 145
  explained, 282
  mailing lists about, 293
  relevance feedback, 290
  sample session, 283-91
  stopwords, 289-90
  via World Wide Web, 312
WAN (Wide Area Network), 490
War of the Worlds, 159
Washington's Farewell Address, 156
Weather Underground, 231
whatis command (archie), 252
white pages, 490. *See also* directory services.
whois
  whois command, 334, 490
  whois servers, list of, 334
  whois@nic.ad.jp, 324, 335
  whois@nic.ddn.mil, 324, 334
   via Knowbot, 327
WIDE (network), 13
Wide Area Information Server (WAIS). *See*
 WAIS.
Wide Area Network (WAN), 490
wildcards
  and FTP, 91-92
  and OPACs, 168
  standard symbol (*), 469
WOCE (World Ocean Circulation Experiment),
 233
World Wide Web, 307-19, 490
  and archie, 312
  and Gopher, 312
  and hypertext, 308-10
  and WAIS, 312
  client software, 310
  home page, 311

  line browser, 310
   commands, 314
   eies2.njit.edu (United States), 310
   info.cern.ch (Switzerland), 310
   vms.huji.ac.il (Israel), 310
  sample session, 310-17
World, The (Internet Service Provider), 157
wuarchive (Washington University Archives), 190
wugate.wustl.edu (Services), 369
  and OPAC access, 169
Wuthering Heights, 157

X

x-ray crystallography
  supercomputer software, 423
X-windows, 491
X.400, 62, 491
X.500, 491
  directory services, 326, 332
   via Knowbot, 327
  technical references, 343
X11, 491
xgopher, 261

Y

Yale Bright Star Catalog, 200
Yale University
  Instant Math Preprints, 226
  Usenet newsgroups, 110
Yeats, W.B., 157, 251
yellow pages. *See* directory services.

Z

Z39.50, 491
Zen and the Art of the Internet, 159
Zimbabwe
  and K-12 networking, 360
ZOO
  files, 102
  program, 102

Order Form

The Internet Passport:
NorthWestNet's Guide to Our World Online 4th ed.

By Jonathan Kochmer and NorthWestNet. Published by NorthWestNet and the Northwest Academic Computing Consortium, Inc., Bellevue, WA. March 1993. (ISBN 0-9635281-0-6) Based on the *NorthWestNet User Services Internet Resource Guide (NUSIRG) 3rd ed.*

Topics include:

Internet Overview, E-mail, Mail Servers, Etiquette, Mail Gateways, Telnet, FTP, File Archives and Compression, Usenet, LISTSERV, Mailing Lists, E-Journals, E-Books, OPACs, Databases, Archie, Gopher and Veronica, WAIS, CWIS, World Wide Web, Directory Services, K-12, Supercomputers

To order your bound copy of *The Internet Passport* send this form with check or money order payable to NorthWestNet:

NorthWestNet: Internet Passport
15400 SE 30th Place, Suite 202
Bellevue, WA 98007

e-mail: **passport@nwnet.net**
phone: (206) 562-3000
fax: (206) 562-4822

Please send e-mail or call for information on bulk orders or electronic versions of *The Internet Passport*.

The Internet Passport:
NorthWestNet's Guide to Our World Online

Name: _____
Institution: _____
Address: _____
City: _____
State or Province: _____ Zip: _____ Country: _____
Phone: _____

	Quantity			Total
Retail Price	_____	@ $39.95 ea.	=	_____
Discount Price: Not-for-Profit Organizations and Education	_____	@ $19.95 ea.	=	_____
Discount Price: NorthWestNet Member Institutions	_____	@ $16.95 ea.	=	_____
Shipping and handling:				
Within U.S. - book rate	_____	@ $3.00 ea.	=	_____
Within U.S. - 1st class	_____	@ $5.00 ea.	=	_____
Outside U.S. - surface rate	_____	@ $5.00 ea.	=	_____
			Subtotal	_____
		WA orders add 8.2% sales tax on subtotal		_____
			Total enclosed	_____